The Essential PowerPoint® 97 Book

How to Order:

For information on quantity discounts contact the publisher: Prima Publishing, P.O. Box 1260BK, Rocklin, CA 95677-1260; (916) 632-4400. On your letterhead include information concerning the intended use of the books and the number of books you wish to purchase. For individual orders, turn to the back of this book for more information.

microsoft
POWER
The Essential PowerPoint® 97 Book
Faithe Wempen
PRIMA PUBLISHING

P is a registered trademark of Prima Publishing, a division of Prima Communications, Inc. Prima Publishing is a registered trademark of Prima Communications, Inc. Prima Publishing, Rocklin, California 95677.

Publisher: Matthew H. Carleson
Managing Editor: Tad Ringo
Acquisitions Editor: Debbie Abshier
Development Editor: Jan Snyder
Project Editor: Theresa Mathias
Technical Reviewer: Lawrence MacDonald
Layout: Marian Hartsough
Cover Design: Mike Tanamachi
Indexer: Sherry Massey

IMPORTANT: If you have problems installing or running Microsoft PowerPoint 97, notify Microsoft Corporation at (206) 635-7056. Prima Publishing cannot provide software support.

ISBN: 0-7615-1182-2
Library of Congress Catalog Card Number: 97-67400
Printed in the United States of America
97 98 99 AA 10 9 8 7 6 5 4 3 2 1

To my big sister Julie. You can do it!

Contents at a Glance

Window Help
Standard
Custom
Colors:
Fill Effects
Gradient
Texture
Pattern
Picture
Texture:
40
20
30

Contents

Acknowledgments

Once again Prima Publishing has assembled for me a first-rate editorial team. Thanks to Debbie Abshier, my acquisitions editor, for all the usual reasons I thank her in all my books: professionalism, friendliness, and the occasional good bit of publishing industry gossip. Thanks also to Jan Snyder, a great development editor, for a strong content editing pass on very quick turnaround. And finally to Theresa Mathias, who edited out my inconsistencies and spelling mistakes and coordinated the project successfully through production. Great work, everybody.

About the Author

Faithe Wempen, M.A., is the owner of Wempen Editorial Services, an Indianapolis-based company that provides writing and editing support to the computer book publishers and OEM software developers. Faithe also teaches hardware and software classes, provides one-on-one computer training, and troubleshoots and repairs computers. She has written 20 computer books, including Prima's *The Essential Excel 97 Book*, and has edited over 250 more.

Introduction

Besides being an author, I'm also a software instructor—I talk to businesspeople every week who are struggling with PowerPoint. Their complaints are nearly always the same: "I want to know more about the program, but I don't have any time to spend figuring it out!"

It's ironic. The software developers, in the race to make their product the easiest to use, add more and more time-saving features to their products with every release. But the average user doesn't have the time to spend learning the new versions and understanding the new commands, so some of the best time-saving features seldom get used. This is especially true with PowerPoint users because they tend to be very busy people who are constantly on the move.

PowerPoint is a tool—like a hammer or a briefcase. It doesn't have any value except in how it can help you create your next presentation. You don't need to know every little detail about PowerPoint to use it effectively, just as you don't have to know what kind of thread holds your briefcase together, or what its maximum capacity is, to carry your papers around in it. That's why in this book, I won't bog you down with useless trivia. In *The Essential PowerPoint 97 Book*, I'll focus only on the most important, most useful features of the program, and I'll show you the easiest method of getting things done, not every single method PowerPoint includes.

Is This Book for You?

This book is designed for business professionals, not computer scientists. I won't try to make you into a computer guru, because I know you have other goals to reach. Instead, I'll guide you through the features of PowerPoint that you most likely will need to use it effectively as a tool toward your *real* goals: like convincing your top client to invest in your company's services for another year.

That doesn't mean you won't come away with a thorough understanding of PowerPoint when you're finished with the book. If you learn everything in this book, you will have knowledge equivalent to almost an entire week of intensive PowerPoint in-lab training. You won't have to humble yourself and seek out your company's PowerPoint expert nearly as often, and people in your office might actually start coming to *you* for help with PowerPoint!

Whether you're a first-time PowerPoint user or an experienced user of a previous version, this book is for you:

- *New users* should check out the first few chapters, to get grounded in some basic skills, such as using the PowerPoint interface, working with files, and understanding how slides fit together to make a presentation.
- *More experienced users* will appreciate the intermediate-level discussions toward the middle and end of the book on such topics as animation, file linking, and the Internet.
- *All levels of users* will appreciate the "real-world" focus of each chapter, including not only how to use each feature but why and under what circumstances.

Conventions Used in This Book

The conventions used in this book should help you learn PowerPoint quickly and easily. You can select most PowerPoint commands with either a mouse or the keyboard. I've written the instructions in this book in a way that enables you to choose the method you prefer. For example, if the instruction reads "Choose File, Open," you should point the mouse to the word File on the menu bar, click the left mouse button, and then click on the word Open in the drop-down menu.

Notice that in each menu command, there is an underlined letter, both on-screen and in the book. That's the *selection letter.* If you prefer to use the keyboard instead of the mouse, you can hold down the Alt key and press the underlined letter in the menu name to open it. For example, to open the File menu, press Alt+F. After a menu is open, press the underlined letter in the command name to select a command. For example, when the File menu is open, press O to select the Open command.

When two keys are to be pressed together (that is, you hold down the first key while you press the second key), a plus sign (+) is used to show the combination: Alt+F or Ctrl+Z.

Often the quickest way to access a feature is by clicking a button on the toolbar. (You'll learn all about the toolbar in Chapter 1.) In the text, I'll refer to the button using the same name that appears on-screen when you point to a toolbar button.

Bold text is used to indicate text you should type. On-screen messages appear in "quotation marks."

Throughout the book I'll assume that you're familiar with certain common mouse actions:

- *Point.* To move the mouse so the tip of the pointer on-screen touches the object.
- *Click.* To press and release the left mouse button once.
- *Double-click.* To press and release the left mouse button twice quickly in succession.
- *Right-click.* To press and release the right mouse button once.
- *Drag.* To press and hold down the left mouse button while pointing at an object and then move the mouse until the object moves to a new location.
- *Right-drag.* Same as drag but with the right mouse button.

Special Elements

Along the way, you will find several special elements that will make using this book easier:

Whenever I mention a feature that's covered more thoroughly in another chapter, you'll see a gray box in the margin that indicates where the other information can be found.

Hands On: Accomplishing a Specific Task

Occasionally you'll find that it's easier to begin learning a feature by following a specific example rather than learning a general procedure. For example, in Chapter 1 you'll use a Hands On to learn how to ask the Office Assistant (a Help system) a question about using PowerPoint.

Sidebars for that Extra Touch

You'll see sidebars throughout the book. Sidebars provide discussions about how you can best use a particular feature. For example, in Chapter 3, a sidebar explains what happens inside your computer when you save your work, and how that process affects the steps you take.

Tips are short hints that provide shortcuts or recommendations on the best way to use a feature.

Notes provide further information—often of a more technical nature—on how a feature works or its uses or limitations.

As you might expect, cautions tell you what to watch out for when using a feature.

PART I
Finding Your Way Around PowerPoint

1

Introducing PowerPoint

In This Chapter

- Starting PowerPoint
- The Parts of the PowerPoint Interface
- Using Dialog Boxes
- Getting Information from the Built-In Help System
- Exiting PowerPoint

PowerPoint is the best-selling presentation graphics program in the world—and with good reason. It's the perfect combination of power and ease-of-use. If you've never used PowerPoint before or are unfamiliar with how Windows programs work, this chapter is the place to start.

Starting PowerPoint

Before you can use PowerPoint, you must start the program. (Of course, the program must already be installed on your computer or on a network that your computer is connected to; if you need help installing, see Appendix A.)

There are many ways to start PowerPoint, but here is the easiest method:

1. Click on the Start button.
2. Move the mouse pointer up to Programs. A submenu appears.
3. Move the mouse onto the submenu and then up or down to Microsoft PowerPoint (see Figure 1.1). Microsoft PowerPoint is highlighted.
4. Click on Microsoft PowerPoint. PowerPoint starts.

Here are some other ways to start PowerPoint in Windows 95:

- Double-click on the PowerPoint program file (Powerpnt.exe) in the My Computer or Windows Explorer window. (It's in the Program Files folder, in a folder called Microsoft Office.)
- To open an existing PowerPoint presentation and start PowerPoint at the same time, double-click on the presentation's name in the My Computer or Windows Explorer window.
- Create a shortcut for PowerPoint on your Desktop and then double-click on that shortcut to start the program. To create a shortcut

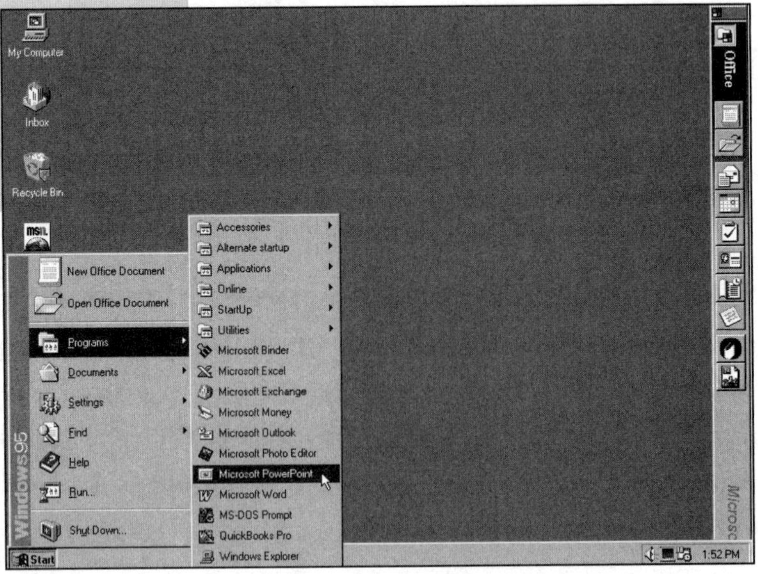

Figure 1.1 Choose PowerPoint from the Start button's menu system to start the program.

for PowerPoint, find the program file (Powerpnt.exe or just Powerpnt) in Windows Explorer or My Computer and drag it to the Desktop.

- If there is a particular presentation that you open frequently, create a shortcut for that presentation file on your Desktop, as described previously, and then double-click on that shortcut to start PowerPoint and open that presentation at the same time.

For more information about starting a new document or opening an existing document with the Microsoft Office Shortcut Bar, see Chapter 3.

If you use Microsoft Office 97, you have access to the Shortcut Bar if you installed it. Here are some ways to start PowerPoint using the Microsoft Office Shortcut Bar:

- Click on the New Office Document button. Select Blank Presentation from the New Office Document dialog box that appears, and click on OK.
- To start PowerPoint and open an existing document at the same time, click on the Open Office Document button. In the Open Office Document dialog box that appears, select the presentation to open and click on OK.
- Add a button to the Microsoft Office Shortcut Bar for the PowerPoint program and then click on that button to start the program. An easy way to do this is to drag an icon from the Desktop to the Microsoft Office Shortcut Bar.

Note

If the Microsoft Office Shortcut Bar feature is not installed, rerun the Microsoft Office 97 Setup program, choose the Custom installation, and make sure you place a check mark beside Microsoft Office Shortcut Bar. For more information about the installation program, see Appendix A.

Finding Your Way Around the Screen

When you start PowerPoint, the first thing you see is the PowerPoint dialog box shown in Figure 1.2. It helps you decide what to do first by giving you some very basic choices: start a new presentation (in one of three different ways) or open an existing presentation. You'll learn all about each of these choices in Chapter 3, but for now you can just choose the easiest one so you can get to the main PowerPoint screen.

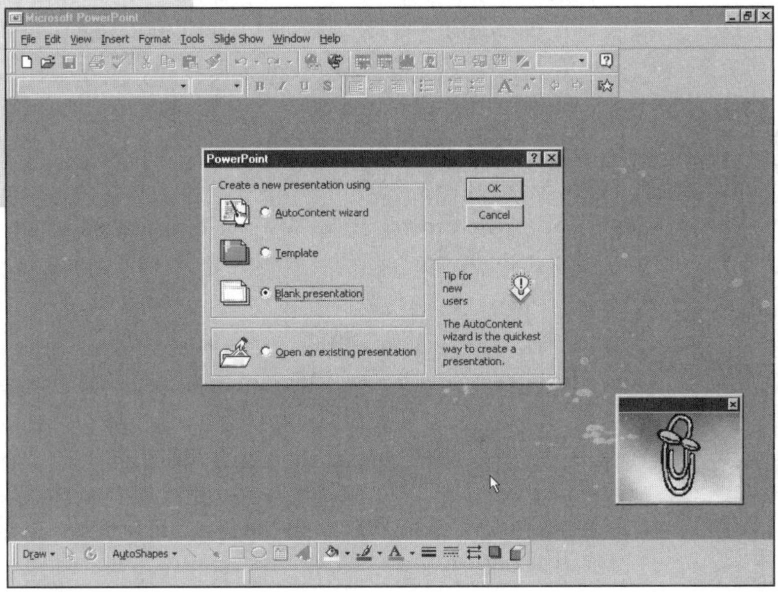

Figure 1.2 The PowerPoint dialog box is the first thing you see when you start the program.

Note

The first time you start PowerPoint, the Office Assistant (the talking paper clip) might ask you if you need help. Just click on Start Using PowerPoint Now; I'll tell you about the Office Assistant later in this chapter. You also might see a Tip of the Day box that you have to close before you can move on.

Hands On: Starting a Blank Presentation

1. In the PowerPoint dialog box, click on the Blank presentation option button.
2. Click on OK. The New Slide dialog box appears.
3. Click on OK again to accept the default slide layout. Now your screen looks like the one shown in Figure 1.3, which is just where you need to be to follow along in this chapter.

In many ways, PowerPoint is much like any other Windows program; it contains the standard elements that users expect to see, such as a title bar, toolbars,

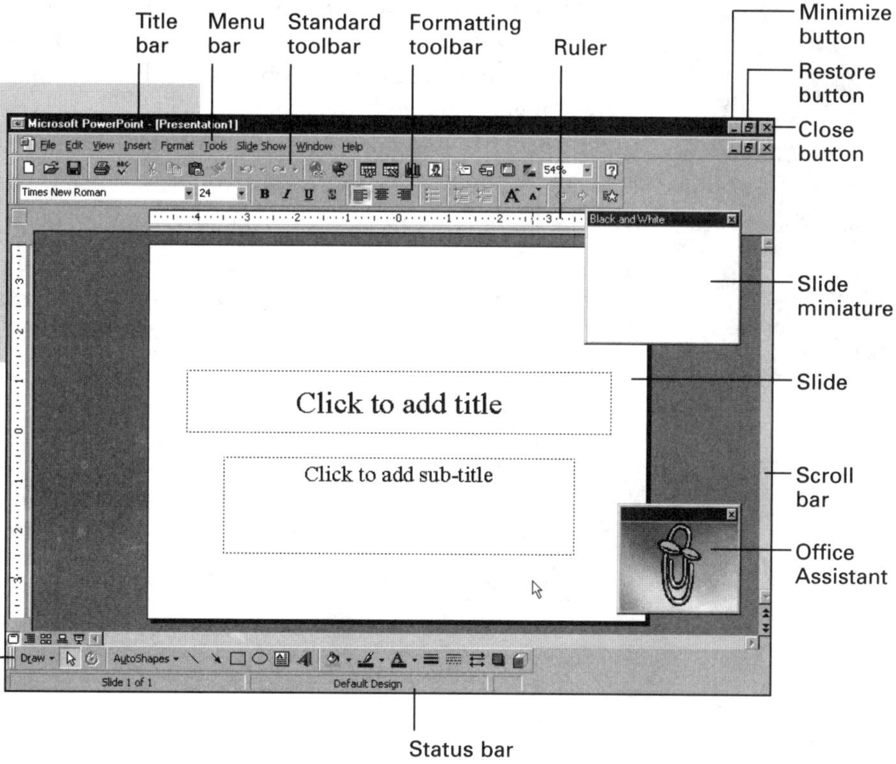

Figure 1.3 The PowerPoint screen contains many familiar Windows elements, plus a few controls that might be new to you.

a menu bar, and window control buttons (Minimize, Maximize, and Restore). If you are already familiar with these controls, feel free to skip the rest of this section. Figure 1.3 shows the initial PowerPoint screen and points out some of its parts; I explain these parts further in the following sections.

Slides

You'll learn all about creating presentations in Chapter 3. Chapter 5 covers adding slides to presentations.

That big white thing in the middle of the PowerPoint window is the *slide*. The slide is the heart of the PowerPoint screen. Slides are like pages in a book (or *presentation*, as the case is in PowerPoint). Each presentation can contain as many slides as you want. When you create a presentation using a template, you have a fixed number of slides to start with; when you create a presentation from scratch (as you did in the preceding Hands On), you must add each slide individually. (That's what you were doing in step 3, in the New Slide dialog box—adding a slide to the presentation.)

You'll learn about the various views available in Chapter 2. Chapter 5 covers placing text on a slide.

Each slide is a blank canvas, on which you place objects. Depending on the slide layout you choose in the New Slide dialog box, your slide might already have some pre-made boxes for objects. (In PowerPoint lingo, an *object* is anything that goes on a slide: text, graphics, a chart—anything.) The *layout* is the arrangement of pre-made boxes on a slide. The layout in Figure 1.3 is for a title slide, and contains two text boxes.

It's very simple to add text or graphics to this kind of pre-made text box—you just follow the directions. In Figure 1.3, you would just click inside the text boxes and type your text. But wait—I'm getting ahead of you! I'll save the slide creation for Chapter 5, after you've nailed the rest of the PowerPoint fundamentals.

Note

If your screen doesn't have one big slide on it in the middle, you're probably in a different view. Choose View, Slide to catch up with the rest of us.

Title Bar

Every Windows program has a *title bar*, the colored bar across the top of the application window. It's called the title bar because, obviously, it contains the title of the program (Microsoft PowerPoint). When a presentation window is maximized, as it is in Figure 1.3, the name of the presentation also appears in the title bar. (In Figure 1.3 it is "Presentation1." Not much of a name, but you'll assign a better one in Chapter 3, when you save the file.)

Menu Bar

Immediately below the title bar is the *menu bar*. All Windows programs use drop-down menus to help you issue commands to the program. The menu bar contains the names of the menus you can open. To open a menu, simply click on its name. Figure 1.4 shows an open menu. When a menu is open, click on a command to choose it (this also closes the menu). If you open a menu and decide not to choose a command from it, press the Esc key or click anywhere outside the menu.

Figure 1.4
This is a typical menu in PowerPoint.

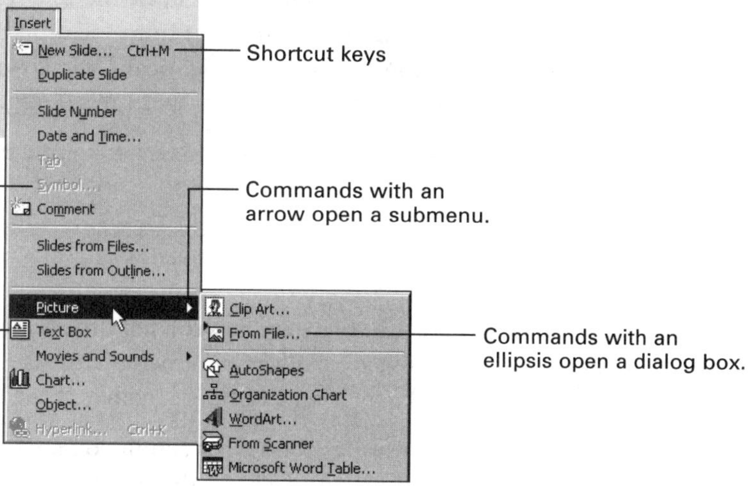

> **You learn how to minimize, maximize, and restore windows in Chapter 2. Chapter 3 shows you how to save the presentation under a more descriptive name.**

Here's a quick look at the features you can find on a menu:

- *Shortcut keys.* In Figure 1.4, for example, the New Slide command has Ctrl+M next to it. That means that instead of choosing Insert, New Slide, you can simply hold down the Ctrl key on the keyboard and press the M key (without opening the menu).
- *Unavailable commands.* These commands are grayed out—that is, they appear in gray letters rather than black in most Windows color schemes. In Figure 1.4, for example, the Symbol command is unavailable.
- *Toolbar button equivalents.* If a command corresponds to a toolbar button, a picture of the button appears to its left. In Figure 1.4, the Clipart command has a toolbar button equivalent.
- *Right-pointing arrows.* In Figure 1.4, for example, the Picture and Movies and Sounds commands both open submenus. The Picture submenu is open because the mouse is pointing at it.
- *Ellipses.* Commands with an ellipses (. . .) following them open *dialog boxes,* which request more information about the action you want to take. For example, choosing Slides from Files in Figure 1.4 would open a dialog box. You learn about dialog boxes later in the chapter.

Opening menus with the mouse is the easiest way, but there is an alternative way. Hold down the Alt key and press the underlined letter (the *selection let-*

ter) in the menu name. For example, to open the File menu, hold down Alt and press F; then, to choose a command from the drop-down menu, type the underlined letter in the command name, or use the down arrow key to move the highlight to the command you want and press Enter.

Throughout this book, the selection letters for each menu and command appear underlined, in case you want to use them.

Toolbars

As you saw in Figure 1.3, there are two rows of little pictures (icons) across the top of the screen. Those are *toolbars*, and each picture is a *button*. To use a button, just click on it. There is an additional toolbar at the bottom of the screen.

WordArt is covered in Chapter 7; pictures in Chapter 8; and charts in Chapter 10.

Different buttons appear based on what action you are performing. For example, when you're working on a chart, the Standard toolbar contains special charting buttons. There also are toolbars that appear when needed, such as the Picture and WordArt toolbars. When you first start a new presentation (refer to Figure 1.3), you can see three toolbars: the Standard and Formatting toolbars at the top, and the Drawing toolbar at the bottom.

Not all toolbar controls are buttons; some are *drop-down lists*—text with a down arrow to the right. To open a drop-down list, click on the down arrow. A list of choices appears; just click on your selection. For example, the first two controls on the left end of the Formatting toolbar are drop-down lists for Font and Font Size, respectively.

Some controls are a combination of a button and a drop-down list—buttons with down arrows next to them. If you click on the button portion, it executes the current setting. For example, if you click on the Font Color button in the Drawing toolbar (the button with the underlined A), the currently chosen font color is applied. (The current color is the color of the underline under the A.) To change the current setting (for example, the current font color), click on the down arrow to open a list of available settings.

Still other controls look like regular buttons but are actually pop-up menus in disguise. Most of the buttons at the right end of the Drawing toolbar are like that. When you click on one of those, a list of options pops up from which you can select a command. The Draw and AutoShape buttons on the Drawing toolbar open pop-up menus, too.

Tables 1.1, 1.2, and 1.3 show the buttons on the Standard, Formatting, and Drawing toolbars and explain what each one does. Don't worry if you don't understand the explanations fully now; all of these buttons will be covered later in the book.

Tip

Throughout the book, I'll be referring to these toolbar buttons by the names shown in these tables. They're the same names you see in the ToolTip that appears when you rest the mouse pointer over the buttons. You may want to mark this page with a sticky note for easy reference to these tables.

Table 1.1 Controls on the Standard Toolbar

Button	Name	Purpose
	New	Starts a new presentation.
	Open	Opens an existing presentation.
	Save	Saves the active presentation to disk.
	Print	Prints the currently displayed slide of the active presentation.
	Spelling	Runs a spelling check.
	Cut	Removes the selected data to the Clipboard.
	Copy	Copies the selected data to the Clipboard.
	Paste	Pastes the Clipboard contents into the worksheet.
	Format Painter	Copies the formatting of the selected text and applies it to the text you select next.
	Undo	Reverses the last action. Opens its drop-down list to choose multiple previous actions to undo.
	Redo	Redoes the last reversed action. Opens a drop-down list from which you can choose multiple "undos" to redo.

Table 1.1 Controls on the Standard Toolbar *(continued)*

Button	Name	Purpose
	Insert Hyperlink	Opens the Insert Hyperlink dialog box.
	Web Toolbar	Displays or hides the Web toolbar.
	Insert Microsoft Word table	Creates a table linked to Microsoft Word.
	Insert Microsoft Excel worksheet	Creates a worksheet linked to Microsoft Excel.
	Insert Chart	Opens Microsoft Graph.
	Insert Clipart	Opens the Clip Gallery.
	New Slide	Enables you to insert a new slide.
	Slide Layout	Enables you to change the current slide's layout.
	Apply Design	Opens the Apply Design dialog box, in which you can select a different slide design.
	Black and White	Toggles the slide display between color and black and white.
54%	Zoom	Opens a drop-down list from which you can choose a magnification at which to view your slide.
	Office Assistant	Opens the Office Assistant, which provides program help information.

Table 1.2 Controls on the Formatting Toolbar

Button	Name	Purpose
Times New Roman	Font	Opens a drop-down list to choose a font.
28	Font Size	Opens a drop-down list to choose a font size.
B	Bold	Toggles the Bold attribute on/off.
I	Italic	Toggles the Italic attribute on/off.
U	Underline	Toggles the Underline attribute on/off.
S	Shadow	Toggles the Shadow attribute on/off.
	Align Left	Aligns text to the left side of the text box.
	Center	Centers text in the text box.
	Align Right	Aligns text to the right side of the text box.
	Bullets	Toggles the Bullet attribute on/off.
	Increase Paragraph Spacing	Increases the blank space between lines in the selected paragraph.
	Decrease Paragraph Spacing	Decreases the blank space between lines in the selected paragraph.
A	Increase Font Size	Increases the size of the selected text.
A	Decrease Font Size	Decreases the size of the selected text.
	Promote	Promotes the selected paragraph in the slide's outline.
	Demote	Demotes the selected paragraph in the slide's outline.
	Animation Effects	Toggles the Animation Effects toolbar on/off.

Table 1.3 Controls on the Drawing Toolbar

Button	Name	Purpose
	Draw	Opens a menu of drawing commands.
	Select Objects	Changes the mouse pointer to a selector arrow.
	Free Rotate	Enables you to rotate drawn objects.
	AutoShapes	Opens a menu of pre-drawn shapes that you can place in the slide.
	Line	Draws a straight line.
	Arrow	Draws a straight line with an arrow on the end.
	Rectangle	Draws a rectangle.
	Oval	Draws an oval.
	Text Box	Inserts a text box in which you can enter text.
	Insert WordArt	Opens the WordArt dialog box, in which you can select a WordArt type to place in the slide.
	Line Color	Applies the selected line color, or opens a drop-down list to select a different color.
	Fill Color	Applies the selected fill color, or opens a drop-down list to select a different color.
	Font Color	Applies the selected font color, or opens a drop-down list to select a different color.
	Line Style	Opens a pop-up list of line style choices.
	Dash Style	Opens a pop-up list of dashed line choices.
	Arrow Style	Opens a pop-up list of arrow choices.
	Shadow	Opens a pop-up list of shadow choices.
	3-D	Opens a pop-up list of 3-D effect choices.

In Chapter 2, you learn how to display or hide various screen elements, including toolbars. In Appendix A, you learn to customize the toolbars with different buttons and even create your own toolbars.

Tip

If at any time you need a quick reminder of a button's name, just move the mouse pointer over it. A ToolTip will pop up telling you the name of the button, as shown in Figure 1.5. You also can get information about a button using the What's This? feature described later in this chapter.

Ruler

The ruler is just underneath the toolbars at the top of the screen. In some views (such as the Slide view), a vertical ruler also appears, running down the left side of the window. These rulers have several uses.

Tip

If you have the ruler turned off in another Office program, PowerPoint's ruler may not appear by default either. If you don't see the ruler, choose View, Ruler.

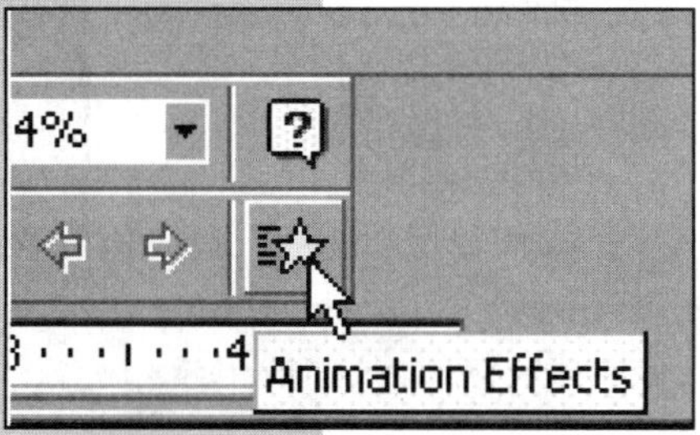

Figure 1.5 ToolTips remind you what a button's name is—you don't have to refer back to Tables 1.1, 1.2, and 1.3 if you forget a button's purpose.

Don't mess with the indent markers right now. You'll take a look at them again in Chapter 7.

You might notice that part of the ruler is gray and part of it is white. The gray area of the ruler is the area outside the slide margins; the white area of the ruler is the area inside the slide margins. If you select a particular object on the slide, such as a text box, the white and gray areas on the ruler show the boundaries of that object rather than the boundaries of the whole slide.

The ruler also shows the position of the mouse pointer. Move the mouse pointer around on-screen, and watch the rulers. A dotted line on each ruler moves to show the position of the mouse pointer relative to the whole slide. If you click in one of the text boxes, indent markers appear on the ruler, as shown in Figure 1.6. You can drag the indent markers to change the indentation of the text.

You'll learn how to change the zoom in Chapter 2.

You may not think these features are particularly useful right now—and when you're looking at the slide in a view like the one in Figure 1.6, you're right. You can already see all sides of the slide, so you don't need any help knowing where the margins are. However, if you zoom the view in, so you see one small area of the slide magnified, it becomes easy to get "lost" and the rulers can help you find your bearings.

Figure 1.6 The ruler has several uses in PowerPoint.

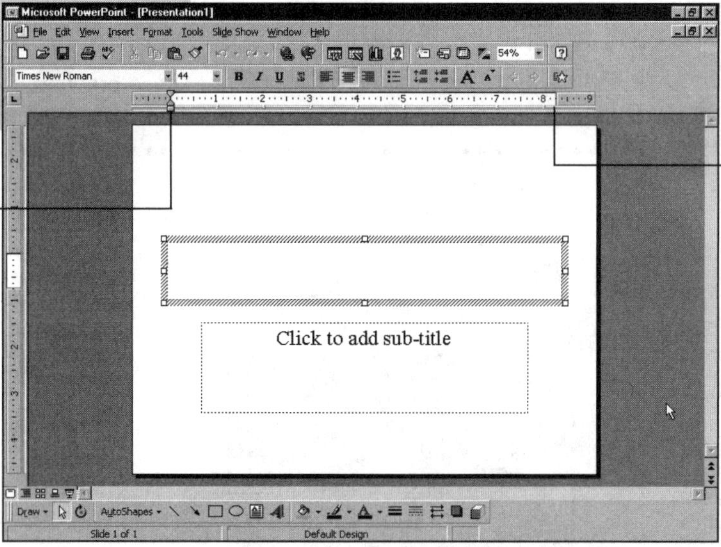

These triangles are indent markers that you can drag.

The margins are where the gray and white areas meet.

Status Bar

The *status bar* is the thin, usually gray bar across the bottom of the PowerPoint window. It gives you two vital pieces of information:

- The slide currently displayed, and the total number of slides in the presentation—for example, Slide 3 of 5.
- The name of the design template that's applied to the presentation—for example, Default Design.

There also is a little book with a check mark in it on the status bar. That is a pagination indicator. When the program is doing automatic repagination, you'll see an animation here that looks like pages turning and a pencil writing. When it's finished, it returns to the static book with a check mark.

Scroll Bars

You'll learn how to add more slides to your presentation in Chapter 5, and how to zoom in for a closer view of a slide in Chapter 2.

Scroll bars help you move different parts of the slide or different parts of the presentation into view. If you have only one slide in the presentation and you already can see all of it (such as the presentation shown in Figure 1.6), the scroll bars don't have much use. However, when you have more slides, or are viewing a slide in a zoomed view, the scroll bars can take you from place to place on the slide and from one slide to the next.

There are several ways to use scroll bars, as shown in Figure 1.7. The simplest is to click on the arrow buttons at the ends to scroll the display up, down, to the left, or to the right. If you hold down the mouse button while pointing at one of the arrow buttons, the display scrolls quickly.

Note

If there is nothing more in the presentation than what currently is shown on-screen, the scroll bars are inactive. I added a few more slides to the presentation before I took the picture shown in Figure 1.7 so you could see the scroll bars in action. If you want to do the same so you can play with the scroll bars now, click on the New Slide button on the Standard toolbar and then click on OK. Do this twice, and you'll have three "dummy" slides in your presentation—more than enough for a scroll bar experiment.

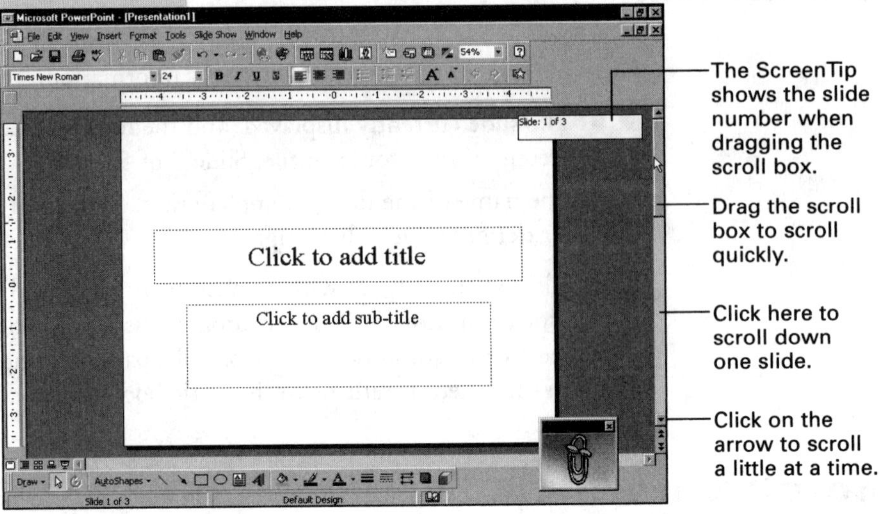

Figure 1.7 Use scroll bars to change which slide is displayed (and what part of it, if applicable).

You learn more about moving around within a presentation in Chapter 5.

Another way to use a scroll bar is to drag the gray box (the *scroll box*) with your mouse. You will move quickly through the presentation. For example, to scroll quickly to the first slide of the presentation, drag the scroll box on the vertical scroll bar to the top of the scroll bar. As you drag, a ScreenTip appears telling you what slide you'll be on if you release the mouse button at that point.

You also can scroll one screenful at a time by clicking on the scroll bar above or below (or to the right or left of) the scroll box. For example, to move one screenful down, click in the space below the scroll box on the vertical scroll bar.

Using Dialog Boxes

As you learned earlier in this chapter, some menu commands and toolbar buttons open *dialog boxes*. Dialog boxes are simply requests for more information or opportunities for you to change default settings before a command is executed.

Figure 1.8 shows some common dialog box controls you may encounter. The following list summarizes these controls:

- *Option button.* When you must choose one out of a group of options, these round option buttons appear. They are like buttons on a car

Figure 1.8
Here are some of the most common dialog box controls you will need in PowerPoint.

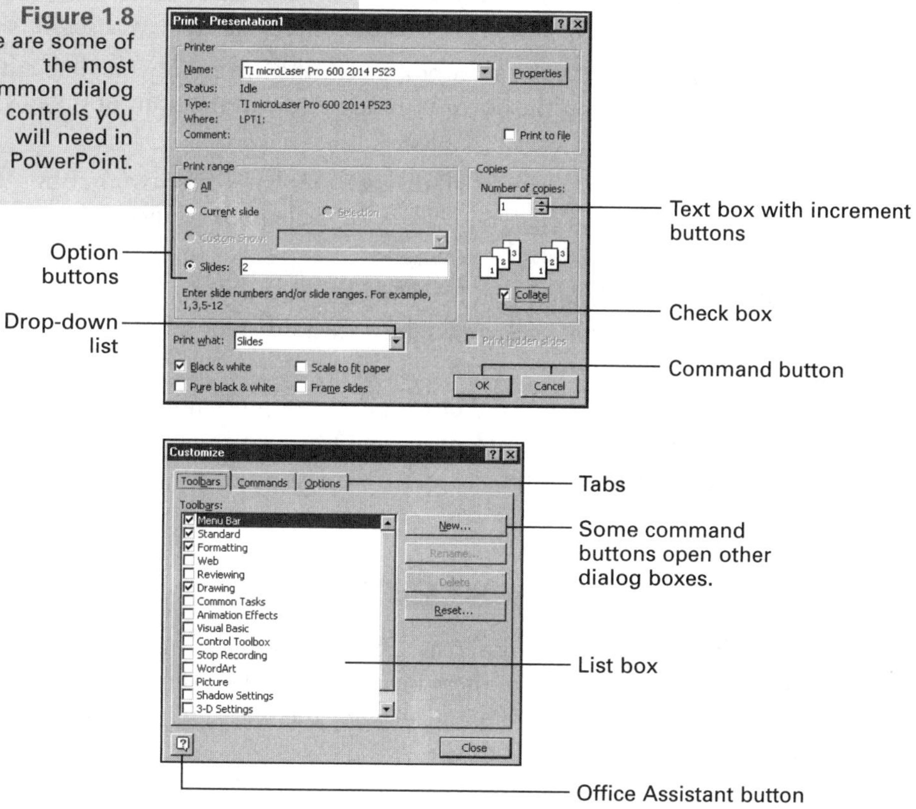

radio—you can select only one at a time. When you click on one, the prior selection becomes deselected.

- *Text box.* You type text into a text box.
- *Increment button.* Text boxes in which you enter a number often have increment buttons. Click on the up arrow to increase the number by one (from 1 to 2, for example); click on the down arrow button to decrease the number by one.
- *Check box.* Check boxes are on/off switches for certain features. Click on the box to place or remove the check mark.
- *Command button.* Command buttons take you somewhere else. Some buttons, such as the Preview button, take you to an entirely different screen and close the dialog box. Some command buttons open other dialog boxes. Usually, but not always, such buttons have ellipses (. . .) on them. Command buttons with >> on them open additional sections of the same dialog box.

- *List box.* A list box is very simple—it's a box with a list in it. If the list is too long to fit in the allotted box space, it may have a scroll bar.
- *Drop-down list.* Like a list box except the box is only one line tall. You have to click on the down-pointing arrow to the right of the box to open it up and see the choices.
- *OK and Cancel.* Almost all dialog boxes have these two buttons. OK accepts your changes and closes the dialog box; Cancel rejects your changes and closes the dialog box.
- *Tab.* Some dialog boxes have too many controls to fit in the box; in those cases, you click on a tab to see a different set of controls in the same dialog box.
- *Office Assistant button.* For certain tricky procedures, this button is available. Click on it to open the Office Assistant, which is described in the following section.

Using the Help System

Because every person is different, PowerPoint offers many ways to get help with the program. Some of these Help methods will be familiar to experienced Windows users; others are brand-new for the Office 97 products. You can do the following:

- Ask the Office Assistant for help
- Choose what you're interested in learning about from a series of Help Topics
- Get help on a particular element you see on-screen with the What's This? tool
- If you are connected to the Internet, access the Microsoft on the Web feature to view Web pages containing Help information

The Office Assistant

The Office Assistant is that little paper clip character that popped up the first time you started PowerPoint. It might look silly, but behind it is a powerful Help system.

By default, the Office Assistant starts whenever you start PowerPoint and sits in a little box on top of whatever you're working on, as shown in Figure 1.9. If you ignore him for awhile, his box gets somewhat smaller and less obtrusive. You can turn it off by clicking on the Close (X) button in its upper-right corner.

Figure 1.9 The Office Assistant appears in its own window on top of the PowerPoint window.

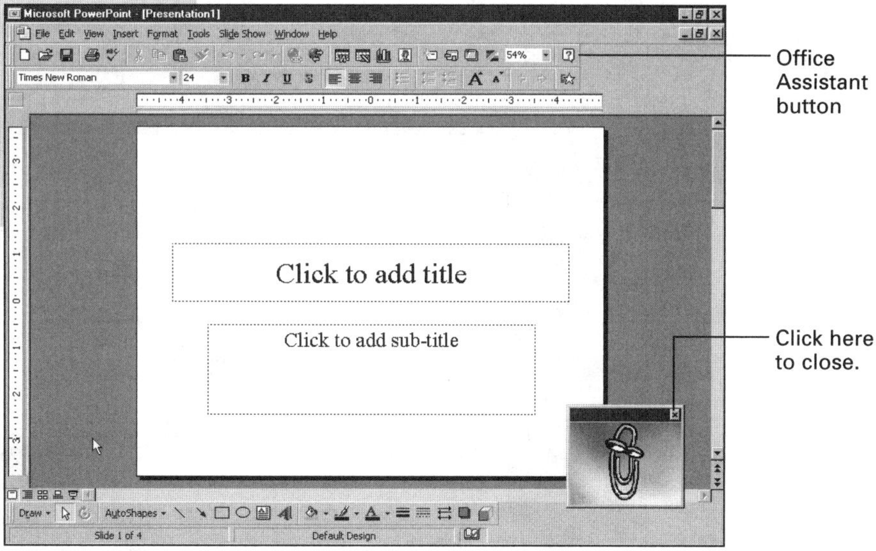

Note

The Office Assistant has replaced the Answer Wizard feature in PowerPoint for Windows 95.

To turn the Office Assistant on again, click on the Office Assistant button in the Standard toolbar or choose Help, Microsoft PowerPoint Help.

Tip

If you don't like the paper clip, you can choose one of the other Office Assistants. Right-click on the Office Assistant and choose Choose Assistant from the short-cut menu. Click on the Back and Next buttons to find an assistant you prefer; then click on OK to change the character. If you get a message telling you the file cannot be located, insert your installation disk in your drive and try again.

When you turn on the Office Assistant, or when you click on it if it's already open, a bubble appears next to (or above) its box asking you what kind of help you want (see Figure 1.10). You can do any of the following:

- Type a question in the text box to tell the Office Assistant what kind of help you need.

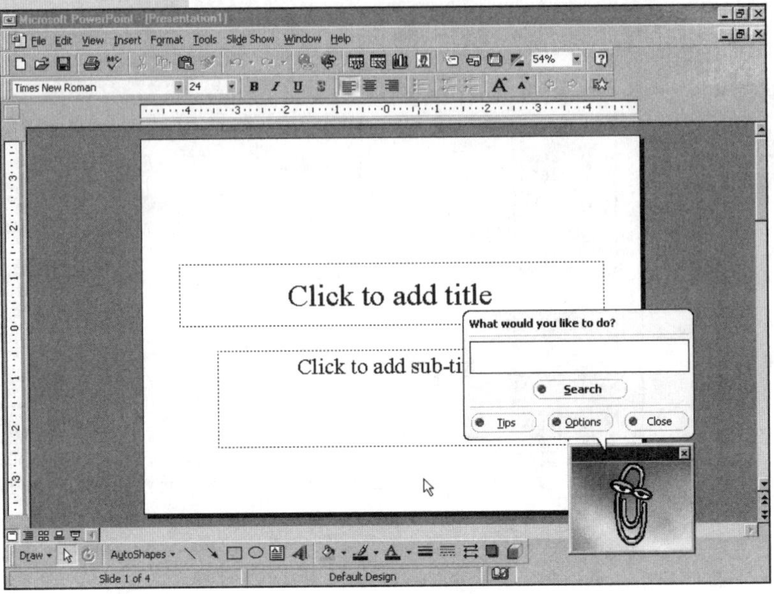

Figure 1.10 Office Assistant asks what you need help with.

- Select one of the Office Assistant's "guesses" about what you need help with, if any appear.
- Type what you want help on and click on the Search button.
- Click on the Tips button to get any tips the Office Assistant can provide for the task you're performing.
- Click on the Options button to customize the way the Office Assistant works.
- Right-click on the Office Assistant window to select options from a shortcut menu.
- Click on the Close button, (not the X button) to close the bubble (but leave the Office Assistant on-screen).

If you close the help bubble, you can reopen it at any time by clicking on the Office Assistant button on the Standard toolbar; pressing F1; choosing Help, Microsoft PowerPoint Help; or clicking on the Office Assistant window.

Tip

If a light bulb appears next to the Office Assistant, it means the Office Assistant has a suggestion for you. To get the suggestion, click on the light bulb. Click on the Close button when you're finished reading the suggestion.

Hands On: Asking the Office Assistant a Question

If you need help on a particular topic, simply type a question in the text box shown in Figure 1.10. Follow these steps:

1. If the Office Assistant's help bubble isn't on-screen, click on the Office Assistant button on the Standard toolbar or click on the Office Assistant window.
2. Type a question in the text box. For example, you might type **How do I save?** to get help saving your work.
3. Click on the Search button or press Enter. The Office Assistant provides some topics that might match what you're looking for. For example, Figure 1.11 shows the Office Assistant's responses to the question "How do I save?"
4. Click on the option that best describes what you're trying to do. For example, I'm going to choose "Save a presentation" from Figure 1.11. A Help window appears with instructions for the specified task. If none of the options describe what you want, click on the See More arrow to view more options, or type a different question in the text box.

The Help window that appears containing the task instructions is part of the same Help system you can access with the Help, Contents and Index

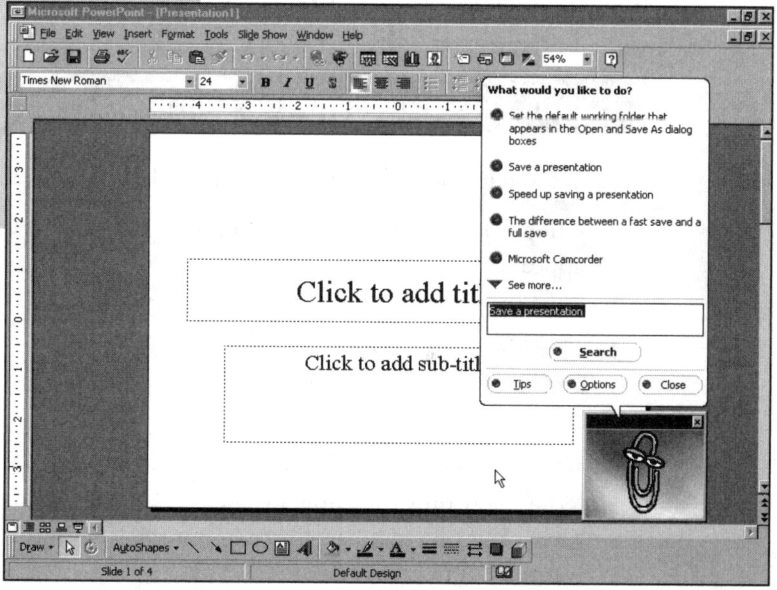

Figure 1.11 The Office Assistant attempts to narrow down exactly what you are trying to accomplish.

command. See the section "Working with Help Information" later in this chapter for information about navigating this window.

Help Topics

If you want a more conventional way to get help, try choosing Help, Contents and Index. The Help Topics dialog box appears. When you open the PowerPoint Help system this way, you move through the listed topics to find the one in which you're interested.

The Help Topics dialog box has several tabs, so you can use Help the way you want it. Click on a tab to display its options.

- *Contents.* Browse the Help system as you would a reference book.
- *Index.* Look up Help topics alphabetically.
- *Find.* Search for a certain word among all the topics in the system.

Complete the steps in the following sections to use the Contents, Index, or Find methods of getting help.

Contents

The Contents tab of the Help Topics dialog box lists a series of "books" you can open. Each book has one or more Help topics in it. Some books contain other subbooks. It's like pulling a real book off the shelf and browsing through it for the topic you're interested in. Figure 1.12 shows the Contents tab.

Hands On: Browsing the Contents Tab

To select a help topic from the Contents tab, follow these steps:

1. Choose Help, Contents and Index. The Help Topics dialog box appears.
2. Click on the Contents tab.
3. Find the book that describes, in broad terms, what you want help with and double-click on it. A list of help topics appears below the book, as shown in Figure 1.12.
4. Double-click on a help topic to display it.
5. When you finish reading a topic, click on the Help Topics button to go back to the main Help screen; or click on the Help window's Close button (X) to exit Help.

Figure 1.12
The Contents tab presents books containing help topics and/or other books.

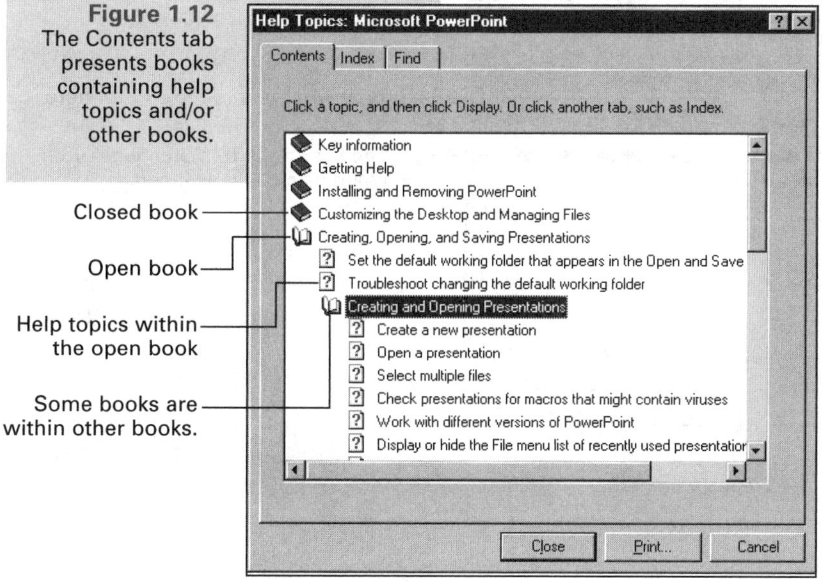

Index

The Index tab is an alphabetical listing of all the Help topics available. It works well if you know the exact term you want to look up, such as Saving or Printing, for example. Use it as you would use the index in a real book (like this one!).

Hands On: Looking Up a Topic in the Index Tab

To use the index:

1. Choose Help, Contents and Index. The Help Topics dialog box appears.
2. Click on the Index tab.
3. Type the first few letters of the topic you're looking for in the first text box. The index list jumps quickly to that spot (see Figure 1.13).
4. Double-click on the topic you want to see.
5. When you finish reading a topic, click on the Help Topics button to go back to the main Help screen; or click on the Help window's Close button (X) to exit from Help.

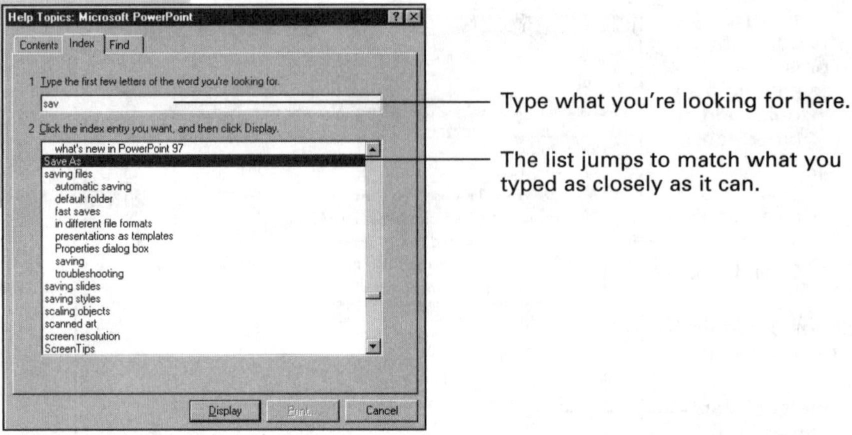

Figure 1.13 The Index tab enables you to browse alphabetically instead of by category.

Find

If you're not sure of the name of the feature you're looking for, use the Find tab. Find searches for the titles of Help topics and for their contents, and retrieves all the topics in which the word(s) you typed appears.

Hands On: Finding a Help Topic in the Help System

To use the Find tab, follow these steps:

1. Choose Help, Contents and Index. The Help Topics dialog box appears.
2. Click on the Find tab. The first time you use Find, it asks you to build the Find index. Click on Next and then click on Finish to create the list.
3. Type the topic you're looking for in the first text box.
4. If more than one line appears in the second box, click on the one that most closely matches your interest. Find considers uppercase and lowercase versions of a word to be different, so in Figure 1.14, for example, there are separate entries for "Save" and "save," as well as for other forms of the word ("saves" and "saved").
5. Browse the topics that appear at the bottom, and click on the one that matches the help you need (see Figure 1.14).

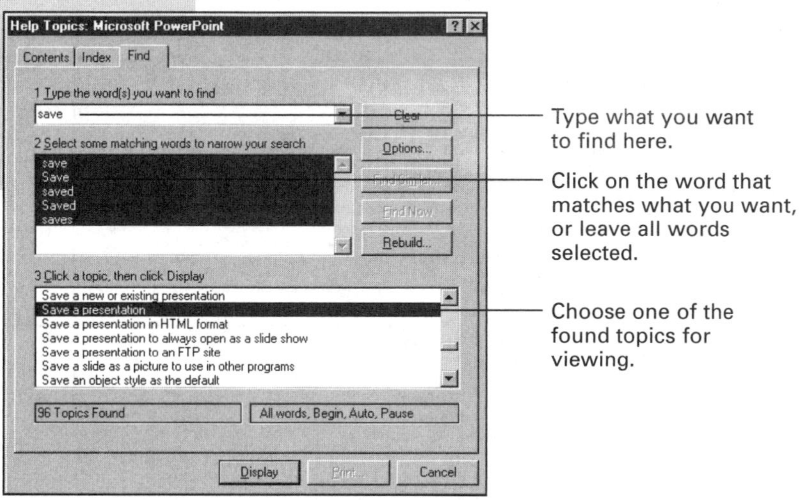

Figure 1.14 Use Find to locate all the help topics that deal with a certain subject.

6. Click on the Display button or press Enter to display the Help information.
7. When you finish reading a topic, click on the Help Topics button to go back to the main Help screen; or click on the Help window's Close button (X) to exit from Help.

Working with Help Information

After you've located the Help topic you need—then what? Read it, of course. All the methods of getting Help described so far end up at the same place—only the journey is different. For example, you could locate the "Save a workbook" information by any of the four methods I've told you about so far and get the same exact information (see Figure 1.15).

After you have a Help topic on-screen, here's what you can do with it:

- Click on an underlined word to see a definition of it (for example, "FTP" in Figure 1.15).
- Click on a button to jump to another Help screen. For example, in Figure 1.15, seven >> buttons are available to take you to screens of related information.
- Print a hard copy of the information by clicking on the Options button and then choosing Print Topic.

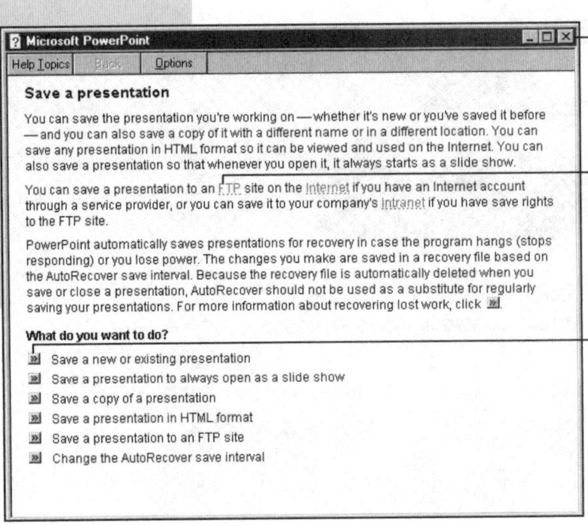

Figure 1.15 After you arrive at the information you need, you can read it on-screen, print it, or move to another Help topic.

- Copy the text to the Clipboard (for pasting into a program, such as Microsoft Word or Windows Notepad) by clicking on the Options button and then choosing Copy.
- Return to the main Help topic that brought you to this subtopic by clicking on the Back button. The Back button is not available if you are viewing a topic you arrived at directly from the Office Assistant, Contents, Index, or Find.
- Return to the main Help Topics screen by clicking on the Help Topics button.
- Close the Help window by clicking on the Close (X) button.

What's This? Help

Sometimes all the words and topics in the world can't help you—for example, if you see something on-screen but you have no idea what it is. How do you look up a toolbar button when all you know is that it looks like a bunch of squiggly lines with a pencil? Or a globe with a piece of chain on it? The answer is the What's This? feature. You can point to an object on-screen and PowerPoint will tell you what that object's purpose is.

Hands On: Finding Out What an On-Screen Element Does

Follow these steps to try out the What's This? feature:

1. Press Shift+F1 or choose Help, What's This?. Your mouse pointer changes to a big arrow with a question mark next to it.
2. Click on the object you want to know about. A box pops up telling you about the object. For example, Figure 1.16 shows the box I saw when I clicked on the Minimize button of the PowerPoint window.

What's This? works well for screen elements in PowerPoint, but it also works for menu commands and dialog box controls.

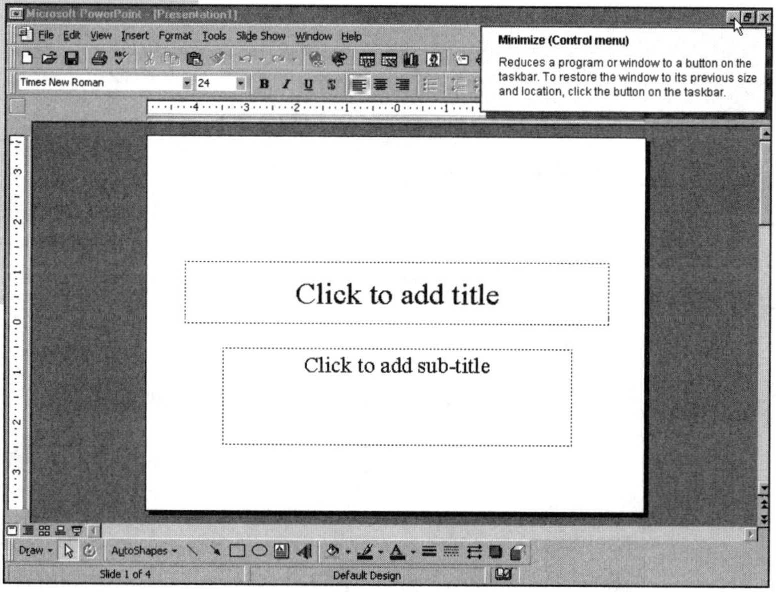

Figure 1.16 What's This? Help spares you the trouble of figuring out the name of an on-screen element. Just press Shift+F1 and then click on the object.

Microsoft On the Web Help

All Microsoft Office 97 applications, including PowerPoint, are tightly connected to the Internet. You get a closer look at the Internet features that PowerPoint provides in Chapter 15, but here's an Internet feature you can take advantage of right away: Microsoft on the Web Help.

Simply put, Microsoft has made available additional Help resources for PowerPoint at its Web site. To access the Web site, just choose Help, Microsoft on the Web, and the document you want to see. (You may have to dial up your Internet service provider first, unless you are already connected or you access the Internet through a LAN.) Your Web browser opens, and the document appears. Figure 1.17 shows the result of selecting the Frequently Asked Questions document.

While you've visiting Microsoft on the Web, you may want to check out what else Microsoft has to offer at its Web site. You can try out all of the menu options on the Help, Microsoft on the Web menu as a start. See the inside back cover of this book for an overview of what's available. When you've exhausted all those sites, try PowerPoint Central, which is described in the following section.

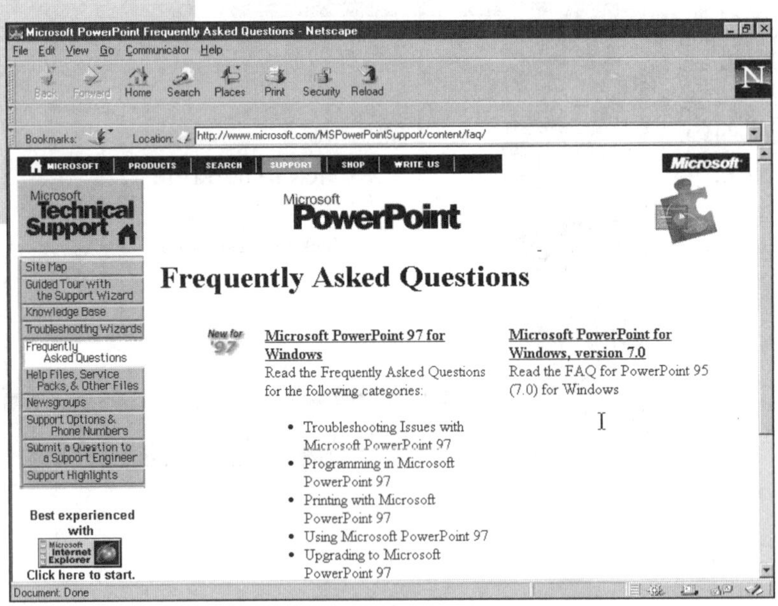

Figure 1.17 One of the many Help documents for PowerPoint available at the Microsoft Web site.

Note

When you access the Web page, it might look different from what you see in Figure 1.17. That's because Microsoft updates these pages periodically with new information. That's the beauty of Microsoft's Internet-provided help—it is never out of date.

Running the Quick Start Tutorial

You'll find a very helpful Quick Start Tutorial in PowerPoint Central. *PowerPoint Central* is a special PowerPoint presentation that contains a wealth of useful information about PowerPoint. It also contains some links to the Microsoft Web site, so you can try it out while your Web connection is running.

The PowerPoint Central presentation resides on your hard disk, but it is integrally connected to the Microsoft Office 97 CD-ROM and to the Internet, and it updates itself regularly from Microsoft's Web site to ensure that you have the most recent information.

Throughout this book, you'll see many uses for PowerPoint Central, such as using it to download additional fonts, clip art, graphics, videos, and more from Microsoft's Web site. This chapter, however, focuses on PowerPoint Central's teaching capability.

Hands On: Running the Quick Start Tutorial

1. Make sure the Microsoft Office 97 CD-ROM is in your CD-ROM drive. This step is not necessary for some other PowerPoint Central features, but it is necessary for running the tutorial.
2. Choose Tools, PowerPoint Central. The PowerPoint Central presentation opens, as shown in Figure 1.18.
3. Click on the Free Stuff button at the top of the page.
4. Click on the big Start graphic in the middle of the slide to begin the Quick Start tutorial.
5. Click on the big Start button in the lower-right corner of the tutorial window. (Don't confuse this with the regular Windows 95 Start button in the lower-left corner!) The tutorial starts.

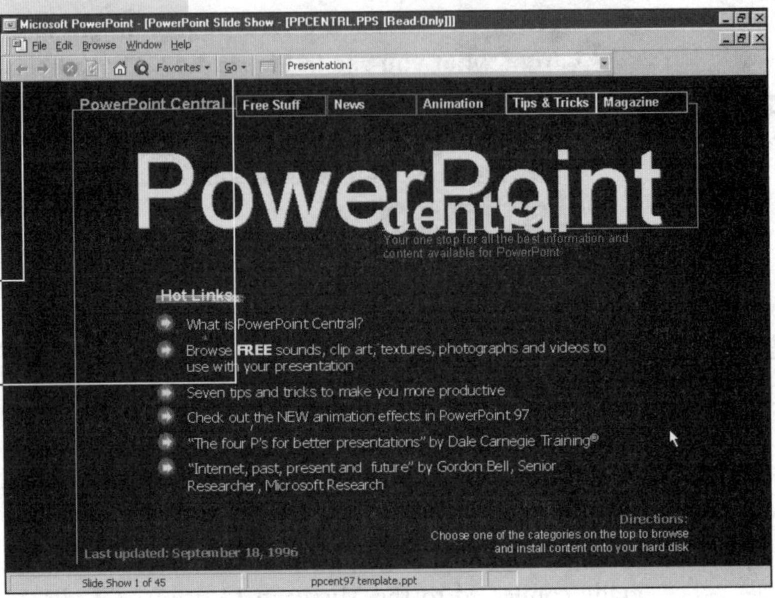

Figure 1.18 One of the many Help documents for PowerPoint available at the Microsoft Web site.

Note

You can end the tutorial early by clicking on the Exit button, or you can jump to a particular part of the tutorial by using the Menu button.

You will explore the PowerPoint Central areas in more detail in the appropriate chapters.

6. Read the first screen, and then click on the right arrow button to move on (see Figure 1.19).
7. Follow the on-screen instructions and read the information presented until you have read the entire tutorial.
8. Click on the Exit button to leave the tutorial.
9. Back in the PowerPoint Central presentation, go ahead and explore some more. Or, if you are finished, go on to the next section of this chapter.

You can close the PowerPoint Central presentation and continue working in PowerPoint if you are not yet ready to exit Excel. Just choose File, End Show, and then click on OK in the dialog box that appears.

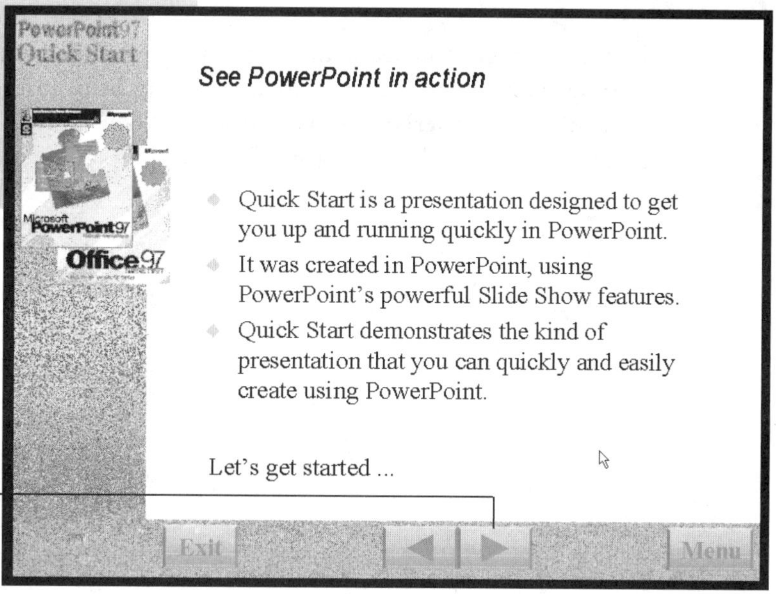

Figure 1.19 Using the Quick Start tutorial is a pleasant and easy way to learn PowerPoint basics.

Click here to advance through the presentation.

Exiting PowerPoint

When you are finished working in PowerPoint, you should close the program to free up system resources for other programs. You can exit PowerPoint in any of these ways:

- Click on the program's Close (×) button in the title bar.
- Choose File, Exit.
- Press Alt+F4.
- Double-click on the program's control icon (the icon at the left end of the title bar)

These methods work equally well. If you have made any changes to a presentation, PowerPoint asks whether you want to save your changes. Click on No. (Of course, if you really have made changes you want to save, click on Yes and see Chapter 3 for more information about saving.)

Summary

In this chapter, you learned the most basic of basics about PowerPoint—starting, moving around, exiting, and getting help. In the next chapter, you'll learn all about PowerPoint's many views and how you can use them to see your presentation in all the right ways.

2

Learning Your Viewing Options

In This Chapter

- Understanding and Using the Views
- Zooming In and Out
- Controlling Windows
- Displaying or Hiding Screen Elements

You've probably heard that old tale about the three blindfolded men who tried to figure out a type of animal by feeling the tusk, foot, and tail, respectively. Each man had a radically different idea of the animal from the others because each had a different perspective. Well, in PowerPoint, your presentation can take on several very different appearances, depending on which view you "grab."

This chapter is all about changing the ways you look at PowerPoint, so you can see your presentation from *all* perspectives. By learning these skills up front, you'll be prepared for whatever comes out of the jungle later.

Understanding Views

A *view*, simply speaking, is a way of seeing your work on-screen. Almost all good-quality programs offer multiple views to serve the needs of the diverse users they support. For example, word processing programs often have Normal view (good for typing), in which the typing area dominates the screen; and Page Layout view (good for seeing graphics), in which page margins, graphic images, multiple columns, and other fancy features are visible.

In word processors, people tend to do a lot of one thing—typing. Therefore, most people pick out one view they're comfortable with and use it most of the time. They don't need the other views to survive. In PowerPoint, however, there isn't one type of task that dominates your time. The average user jumps between many different tasks in a PowerPoint session, from typing new text to adding graphics to rearranging the slides in the presentation. Each PowerPoint view is uniquely suited to certain tasks, so you need to learn how to jump freely between the views to master PowerPoint.

You'll learn more about creating presentation files in Chapter 3.

In this section, you will experiment with PowerPoint's views. To do so, you should have a presentation on-screen. If you've been following along with the examples in the book, all you have on-screen is a single, plain slide, without any text on it. That won't do. If you want to try out the views, use the following Hands On procedure to create a sample file to play with.

Hands On: Creating a Sample File

1. Choose File, New. The New Presentation dialog box opens.
2. Click on the Presentations tab.
3. Double-click on Generic (Standard). A generic presentation opens on-screen.

Now you are ready to start experimenting with the PowerPoint views!

Changing the View

Before I tell you about what each PowerPoint view has to offer, you should know how to change the view. It's very simple to change view, actually, and the process is the same to change to any view.

The easiest way to change the view is to click on one of the View buttons at the lower-left corner of the PowerPoint window:

 Slide View

 Outline View

 Slide Sorter View

 Notes Page View

 Slide Show View

You'll learn more about Slide Show view in Chapter 18.

All views remain active until you switch to another view. Some views have their own toolbar buttons and menu commands that are available only while you're in that view; for example, Outline view has an Outlining toolbar, as you'll see later in this chapter. The exception is Slide Show view, which fills your screen with a preview of the slide show. To exit from Slide Show view (to return to the view you used before you entered Slide Show view), press the Esc key.

The other way to switch views is by using the View menu. Use the following Hands On to try it out.

Hands On: Switching Views with the View Menu

1. Open the View menu.
2. Click on one of the following commands:

   Slide

   Outline

   Slide Sorter

   Notes Page

   Slide Show
3. Note the changes on-screen in the view you selected.
4. Go back and try each of the other views listed in step 2 until you have seen them all.

Slide View: Good for Editing

> See Chapter 7 to learn more about text boxes; Chapter 8 for clip art; Chapter 10 for charts; and Chapter 13 for sound clips.

By default, PowerPoint starts out in Slide view (see Figure 2.1). Slide view shows you one slide at a time. You can zoom the view in and out (as you'll learn later in this chapter) for a closer or farther-away look at the slide.

Slide view is great for adding objects to slides. (An *object* can be anything—a text box, a graphic, a chart, an icon for a sound clip, and so on.) For example, when you want to place a piece of clip art precisely on a slide, Slide view shows you the big picture and helps you get the placement just right. Because you see only one slide at once in Slide view, the slide can appear fairly large, so you can see all the details.

Outline View: Good for Adding Text

> You'll use Outline view extensively in Chapter 5.

If you have lots of text to add to slides, Outline view is the best view to do it. Outline view makes creating bulleted lists on slides a snap, even multiple levels of bullets. As you can see in Figure 2.2, Outline view has its own Outlining toolbar that contains buttons for promoting and demoting lines on a slide, in effect creating a sophisticated, multi-level outline of the presentation. You can print this outline and hand it out to your audience, or use it for your own reference.

Figure 2.1 Slide view shows individual slides so you can place objects on them.

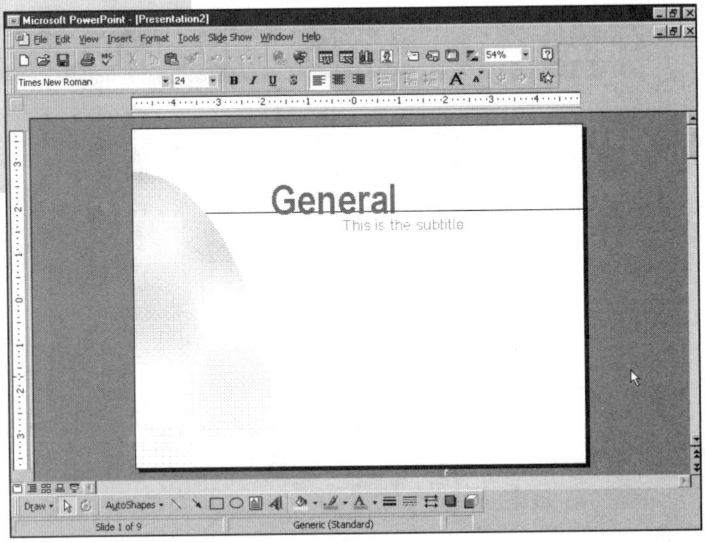

Slide Master View

Most of the time, the text, graphics, or whatever you add to a slide applies only to that one slide—not to all the slides in the presentation. However, sometimes you may want an object—such as a company logo or motto—repeated on every slide in the presentation. You could add this object to each slide manually, but a much better way is to add the object to the Slide Master.

The Slide Master is a special, hidden slide that every presentation has; you can see it only in Slide view. If you are in another view and try to view the Slide Master, your display changes to Slide view. Anything you add to the Slide Master will appear on every slide in the presentation. To display the Slide Master, choose View, Master, Slide Master. To get back to working with an individual slide, click on the Close button that floats above the Slide Master. You'll learn more about the Slide Master in Chapter 6.

Figure 2.2 Outline view is good for adding lots of text to the presentation and organizing it as an outline.

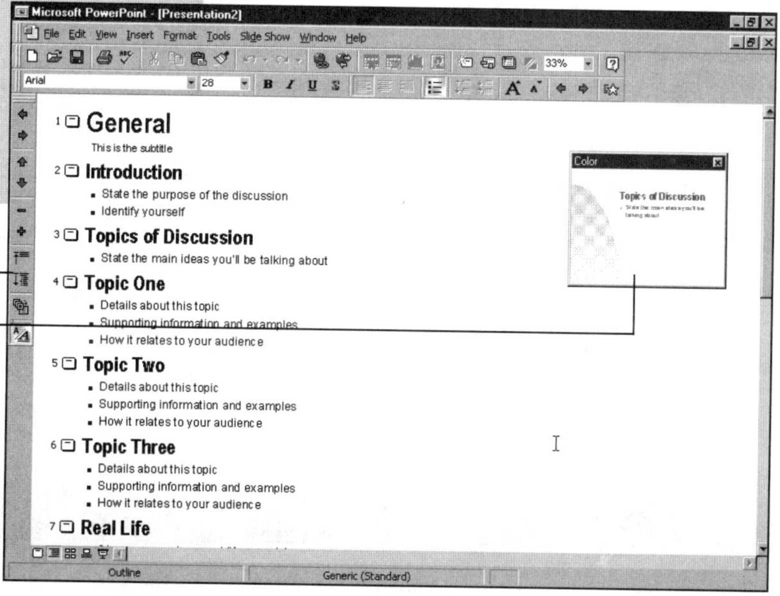

Outlining toolbar

The Slide Miniature window shows the selected slide in graphical form.

Slide Sorter View: Good for Rearranging Slides

In Chapter 16, you'll work with Slide Sorter view as you arrange your slides before a big presentation.

If you have ever worked with real slide-projector-type slides or overhead transparencies, you know that it can be helpful to lay slides out on a big table and plan the order in which you'll show them. You rearrange them, moving this one here, that one there, until the order is just perfect. You might even start a pile of "backups" that you will not show in the main presentation, but will hold back in case someone asks a pertinent question.

That's exactly what you can do with Slide Sorter view. As you can see in Figure 2.3, Slide Sorter view lays the slides out in miniature, so you can see the big picture. You can drag the slides around and rearrange them into the perfect order.

Notes Page View: Good for Organizing Your Notes

When you give a presentation, your props usually include more than just your brain and your slides. You typically have all kinds of notes and backup mater-

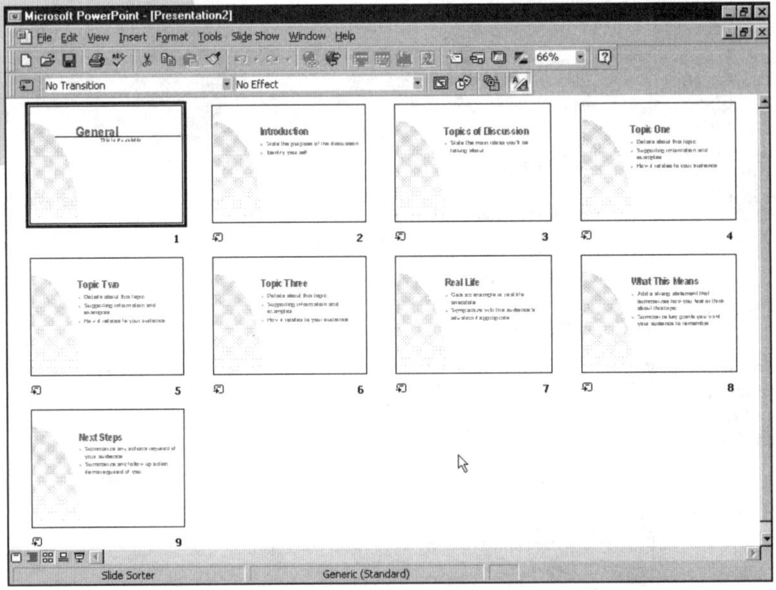

Figure 2.3 Use Slide Sorter view for a birds-eye view of your presentation.

You'll work with Notes Page view in Chapter 16, as you prepare your notes.

ial for each slide—figures on last quarter's sales, sources to cite if someone questions your data, and so on. In the old days of framed overhead transparencies, we used to attach sticky notes to the slide frames for this, and hope that nobody asked any questions that would require diving into the four-inch-thick stack of statistics we brought.

Today, you can type your notes and supporting facts directly in PowerPoint, in the Notes Page view. In Notes Page view, you see a single slide with a special text area, called the *notes area,* below it for your notes (see Figure 2.4). You can refer to these notes as you give an on-screen presentation, or you can print out Notes Page to stack neatly on the lectern next to you during the big event.

Slide Show View: Good for Practicing Your Presentation

When it's time to rehearse the presentation, nothing shows you the finished product quite as clearly as Slide Show view does. In Slide Show view, the slide fills the entire screen (see Figure 2.5). You move from slide to slide by pressing the Page Up or Page Down keys, or by using one of the other movement methods available.

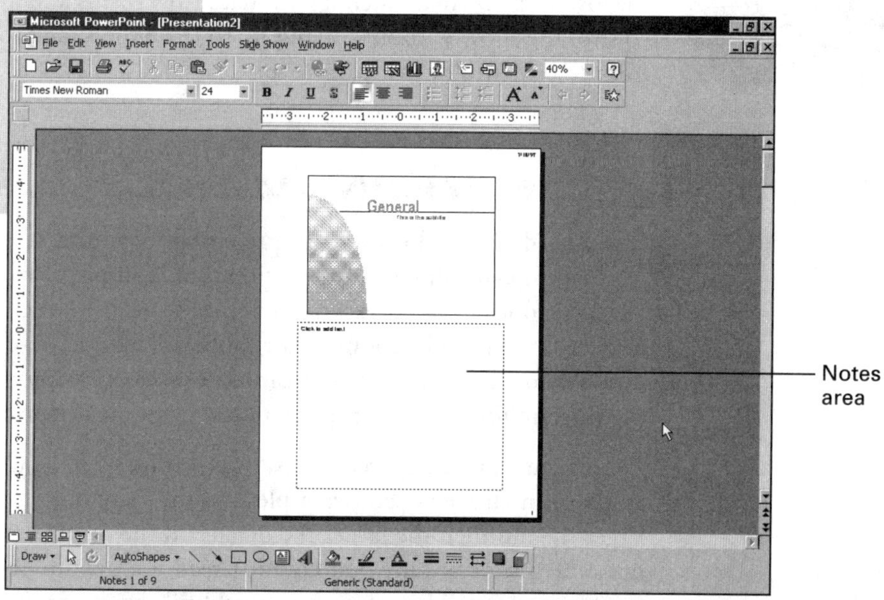

Figure 2.4
Notes Page view offers a special text area for your notes, separate from the slides themselves.

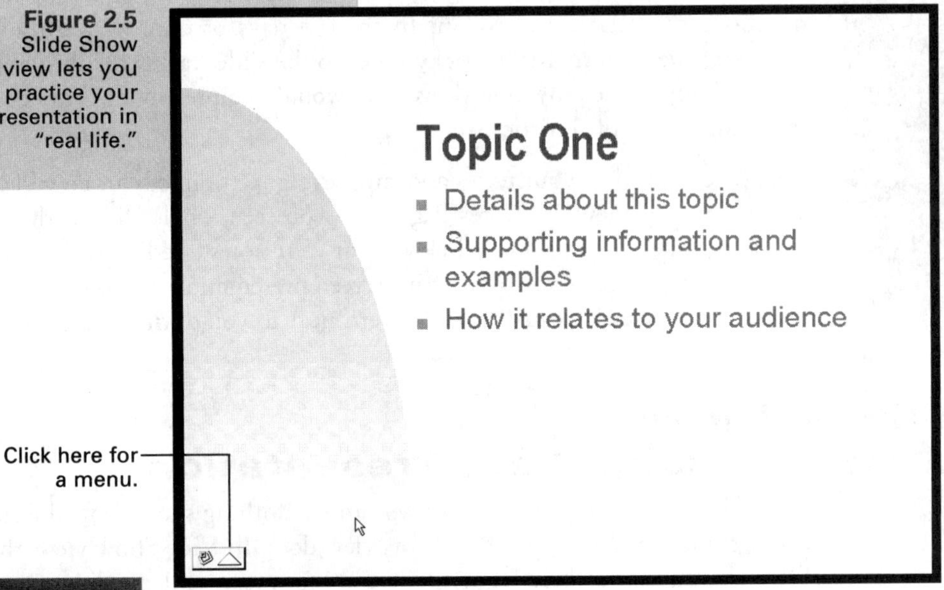

Figure 2.5 Slide Show view lets you practice your presentation in "real life."

You'll learn the many ways to control a slide show in Chapter 18.

If you move your mouse while in Slide Show view, a semi-transparent arrow appears on-screen. If you look closely at Figure 2.5, you can see the arrow in the lower-left corner. Clicking on that arrow opens a menu that enables you to control the show without leaving it. To leave the slide show, choose End Show from that menu, or just press Esc.

Zooming the View In and Out

If you need a closer look at your presentation, you can zoom the view in or out to accommodate almost any situation. For example, if you have trouble getting a graphic object placed exactly at the same vertical level as some text in a box next to it, you might zoom in for more precision. You can view the presentation window at various magnifications on-screen, without changing the size of the surrounding tools or the size of the print on the printout.

Zoom is measured in percentages, from 10% to 400%. (Not all percentages are available in all views. For example Outline view only goes up to 100%.) The larger the number, the larger the details on the display. A zoom of 10% would make each slide so tiny you couldn't read it. A zoom of 400% would make a few letters on a slide so big they would fill the entire screen.

For the Slide and Notes Page views, the default zoom setting is "Fit," which means the number is the highest it can be for you to still see the whole slide on-screen at once. It's the default because that's what most people want in these views: to get a good, complete look at the single slide. On my computer (running at 800 × 600 video resolution), for example, the zoom defaults are:

- 54% for Slide view
- 43% for Notes Page view

You can change the zoom to whatever you like in these views, and then return to the defaults by choosing Fit as the zoom amount.

The other views (Slide Sorter and Outline) don't have "ideal" settings because the zoom level in these views are more a matter of personal preference. Some people like the elements in these views to be larger and more readable; other people prefer to be able to see more items at once on-screen. For example, in Slide Sorter view, at 66% zoom you can see four slides on each line; at 75% you can see three slides on each line, but each slide is larger and more detailed.

If you have less-than-perfect eyesight, you may find yourself squinting to read the text on-screen, especially in Outline view. *Zooming in,* which means increasing the zoom, will make everything larger so you can get a better look at it. Figure 2.6 shows a 75% zoom in Outline view.

Zooming out goes the other way—it decreases the zoom, making everything smaller on-screen. The main advantage of zooming out is to fit more on-screen at once. For example, if I'm working with a lot of slides in Slide Sorter, and I normally can see three slides on each row, zooming out to 33% might let me see eight or more slides on each row, for a total of more than 40 slides per

What Does Zoom Do?

In the PowerPoint classes I teach, beginners have a common misconception that adjusting the zoom changes the size of the type on the printout. It doesn't. Zooming affects only the on-screen display and only the PowerPoint window. It's like holding a magnifying glass up to your monitor.

If you want to make the type larger or smaller on the printout, you must change the font size, a skill that is covered in Chapter 7.

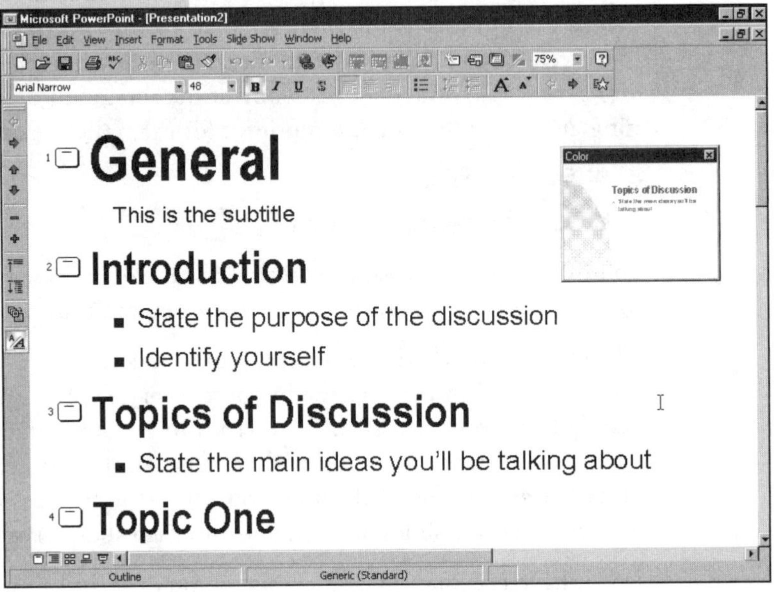

Figure 2.6 Zooming in makes for a close-up view.

screenful. The disadvantage, of course, is that if the slides get too small, as in Figure 2.7, and all the slides look similar except for the text on them, you won't be able to tell them apart.

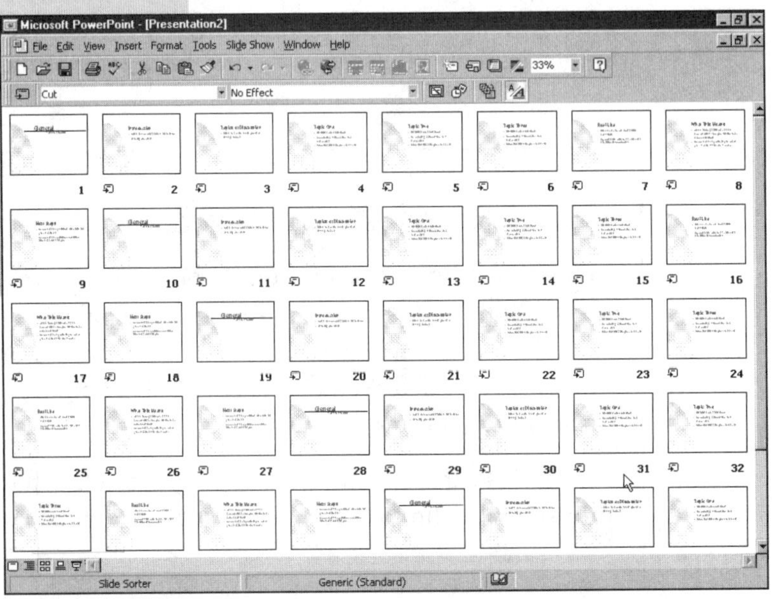

Figure 2.7 Zooming out gives you a birds-eye view in which you can see more of the presentation; however, you sacrifice some readability.

Here's a simple way to remember which is "out" and which is "in"—think of how the view changes when you step toward or away from the monitor. When you step "out" (away), everything looks smaller; when you step "in" (toward the monitor), everything looks larger.

Hands-On

The easiest way to change the zoom is with the Zoom drop-down list on the Standard toolbar (see Figure 2.8). To change the zoom, just do this:

1. Click on the down arrow next to the Zoom text box.
2. Select a different zoom level from the drop-down list.

You also can type a precise zoom number in the Zoom text box; for example, if you like to use 85% zoom, but 85% is not on the list, follow these steps:

1. Click on the current number in the Zoom text box. It becomes highlighted.
2. Type a new number.
3. Press Enter.

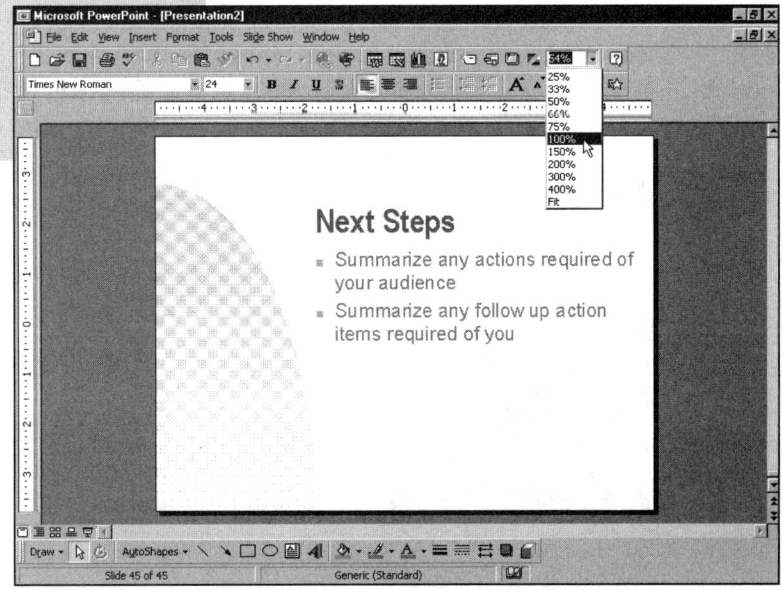

Figure 2.8 Use the Zoom drop-down list to change the zoom.

You also can change the zoom with a menu command: View, Zoom. When you choose this command, the Zoom dialog box appears (see Figure 2.9). Just make your selection by clicking on the appropriate button and then click on OK.

The Zoom dialog box has a couple of things to notice:

- Some of the option buttons in the Zoom dialog box are grayed out (unavailable) in certain views. For example, the Fit button is grayed out when you access the Zoom dialog box from Slide Sorter view.
- You can type a precise zoom percentage in the Percent text box, or use the incrementer arrows to change the amount shown. This is the same as typing a percentage directly into the Zoom text box on the Standard toolbar.

Displaying and Hiding Screen Elements

Different elements are available on-screen depending on the view you are in. When you are in Outline view, for example, the Outlining toolbar appears and the ruler disappears. This system works pretty well, and most people don't manually change the display of screen elements. However, if you like to have things "just-so," you might find the procedures in the following sections helpful.

Displaying or Hiding the Ruler

The vertical and horizontal rulers appear automatically in views where you are working with one specific slide—that is, in Slide and Notes Page views. You can hide the rulers by choosing View, Ruler. This removes the check mark next to Ruler on the menu. You can show the rulers the same way. When you hide the rulers, they stay off in both Slide and Notes Page views until you show them again.

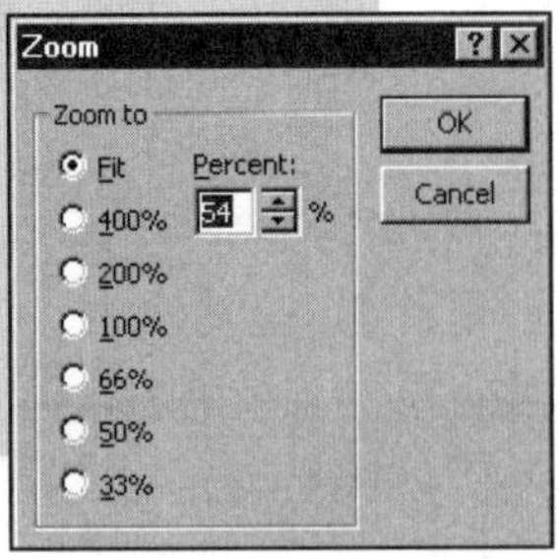

Figure 2.9 You can zoom with the Zoom dialog box rather than the Zoom drop-down list on the toolbar if you prefer.

[Ctrl]+[Y] repeats the last action. If your last action was to turn the ruler on (for example, to take a quick look at a measurement), you can turn it back off again quickly by pressing [Ctrl]+[Y] if you haven't done anything else in the interim.

In all other views, the rulers are unavailable; if you look on the View menu in these views, you'll notice that the Ruler command is grayed out.

If you want the horizontal ruler but not the vertical one, you can hide the vertical ruler. Choose Tools, Options, and click on the View tab. Deselect the Vertical Ruler check box and click on OK.

Displaying or Hiding Guides

Guides are on-screen dotted lines that can help you line up objects on a slide precisely. For example, if you want to center an object exactly in the middle of the slide, you can place the object exactly at the intersection of the guide lines (see Figure 2.10). To turn them on/off, choose View, Guides.

Like rulers, guides are available only in Slide and Notes Page views. In the other views, the command is grayed out on the View menu.

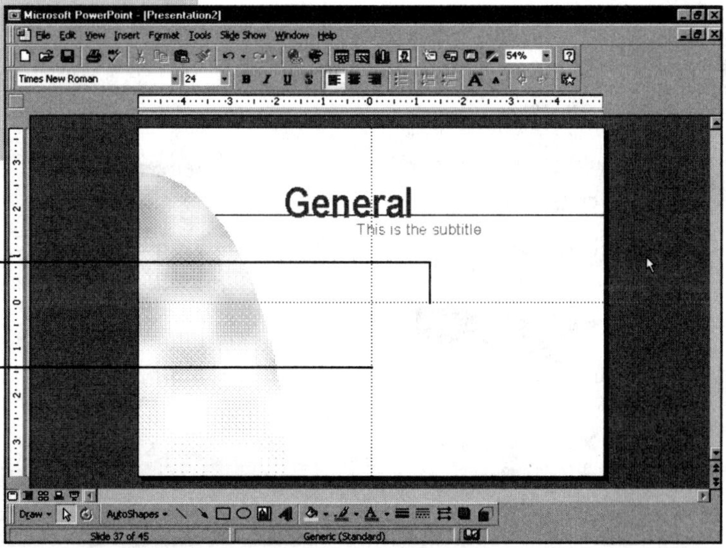

Figure 2.10 Guides can help with object placement in Slide view.

Displaying or Hiding the Slide Miniature Window

The Slide Miniature window shows you a mini-view of a particular slide, in either black and white or color (your choice). It's useful in several ways:

- In Outline view, the Slide Miniature window gives you a graphical view of the selected slide so you don't have to change to Slide view to see the results of your typing (see Figure 2.11).
- In Slide view, the Slide Miniature window shows you how your slide will look in black and white if the main slide is color, or you will see how the slide will look in color if the main slide is in black and white.
- In Notes Page view, you can see how much text will appear under the slide on a regular printed page in Portrait orientation.
- If you're zoomed in for close-up work, the Slide Miniature window can show you the big picture of the entire slide.

Portrait Orientation is covered in Chapter 17.

The Slide Miniature window is not available in Slide Sorter view because it's not needed—*all* the slides in Slide Sorter view are miniature.

To turn on the Slide Miniature window, choose View, Slide Miniature. To turn it off again, do the same thing, or click on the Close (X) button in the Slide Miniature window. PowerPoint remembers your preference, so if you turn it off, it will continue to be off until you turn it back on again.

Figure 2.11 The Slide Miniature window provides an extra perspective on the selected slide.

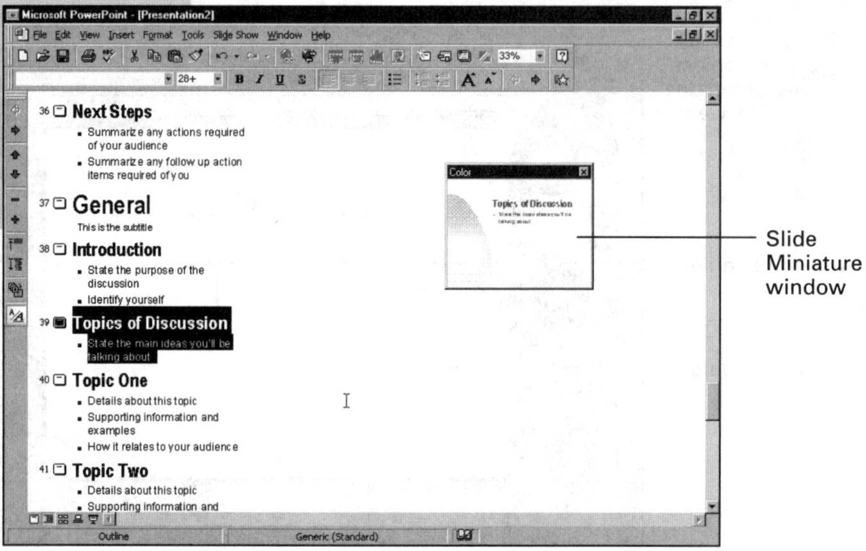

By default, the Slide Miniature window shows the opposite of what's in the presentation: if the presentation is in color, for example, the Slide Miniature will be in black and white. You can set the Slide Miniature's color setting manually, though. Just right-click on the Slide Miniature window and choose Black and White View or Color View from the shortcut menu that appears.

Displaying or Hiding Toolbars

PowerPoint comes with many toolbars, and you can create your own (as you will learn in Appendix A). By default, as you learned in Chapter 1, the Standard, Formatting, and Drawing toolbars appear on-screen in Slide view. Here are the defaults for the other views:

View	Toolbars that Appear
Outline	Standard and Formatting (some commands grayed out), and Outlining
Slide Sorter	Standard (some commands grayed out) and Slide Sorter
Notes Page	Standard and Formatting

In Appendix C, you learn how to customize the buttons on each toolbar and even create your own toolbars containing the buttons you use most often.

Not all toolbars are available in all views, because their buttons simply aren't useful in those views. For example, you can't use the Outlining toolbar in Slide Sorter view, but you would not need to anyway. However, there are some extra toolbars you might find useful in some views. That's why you can display and hide toolbars in each view.

Hands On: Displaying/Hiding a Toolbar

1. Right-click on a visible toolbar. A shortcut menu appears listing all the toolbars available in the current view, as shown in Figure 2.12. A check mark appears beside the ones already displayed.
2. Click on the name of the toolbar you want to display or hide.

Another way to turn toolbars on/off is to choose View, Toolbars. The available toolbars appear in a submenu, just like the shortcut menu in the preceding hands on. Just click on the toolbar you want to use.

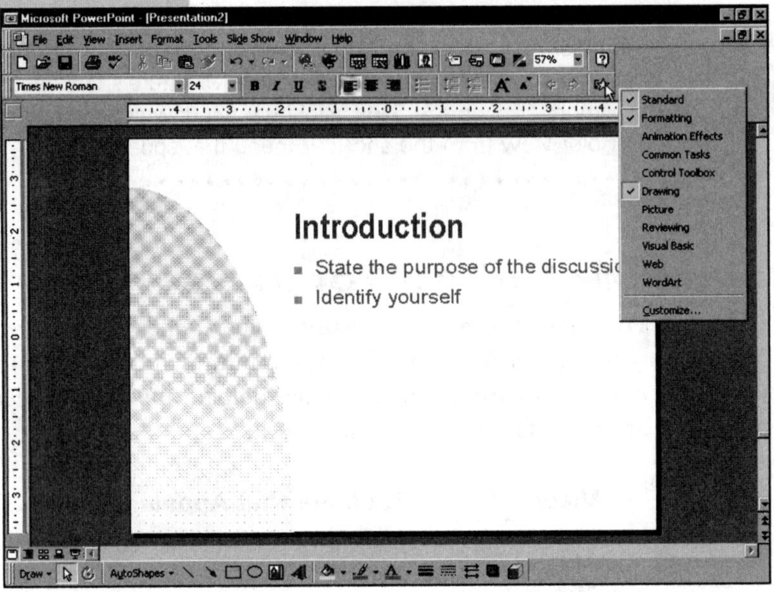

Figure 2.12 Right-click on a toolbar and then select what toolbars you want to see or hide.

Here are some of the toolbars you might find useful. Sometimes the appropriate toolbar will spontaneously open for you at the right time (for example, the Picture toolbar may appear when you're working with a picture); other times you may have to turn the toolbar on yourself.

- *Animation Effects.* Helps you set up animation on slides (see Chapter 14).
- *Common Tasks.* Contains three text buttons that open the dialog boxes used most frequently: New Slide, Slide Layout, and Apply Design.
- *Picture.* Helps you edit clip art and other pictures (see Chapter 8).
- *Reviewing.* Provides buttons for commenting on and revising a presentation.
- *Visual Basic.* Provides buttons for running, recording, and editing macros.
- *Web.* Contains controls to help set up and test Web-based presentations (see Chapter 15).
- *WordArt.* Helps you edit and manipulate WordArt objects (see Chapter 7).

Other Elements You Can Display/Hide

There are a few more elements you can choose to display or hide. Some of them aren't really screen elements, but rather dialog boxes at certain points in the program. To turn these options on/off, follow these steps:

1. Choose Tools, Options. The Options dialog box appears.
2. Click on the View tab (see Figure 2.13).
3. Select or deselect the check box for the option you want to display or hide.
4. Click on OK.

The View tab is divided into two frames: settings for all the "working" views (that is, all the views except Slide Show) and settings for Slide Show view itself.

Here are the options that affect all views except Slide Show:

- *Startup Dialog.* When you started PowerPoint in Chapter 1, recall that a PowerPoint dialog box appeared to help you get started (refer to Figure 1.2). You can turn off this dialog box so that an empty work area appears when you start PowerPoint.
- *New Slide Dialog.* When you add new slides to a presentation, the New Slide dialog box appears. In it, you select what slide layout you want. You can turn off this dialog box to add a totally blank slide each time you call for a new slide.
- *Status Bar.* You can save about a half inch of on-screen space by turning off the status bar. This enables you to make the Zoom setting about 3% larger. Is it worth it? You decide.

You learn more about adding slides to a presentation in Chapter 5.

Figure 2.13 The View tab in the Options dialog box lets you specify what you do or don't want to see.

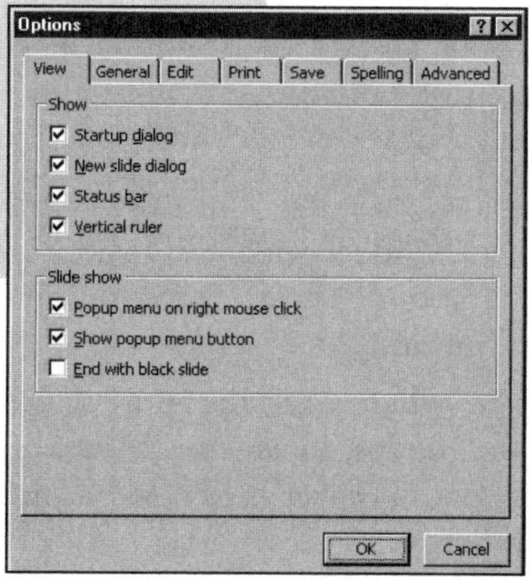

- *Vertical Ruler.* You saw this one earlier in the chapter; you can turn off the vertical ruler so only the horizontal ruler appears when you use the Ruler command.

The following options affect only Slide Show view:

- *Popup Menu on Right Mouse Click.* Normally, as you've seen, you can right-click on things in PowerPoint to make shortcut menus appear. You can disable this capability in Slide Show view if you want. It may deter a capricious user from tampering with your presentation if it is self-running.
- *Show Popup Menu Button.* As you saw in Figure 2.5, an arrow appears on-screen when you move your mouse in Slide Show view; you can click on the arrow to open a menu. You can disable that capability here by deselecting this check box. Again, it may deter tampering.
- *End with Black Slide.* If you want your presentation to end by displaying a black screen, leave this check box selected. (It's a nice touch, in my opinion.)

Controlling Windows

If you are a long-time Windows user, you can safely skip this section; it's all about controlling the windows of Windows 95. I've included it here because without a basic knowledge of how to control a window, your PowerPoint productivity can be severely hampered, especially when you begin working with more than one presentation at a time.

Minimizing, Maximizing, and Restoring

Before you can learn about how to use windows in PowerPoint, you must understand a few basic terms: *minimize*, *maximize*, and *restore*. These are standard Windows operations, but if you aren't sure what they mean, refresh your memory here:

A *minimized* window is reduced to an icon or a small rectangle. You minimize a window by clicking on its Minimize button.

A *maximized* window fills the entire screen (or the entire space of the window in which it resides, if it's a window in a window). You maximize a window by clicking on its Maximize button.

If a window is already maximized, you *restore* it to the size and shape it was before being maximized by clicking on the Restore button.

You can close a window by clicking on its Close button.

Understanding PowerPoint's Window Structure

Windows are used within windows in PowerPoint, as in most Windows applications. The outer window is PowerPoint itself. The inner windows are any presentations you have open. In Figure 2.14, for example, the PowerPoint application window is maximized; it fills the entire computer screen. Within it, two presentation windows are open: Presentation1 and Presentation2. The Presentation1 window is minimized, and the Presentation2 window is restored (that is, not maximized). Contrast this to the maximized presentation window in Figure 2.15. Notice that when a presentation window is maximized, it shares a title bar with the PowerPoint application window; when it's restored, it has its own title bar. Notice also in Figure 2.15 that when a presentation is maximized within the PowerPoint window, its window control buttons (Minimize, Restore, and Close) appear directly below those for the PowerPoint window itself rather than in the title bar.

Figure 2.14 This PowerPoint window has two open presentations: one minimized and one restored.

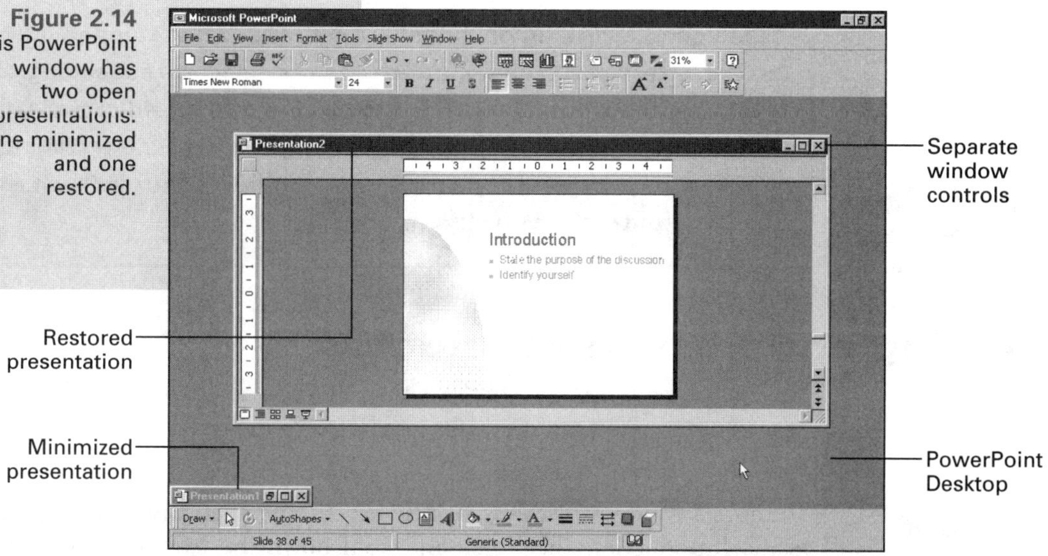

Figure 2.15 This PowerPoint window has a maximized presentation.

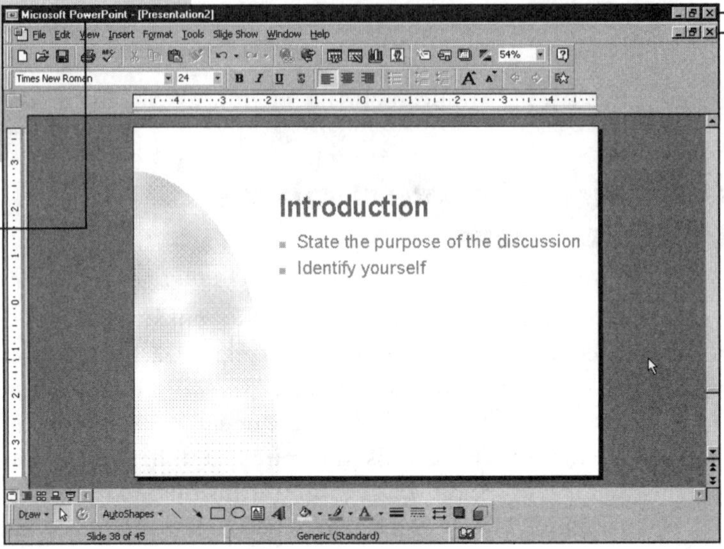

When a presentation window is minimized, it sits as a rectangular icon on the PowerPoint window's *Desktop*—the gray area behind the presentations. To reopen a minimized presentation, you just double-click on it. If another window is obscuring it, press Ctrl+Tab until it appears.

When double-clicking on a minimized presentation to open it, click on the letters of the name, not on the right end of the rectangle. That's because when you click once on the minimized presentation, window control buttons appear at the right end of the rectangle, and you may accidentally click on one of those controls (such as the Close button) if you click on the right end.

Moving and Resizing Windows

You can move and resize windows that are restored (that is, aren't minimized or maximized). You can do this to the PowerPoint window itself too, or to any window, for that matter.

To move a window, just drag its title bar. (Remember, I told you how to drag in the Introduction? Just click and hold down the left mouse button while you're pointing at the object you want to drag.)

To resize a window, position the mouse pointer over any border of the window, so the mouse pointer changes to a double-headed arrow (see Figure 2.16). Drag the border until the window is the size you want it to be. As you drag the window, it changes size.

Most windows in Windows 95 programs have a little gray tab in the lower-right corner designed especially for resizing the window; you can drag any of the sides or corners, but dragging the gray tab is very easy because it is large and easy to position the mouse pointer over, and because it resizes both sides at once.

Tip

To resize a window so the active slide exactly fits in the window, choose Window, Fit to Page. To try it out, first switch to Slide view and then issue the command.

Opening a New Display Window

Have you ever wished you could be in two places at once? Well, in PowerPoint, you actually can. PowerPoint provides a way to view two different spots in a presentation at the same time by opening a new window. You can use any view with any window, so you can have two different slides in Slide view at once, or Slide view and Outline view, or any other combination (see Figure 2.17). Both windows contain the same presentation, so any changes you make in one window are reflected in the other window.

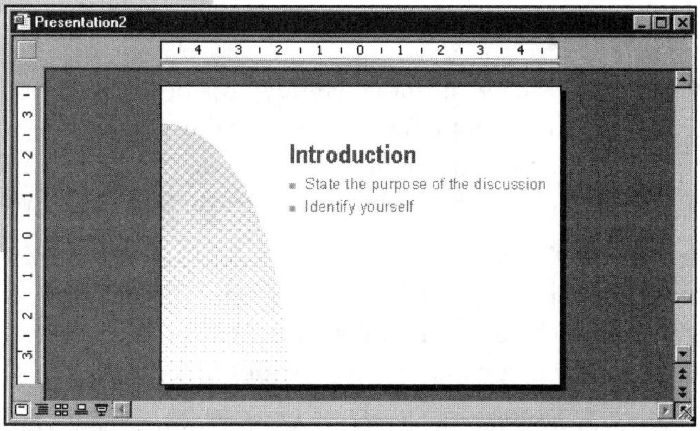

Figure 2.16 To resize a window, drag the gray tab in the lower-right corner, or any side or corner of the window.

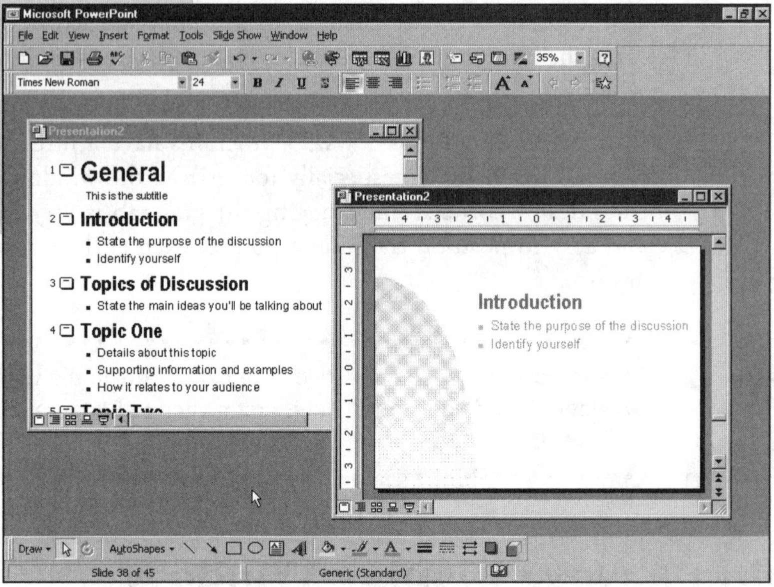

Figure 2.17 Two windows both contain the same presentation, so you can see different views at once.

Note

In Figure 2.14, you saw two windows open at once, but that was two separate presentations: Presentation1 and Presentation2. In Figure 2.17, you see two views of the same presentation.

Arranging Windows

When you have two or more windows open, whether they are for the same presentation or different ones, you will need to arrange them for optimal viewing. You saw earlier in this chapter how to resize a non-maximized window, but did you know that PowerPoint can do some arranging for you?

Almost all Windows-based programs (at least the ones that allow you to have more than one data window open at once within them) have a Window menu with some commands that help you arrange the windows. When you want to arrange the open windows, do one of the following:

- Choose Window, Arrange All to tile the open windows so there is no overlap (see Figure 2.18).

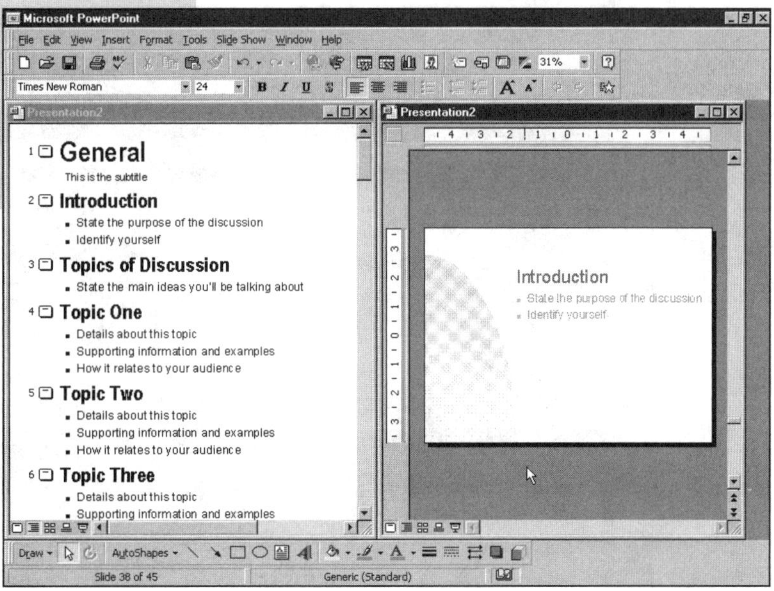

Figure 2.18 The Arrange All command tiles the windows within the PowerPoint window.

Note

The Window, Arrange All command is like the Tile command in some other Windows-based programs.

- Choose Window, Cascade to arrange the open windows so the title bars "cascade" from upper-left to lower-right on-screen, as shown in Figure 2.19. Click on a title bar to activate the window.

Note

Don't worry if you don't know how to open multiple presentations yet; you learn all about it in Chapter 3. If you want some presentation windows to practice on now, click on the New button on the Standard toolbar and then click on OK to open a new blank presentation.

Figure 2.19 The Cascade command arranges the windows so all title bars are visible.

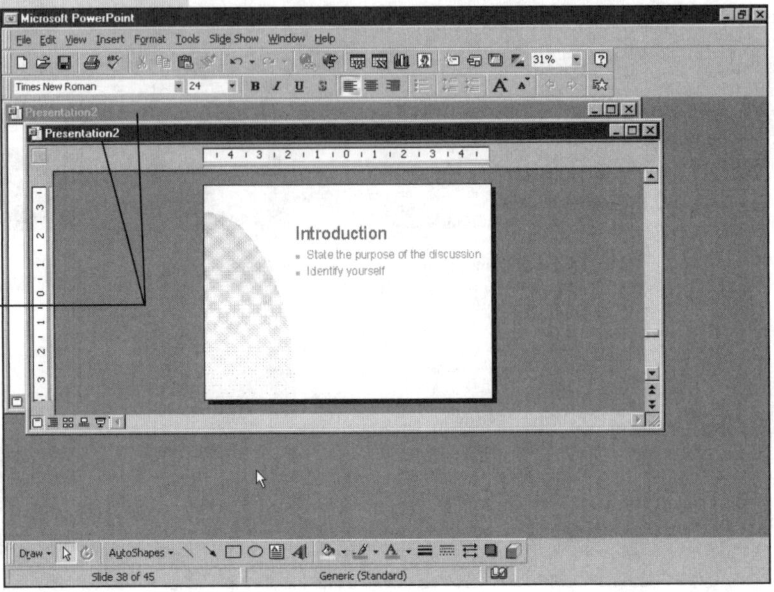

The Arrange All and Cascade commands on the Window menu do not apply to minimized windows. If you want to include an open presentation in the arrangement, make sure you restore it from its minimized state first, if needed.

Switching Among Open Windows

If you have more than one window open and all the windows are at least partly visible on-screen, you can switch among them by clicking on any visible portion of the one you want to see. It moves to the top of the pile.

If you have one of the windows maximized, or if another window is completely obscuring the one you want, you have to use another method: the Window menu. Open the Window menu, and notice that at the bottom of it, all the open windows are listed (see Figure 2.20). Just choose the one you want to switch to from that list.

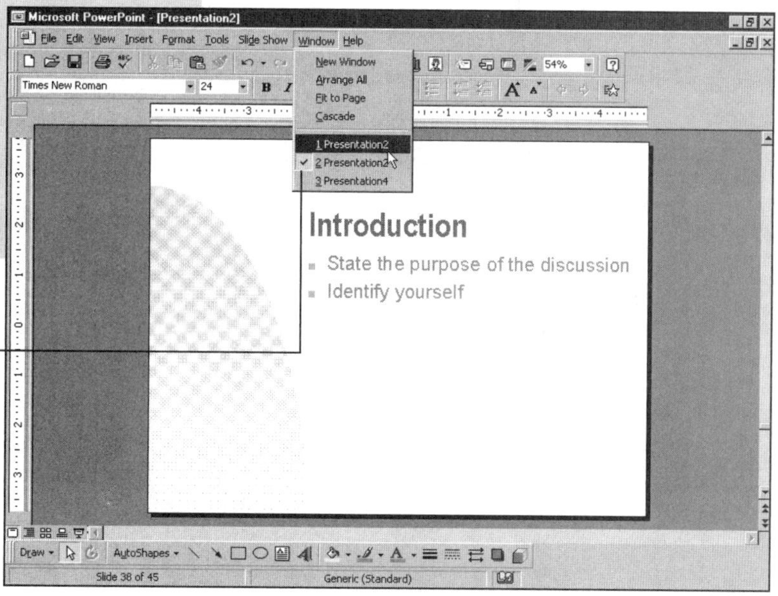

Figure 2.20 One of the best ways to switch among open windows is to choose the one you want from the Window menu.

The currently active window has a check mark next to it.

Summary

In this chapter, you learned several ways to look at a PowerPoint presentation, including different views, different zoom levels, and with different screen elements present. In the next chapter, you'll start working with presentation files, and you'll start thinking about how to organize your presentation.

3

Working with Presentation Files

In This Chapter

- Creating New Presentations
- Saving and Opening Presentations
- Opening a File from Another Program
- Duplicating a Presentation
- Deleting a Presentation

Presentation files are the heart of PowerPoint; they're the files into which the program saves your data. Just as you must understand suitcases before you can pack your bags for an exciting trip, you must understand how to handle presentation files before you can begin your journey with PowerPoint.

What Is a Presentation?

In Chapter 6, you'll learn how to make your slides work as a group.

A *presentation* is a file containing a group of slides. Generally, you group all the slides for a particular event together in a presentation. However, if you are planning a huge event, such as an all-day meeting, you might want to break down the slides for individual sessions in their own presentation files.

All of the slides in a presentation typically have a common look and feel, so they seem like a cohesive group.

Creating a New Presentation

Each time you start PowerPoint, the PowerPoint dialog box prompts you to start a new presentation or to open an existing one. There's a good reason for this: you can't do anything in PowerPoint unless at least one presentation file is open.

Creating a presentation is not the same as saving one. When you create a presentation, it has a generic name, such as Presentation1. The presentation exists only on-screen and in the computer's temporary memory. When you save your work, you save it with a more descriptive name and a copy is placed on your computer's hard disk, where it is safe from power outages and program errors.

Ways to Start a New Presentation

If you just started PowerPoint, and the PowerPoint dialog box is still on-screen, that's the easiest way to go (see Figure 3.1). Just click on the appropriate button for the type of help you need (AutoContent Wizard, Template, or Blank Presentation) and click on OK. I'll explain each of these more in upcoming sections.

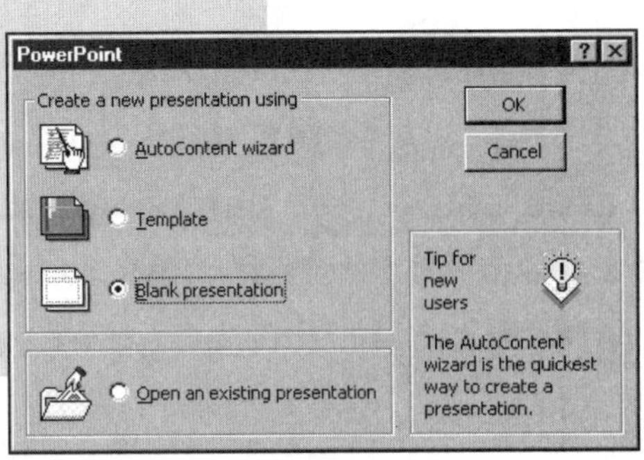

Figure 3.1 When you first start PowerPoint, this dialog box is available for starting a new presentation or for opening an existing one.

But if you have been following along in the preceding chapters, this dialog box is long gone. You could exit and restart PowerPoint to get it back, but it's easier to use one of the following methods instead to access the New Presentation controls:

- Click on the New button on the Standard toolbar.
- Press Ctrl+N.
- Choose File, New.

You'll learn more about templates in Chapter 4.

With the first option, you don't get to choose a presentation design—you get a blank presentation. That's because the New button creates a new presentation based on the Blank Presentation template. As you'll learn in Chapter 4, a *template* is a set of specifications (such as the margins, background colors, number of slides, and other options) on which a new presentation can be based. New presentations based on the Blank Presentation template are just that: blank, dull, and plain.

Note

When you use the Blank Presentation template, you get a plain, boring presentation with no special fonts or backgrounds or images. Why would anyone want this? Well, some people like to add their own backgrounds and customizations, and any existing ones get in their way. By starting with the Blank Presentation template, they can start from scratch on a blank canvas.

The other two methods, choosing File, New and pressing Ctrl+N, open the New Presentation dialog box shown in Figure 3.2. As you can see, this dialog box has four tabs: General, Presentation Designs, Presentations, and Web Pages. These tabs contain the available templates.

What Kind of Presentation Should I Start With?

To confuse matters even more, not only are there several ways to start the presentation-creation ball rolling, but there are several kinds of new presentations you can create, depending on the level of help you need:

- The AutoContent Wizard offers the highest level of help. It asks you a series of questions and then creates a pre-formatted presentation for

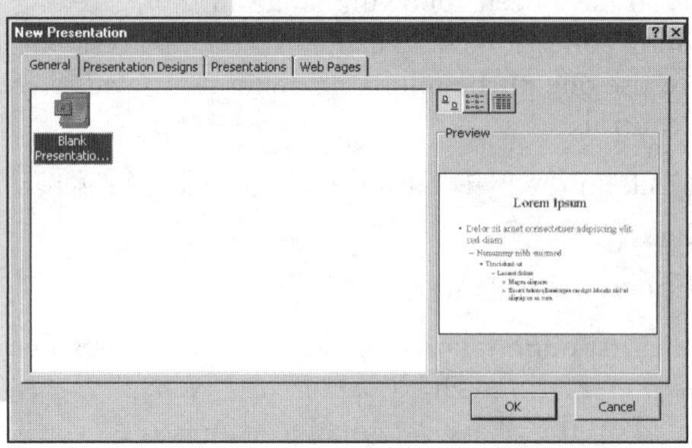

Figure 3.2 The File, New command opens the New Presentation dialog box, in which you can choose a template on which to base your new presentation.

Chapter 4 showcases all the templates available in PowerPoint and tells you how to get more.

you, complete with slides that contain sample content appropriate for your event.

- Presentation templates are the next level down. They too offer preformatted slides with sample text, but there are no questions beforehand to help determine your needs. You have to know enough to be able to select the appropriate presentation template on your own.
- If you need help with formatting but not content, you can use a Presentation Design template. These are pre-made designs that will automatically be applied to the slides you create.
- The Blank Presentation template, as you've seen, is a completely blank canvas. There is no sample design and there is no sample text.

Each of these possibilities is appropriate for certain circumstances. The following sections look at each one in more detail.

Creating a New Presentation with AutoContent Wizard

If you're brand-new to PowerPoint and don't have a clue what to do, the AutoContent Wizard is definitely the place to start. The AutoContent Wizard holds your hand every step of the way, and provides great ideas.

1. Start the AutoContent Wizard in one of the following ways:
   - In the PowerPoint dialog box that appears when you first start PowerPoint, click on AutoContent Wizard and click on OK.
   - Choose File, New. In the New Presentation dialog box, click on the Presentations tab, and double-click on AutoContent Wizard.

2. In the Start screen of the AutoContent Wizard, click on Next to begin. You see the Presentation Type screen of the AutoContent Wizard shown in Figure 3.3.
3. Click on the button for the type of presentation you want. For example, click on Projects. All the available presentation templates in that category appear on the list.

If you don't know what type to pick in step 3, click on All. This shows a full list of all available templates.

4. Click on the presentation template that best describes what you want (for example, click on Project Overview); then click on Next to continue.
5. In the Output Options screen of the AutoContent Wizard, choose one of the following option buttons, and then click on Next to continue:
   - *Presentations, Informal Meetings, Handouts.* Choose this option button if you want to create a traditional presentation that will have a presenter.
   - *Internet, Kiosk.* Choose this option button if you want to create a self-running presentation.
6. In the Presentation Style screen of the AutoContent Wizard, click on the appropriate option buttons to choose the type of output you want and whether you want handouts. For example, choose On-screen presentation and Yes. Click on Next to continue.
7. In the Presentation Options screen of the AutoContent Wizard, enter your name, company name, and anything else you want to appear on the title slide (see Figure 3.5). Click on Next to continue.

Figure 3.3 The first task is to tell AutoContent Wizard what kind of presentation you want.

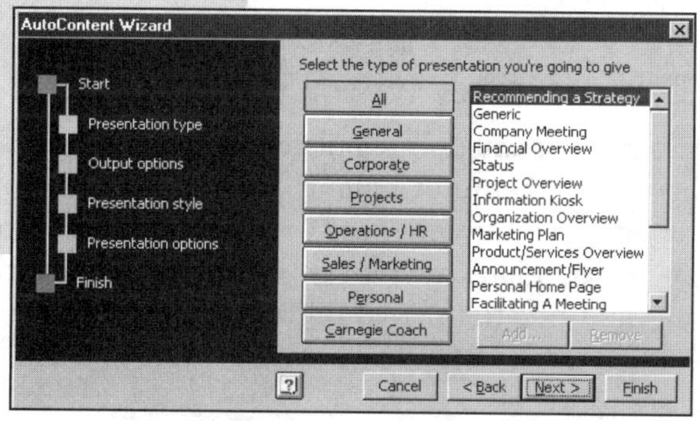

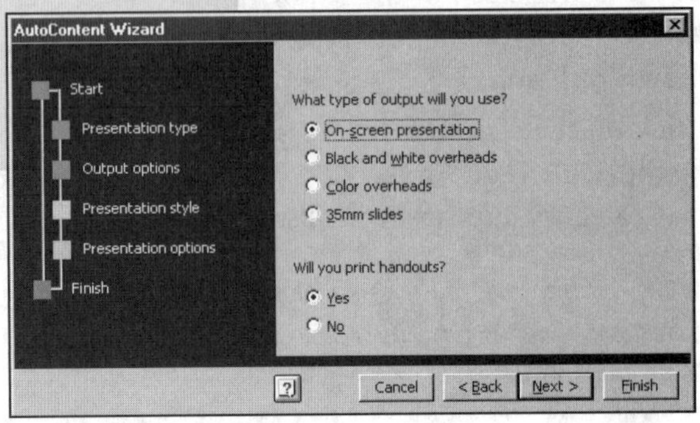

Figure 3.4 Choose the type of output you'll need.

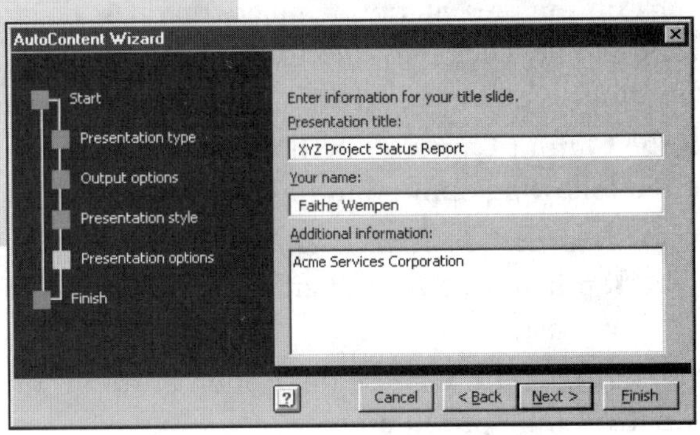

Figure 3.5 The information you enter here will appear on the title slide of the presentation.

8. Click on the Finish button. PowerPoint generates the presentation, which appears in Outline view.

From here, you can begin changing the text on the slides to make it your own and customizing the presentation in other ways. See Chapters 5 through 14 to see what's possible.

Creating a New Presentation with a Presentation Template

As mentioned, presentation templates are the next step down in the "full service" chain from the AutoContent Wizard. You can browse the presentation templates until you find one that does what you want to do, and then create your new presentation based on it. Except for a few little extras (like having your name and title transferred onto the title slide), the result is just like the result you get with the AutoContent Wizard. In fact, the same sample presentation templates that the AutoContent Wizard uses are available this way.

Another nice thing about the presentation templates is that you can browse them not only for appropriate purpose but also for design and color scheme. With the AutoContent Wizard, a template is assigned to you "sight-unseen." You don't get to check out its colors and patterns before you choose it. With the presentation templates, you can see what you're getting ahead of time.

1. Open the New Presentation dialog box in one of the following ways:
   - In the PowerPoint dialog box, click on Template and click on OK.
   - Choose File, New.
2. Click on the Presentations tab.

Note

On the Presentations tab, you'll see two versions of every template: Standard and Online. The Online versions are for presentations that will be presented in an interactive, self-running way, such as on the Internet. Unless that's the type of presentation you need to create, stick with the Standard presentations.

3. Click on a presentation to see a preview of it (see Figure 3.6). Continue clicking on presentations until you find the one you want to use.
4. Click on OK. The presentation opens to show the first slide in Slide view.

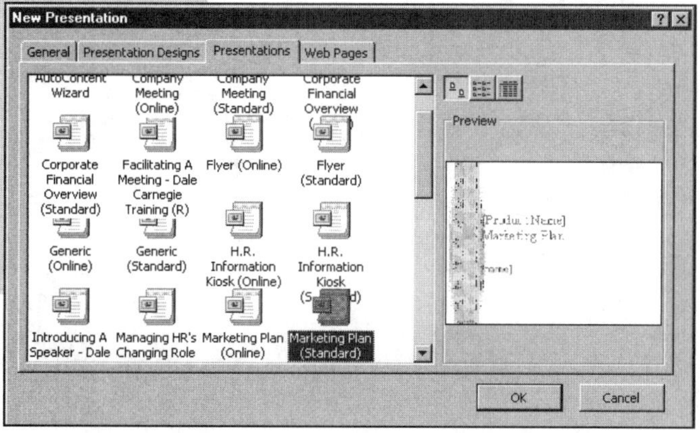

Figure 3.6 Choose the presentation template that fits your presentation purpose—and that matches your idea of a good design.

Now go ahead and customize the presentation to your own tastes, changing text and adding features as needed. Chapters 5 through 13 offer all the help you need.

Creating a New Presentation with a Presentation Design Template

If you like having the colors and patterns picked out for you, but you don't want to be told what slides to include, then the presentation design templates are ideal for you. These are just what the name says: designs. You add your own slides.

1. Open the New Presentation dialog box in one of the following ways:
   - In the PowerPoint dialog box, click on Template and click on OK.
   - Choose File, New.
2. Click on the Presentation Designs tab.
3. Click on a presentation design to see a preview of it (see Figure 3.7). Continue clicking on presentation designs until you find the one you want to use.
4. Click on OK. The New Slide dialog box opens, in which you can choose the layout of the first slide to add to the presentation.
5. Click on a slide layout and click on OK.

Now go on to Chapters 5 through 13 to add more slides to the presentation and dress them up just the way you want.

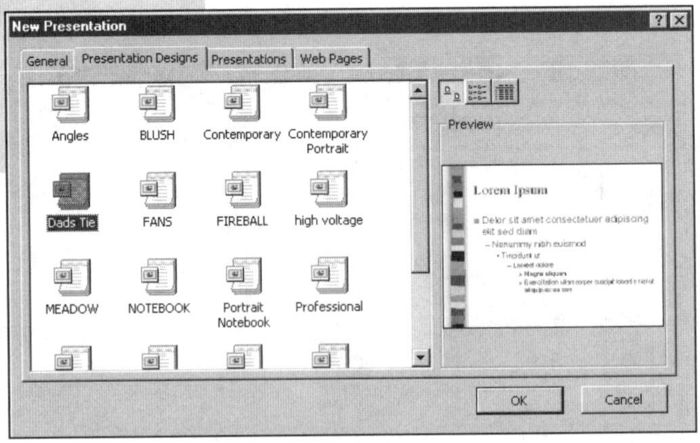

Figure 3.7 Select the presentation design you want to use.

Creating a Blank Presentation

A blank presentation is really nothing more than a presentation created with the Blank Presentation design template. Just follow the steps below to see for yourself.

1. Start a blank presentation in one of the following ways:
   - In the PowerPoint dialog box, click on Blank Presentation and click on OK.
   - Choose File, New. In the New Presentation dialog box, click on the General tab, and double-click on Blank Presentation.
2. The New Slide dialog box opens, in which you can choose the layout of the first slide to add to the presentation. Click on a slide layout and click on OK.

Importing Text from Word

Often you will have at least the basic shell of your presentation outlined in a text-based program, such as Microsoft Word. Luckily, you don't have to retype all this information; PowerPoint accepts the information without a hitch, provided you set up the text in an outline. Word works great for organizing your thoughts in outline form because of its special Outline view. In this view, you can create multi-level outlines that import into PowerPoint very well. The following Hands On shows you how to set up your outline in Word (assuming you have Word). You can import from almost any text-based program, so other word processors will work too.

Hands On: Creating an Outline in Microsoft Word

1. Start Microsoft Word.
2. Choose View, Outline to switch to Outline view.
3. Type your outline, as shown in Figure 3.8. Use the following to set up the multiple levels:

   Press Tab to indent (demote) a line one level in the outline.

   Press Shift+Tab to outdent (promote) a line one level in the outline.
4. Choose File, Save to save your work.
5. Choose File, Exit to exit Word.

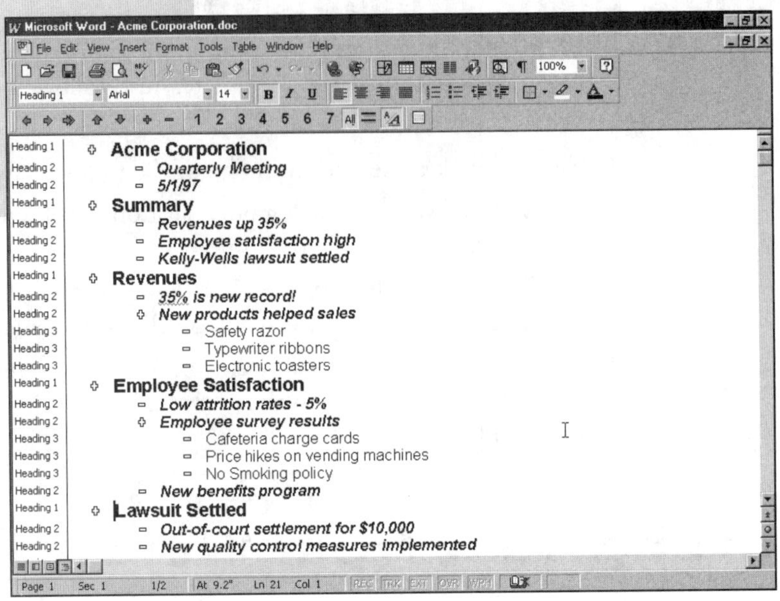

Figure 3.8 If you have Word, you can create an outline in it that imports seamlessly into PowerPoint.

> **You'll learn about PowerPoint's Outline view, and how to change outline levels in it, in Chapter 5.**

You can create your outline in Word without using Outline view and the multiple levels. If you do so, each line will be on a separate slide when you import the outline into PowerPoint, and this is seldom what you really want. You can fix this by modifying outline levels in PowerPoint's Outline view, but it's easier to just do it right in Word in the first place.

Once you have a Word outline ready to import, use the following Hands On to import that outline into your PowerPoint presentation.

Hands On: Importing a Word Outline into a Presentation

1. In PowerPoint, choose Insert, Slides from Outline. The Insert Outline dialog box appears (see Figure 3.9).
2. Navigate to the Word file containing the outline and double-click on it. (See "Changing the Folder or Drive" later in this chapter if you need help switching folders in a dialog box.)

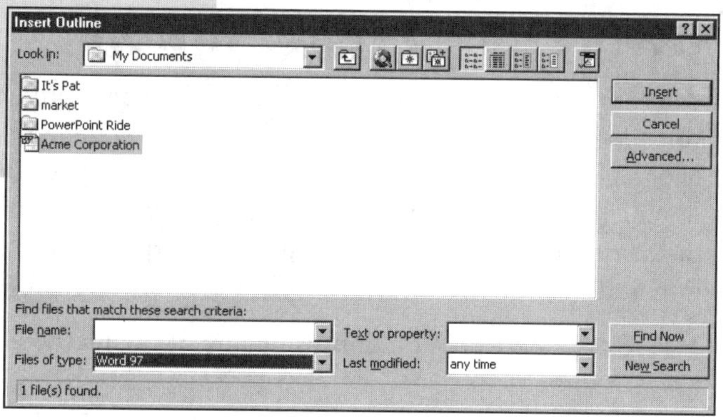

Figure 3.9 Choose the file containing the outline from this dialog box.

If you want to narrow the list of files shown to only Word files (files with the .doc extension), open the Files of Type drop-down list and choose Word 97. Figure 3.9 shows the dialog box with only the Word 97 files showing.

The outline items are placed on new slides in your PowerPoint presentation. Top-level outline items get their own slide, and subordinate items are placed as bullets on the slides, as you can see in Figure 3.10.

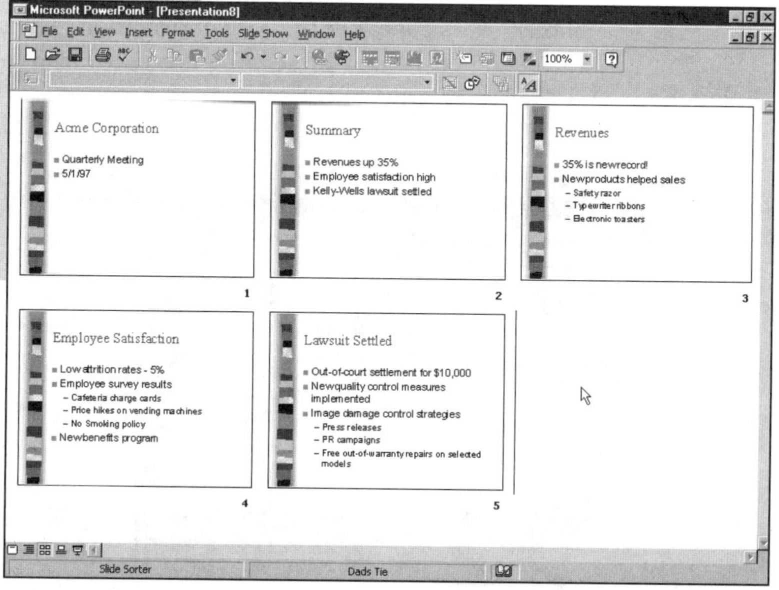

Figure 3.10 As you can see in Slide Sorter view here, the text has been placed on multiple slides according to its outline level in Word.

Importing Slides from Another PowerPoint Presentation

You also can copy slides from other PowerPoint presentations into the one you're working with. If you frequently give presentations, for example, you may have a certain number of slides with which you always open a presentation. These slides might include your company name and a summary of your major products. You can set up these boilerplate slides in a generic presentation and then import them as needed into the new presentation.

1. Start a new presentation using any of the methods you learned earlier in this chapter.
2. Choose Insert, Slides from Files. The Slide Finder dialog box appears.
3. Click on the Browse button. The Insert Slides from Files dialog box appears.
4. Navigate to the PowerPoint file from which you want to copy slides and double-click on it.
5. Click on the Display button. The slides in the selected presentation appear in the Slide Finder dialog box, as shown in Figure 3.11.
6. In the Select Slides area, click on each slide you want to copy. Use the horizontal scroll bar under the slide images if needed to see more slides.
7. Click on the Insert button to insert the selected slides into the current presentation.
8. Click on the Close button to close the Slide Finder dialog box. The chosen slides appear in the new presentation. The new slides take on the design of the new presentation so they blend in with the existing slides (see Figure 3.12).

Figure 3.11 Select the slides you want to copy by clicking on them.

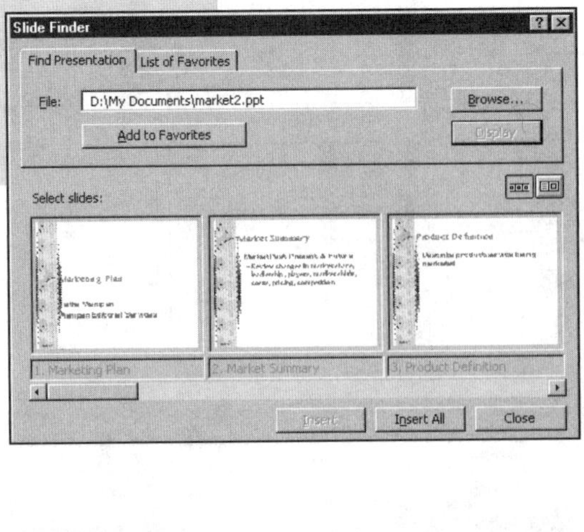

Figure 3.12 Imported slides take on the same formatting as the existing ones.

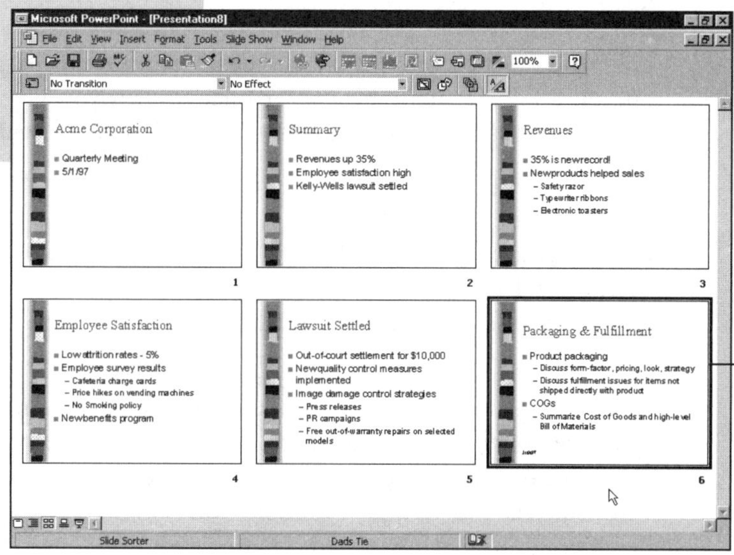

This is the imported slide.

Saving a Presentation

Skip ahead a moment and pretend you have created something in your presentation worthy of saving. (That's what the rest of the book will help you do.) After you've entered something you want to preserve, you need to save it.

What Happens When You Save?

You can think of your computer's memory as the top of your desk and your hard disk as a drawer in the desk. When you work in PowerPoint, you're working on the top of the desk, just as you would when you write a letter or add numbers by hand. When you exit PowerPoint or turn off your computer, it's like a janitor coming in and scooping everything from your desk surface into the garbage. Everything in memory is wiped out. If you want to preserve something you've been working on, you have to copy it to the hard disk, so that it's safely stashed away in a "drawer" where the "janitor" can't get it. Copying it to the hard disk is called *saving*.

As you've seen, when you're working with a new presentation, it has a generic name, such as Presentation1, Presentation2, and so on. PowerPoint assigns these names to prevent you from getting confused when you have more than one unsaved presentation open at once. When you save a presentation, you give it a "real" name, something more descriptive that will help you remember its purpose.

Names can be up to 255 characters and can include spaces. For practical purposes, however, you should keep the names reasonably short, such as Acme Marketing 1997 or Henson Sales Pitch. You can include spaces in your file names, and most symbols (although not < > ? or *). You don't have to type .ppt at the end of the name; PowerPoint adds that automatically.

After a presentation has been saved, a copy exists on your hard disk that you can "open," which you'll learn to do later in the chapter. The copy stays on your hard disk until you delete it (also covered later in the chapter). Each time you make changes to a presentation, you must save it again for the changes to be reflected in the copy stored on your hard disk.

Save versus Save As

There are two procedures for saving: Save and Save As. If you have never saved the presentation before, they are identical: they both ask for a name and location for the file. After you have saved the presentation, Save re-saves the presentation with the same name and location you initially entered, whereas Save As gives you the opportunity to save the presentation with a different name and/or location.

The first time you save a presentation, you assign it a name and a location so you can retrieve it later. The following steps show you how to save a presentation for the first time.

1. Do any of the following to open the Save As dialog box:
   - Click on the Save button on the Standard toolbar.
   - Press [Ctrl]+[S].
   - Choose File, Save or File, Save As. (They work the same if you have never saved this presentation before.)
2. In the Save As dialog box, enter a name for the presentation in the File Name text box (see Figure 3.13).
3. (Optional) To save the presentation in a different folder, use the navigation buttons in the dialog box to change the folder and/or drive. (See the following section for help with this.) The default is the My Documents folder on the same drive on which Windows 95 is installed.

Figure 3.13 Use the Save dialog box to specify a file name and location.

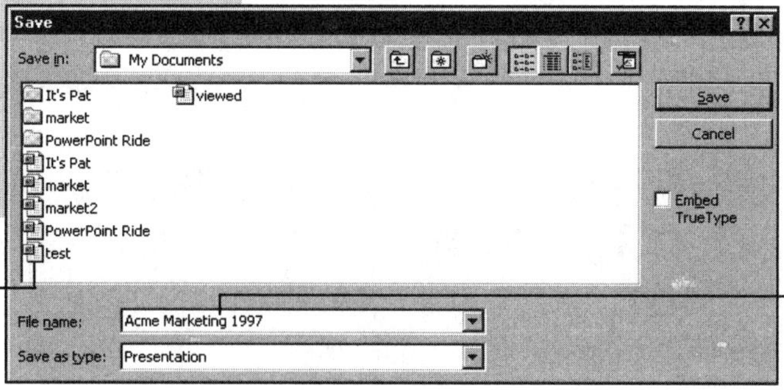

4. Click on the Save button in the dialog box. The presentation is saved to disk, and the new name of it appears in the title bar.

Changing the Folder or Drive

If you have not used many Windows 95 programs, the file navigation system might seem foreign at first. You must use it whenever you need to change the drive and/or folder in a dialog box that saves or opens files. You'll encounter it in the Save As dialog box and in the Open dialog box, which is covered later in the chapter.

To change to a different drive, you must open the Save In or Look In drop-down list. (The name changes depending on whether you're saving or opening a file.) Figure 3.14 shows this drop-down list in the Save As dialog box. From the drop-down list, choose the drive on which you want to save the file.

Next, you must select the folder in which you want to save the file (or open it from). When you select the drive, a list of the folders on that drive appears. Double-click on the folder to select it.

Figure 3.14 Use this drop-down list to choose a different drive.

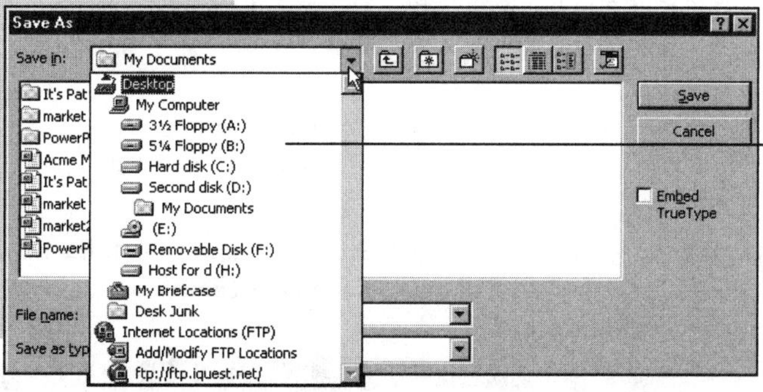

Table 3.1 explains the buttons and other controls you see in the Save As and Open dialog boxes, as well as in other Windows 95 dialog boxes you might encounter.

Table 3.1 Buttons for Changing Drives and Folders in Windows 95 Dialog Boxes

Button	Name	Purpose
	Up One Level	Moves to the folder "above" the one shown in the Save In box (that is, the folder in which the current one resides).
	Look in Favorites	Shows the C:\WINDOWS\FAVORITES folder, no matter which folder was displayed before.
	Create New Folder	Creates a new folder (Save As dialog box only).
	List	Shows the folders and files in the currently displayed folder in a list.
	Details	Shows details about each file and folder.
	Properties	Shows the properties of each file and folder.
	Preview	Shows a preview of the current file (Open dialog box only).
	Commands and Settings	Opens a dialog box of settings you can change that affect the dialog box.
	Add to Favorites	Adds a shortcut to the currently displayed folder to the Favorites list (Open dialog box only).
	Search the Web	Enables you to search the Internet for documents to open (Open dialog box only).

Tip

Notice in Figure 3.14 that you can select Internet Locations at which to save a file from the Save In drop-down list. If you are connected to an Internet FTP site, you can save the file directly to that server's disk drive rather than your own hard drive. You learn more about this in Chapter 15.

Saving a Presentation Subsequent Times

After you have saved a presentation, you can re-save it using the same file name and location by doing any of the following:

- Click on the Save button on the Standard toolbar.
- Press Ctrl+S.
- Choose File, Save.

If you need to, you can reopen the Save As dialog box to specify a different name or location (for example, choose File, Save As) and then save the file as you did the first time.

Saving in Other Formats

You might have noticed the Save as Type drop-down list in the Save As dialog box; it enables you to save your PowerPoint presentation in a variety of foreign formats. For example, suppose you have a coworker who uses an earlier version of PowerPoint. You could export your presentation in that format (for example, PowerPoint 4.0) so your coworker could use it. You can export to almost every older version of PowerPoint, as well as to GIF and JPEG images.

You also can export to HTML format, but there's a separate command that covers that: File, Save As HTML. I'll cover that feature in Chapter 15.

PowerPoint does not enable you to save in the native formats of competing products, such as Harvard Graphics or Freelance, but if you need to export data to one of those programs, you might try some of the following ideas:

- *Save in Text format.* Almost all programs import text.
- *Save in HTML format.* Most newer programs accept HTML imports.
- *Try opening your PowerPoint file in the other program.* Many programs can open more file formats than they save to.

To save in another format, just save the file normally using the Save As dialog box, but before you click on Save, open the Save as Type drop-down list and select a different type, as shown in Figure 3.15. Then click on Save.

Figure 3.15 You can save your work in other formats for compatibility with other programs.

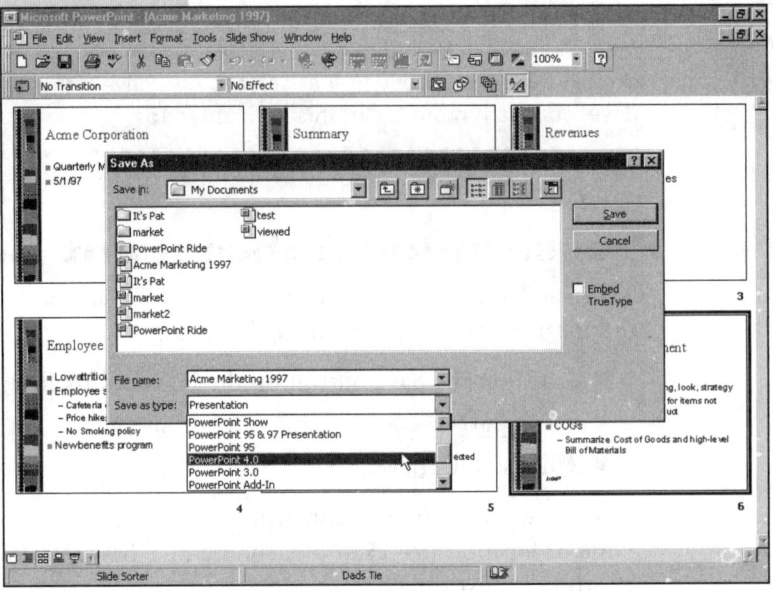

If you save in another format, you risk losing some of the unique PowerPoint 97 features, such as animations. If you save in a graphic format (such as GIF or JPEG), you lose even more—each slide is saved in a separate graphic file. Your presentation isn't a "whole" anymore, but a series of "stills." Therefore, think carefully before you save in other formats.

Closing a Presentation

When you save a presentation, it remains on-screen so you can continue to work on it. When you finish working with the presentation, you can close it in either of two ways:

- You can exit PowerPoint. The presentation closes when PowerPoint closes.
- You can close the presentation and keep working in other PowerPoint presentations.

Changing the Default Save Location

If you find yourself changing the location where you save your files each time you save a file, perhaps you should set a different folder to be the default folder in which PowerPoint saves. Normally it's My Documents, but you can change it to any folder. For example, I chose a folder I created, called Books, because the PowerPoint files I work with are used in the books I write.

To change the default file location, choose Tools, Options, and click on the Advanced tab. In the Default File Location text box, type the path to the folder you want to use and click on OK.

You already learned how to quit PowerPoint in Chapter 1: just choose File, Exit or click on the PowerPoint window's Close (X) button. To close a presentation and leave PowerPoint open, do any of the following:

- Click on the presentation window's Close (X) button. If the presentation window is maximized, the Close button is the lower of the two Close buttons in the upper-right corner. If the presentation window is not maximized, the Close button is at the right end of the presentation window's title bar.
- Choose File, Close.
- Press Ctrl+W.

If you have made any changes to the presentation since you last saved it, you'll be asked if you want to save your work when you close the presentation (see Figure 3.16). Click on Yes or No, depending on what you want. If you click on Yes and the presentation has not yet been saved, the Save As dialog box opens, which you learned about earlier in this chapter.

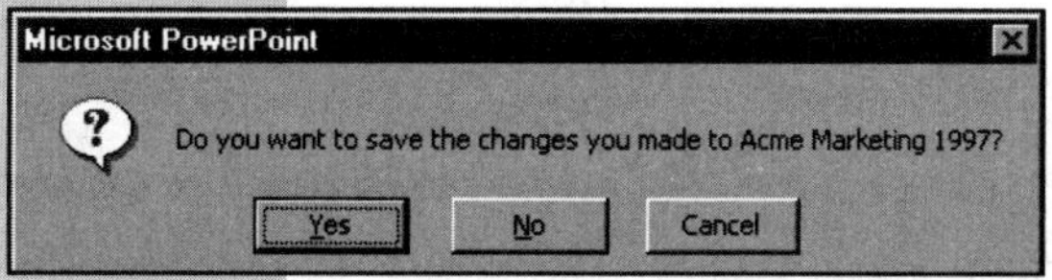

Figure 3.16 If you try to close a presentation without saving your changes, you'll get a warning like this one.

Opening a Presentation

There's no point in saving your presentations to your hard disk unless you are, at some point, going to open them again. When you open a file, you redisplay it on-screen, where you can modify it further if you want. The following steps show you how to open a saved PowerPoint file.

1. Do one of the following to open the Open dialog box shown in Figure 3.17:
   - Click on the Open button on the Standard toolbar.
   - Choose File, Open.
   - Press Ctrl+O.
2. If the file you want to open appears, click on it. Otherwise, change the drive and folder displayed as needed to find it. (Refer to "Changing the Folder or Drive" earlier in this chapter for help.)
3. Click on the Open button, or double-click on the presentation file. The presentation opens on-screen.

Note

If you use the Microsoft Office Shortcut Bar, you can open a presentation from it. Just click on the Open Office Document button on the Shortcut Bar and then navigate through the drives and folders to find the file you want. When you find and select it, click on Open.

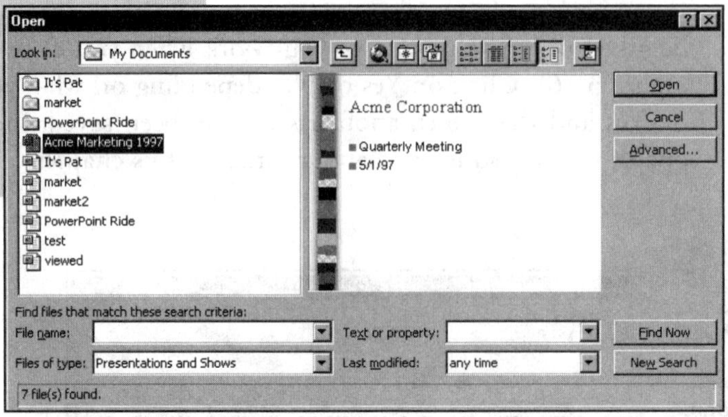

Figure 3.17 Choose the saved file you want to open and then click on the Open button.

Finding a Presentation to Open

If you're having trouble locating your presentation, PowerPoint can help you look. Perhaps you forgot which folder you saved it in, or you have moved it in Windows 95 since you saved it? No matter what the reason, PowerPoint's Find feature can rescue you. The following steps show you how to find a file.

1. Open the Open dialog box if is not already open.
2. In the File Name text box, type the name of the file you're looking for (see Figure 3.18).

You can use wildcards if you don't know the entire name of a file. The asterisk (*) wildcard character stands in for any character or set of characters, and the question mark (?) wildcard character stands in for any single character. For example, if you know the file begins with "A," you could type **A*.ppt**, as shown in Figure 3.18, to find all PowerPoint files that begin with "A."

3. (Optional) Enter other search criteria:
   - If you're looking for a different file type, choose it from the Files of Type drop-down list.
   - If you're looking for a file containing certain text, type that text in the Text or Property box.
   - If you know when you last modified the file, choose the time interval from the Last Modified drop-down list.
4. Click on the Advanced button. The Advanced Find dialog box appears (see Figure 3.19).

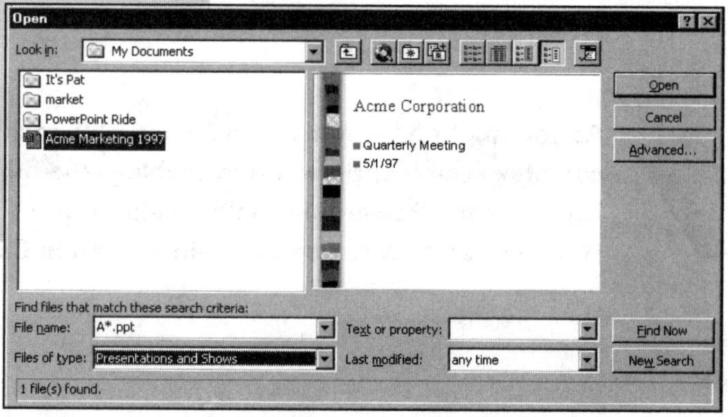

Figure 3.18 If you are not sure where a file resides, search for it by entering the portion of the name you know.

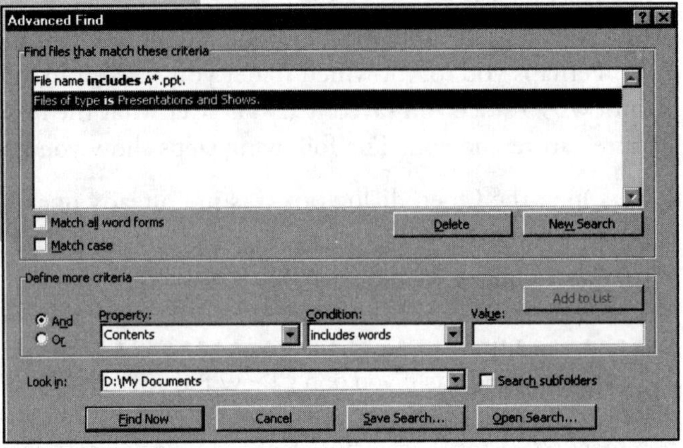

Figure 3.19 Use the Advanced Find dialog box to select the folders and drives in which you want to search.

5. In the Look In section at the bottom of the Advanced Find dialog box, narrow the search area as much as possible using these techniques:
   - If you are sure the file is in a certain folder, type that folder's path (such as C:\WINDOWS) in the Look In box.
   - If you are sure the file is on a certain drive, select that drive from the Look In drop-down list.
   - If you don't know which drive contains the file, select My Computer from the Look In drop-down list.
6. Make sure the Search Subfolders check box is marked. If it isn't, click on it.
7. Click on the Find Now button. The Open dialog box reappears and displays the files that match your search criteria.
8. Double-click on the desired file to open it.

Note

As you might have noticed in Figure 3.19, many more complex search options are available—too many to cover here. See the PowerPoint online help for more details. (You learned how to use the Help system in Chapter 1.)

Switching Among Open Presentations

In Chapter 2, I talked a little about presentations and windows. When you have more than one presentation open at once, each has its own window. When a presentation is at the top of the stack, it becomes the *active* presentation. Any commands you issue or changes you make apply to the active presentation.

Note

If you have more than one window displaying the same presentation (by using the Window, New Window command), any changes you make to one window affect the other window equally, because they are the same presentation.

You can switch to a specific open window by following this procedure:

1. Open the Window menu.
2. Click on the name of the presentation whose window you want to see.

Another way to switch among the open windows is to press Ctrl+Tab. Each time you press Ctrl+Tab, the display toggles to the next window in the list of open ones. Keep pressing Ctrl+Tab until the one you want comes into view.

If the windows are not maximized and you can see any part of a window "behind" another one, click on the part you can see to bring that window to the top of the stack.

Duplicating a Presentation

Suppose you want to make a copy of a great presentation. You could make a copy in Windows Explorer, but it might be easier to do the copying right in PowerPoint.

1. Choose File, Open to open the Open dialog box.
2. Change the drive and/or folder if needed to bring the file's name into view.
3. Right-click on the file you want to copy and choose the Copy command from the shortcut menu that appears.

4. Change the drive and/or folder if needed to display the folder in which you want to place the copy.
5. Right-click on any empty area of the folder window and choose the Paste command from the shortcut menu that appears. The copy is pasted into that folder.
6. (Optional) If you want to change the name of the copy, click on it once, press F2, and type a new name for it. Press Enter when you finish typing.
7. Click on Cancel to close the Open dialog box.

Using Properties to Manage Your Documents

Each presentation file has *properties*, which are overall attributes that apply to the file itself rather than to its contents. With a little care and thought, you can create a useful document management system by setting up properties for each presentation file.

1. Open the presentation for which you want to set the properties.
2. Choose File, Properties. The Properties dialog box appears, as shown in Figure 3.20.
3. Click on the Summary tab if it is not already displayed.

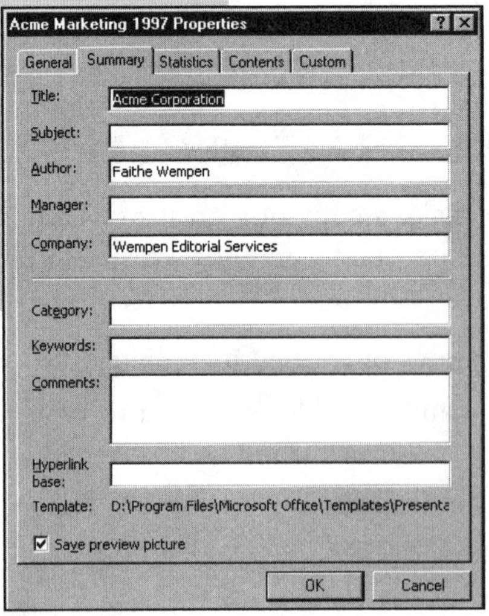

Figure 3.20 You can enter information in any of the text boxes to help you organize your presentation filing system.

4. Fill in any information you want in the text boxes on the Summary tab. You can use this information to search with the Advanced searching methods in the Open dialog box.
5. Click on OK.

If you want to get really fancy with your document properties, check out the Custom tab in the Properties dialog box. There you can specify values for dozens of special-use properties, such as Language, Client, Typist, and so on. This might seem like overkill if you have just a few dozen presentations on your computer, but if over the years you end up with hundreds of presentations, using properties to organize your system can be really useful.

Deleting a Presentation

Just as you can copy files from the Open dialog box, you can delete files from there. This makes it very convenient to clean up unwanted files without leaving PowerPoint.

To delete a file from within PowerPoint, follow these steps:

1. Choose File, Open to open the Open dialog box.
2. Change the drive and/or folder if needed to bring the file's name into view.
3. Click on the file you want to delete and then press the Delete key.
4. A warning appears asking whether you are sure you want to delete the file. Click on Yes. The file is gone.
5. Click on Cancel to close the Open dialog box.

You can delete multiple files at once from the Open dialog box; just click on the first one and then hold down the Ctrl key while you click on others. When they are all selected, press the Delete key to delete them as a group.

If you accidentally delete something you shouldn't have, you can get it back in Windows 95. Double-click on the Recycle Bin icon on the Desktop and then click on the file you want to retrieve. In the Recycle Bin, choose File, Restore.

Summary

In this chapter, you learned about files: opening them, saving them, finding them, and more. You'll use these skills every time you work with PowerPoint, and in many other programs too. In the next chapter, you'll take a look at some special templates that can make the work of creating your PowerPoint presentation much easier.

4

A Look at the PowerPoint Templates

In This Chapter

- How Templates Work
- Presentation Templates versus Presentation Design Templates
- How to Get More Templates
- Creating Your Own Templates

For abstract, creative-type people with lots of spare time, starting with a blank presentation file is really the most fun way to create a presentation. However, for the rest of us (like those of us with real jobs to do and no free time!), it pays to become familiar with PowerPoint's gallery of templates. You can pick through them on an as-needed basis, or you can learn about them all at once in this chapter.

How Templates Work

Have you ever seen a professional sign painter at work? When one of his signs must include some standard lettering, he doesn't attempt to paint it freehand, measuring out each letter separately. Instead, he uses a stencil for each letter, a pattern with the exact height and width of the letter predetermined. This saves the professional sign painter a tremendous amount of time by making the ordinary and boring part of the job go faster. That way, he can focus his attention on the special or tricky parts of the particular job. That's exactly what a template does for a PowerPoint user. A template helps you zoom quickly through the mundane parts of presentation creation, so you have more time to focus on the special parts.

Don't be deceived by the fact that PowerPoint calls different kinds of templates by different names (AutoContent, Presentations, and Presentation Designs), as you saw in Chapter 3. At the basic level, all PowerPoint templates are alike: they're collections of saved settings (and sometimes slides too) that give you a head-start on a presentation. The differences are only a matter of degree:

You learned how to create a new presentation with the AutoContent Wizard in Chapter 3.

- *Presentation templates* are templates that include sample slides.
- *Presentation design templates* are templates that do not include sample slides.
- *The AutoContent Wizard* isn't a template in the true sense of the word; it's a program that helps you select the appropriate presentation template for your situation.

Templates don't do anything that you can't do for yourself. You'll learn to do all the same things manually later in this book. These include:

- Sample text
- Background designs (Chapter 6)
- Text attributes (Chapter 7)
- Hyperlinks (Chapter 15)
- Buttons and other on-screen controls (Chapter 15)

But even if you can set up all these things manually, do you really want to spend the time doing so? It's a little like changing the oil in your car: some things it's nicer to have someone do for you.

How Presentation Design Templates Work

Chapter 6 covers using Slide Masters.

Presentation design templates contain the basic background and layout settings for a presentation, but no actual slides. Where do those settings and backgrounds come from, and where are they stored? In a Slide Master.

Every presentation has a Slide Master, which is, as its name implies, a "master slide" on which all other slides are based. It's a great feature, because you can make a change to the Slide Master (for example, add a logo or change a margin) and that change is automatically applied to all the slides in the whole presentation.

The Slide Master is not actually a part of the presentation, in that it's not a slide you can display in Slide Show view. But it looks and acts just like a regular slide when you view it in Slide Master view, as you can see in Figure 4.1. (To display the Slide Master, choose View, Master, Slide Master. To close the Slide Master, click on the floating Close button.)

Note

You also can use the *Title Master,* a special Master for the title slide in the presentation. You can use it to apply different settings to the title slide than to the rest of the presentation. There also is a Handout Master and a Notes Master.

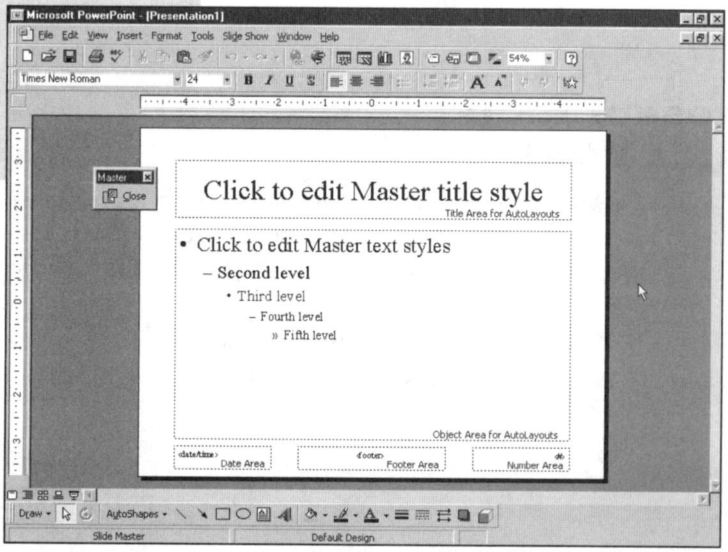

Figure 4.1
Here's the Slide Master for the Blank Presentation template.

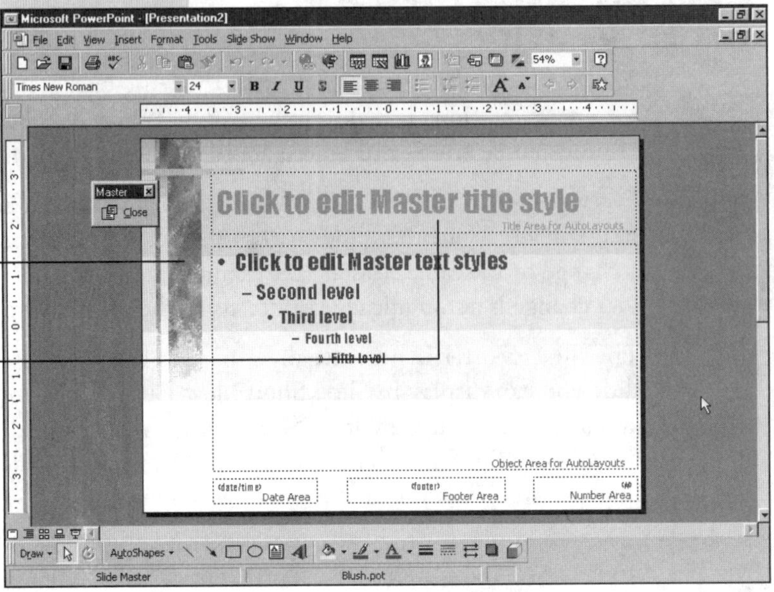

Figure 4.2 Here's the Slide Master for the Blush presentation design template.

Okay, I told you all of that so that I could tell you this: a presentation design template is nothing more than the Blank Presentation template that has a special background and some format settings applied to its Masters (Slide, Title, and so on). For example, Figure 4.2 shows the Slide Master for a presentation created with the Blush presentation design template.

How Presentation Templates Work

Presentation templates include slides. With a presentation template, you get everything that comes with a presentation design template, and you get a series of slides with sample text appropriate for a particular type of presentation. For example, Figure 4.3 shows a presentation created based on the Marketing Plan (online) presentation template. I set the view to Slide Sorter so you can see the pre-designed slides that the presentation template has automatically generated.

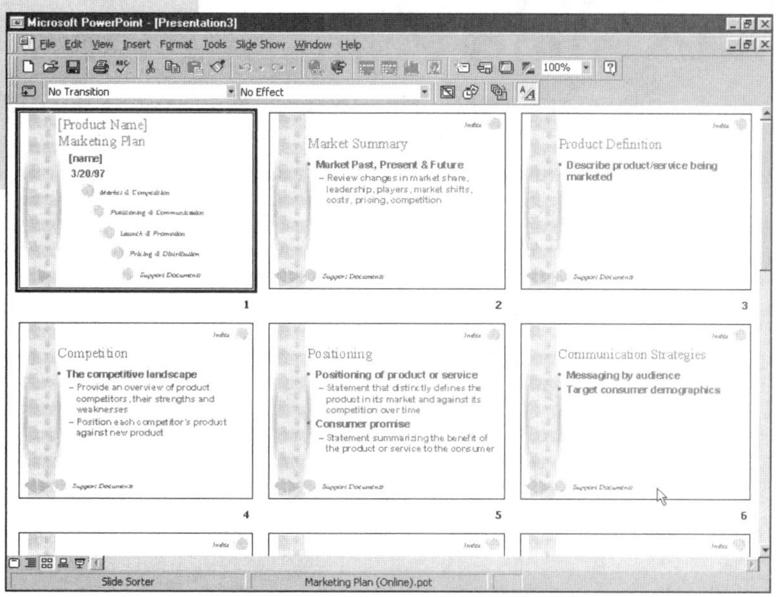

Figure 4.3 Presentation templates give you both designs and sample slides.

Refresher: Starting a New Presentation with a Template

You learned how to start a new presentation based on a template in Chapter 1, but in case you've forgotten, here's a quick reminder:

1. Choose File, New. The New dialog box appears.
2. Click on the tab that represents the type of template you want.
3. Click on a template to see a preview of it.
4. When you have selected the one you want, click on OK.

Note

The Web Pages tab contains a couple of Web page banner samples you can experiment with if you're a Web page designer. You would think PowerPoint would include all of the "online" versions of the presentation templates on the Web Pages tab too, but that's not the case—they're mixed in with their Standard equivalents on the Presentations tab.

Applying a Template to an Existing Presentation

You can't directly apply a template to an existing presentation. You must use a template when you create a presentation. However, you can do the next-best thing: you can "borrow" the design from a template (that is, all the attributes of the Slide Master) and apply it to an existing presentation. Because a presentation design template is nothing more than a dolled-up Slide Master, this has the exact same end result as if you chose that template originally when you created the presentation.

You also can copy the design of a presentation template (those are the ones that contain slides, remember), just as you can with a presentation design template. If you really like the design of a presentation template, but you don't want all of its sample slides, you can create your own slides and apply that template's design to the presentation. The following Hands On shows you how to "borrow" a design from a template for your existing presentation.

Hands On: Changing an Existing Presentation's Design

1. Choose Format, Apply Design. The Apply Design dialog box appears (see Figure 4.4).
2. By default, the Presentation Designs folder appears in the Look In box. Do one of the following:
   - If you want to take the design from one of the presentation design templates, do nothing.

Figure 4.4 Use this dialog box to choose a template from which to take a design.

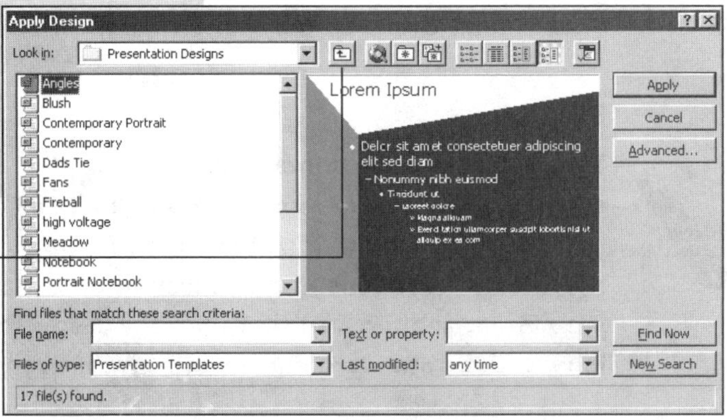

Up One Level button

You learned how to change drives and folders in a dialog box in Chapter 3.

- If you want to take the design from one of the presentation templates, click on the Up One Level button, and then double-click on the Presentations folder.
- If the template is located somewhere else on your computer, use the dialog box controls to navigate to that folder.

3. Click on a template and check the preview box to see if it looks like the one you want.
4. When you have selected the one you want, click on Apply. The template's design is applied to your presentation's Masters.

What Templates Does PowerPoint Offer?

Now comes the fun part of this chapter: you get to look at all the templates and designs that PowerPoint has to offer. I've included this section so you don't have to go through the New Presentation dialog box and click on each template to see the choices that PowerPoint provides.

Presentation Design Templates

Each of the presentation design templates offers a unique "feel" through the combination of background, fonts, and coloring. In the following listing, I've tried to not only show you what the template looks like, but to give you an idea of the "feel" of the design and what it might be useful for.

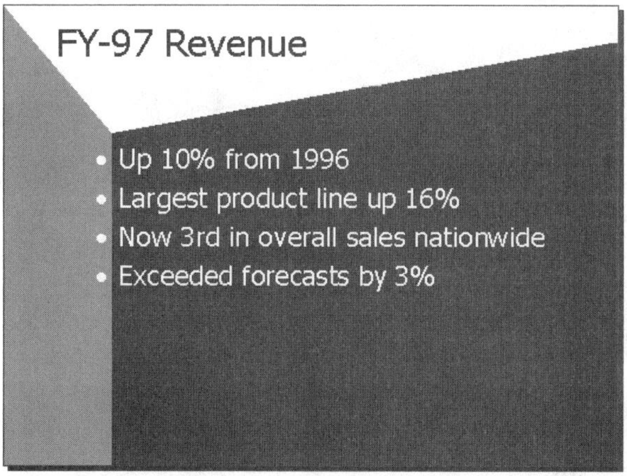

Angles. A dramatic red, white, and black design that emphasizes angularity. Artistic without being too "busy," but watch that the black background does not overwhelm your text.

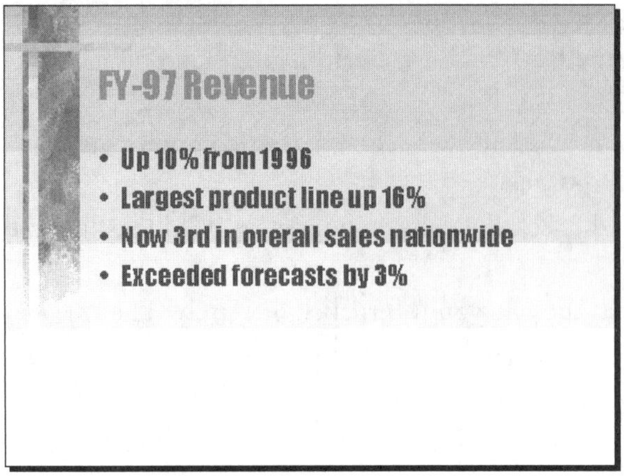

Blush. A graduated blend of peach and pink, with purple headings. Adds a feminine, almost floral touch to the presentation. A nice design, but not appropriate for many industries.

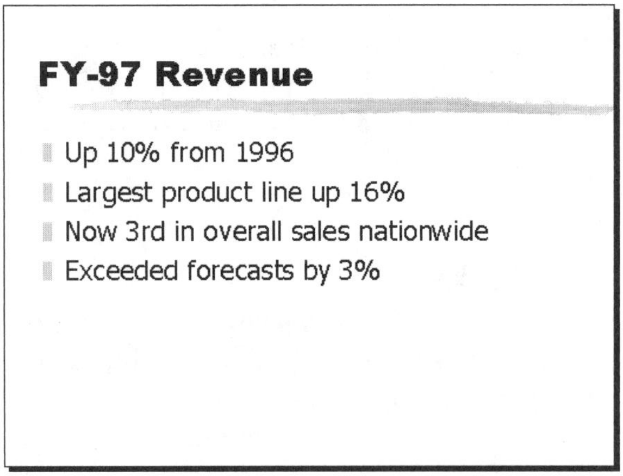

Contemporary Portrait. Very sparse and minimalist, with only a touch of yellow accent. Looks casual and relaxed, and black-and-white printouts look very much like the original slides.

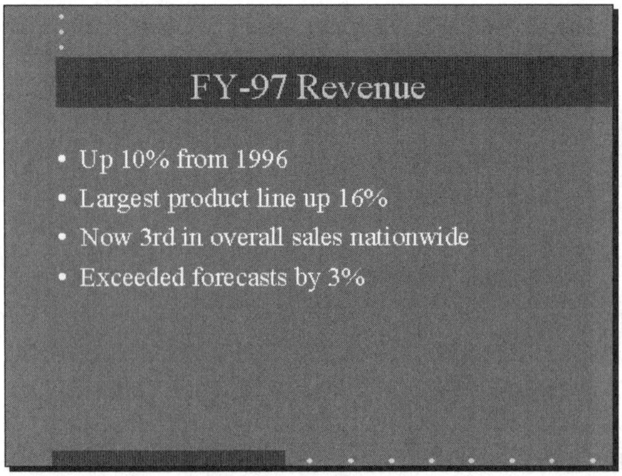

Contemporary. This design is all blue, with various shades providing the design. It may be too dark for black-and-white use, but in its native color format it is attractive.

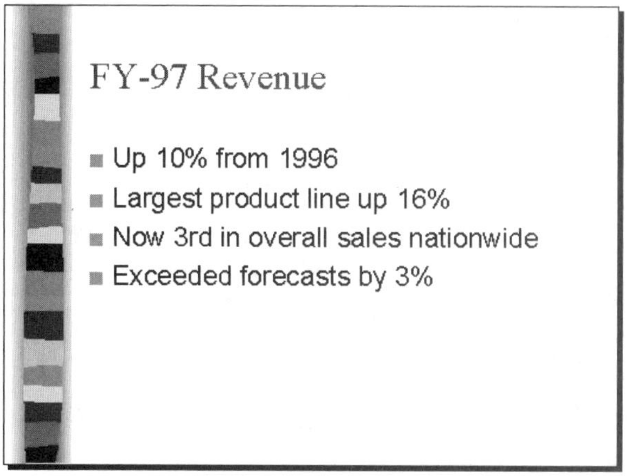

Dad's Tie. The design resembles a casual striped necktie in blues and contrasting colors. This also is a casual design, although less casual than Contemporary Portrait.

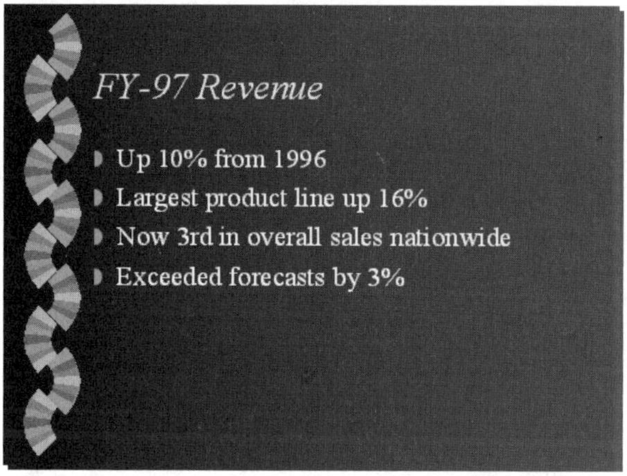

Fans. This black-background design plays up splashes of bright color. It's pretty, but the audience may spend too much time admiring the intricate fan patterns and too little time reading the slides.

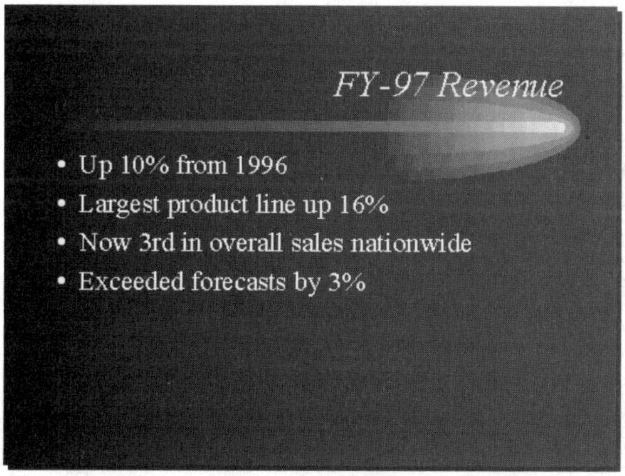

Fireball. The yellow fireball streaking across a black slide makes a dramatic impression. The fireball image also creates a feeling of movement and urgency.

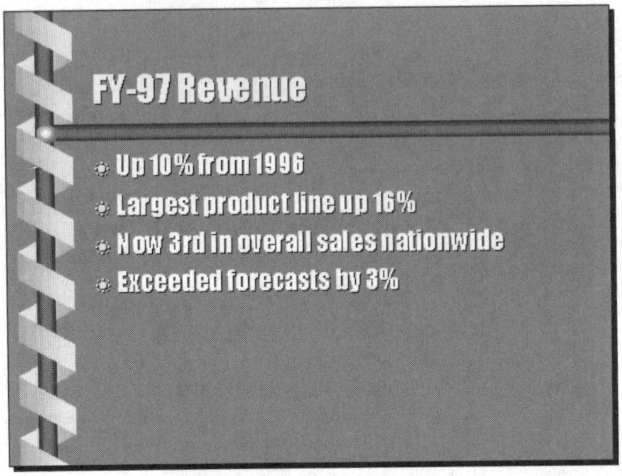

High Voltage. The activity of the graphics are balanced by the serene blues of the background in this design, leaving a well-balanced image that's good for overheads and 35mm slides.

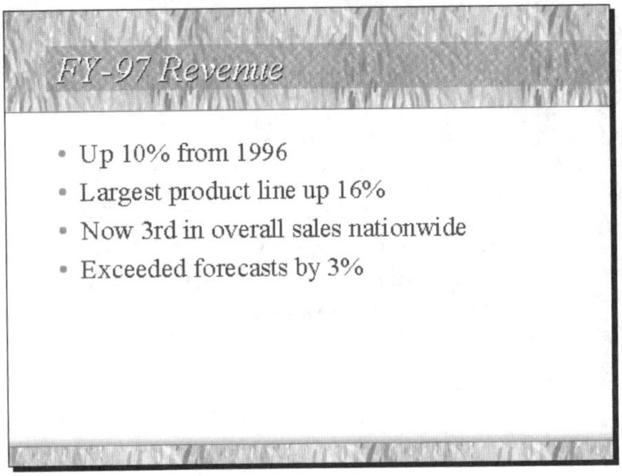

Meadow. The pattern on the slide, although you can't see it very well here, is a green meadow. Not the most attractive design, in my opinion, but good for a nature/environmental tie-in.

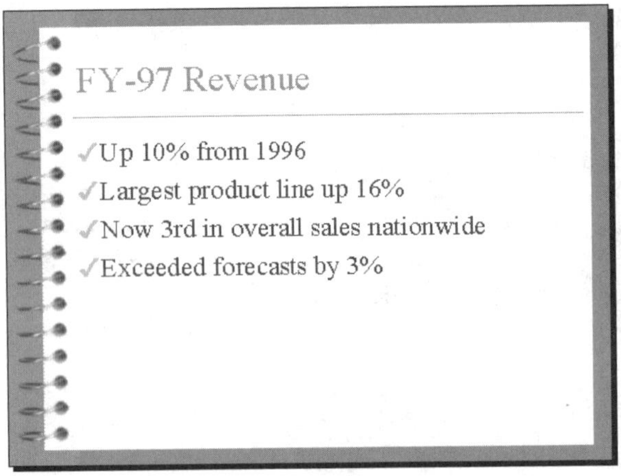

Notebook. Two notebook designs are available; this one shows unlined, light-gold pages. Nice tie-in for presenting status reports or research findings.

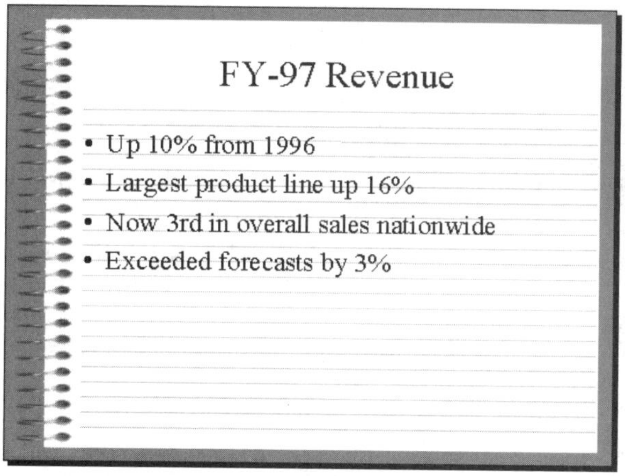

Portrait Notebook. This is the other notebook design; it has lined white pages that look like lined writing paper. The notebook paper provides a tie-in for academic-themed presentations.

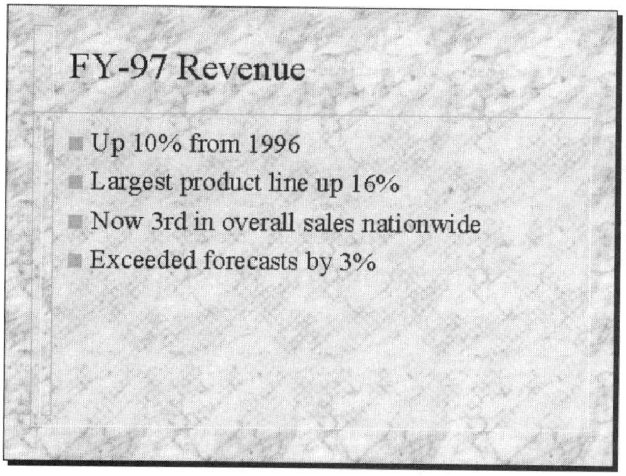

Professional. The tasteful gray marble background on this design is suitable for any conservative industry, such as banking.

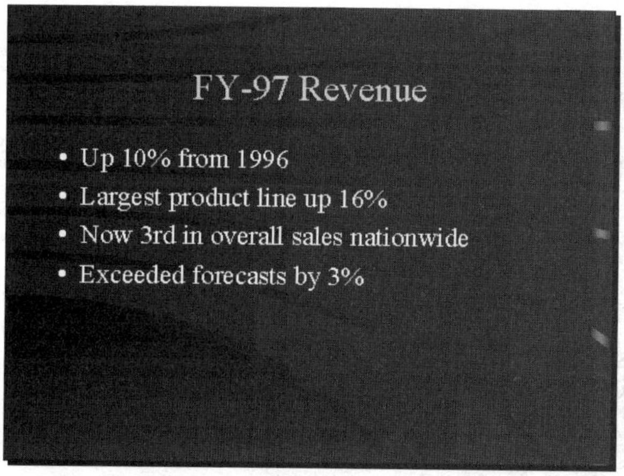

Pulse. Dark blue with a sweeping "swoosh" design, this is a beautiful design for 35mm slides, but can be too dark in some other mediums.

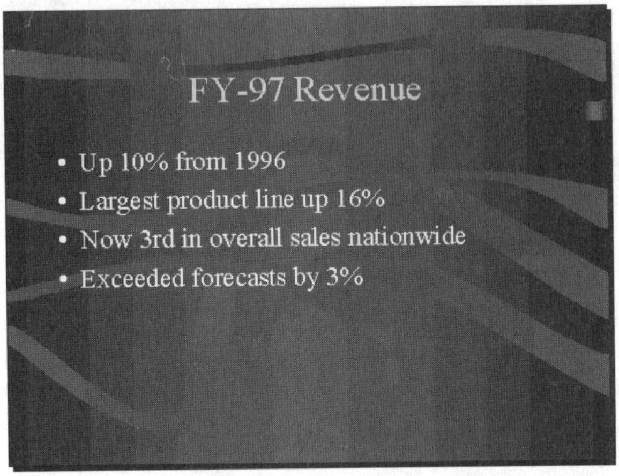

Ribbons. This cranberry-colored background with waving ribbons looks like a celebration—in a reserved, businesslike way, of course.

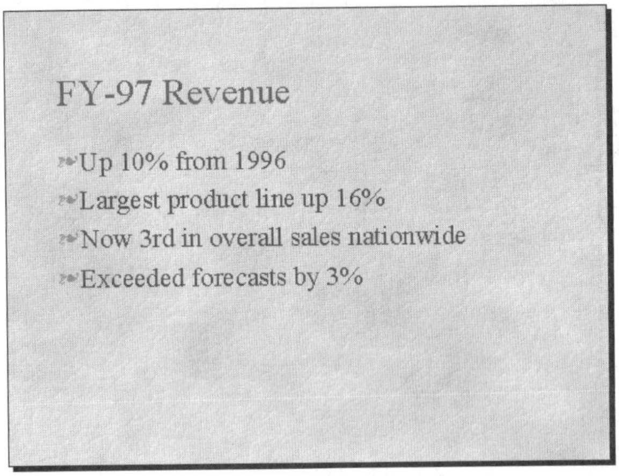

Serene. Zzzzzz . . . oops, sorry, dozed off there. This design's mottled light-green background is easy on the eyes and very peaceful, but may say "wishy-washy" to your audience.

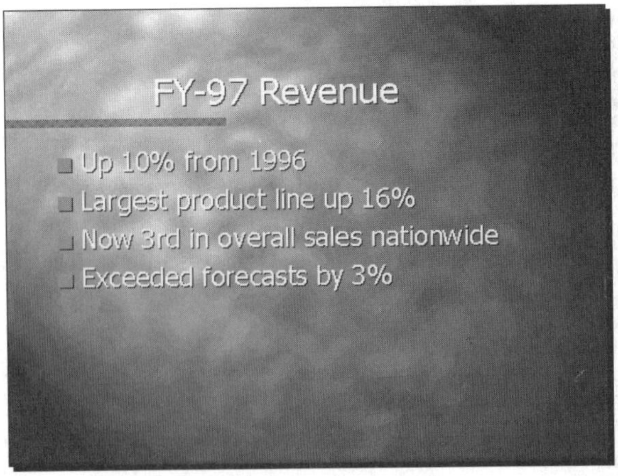

Whirlpool. If you lay on the bottom of a swimming pool and look up toward the sun, this blue design is what you see. It draws the viewer's attention to the light area in the middle, so make sure your text goes there.

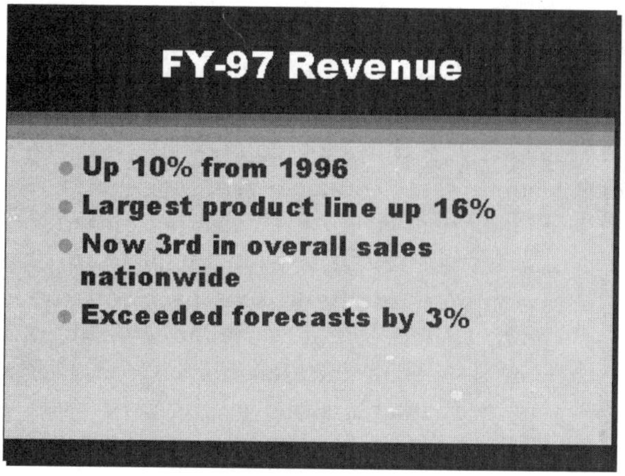

Zesty. Nothing subtle here—a bright orange background with black, red, and purple accents. Looks like a Mexican blanket, and adds a fun mood to the presentation. However, it could become overwhelming if used on every slide of a big presentation.

Presentation Templates

You'll learn all about applying different design templates to a presentation in Chapter 6.

While presentation designs are focused on the colors and background that they provide, the presentation templates have an added element: the sample content. You may not find a presentation template that has the content *and* the background you want, so choose content first, and don't worry too much about the background. You can always apply one of the presentation design templates to the presentation later to change the background.

For each presentation template, there are two versions: Standard and Online. For a presentation that will be presented by a live speaker, use the Standard template; for self-running presentations, use the Online template. The difference is that the Online versions have special navigation buttons built into the Slide Master that help the user move from slide to slide on his own.

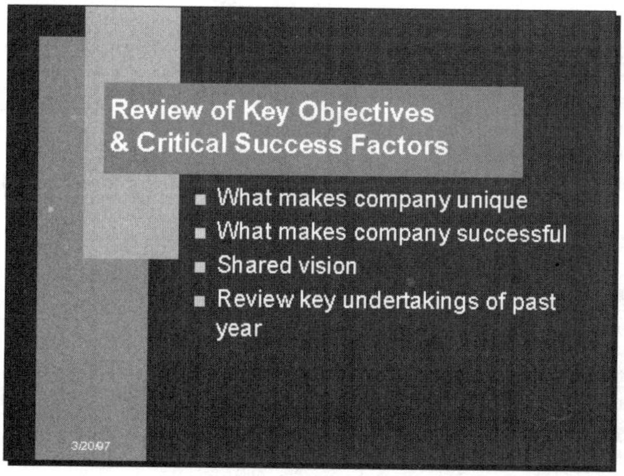

Company Meeting. Contains slides that outline a typical company meeting, a presentation given to an audience of employees. The dark green background looks soothing, while the colorful blocks add some interest.

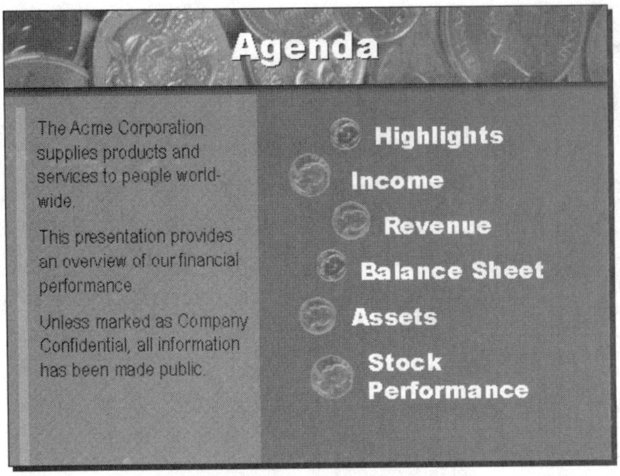

Corporate Financial Overview. Although it's hard to see from this small picture, this template uses a money motif. All the bullets are actually pictures of coins. This template's sample slides contain a variety of special elements, including Word tables and Microsoft Graph charts. It's a good template to base your presentation on if your presentation is going to have lots of charts and tables in it. If you don't like the design, you can always apply a different one, keeping the sample charts.

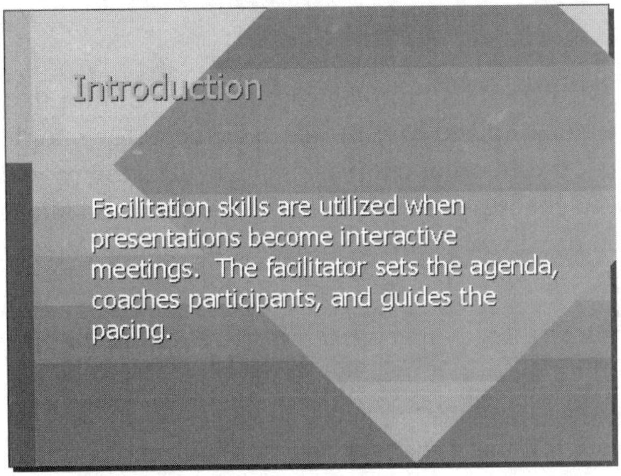

The Dale Carnegie Templates. PowerPoint includes a number of templates that contain information and advice from the Dale Carnegie Institute. They include Facilitating a Meeting (shown here), Introducing a Speaker, Managing Human Resources' Changing Role, Motivating a Team, Presentation Guidelines, Presenting a Technical Report, Selling Your Ideas, and Thanking a Speaker. All of these use the same design. You may want to create presentations using these templates just so you can read the advice on the sample slides!

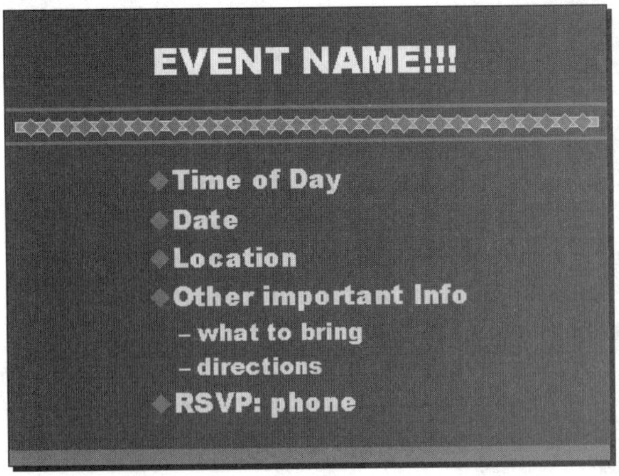

Flyer. This template is different from most of the others, in that it isn't meant to be used for a real presentation. Instead, it's a template for creating an invitation or announcement. There are only two slides: one for the front of the flyer and one for the back.

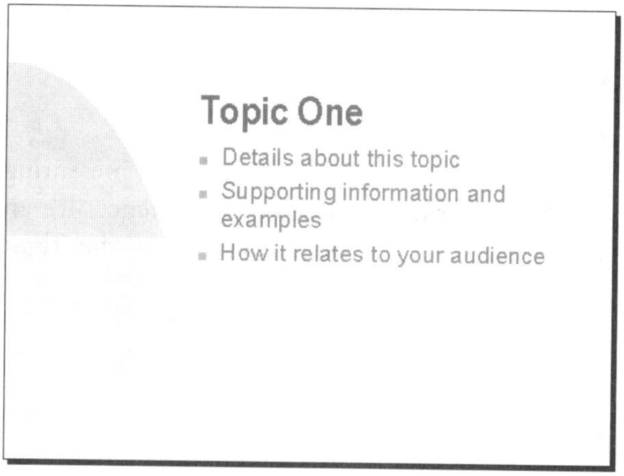

Generic. Provides an outline that can be used for almost any type of meeting. It also has a very nice white-background design, one of my personal favorites among those that PowerPoint provides. You'll be seeing it in some of the examples later in the book.

Use dark background designs when creating slides that are going to be viewed on-screen or as 35mm slides or overheads. Use light background designs when creating a presentation that will be printed and distributed in hard-copy form.

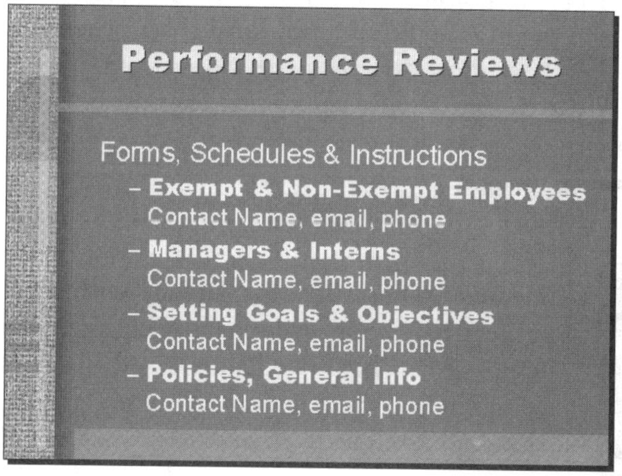

H.R. Information Kiosk. Helps you put together an informative presentation about your organization's human resources policies and procedures. The soothing blue background helps put employees at ease.

PowerPoint comes with Microsoft Organization Chart, a program that can create the "standard" type of organizational charts. See Chapter 11 for details.

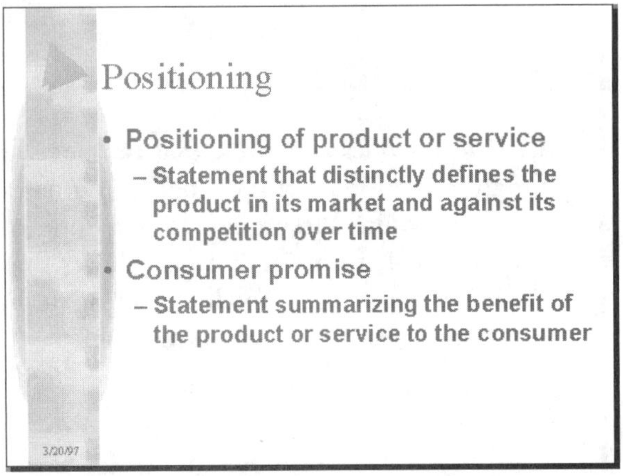

Marketing Plan. Provides slides for presenting your marketing goals to an audience. It's an attractive, airy design with just the right touch of color along the side.

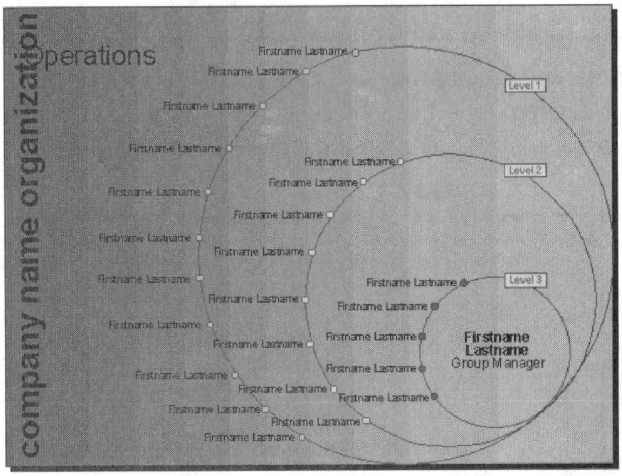

Organization Overview. This template is particularly interesting, not because of its design but because it contains many sample slides showing all kinds of ways that organizational information can be presented. You aren't limited to simple organizational charts when you have these designs to take ideas from!

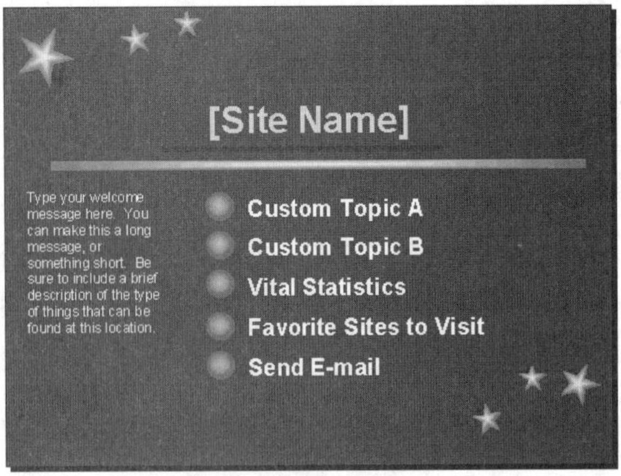

Personal Home Page. For anyone with aspirations to having their own Web site, this template can be a good starting-off place. It comes in both Standard and Online versions, although Online is most likely what you'll want.

You'll learn more about creating a Web page with PowerPoint in Chapter 15.

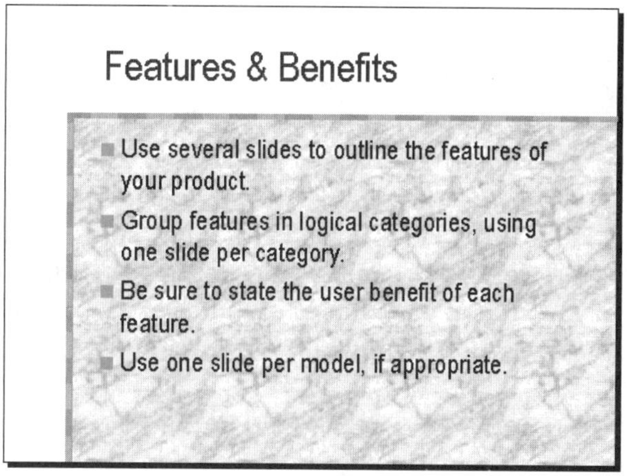

Product Overview. This template's slides start you out talking about your product, although you will probably want to augment them with more detailed slides specific to your industry or your product. The gray marble background gives it a classy look, too.

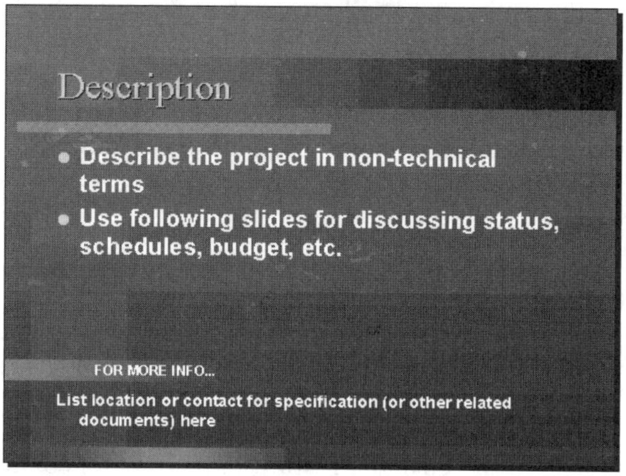

Project Overview. These slides take you through a description of a project (that is, something that's going on, as opposed to a product, which is something that just sits there). The graduated blue background looks good on a screen, and some slides (like the one shown here) show you innovative ways to handle special elements, such as footnotes.

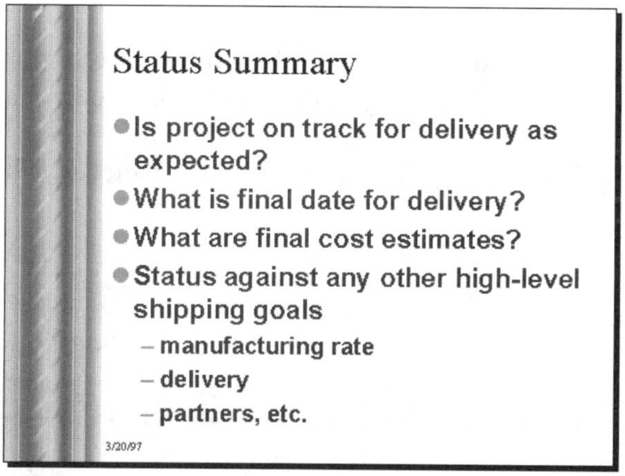

Project Status. These slides explain a project, like the preceding one, but the audience is different. For the Project Overview, the audience is just now learning about the project; for Project Status, they are already familiar with the project and you are bringing them up to speed on the latest developments. The gold and white design is simple and understated, good for a conservative industry.

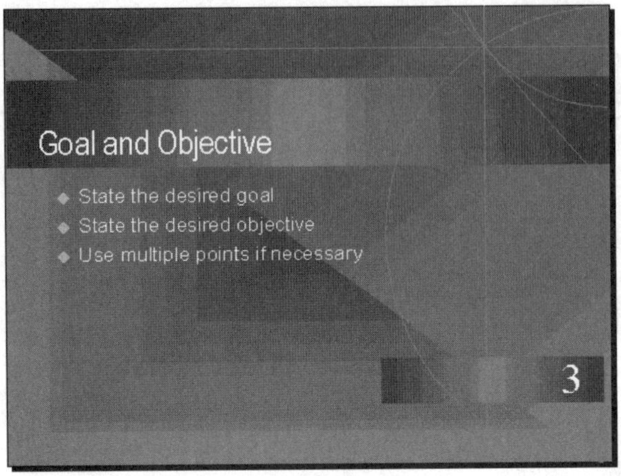

Recommending a Strategy. Although I can't recommend this design wholeheartedly (it consists mostly of brown gradations, and doesn't look too good either on-screen or in print), the sample slides provide helpful direction on making your pitch for a particular action plan in your organization.

I Want More!

If none of the presentation designs you've seen in this chapter are exactly what you want, don't despair! There are a number of things you can do, described in the following sections.

Customizing the Templates

See Chapter 5 to learn how to change the color of a background, and how to change fonts in Chapter 7.

One is to start out with a template and then customize it. For example, if you like the design of the Recommending a Strategy template but can't stand the color brown, you can easily change the background color to blue or pink or whatever you want. You also can change the font, font size, and color, add graphics, and lots more. Just use the skills you'll learn in the upcoming chapters.

If you are sure you prefer a certain template to always be a different way (for example, if you always want the Recommending a Strategy template to have a blue background), you can change the template itself, rather than the presentation based on it; that way, all future presentations based on that template will reflect your changes.

Tip

If you alter a template and then decide you want it back the way it was originally, reinstall the template from the Microsoft PowerPoint 97 (or Office 97) CD-ROM or distribution disks (see Appendix A).

See Chapter 3 if you need help navigating the folders on your disk.

See Chapter 5 to learn how to modify a template's design and add or delete slides.

Hands On: Altering a Template

1. Choose File, Open. The Open dialog box appears.
2. Open the Files of Type drop-down list and choose Presentation Templates.
3. Navigate to the Program Files/Microsoft Office/Templates folder on your hard disk.
4. Double-click on the folder containing the template you want to modify. For example, if you want to modify Recommending a Strategy, double-click on Presentations because it is a presentation template.
5. Double-click on the name of the template you want to open.
6. Make changes to the template's design. Add or delete slides too, if you want to.
7. Choose File, Save As and save the template under a new name. (This is better than saving over the original template, which you may want to use in its original form someday.)
8. Choose File, Close to close the template. The next time you use the template, it will reflect your changes.

Do not use the template like a regular presentation. That is, do not make changes to the template file that you do not want to be reflected in every single presentation that this template will be the basis for in the future.

Getting More Templates from the CD-ROM

If you want more templates to choose from, and you purchased the CD-ROM version of Microsoft Office or Microsoft PowerPoint, you're in luck. There are lots and lots more templates to choose from.

In the following Hands On, I will walk you through the procedure for grabbing those extra templates in the way that I do it: spending some time looking at what's there first, before copying every single template wholesale. Some people think that, like fonts, you can never have too many templates, but I disagree. If I will never use a template in my job, I don't want it taking up space on my hard disk.

Tip

Remember PowerPoint Central, which you saw in Chapter 1? It's a special information presentation built into PowerPoint. You can access it (choose Tools, PowerPoint Central) and browse in it to read about the templates available on the CD-ROM, but you can't actually transfer them to your hard disk from there; you have to use the procedure in the following Hands On.

Hands On: Retrieving Extra Templates from the CD-ROM

1. Make sure the Office 97 or PowerPoint 97 CD-ROM is in your CD-ROM drive.
2. In PowerPoint, click on the New button on the Standard toolbar. A new, blank presentation opens, and the New Slide dialog box appears.
3. Click on any slide in the New Slide dialog box and click on OK. (You just need something on-screen; it doesn't matter what.)
4. Choose Format, Apply Design. The Apply Design dialog box opens.
5. Open the Look In drop-down list and choose the CD-ROM drive.
6. Navigate to Valupack\Template\Present. That's where the other presentation templates are. You can't tell what sample slides they contain, but you can see their designs and get a general idea from the sample slide what each one does.
7. Browse through each of the templates in this folder, making notes to yourself of which ones you will want to copy to your hard disk later.
8. When you are finished looking at these templates, click on the Up One Level button and then double-click on the Designs folder. This is where the additional presentation design templates are kept.
9. Repeat step 7 for these templates.
10. When you have a comprehensive list of all the templates you want, click on Cancel.
11. Minimize the PowerPoint window.
12. Click on the Start button and choose Programs, Windows Explorer. The Explorer opens.
13. In the Explorer, navigate to one of the folders that contained the templates you wanted. For example, in Figure 4.5, I'm displaying the ValuPack\Template\Designs folder.

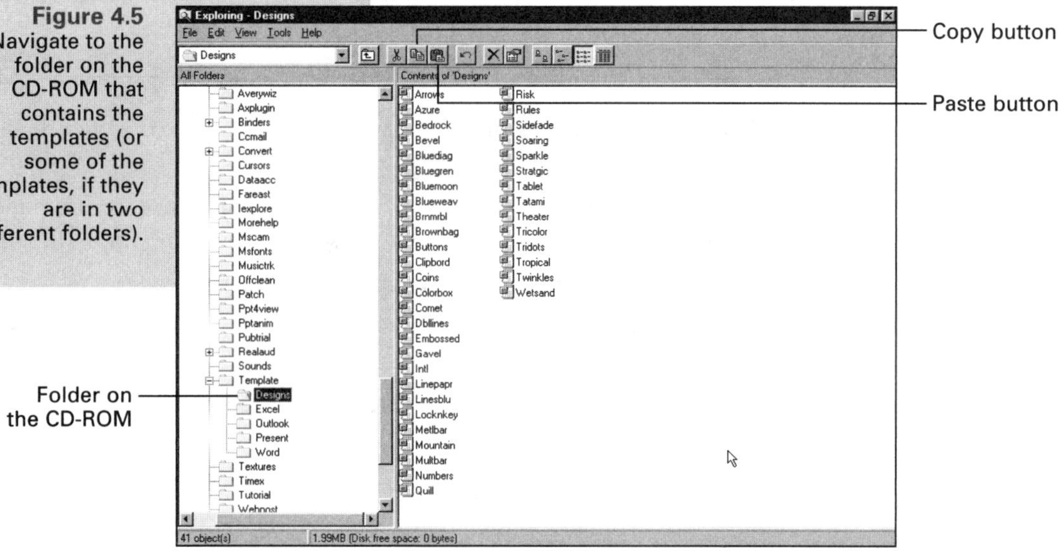

Figure 4.5 Navigate to the folder on the CD-ROM that contains the templates (or some of the templates, if they are in two different folders).

14. Hold down the Ctrl key and click on all the names of the templates you want. Release the Ctrl key when they are all selected.
15. Click on the Copy button in Windows Explorer, or press Ctrl+C. The selected templates are copied to the Clipboard.
16. Navigate to the Program Files\Microsoft Office\Templates folder, and then to either the Presentations or Presentation Designs folder, depending on the type of templates you just copied.
17. Click on the Paste button in Windows Explorer, or press Ctrl+V. The templates are copied into that folder, and are now ready for your use in PowerPoint.
18. Repeat steps 13 through 17 if you need to copy from an additional folder on the CD-ROM. Otherwise you are done.
19. Restore the PowerPoint window and apply the new templates as you would any other ones.

Getting More Templates from the Internet

Still not satisfied with the available templates? You can get even more of them from Microsoft's Web site if you have an Internet connection. (If you don't have an Internet connection, Microsoft will be glad to set you up with one via the Microsoft Network; just double-click on the Microsoft Network icon on your Desktop and follow the instructions.)

To get additional templates from the Internet, follow these steps:

1. Start your Internet connection if it is a dial-up one (that is, if you use a modem to connect).
2. Start your favorite Web browser. (Microsoft, of course, recommends their own Internet Explorer, but Netscape Navigator works fine too.)
3. Enter the following URL in your Web browser:

   http://www.microsoft.com/officefreestuff/powerpoint/templates/default.htm.

   A page appears listing various categories of templates available to download (see Figure 4.6).
4. Click on a category (for example, Communications Templates).
5. You may see a Registration Wizard screen like the one shown in Figure 4.7. If you do, click on Next to begin registration.
6. Complete the registration process (just follow along with whatever screens appear; I'm not going to describe it in detail here because

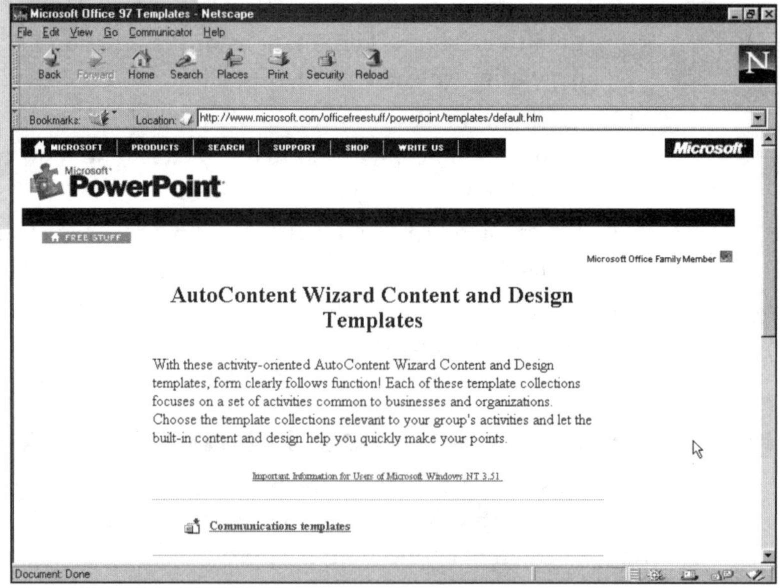

Figure 4.6 Here's the PowerPoint Free Stuff page; it may have changed slightly by the time you access it.

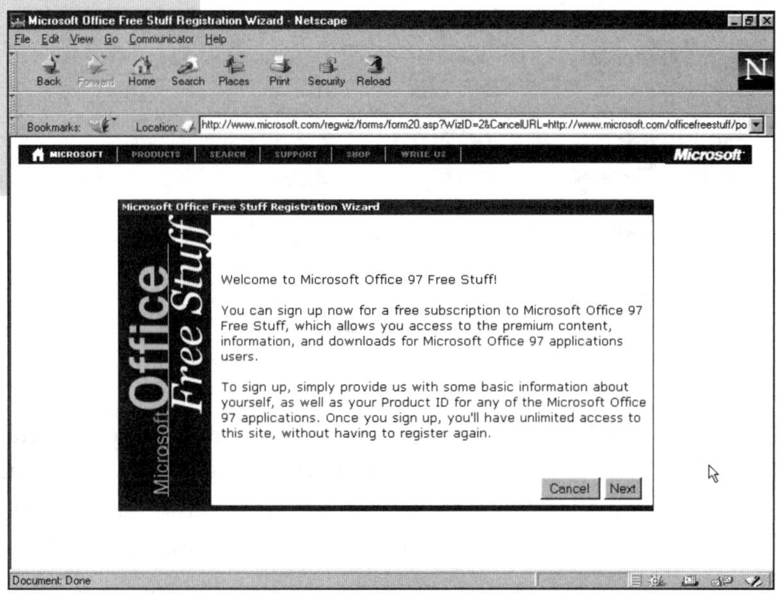

Figure 4.7 If asked to register, click on Next and follow the instructions to comply.

Note

Microsoft asks you to register before receiving free stuff because they want to restrict it to people who are legitimate users of Microsoft Office products.

Microsoft may change the procedure between now and the time you read this). When you finish, you'll end up back at Figure 4.6. Click on the category again, and go on to step 7.

7. The Save As dialog box opens, so you can save the selected template collection to your hard disk (see Figure 4.8). Click on the Create New Folder button and create a new folder on your hard disk called Temptemp (short for "Temporary storage space for Templates"). Then double-click on that folder and click on Save. A Saving Location message box shows you the progress of the download.
8. Wait for the file to transfer to your hard disk. You can tell it's done when the Saving Location message box goes away.
9. If you want to download another category of templates, click on another category. When the Save As dialog box appears again, just click on Save. (The folder will already be correct).

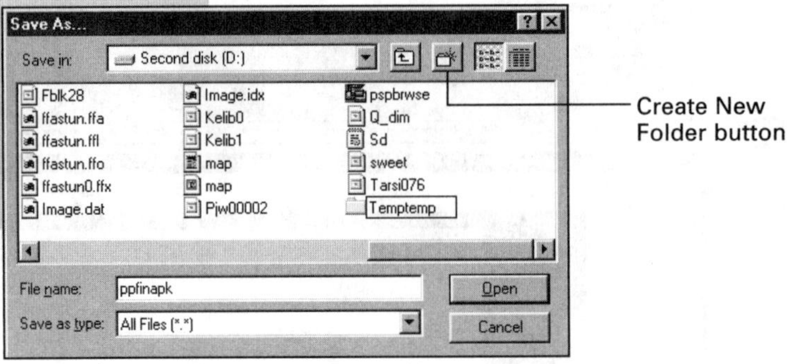

Figure 4.8 Create a new folder (I called mine Temptemp) to hold the downloaded files.

10. When you are finished downloading templates, close your Web browser and terminate your Internet connection if it's a dial-up.
11. In Windows Explorer, navigate to the Temptemp folder and double-click on one of the downloaded files. An installation program begins.
12. Follow the steps on-screen to complete the installation process. Depending on what you downloaded, a DOS window may appear as part of the setup program; this is normal. Just follow the directions you see there.
13. Repeat steps 11 and 12 if you downloaded more than one set of templates.
14. In the Explorer, delete the files you downloaded. You don't need them anymore now that you've run the setup programs; they are just taking up space on your hard disk.

Summary

This chapter showcased PowerPoint's templates. You can use this chapter as a reference when you aren't sure which template you want to use. The next chapter starts a whole new part of the book, and a whole new part in your PowerPoint education. You'll start your first real presentation and begin editing slides.

PART II

Building Great Slides

5 Starting a Basic Slide Presentation

In This Chapter

- Developing Your Plan
- Adding and Deleting Slides
- Moving Between Slides
- Editing the Text
- Working with Slide Objects

Even if you're planning a huge, elaborate presentation with multimedia, you have to start with the basics and build from a solid foundation. You began that foundation in Chapters 3 and 4, when you chose the template on which your presentation would be based. In this chapter, you'll start forming that rough outer shell into a presentation with content that is really your own.

Assessing What's Already There

At this point, you have a presentation on-screen you created with a template. If you used a presentation template, you have some sample slides; if you used a presentation design template, it's just you and your Slide Master, ready to add the slides you need. That difference will be important later in the chapter, but at this point, users of all templates have to make some decisions.

> If you need more help with the following tasks, refer back to Chapters 3 and 4.

- *Are you happy with the sample slides?* If you used a presentation template in Chapter 3 to start the new presentation (as opposed to a presentation design template), you received some sample slides with it. Switch to Outline view and take a look at the text on those sample slides. Naturally you will want to customize much of the text later, but if the overall structure seems all wrong for the presentation you want to give, now is a good time to start over with a different presentation template. If you don't have any sample slides, but want some, you might want to start over and, this time, use a presentation template rather than a design template.
- *Do you like the background and fonts?* Choose View, Master, Slide Master and examine the background and fonts being used. If you don't like them, close the Slide Master (click on the Close button) and choose Format, Apply Design and choose a different template for the design.
- *What content do you need to add?* If you started with a presentation design template, the answer to this question is: Everything. You have no content yet. If you started with a presentation template, you have some text on sample slides, but you will definitely have to customize it to meet your own needs. Think now about the information you need to present and how it can be best organized on slides.

> You'll learn more about changing backgrounds in Chapter 6.

After you have given these three points some careful thought, and made any template changes needed, you're ready to begin working on your presentation.

Changing Which Slide Is Active

If you already have more than one slide in your presentation, then when you issue a command, PowerPoint needs to know which slide you want that command to act upon. That's why you need to learn how to *select* a slide, making it *active*. (If you don't have more than one slide yet in your presentation, skip ahead to the section "Adding New Slides to a Presentation" later in this chapter.)

In Slide and Notes Page view, only a single slide can be active, or "selected," at once. There is never any doubt as to which slide is selected—it's the one showing on-screen at the time. When you issue a command in one of those views, it acts upon the active slide.

Making a particular slide active is somewhat different in views that show multiple slides at once. In such views (like Slide Sorter and Outline), you can select a single slide or several slides before you issue a command. Therefore, in Slide Sorter and Outline views, you are not so much switching slides as you are selecting or deselecting them. Take a look at these two separate but related procedures.

Switching Slides Single-Slide Views

Slide and Notes Page view are similar in that they both show only one slide at a time. Consequently, their procedures for moving from slide to slide are the same. Use whichever of the following methods you find the easiest to switch slides in either of these views:

- Drag the vertical scroll box or click on the vertical scroll bar's up and down arrows until the new slide comes into view. By dragging the scroll box, you can move several slides at a time.
- Press the Page Up and Page Down keys on the keyboard once for each slide you want to move back or forward in the presentation.
- Click on the Next Slide and Previous Slide buttons on-screen (see Figure 5.1).

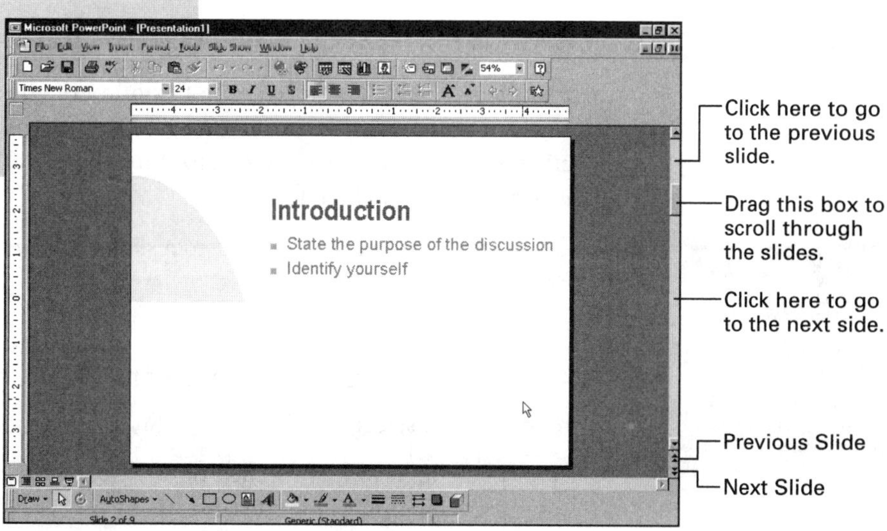

Figure 5.1 There are several ways to change slides in Slide view.

Movement Buttons and Keys: What's the Difference?

The on-screen controls all appear to work the same way, but that's not always the case. It gets a little bit complicated.

When you're scrolling through the presentation, it's as if your whole presentation were on one giant scroll (like form-feed paper) and the scroll bar controls what point on the scroll you see.

The scroll bar itself deals in "screenfuls." When you click above or below the scroll box, you scroll the display up or down one screenful. If the Zoom is set so that an entire slide fits on-screen at once, then a screenful is the same as a slide, so it looks like you are moving through one slide at a time. However, that's just a coincidence that a screenful happens to equal exactly one slide.

If you set the zoom higher, so that one slide requires two or more screenfuls, clicking above or below the scroll box moves you up or down on the slide, but not to the next slide until you are at the very bottom of the current one.

In contrast, the Previous Slide and Next Slide buttons (and the Page Up and Page Down keys) always take you to a whole different slide, no matter what the zoom.

Selecting Slides in Multiple-Slide Views

In these multi-slide views, you have the flexibility of choosing a single slide or multiple slides to which the commands you issue will apply. For example, if you wanted to assign a transition effect to three slides, you could select all three of them and then apply the effect.

Chapter 13 covers transition effects.

In views like that, rather than "switch" to a slide, you "select" it. The net result is the same—the slide becomes active.

Selecting Slides in Slide Sorter View

Here are some slide-selecting methods for Slide Sorter view:

- To select a single slide, just click on it. A black frame appears around it.

- To select multiple slides, hold down the Shift key as you click on each one you want. A black frame appears around each one.
- Use the following Hands On to select a rectangular block of slides.

Hands On: Selecting a Block of Slides

In the following procedure, you will select the four slides in the upper-right corner of Slide Sorter view.

Note

This procedure assumes you have a presentation with several slides in it already. If you don't, start a new presentation using one of the presentation templates that includes sample slides, as described in Chapter 3.

1. Switch to Slide Sorter view if you're not already there.
2. Click and hold down the mouse button slightly above and to the right of the slide in the upper-right corner of the range you want. For example, notice the pointer position in Figure 5.2.

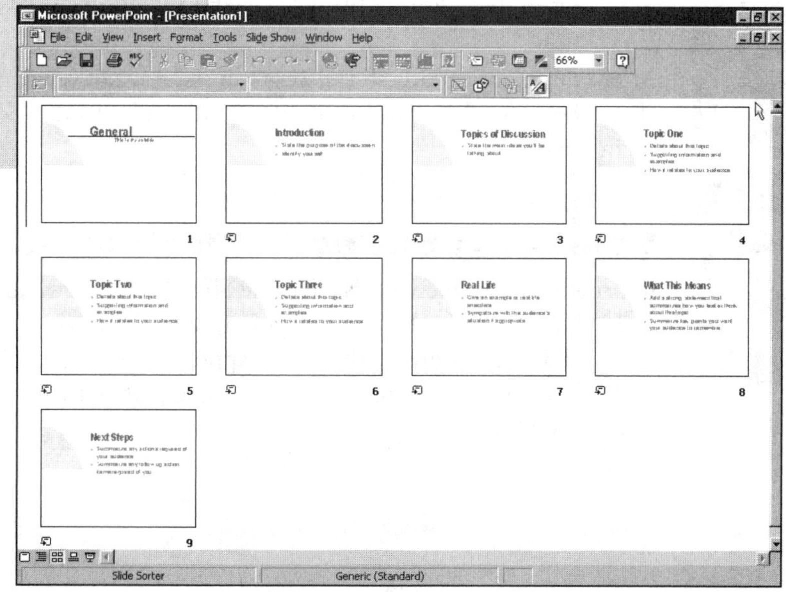

Figure 5.2 Position the mouse pointer at one corner of the range to select.

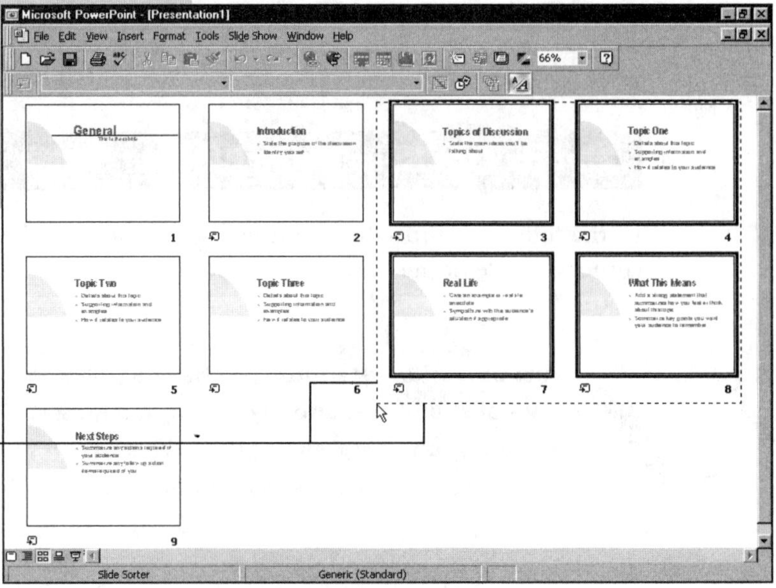

Figure 5.3 When you drag to the opposite corner of the range, all slides in the range become selected.

The dotted lines show the range.

You'll learn the wide range of things you can do to a slide or groups of slides in upcoming chapters, especially Chapter 6.

3. Hold down the left mouse button and drag the mouse pointer to the opposite corner of the range (see Figure 5.3). All the slides in the range become selected.
4. Release the mouse button. Selected slides appear with thick black borders.

After you select certain slides, you can issue whatever command you want to affect the slides. You can format them, add animation or special effects, delete them, and so on.

Selecting Slides in Outline View

In principle, Outline view is a lot like Slide Sorter view, but in practice, it looks and behaves differently. For one thing, in Outline view, you see only the text of the slide; for another, the slides appear in a single column rather than in multiple rows. Therefore, it's not surprising that the procedure for selecting slides is different.

As you can see in Figure 5.4, each slide in Outline view has a slide icon next to it. Those icons help you see at a glance where the text for one slide stops and the text for the next slide begins. To select a slide in outline view, just click on its slide icon. This highlights (selects) the entire slide and all its text, as shown in Figure 5.4.

To select multiple slides in a row, hold down the Shift key as you click on the first and last one you want. You can't select non-contiguous slides in Outline view, so if, for example, you click on slide 1 and then on slide 4 (with the Shift key down), slides 2 and 3 will become selected too.

Figure 5.4 To select a slide in Outline view, click on its slide icon.

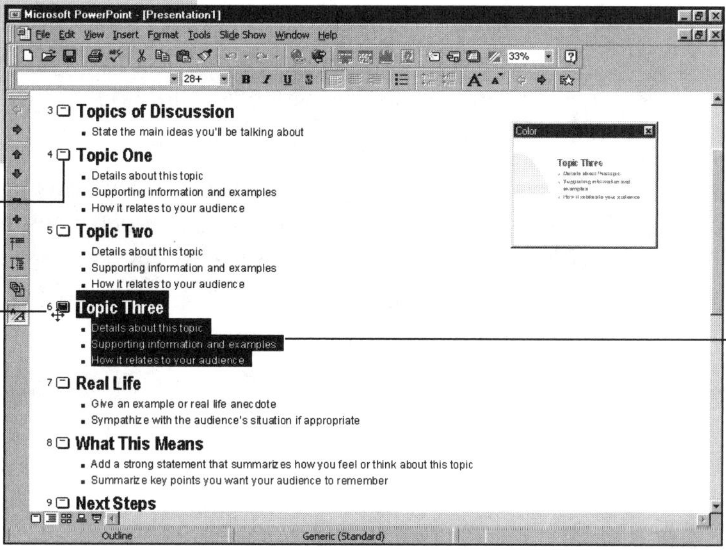

Note

Notice in Figure 5.4 that the mouse pointer is a four-headed arrow. When you move the mouse pointer over the slide icons, it changes to this to indicate that you can move the slide up or down in the presentation by dragging it by its icon, as you'll see later in this chapter.

PowerPoint's Unusual Selection Style

I must take a moment here to warn you about PowerPoint's unconventional use of the Shift key for selecting multiple slides. It's not what you may be used to.

In most Windows programs, when you want to select more than one of some item, you hold down the Shift key for contiguous blocks and the Ctrl key for non-contiguous ones. However, when selecting slides in PowerPoint, the Ctrl key has no effect. Further, what you get with the Shift key is based on what view you're in.

In Slide Sorter view, the Shift key selects non-contiguously (like the Ctrl key does in other applications). In other words, to select multiple slides in Slide Sorter view, you hold down the Shift key and then click on each slide individually.

In Outline view, the Shift key selects contiguously. In other words, to select multiple contiguous slides, you click on the first one, then hold down the Shift key and click on the last one. All the slides in-between those two are selected. There is no way to select slides non-contiguously in Outline view.

Adding New Slides to a Presentation

If you used a presentation design template or started with a blank presentation, you don't have any slides yet. You either have the New Slide dialog box onscreen right now, or you got rid of it by clicking on OK or Cancel when you saw it. At any rate, you need some slides.

If you started your presentation based on a presentation template, you already have some slides, but they may not be enough. You will probably want to add more to go along with them. (I'll talk about changing the text on the existing slides later in this chapter.)

You can add slides to your presentation in any view, but let me make some suggestions:

- If the new slide will be primarily graphical (for example, a chart or picture with very little text), add it in Slide view. Slide view is best for positioning objects, especially graphics.
- If the new slide will be primarily text, add it in Outline view. Outline view makes adding new text slides extremely easy. If you have the New Slide dialog box on your screen right now, go ahead and use the Slide view method for one slide, but then switch to the Outline view method for the rest of them.

Why not use the other two views? When you add a slide in Slide Sorter view, it's too small to really see anything on it or do any editing. And when you add a slide in Notes Page view, it's unnecessarily small because the notes area has to be shown.

Adding Slides in Slide View

For more information about displaying different slides, see the section "Changing Which Slide is Active" earlier in this chapter.

When you start a new presentation that's either blank or based on a template that contains no samples, the New Slide dialog box opens immediately, prompting you to choose an AutoLayout for the first slide (see Figure 5.5). If you see this dialog box on-screen right now, skip to step 3 of the following steps; you don't need the first two.

If you're working with a presentation that has at least one slide already, you won't see the New Slide dialog box automatically. You'll need to open it by starting with step 1 of this procedure:

1. In Slide view, display the slide that the new slide should come *after*. (Use the [Page Up] and [Page Down] keys to change which slide is displayed.)
2. Do any of the following to open the New Slide dialog box (see Figure 5.5):
   - Click on the New Slide button on the Standard toolbar.
   - Choose Insert, New Slide.
   - Press [Ctrl]+[M].
3. Click on the AutoLayout you want to use. For example, to create a title slide, click on the AutoLayout in the upper-left corner of the dialog box.
4. Click on OK.

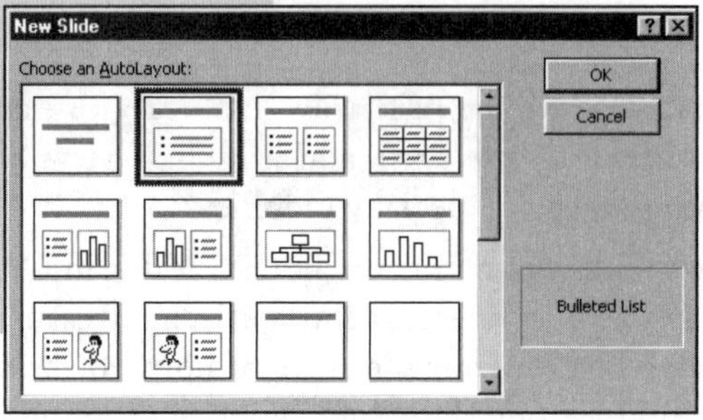

Figure 5.5 The New Slide dialog box prompts you to choose the AutoLayout for the new slide to insert.

5. Follow the instructions in the boxes provided to fill in the slide. For example, in Figure 5.6, click on the words "Click to add title" and type a title for the presentation.

These "AutoLayouts" in the New Slide dialog box are pre-designed starter layouts for the most popular types of slides. They contain text and graphic boxes with special advice and helps in them that make it easy for you to "fill in the blanks." (One of the choices is a totally blank AutoLayout, so you aren't forced into using PowerPoint's AutoLayouts if you don't want them for some reason on a slide.)

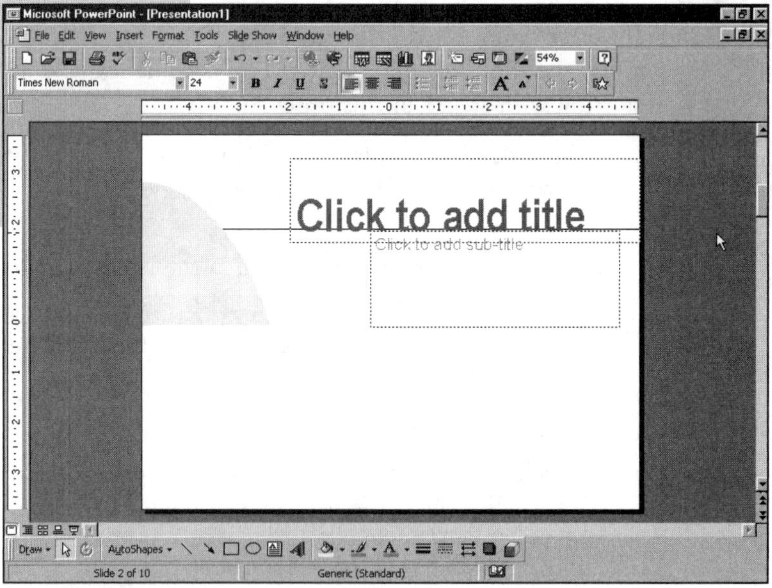

Figure 5.6 This slide's two text boxes (one for the heading and one for the subheading) were created by PowerPoint.

Caution

You can't delete text boxes that are put on a slide with one of the AutoLayouts. That's because they take their properties from your Slide Master (which you may remember from Chapter 4). If you want total control over every element on your slide, including the ability to delete every element, you are better off creating a slide based on the blank AutoLayout and then manually adding each text box, as you'll learn to do in Chapter 7.

Adding Slides in Outline View

As you saw in the preceding section, adding a new slide in Slide view is a fairly big production. You have to open a dialog box, choose a layout, and click on several things before you can type your slide text. This can be a real pain if you have to create a lot of text slides!

Luckily, there's an easier way: Outline view. To add a slide in Outline view, you just position your cursor and press Enter, and then type your text. It doesn't get much easier than that. The only catch is that you don't have a lot of choice about what kind of slide you create—if you create a slide in Outline view, it's always a slide with a title and a bullet list. That's why I said earlier that creating slides in Outline view is good primarily for creating text slides.

Hands On: Creating New Text Slides

Try it out with the following steps:

1. Switch to Outline view if you're not already there.
2. Click to position the insertion point at the beginning of the slide *before* which the new slide should go. For example, in Figure 5.7, I wanted the new slide to go before the current slide 3, so I positioned the insertion point at the beginning of slide 3.

Note

If you want the new slide after the last slide, position the insertion point at the end of the last line on the last slide.

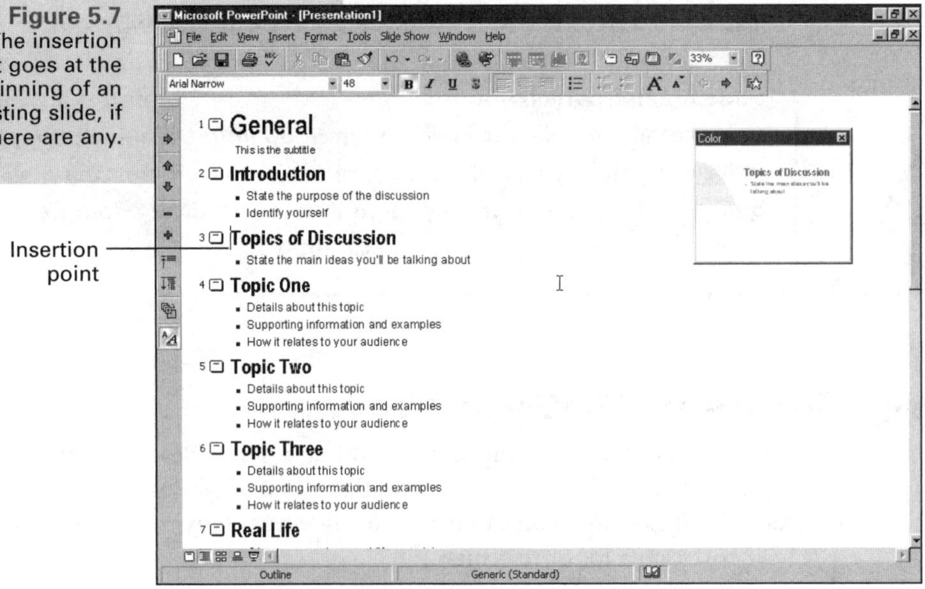

Figure 5.7 The insertion point goes at the beginning of an existing slide, if there are any.

3. Press Enter. The existing slide moves down and a new, blank slide appears (see Figure 5.8).

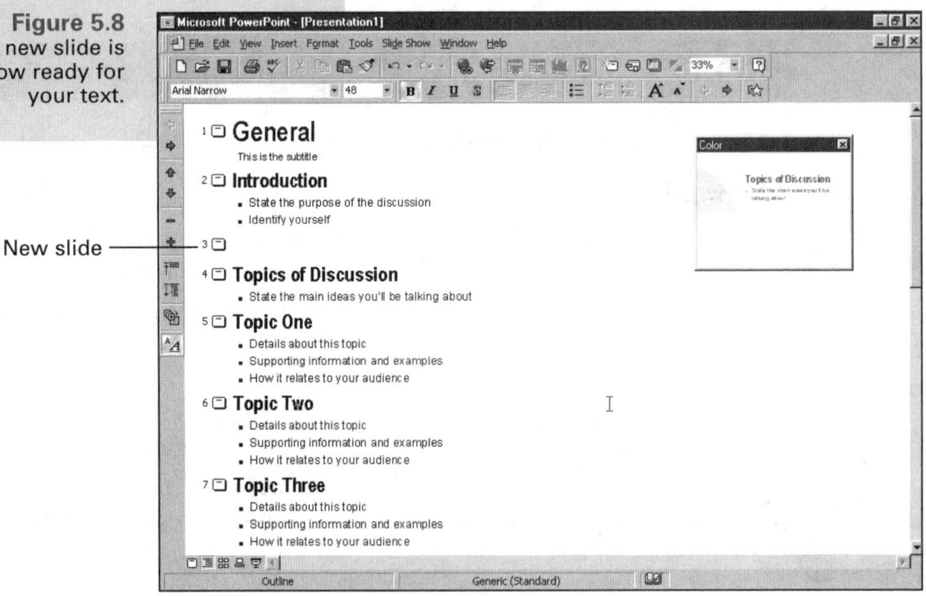

Figure 5.8 A new slide is now ready for your text.

4. Press the [↑] key once to move the insertion point up to the blank slide you just created.
5. Type the title text for the new slide.
6. Press [Enter]. Another new line is created.
7. Press [Tab] to make the newly-created line subordinate to the title you typed in step 5 (see Figure 5.9).
8. Type the first bullet point for the slide, and press [Enter].
9. Type additional bullet points for that slide.
10. When you are done typing the bullet points for that slide, press [Enter], and then press [Shift] + [Tab] to promote the next line to be a separate slide on the outline.
11. Repeat steps 5 through 10 for the next slide you need to create if you need more slides.

Tip

If you have a slide that is will be mostly text but with a small image or other element on it, create it in Outline view and then switch to Slide view to add the additional objects.

Figure 5.9
I pressed [Tab] to make this line subordinate to the new slide's title, and therefore a bullet point under it.

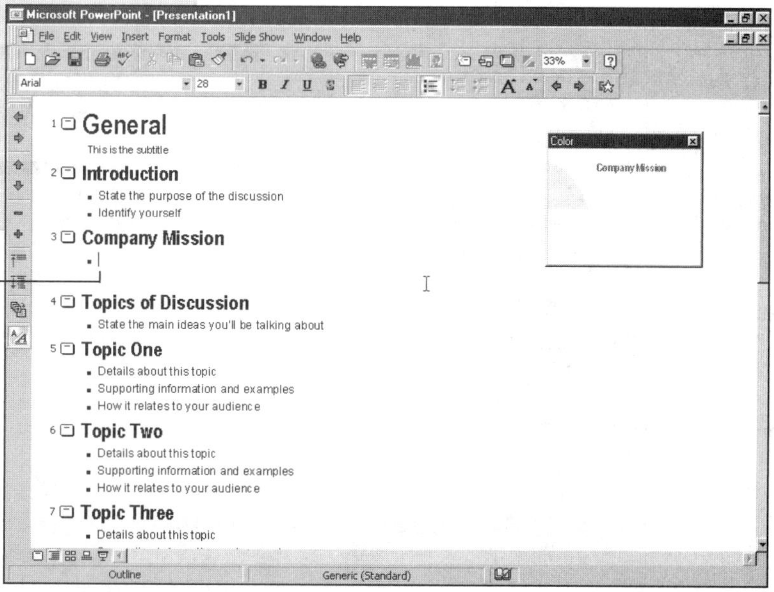

Creating a Summary Slide

Here's a nifty little trick you may never need, but if you do, you'll be glad to have it at your disposal. Suppose you have four slides in the presentation that each cover a certain discussion point. Many presenters find it useful to introduce upcoming topics on a summary slide before delving into the details, so the audience can see where the presentation is headed. You could create such a summary slide and place it right before these four slides in your presentation.

PowerPoint's Summary Slide feature takes the titles of each of the slides and makes it a bullet point on the summary slide. Follow these steps to create one:

1. In Outline view, select the slides you want to summarize.
2. Click on the Summary Slide button on the Outlining toolbar. The new slide appears, as shown in Figure 5.10, with the selected slides' titles as its bullets.

There is no link maintained between the summarized slides and the summary slide. That means that if you change any of the slide titles, you will need to update the summary slide. You can't update it with the Summary Slide button, however; you must manually edit the text on the summary slide or delete it and regenerate it.

Figure 5.10 Creating a summary slide is a quick shortcut when you need an introductory slide for part of your presentation.

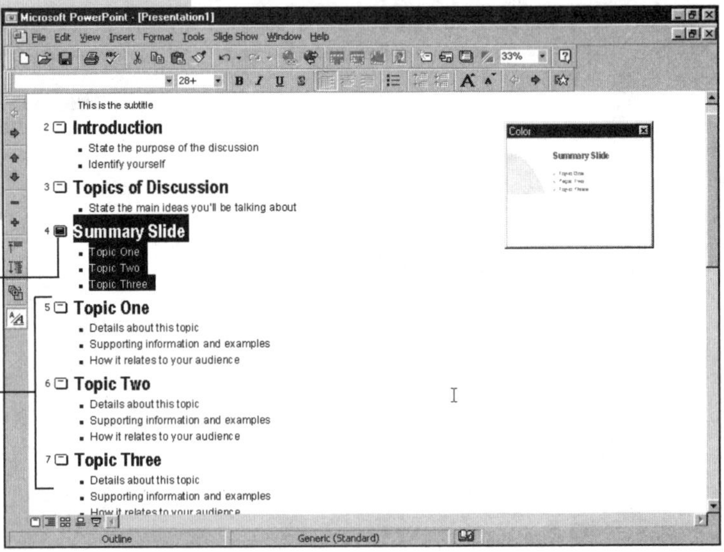

Deleting Slides from a Presentation

Especially if you started with a template that contained slides, you might find that some slides should go away. Maybe you don't need them, or maybe they never should have been included in the first place. Whatever the reason, deleting a slide is a simple matter.

If you think there is any possibility that you might use the slide, try hiding it rather than deleting it. That way, if you do need it, you can unhide it later rather than recreating it from scratch. Chapter 15 covers hiding slides, but you can quickly hide a slide by choosing Slide Show, Hide Slide.

- To delete a slide from a single-slide view (Slide or Notes Page), display the slide you want to delete and choose Edit, Delete Slide.
- To delete a slide (or multiple slides) from a multi-slide view (Slide Sorter or Outline), select the slide(s) as you learned to do in the preceding section and press the Delete key. (If you prefer, you can choose Edit, Delete Slide here instead. The Delete key is faster, however.)

Rearranging Slides

Both Slide Sorter and Outline views work well when you need to change the order in which slides appear in the presentation. Each method has a different "feel" to it, so you may find that you prefer one method over the other. Take a look at both methods, so you can see what method works best for you.

Rearranging Slides in Slide Sorter View

Slide Sorter view is like spreading out your whole presentation on a giant table, and being able to get an eagles-eye view of the whole thing. From there it's often easy to see what needs to change position for the whole presentation to work smoothly.

Go ahead and try it out—rearrange the slides in whatever presentation you have on-screen right now. The following Hands On shows you how.

Hands On: Rearranging in Slide Sorter View

1. Switch to Slide Sorter view if you're not already there.
2. Click on the slide you want to move—for example, move the second slide to the end of the presentation.
3. Drag the selected slide to its new location. The mouse pointer changes to show a little rectangle next to the pointer arrow. You also see a vertical bar, like the one in Figure 5.11. It shows where the slide will go if you release the mouse button at that point.
4. Release the mouse button. The slide moves to its new location.

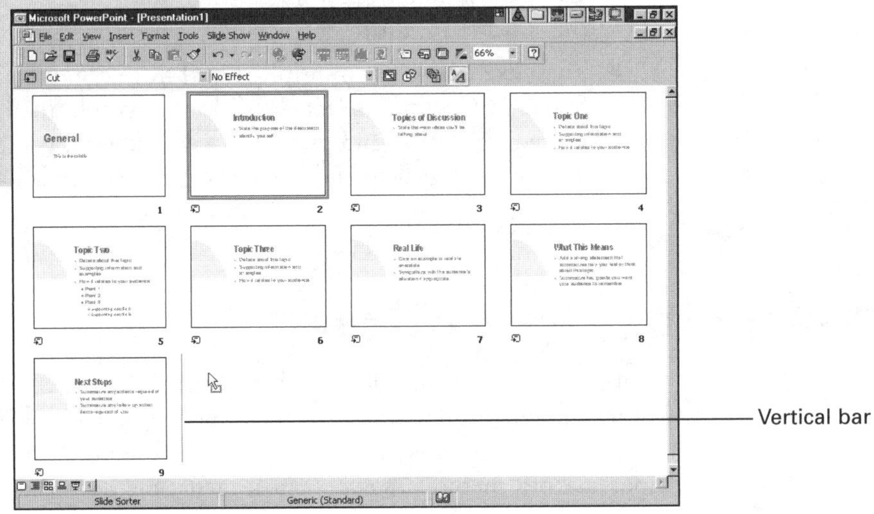

Figure 5.11 As you drag a slide, its new position is indicated by a vertical bar.

Rearranging Slides in Outline View

Rearranging in Outline view is not quite as easy as doing it in Slide Sorter view, but it's a more versatile system. You not only can drag entire slides from place to place, but also individual paragraphs from one slide to another. There also are some special toolbar buttons that help with rearrangement.

To move an entire slide in Outline view:

1. Switch to Outline view if you're not already there.
2. Position the mouse pointer over the slide's icon. The mouse pointer changes to a four-headed arrow.

Figure 5.12 You can drag the slide's icon to move it or use the Move Up or Move Down buttons.

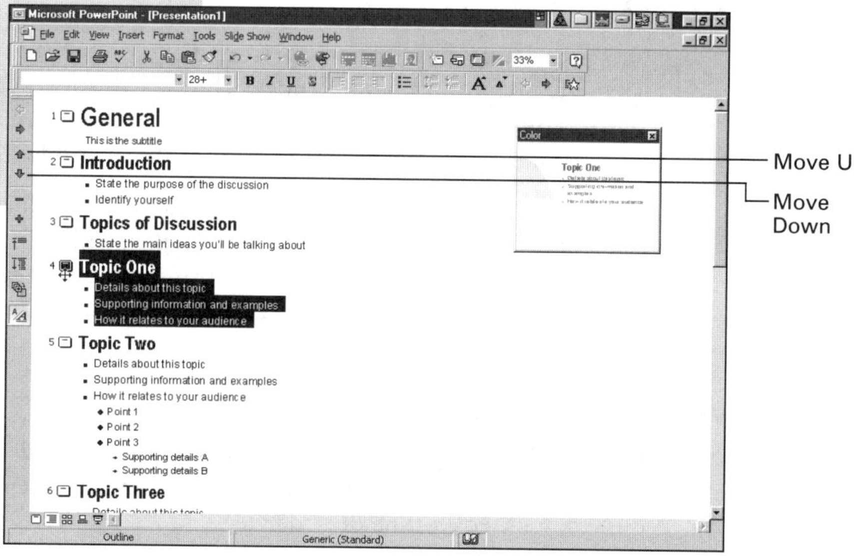

3. Click. The entire text of that slide is selected (see Figure 5.12).
4. Drag the slide's icon to a new position in the outline. As you drag, you see a horizontal line showing where the slide will be if you release the mouse button at that point.
5. Release the mouse button when the horizontal line is at the right place. All the slide's text accompanies it to its new home.

If you prefer, instead of step 4, you can move the slide using the Move Up and Move Down buttons on the Outlining toolbar (refer to Figure 5.12). Just do steps 1 through 3 and then click on one of those buttons to move the slide up or down one slide in the outline.

Some people prefer to use the toolbar buttons to move a slide if the destination is out of view on-screen. That way you don't have to try to scroll and drag at the same time to reach the slide's destination.

There are keyboard shortcuts for moving a slide up and down in the outline. You might find that these are faster than clicking on the toolbar buttons. The shortcuts are Alt + Shift + ↑ to move up and Alt + Shift + ↓ to move down.

Editing Slide Text

Of course, your presentation's heart and soul is not the flashy background—it's the text you put on your slides. Through this text, you convey your message to your audience. Therefore, the first thing most users want to do, after they've added and removed slides as needed, is to add and edit slide text.

The best way to edit your text is in Outline view. Outline view is designed for text work, as you've seen earlier in this chapter. Bullet lists fall into place easily from here, and there are plenty of controls for adding, deleting, and rearranging text. You also can edit text in Slide view if you prefer.

Selecting Text on a Slide

Earlier in the chapter you learned to select entire slides. You also can select individual bits of text on a slide without selecting the entire slide. You can do this from either Outline or Slide view.

Note

When you select some text on a slide (but not the entire slide), if you then issue a command that can apply to only part of a slide (such as Format, Font), only the selected text will be affected. However, if you then issue a command that applies to the entire slides (such as Format, Slide Color Scheme), the whole slide will be affected.

Here's how to select some text on a slide in Outline or Slide view:

- To select a single word, double-click on it.
- To select a single paragraph or bullet point, triple-click on it.
- To select a custom block of text, drag your mouse pointer across it.

Changing, Adding, and Deleting Text on a Slide

If you started your presentation with a template that included slides, you have quite a bit of "dummy" text that needs to be replaced with your own specifics. To change this text, follow these steps:

1. Select the text you need to replace. (Use the procedures from the preceding section.)

2. Type the replacement text. The old text is deleted automatically.

You also can add new text by positioning the insertion point (just click where you want it) and then the new text. To remove a stray extra letter here or there, use the Backspace and Delete keys. Then retype the text the way you want it.

Finding and Replacing Text

Like all Microsoft applications, PowerPoint has a good built-in Find tool. It enables you to search for (and, optionally, replace) a string of text anywhere in your presentation. The feature works the same way in all views (except Slide Show, in which it isn't applicable).

Look at finding first because it's simpler than replacing. Say Bob Smith just got fired this morning. (Poor Bob.) Now you need to go through your presentation and see whether Bob's name was mentioned, so you can take out any lines that refer to him. Follow these steps to find a text string (such as Bob Smith):

1. Choose Edit, Find. The Find dialog box opens.
2. Type what you want to find in the Find What text box, as shown in Figure 5.13.

If you want to find some text that you have searched for before, open the Find What drop-down list and select it. It's faster than retyping it.

3. If you want to find only whole words or to match the case, mark the appropriate check box.
4. Click on Find Next. The display jumps to the first instance of the text in your presentation (starting from wherever your insertion point was positioned and working downward through the presentation, and then looping back to the top).
5. If the found instance was not the one you were looking for, or if you want to see if there are other instances, click on Find Next again until you've seen all the instances. (You'll get a message "The search text was

Figure 5.13 Type what you want to find, and then click on the Find Next button.

not found" when that happens, and you must click on OK to clear that message.)

6. Click on Close when you are finished finding.

You also can do a replace, which is like a "Find plus." It finds the specified text and then replaces it with other text that you specify.

Suppose, for example, that you were preparing a presentation for the Acme Corporation's sales staff. Two days before the presentation, you find out that Acme has just been purchased by Primo Corporation. So you need to go through the entire presentation and change every instance of Acme to Primo.

While you are using the Find feature, as explained in the preceding steps, you can switch to the Replace dialog box by clicking on the Replace button. When you do so, your Find string transfers over, so you don't have to retype it.

To find and replace a text string like this, follow these steps:

1. Choose Edit, Replace. The Replace dialog box appears.
2. Type the text you want to find in the Find What text box. If you have previously used Find or Replace, the most recent text you found appears in the text box already.
3. Type the new text in the Replace With text box. For example, if you were replacing "layoffs" with "downsizing," it would look like Figure 5.14.
4. If you want whole words only or a case-sensitive search, select the appropriate check box.
5. Click on Find Next to find the first instance.
6. If you want to replace that instance, click on the Replace button. The next instance appears automatically.
7. Repeat step 5 to check and selectively replace each instance, or click on Replace All to change all instances at once.

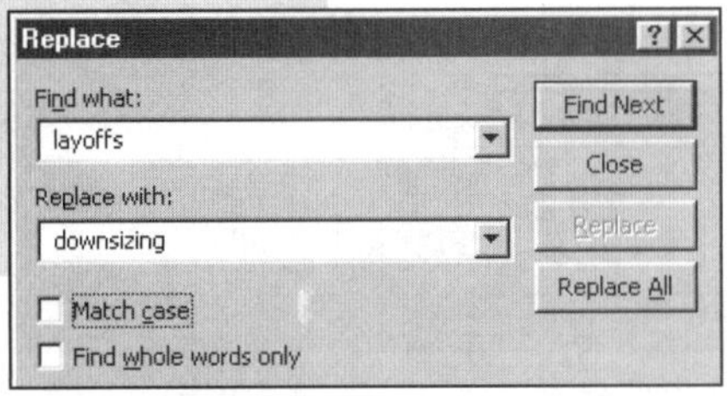

Figure 5.14 Enter what you want to find and what you want to replace it with.

8. When you are finished, click on Close. (You may have to click on OK first to clear a dialog box telling you that the specified text was not found.)

Changing a Paragraph's Outline Level

Most presentations contain many bullet lists. The short, bulleted items make great starters for discussion and lecture topics. And, as you've seen earlier in this chapter, PowerPoint's Outline view makes it a snap to create such slides. But did you know you can rearrange and re-outline these lists in Outline view?

When you're in Outline view, you have access to the Outlining toolbar, shown in Figure 5.15. This toolbar contains many buttons that you can use to control the outline and its appearance.

To change the outline level of a paragraph (or multiple paragraphs), follow these steps:

1. To adjust the outline level of a single paragraph, position the insertion point anywhere within it. Or, to adjust more than one paragraph, select at least part of the text in all the paragraphs you want to affect.
2. Click on the Promote or Demote button on the Outlining toolbar, or press the Tab (to demote) or Shift+Tab (to promote) keys.

In addition to changing the outline levels, you also can change what outline levels are visible on-screen. This can come in handy, for example, if you have

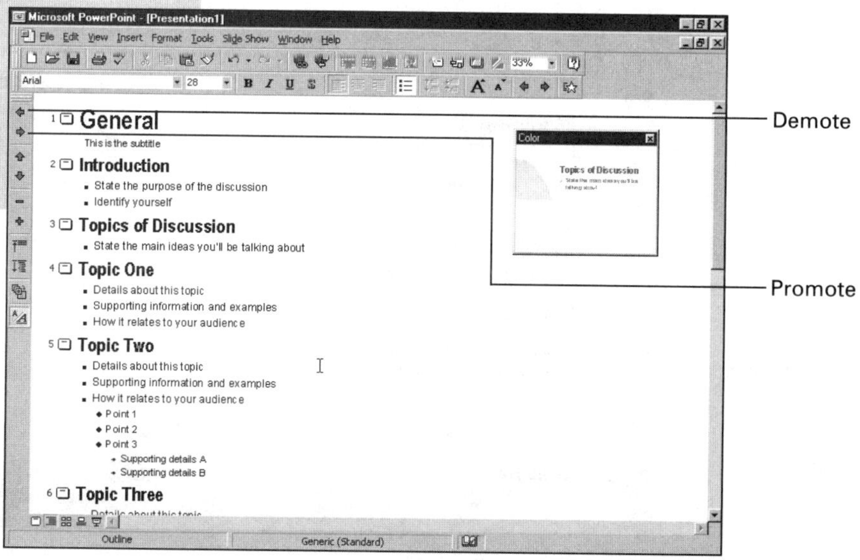

Figure 5.15 Use these buttons on the Outlining toolbar to adjust the outline level of a paragraph.

a big presentation and you just want to see a list of the slide titles and the first-level bullets beneath each one. Figures 5.16 and 5.17 show the difference between a fully collapsed outline and a fully expanded one.

Figure 5.16 The outline is fully collapsed here; you see only the slide titles.

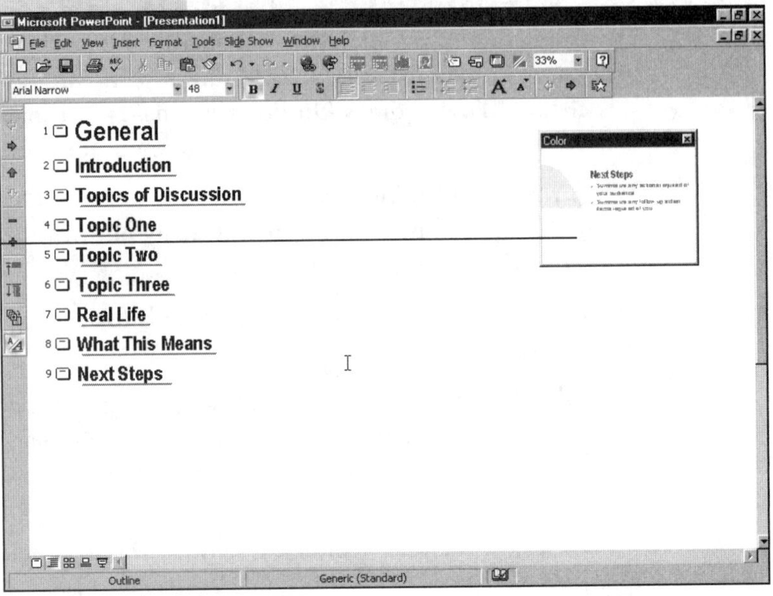

The Slide Miniature shows the full details on the slide.

Figure 5.17 This outline is fully expanded; all outline levels are visible.

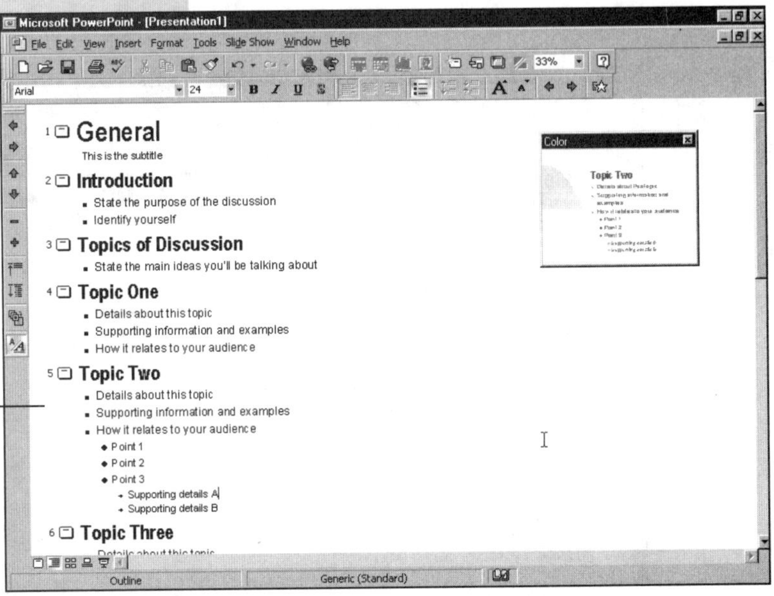

Multiple outline levels

These buttons, also on the Outlining toolbar, control what outline levels appear on-screen in Outline view:

 Collapse the outline one level for the selected slide(s)

 Expand the outline one level for the selected slide(s)

 Collapse the entire presentation's outline fully, down to the first level (the slide titles)

 Expand the entire presentation's outline fully, including all levels. (This is the default.)

Slide View Editing: Everything Is an Object!

So far in this chapter, all the editing you've done has focused on the content of the slides. However, you also can edit from Slide view. Whereas Outline view is best for editing text, Slide view is best for repositioning the text's position on the slide and for adding non-text objects like graphics.

As you learned in Chapter 1, every thing you can possibly put on a slide is considered an *object*. Each object has its own properties and position on the slide. When you were working in Outline view, you didn't notice the objects—all you saw was text. But if you switch to Slide view, your objects become immediately apparent. As shown in Figure 5.18, each object resides in its own box.

Note

In this chapter, all the objects are text boxes because you haven't created anything except text on the slides yet. In later chapters, you'll learn how to place a variety of other objects on slides, including graphs, organization charts, pictures, video clips and so on. When you get to those, keep in mind that they are indeed objects, and that you can work with them in just the same ways as you're learning now.

Figure 15.18 The text beneath the title on a slide is treated as a single object.

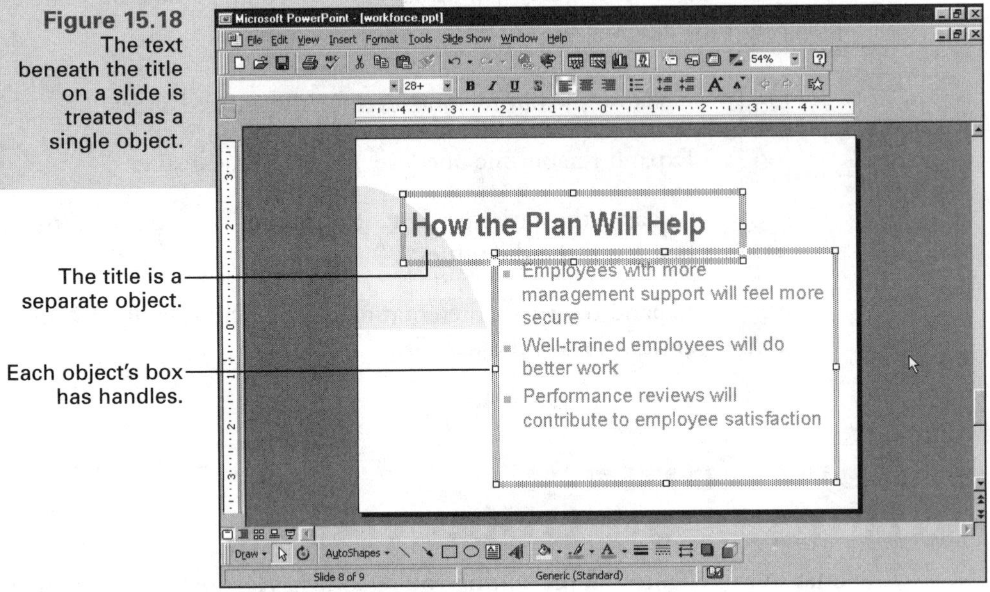

Editing Text on a Slide

Text lies in text object boxes on your slides, as you saw in Figure 5.18. To edit the text, just click on where you want the insertion point and do your editing just like you did in Outline view. It's the same text, and you can handle it in all the same ways.

Selecting Objects on a Slide

Before you can act on an entire object box, you must select it. When you select an object, handles appear around it.

- To select a single object, just click on it, anywhere within its box. The selection handles appear around it.
- To select multiple objects, click on the first one, and then hold down the Shift key while you click on subsequent objects. Release the Shift key when you're done selecting objects.

Editing Selected Objects

The procedure for editing an object depends heavily on the type of object it is. You've already learned to edit text objects in this chapter; you can wait until I introduce you to the various other object types before learning how to edit them.

I will tell you now, however, that in most cases you can right-click on an object to see a shortcut menu that contains the most common commands for that object, and one of them is usually some kind of editing or formatting command. When you aren't sure what you can do with an object to edit it, try right-clicking on it to see what commands appear for your use.

Deleting Objects from the Slide

Deleting an object from a slide is simple: just select it and press the Delete key. If you want to delete more than one object at a time, select all the objects first.

Note

If you press the Delete key and a single character disappears from the text box, you need to click on the perimeter of the box to remove the insertion point from the text.

Okay, time out for an explanation. If you just tried the above procedure—selecting a text box and pressing Delete—then you probably experienced first-hand what I was telling you earlier in this chapter: not all objects are alike. Specifically, the special text boxes on a slide that are placed there by AutoLayouts, or when you create bullet lists in Outline view, cannot be deleted. When you click on their box and then press Delete, all the text disappears from the box and the words "Click on to add text" appear in the box instead. In other words, "deleting" these boxes does not get rid of the box—only the text in it. The box is still there (although it won't show up on a printout or in a slide show if you don't put any text in it).

So what kinds of object boxes can you actually delete completely? Basically, any box that you manually place on the slide yourself can be deleted completely. (You haven't learned to do that yet, so you probably don't have any like that at the moment.)

Hands On: Deleting an Object

To practice deleting an object, quickly place a dummy object on a slide and then delete it.

You'll learn more about the drawing tools in Chapter 8.

1. Click on the Rectangle button on the Drawing toolbar. It's the toolbar at the bottom of the screen, and the rectangle button is (surprise!) the button with the rectangle on it.
2. Drag anywhere on the slide to draw a rectangle. It remains selected after you draw it.
3. Press the Delete key to delete it.

Moving Objects Around on a Slide

See Chapter 6 for information about the Slide Master.

All objects on a slide—bar none—can be moved around. To move an object, follow these steps:

1. Click anywhere in the object's box to select it. Selection handles appear.
2. Position the mouse pointer on the border of the object box, but not on a selection handle. The pointer turns into a pointer with a four-headed arrow.
3. Drag the object's box to a new position. A dotted outline shows where the object is going, as shown in Figure 5.19.

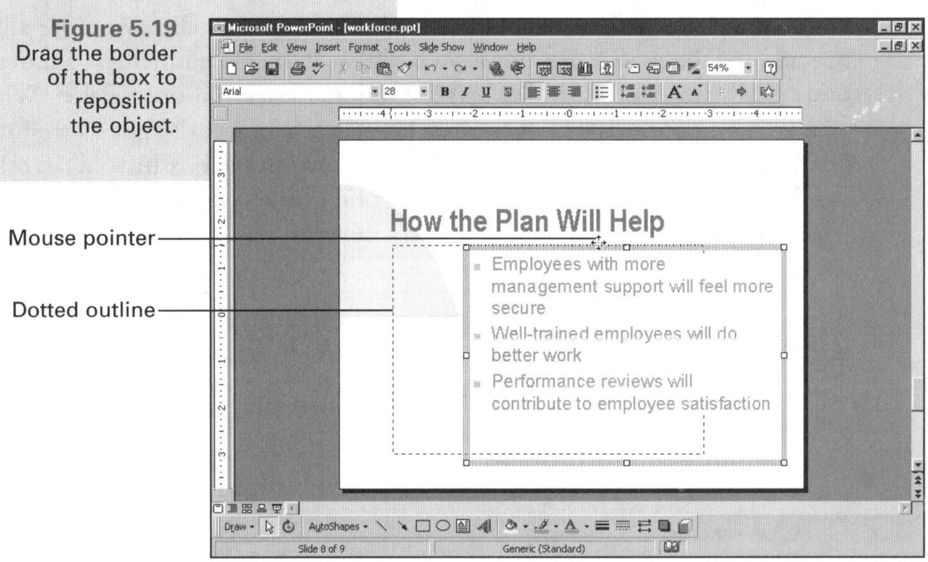

Figure 5.19 Drag the border of the box to reposition the object.

Tip

If you can't select or move a particular object, it's probably on the Slide Master rather than on that individual slide. Edit the Slide Master to alter its position.

Moving Objects Between Slides

Only objects that you have created yourself can be moved between slides. The easiest way to do so is with the Cut and Paste commands. You can access these commands from the Edit menu, but it's much easier to use their equivalent toolbar buttons or shortcut keys.

Hands On: Moving an Object to a Different Slide

Because you don't have any such objects in your presentation yet, create a dummy object and move it from one slide to another.

1. Display any slide in Slide view.
2. Click on the Rectangle button on the Drawing toolbar.
3. Drag anywhere on the slide to create a rectangle.
4. Click on the Cut button on the Standard toolbar or press Ctrl+X to cut the rectangle from the slide.
5. Display a different slide.
6. Click on the Paste button on the Standard toolbar or press Ctrl+V to paste the rectangle onto the other slide.
7. Press the Delete key to delete the rectangle when you're done practicing moving it.

Summary

In this chapter, you got off to a great start with your presentation by creating your first slides. But this is only the beginning; in the upcoming chapters you'll make your presentation into much more than a simple series of text lists by adding graphics, sounds, transitions, and much more.

6

Improving Your Presentation's Appearance

In This Chapter

- Using Slide Masters
- Setting Page Margins
- Applying Designs and Layouts
- Changing Colors and Backgrounds
- Checking Your Spelling
- Analyzing the Presentation's Style

Now that you have a simple presentation with the text-based content you need, it's time to start dressing it up. Later on in the book, you'll look at little extras you can add to individual slides, but in this chapter, you will start the presentation-beautification project by examining some ways you can improve all the slides in the presentation as a whole.

Using the Slide Master to Ensure Consistency

> You saw the Slide Master at work in Chapter 5.

I mentioned the Slide Master earlier in the book, and promised you more detail on it. The Slide Master is essentially a template to which each slide in the presentation adheres. When you apply a design to a presentation, you are really applying it to the Slide Master, and thereby affecting every slide in the presentation. (I'll go over applying a design again later in this chapter, so don't worry if you don't remember how to do it.) Figure 6.1 shows a sample Slide Master.

> You'll learn how to manipulate Handout Master and Notes Master in Chapter 15.

In addition to the Slide Master, there are three other masters: Title Master, Handout Master, and Notes Master. Title Master is just like Slide Master except it is for the title slide in the presentation, that is, the slide(s) formatted with the Title AutoLayout (see Figure 6.2). The Title Master exists because the title slide often needs to be different in font size and placement, and may have other differences too. Handout Master controls the elements that will go on the handouts you print, and Notes Master controls how the notes pages you print will appear. If you created your presentation from a presentation template, you may already have all four of these masters in your presentation. If not, don't worry—you'll learn how to set them up later in this chapter.

Besides applying designs to your Slide Master, you also can manually add, edit, and delete objects on it. You can move things around, change colors and pat-

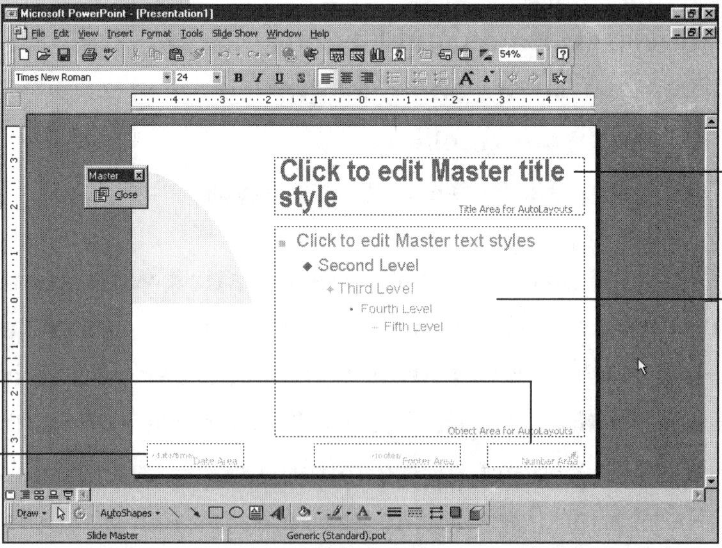

Figure 6.1 The Slide Master holds the elements that will appear on every slide in the presentation.

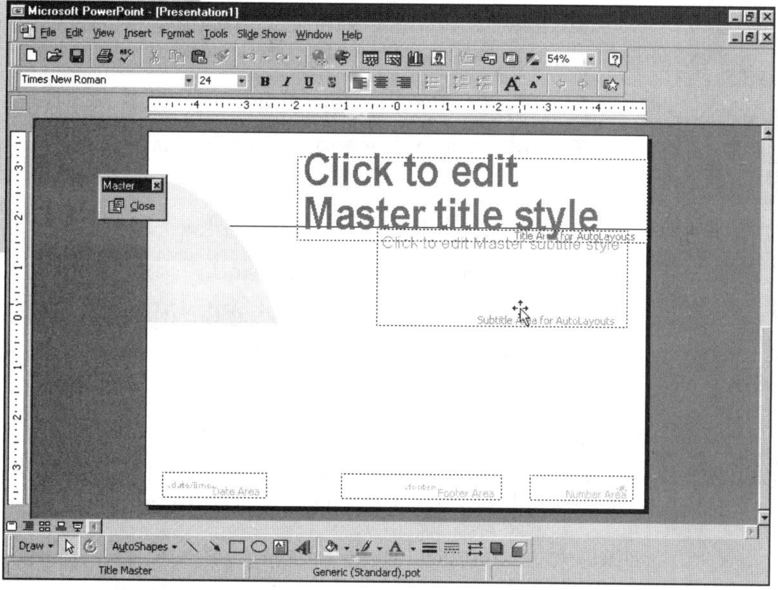

Figure 6.2 The Title Master is just like the Slide Master except it applies only to slides formatted with the Title AutoFormat.

terns, and a lot more. Anything that you can do to a regular slide, you can do to the Slide Master, and thereby affect all the slides in the presentation at once!

But before you dive into that, take a moment to ponder what you want to do and why you think it's best done to the Slide Master. Not all changes are appropriate to make to the Slide Master; some are better made to individual slides. For example, you might add a chart to an individual slide. You certainly wouldn't want that same chart to appear on every single slide! However, other additions do need to appear on every slide—for example, a company logo. It is this latter kind of object that you can add to your Slide Master to save yourself the time and trouble of adding it individually to every slide.

Hands On: Editing the Slide Master

Follow these steps to make a change to the Slide Master:

1. Choose View, Master, Slide Master. The Slide Master appears (refer to Figure 6.1).

To learn how to change the text formatting (font, size, color, and so on), refer to Chapter 7. To learn about placing graphics, check Chapter 8.

2. Add, edit, or delete elements on the Slide Master as desired, and/or change the color scheme and background. Here's a sampling of what you might do:
   - Drag the text boxes around, or even delete them.
   - Add a graphic or some other object.
   - Apply a different slide layout.
   - Apply a different design or color scheme.
   - Assign a different background.
3. When you are finished viewing the Master, click on the Close button to return to the regular presentation. All your changes are applied to each slide.

Keep the Slide Master in mind throughout the rest of the book. As you polish your presentation, if you find yourself doing the same thing repeatedly to each slide, consider doing it to the Slide Master and saving yourself some time.

Most of the changes I'm going to describe in the following sections also can be made to individual slides, if that's what you want, but if consistency is your goal, making the changes to the Slide Master makes the most sense.

Applying a Different Design

By now, you should be quite familiar with design templates and how they work. (If not, refer to Chapter 4.) Design templates give your presentation its backbone of appearance choices: colors, fonts, backgrounds, and so on. You

Creating a Title Master

If you created your presentation from a blank start, you won't have a Title Master automatically. You'll need to create it. Here's how:

1. View the Slide Master.
2. Choose Insert, New Title Master or press Ctrl+M.

A default Title Master appears, which you can change.

can choose a design template when you create the presentation, and/or you can apply one later.

For example, suppose you started out with one template, but then decided that you really like the design of the Generic template. You can "steal" the design from the Generic template using the following Hands On.

Hands On: Changing the Design

1. Select Format, Apply Design. The Apply Design dialog box appears (see Figure 6.3).
2. If needed, change the folder displayed in the Look In text box to the folder containing the template you want. For this example, click on the Up One Level button, and then double-click on the Presentations folder.
3. Double-click on the template name. For our example, click on Generic (Standard).

Note

If you aren't sure which template you want, click on one to see a sample of it and then click on the Apply button when you find the one you want.)

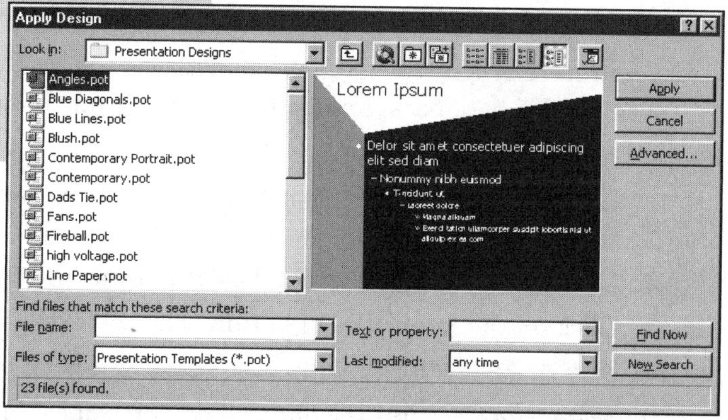

Figure 6.3 You can choose a different design from here.

Understanding Color Schemes and Backgrounds

As you have seen, templates provide a complete package of colors, fonts, text placement, and background. These complete packages are designed to work well together.

To learn how to change the text appearance, see Chapter 7.

But sometimes you may want to change parts of the package. You might want to change the color scheme in use in the presentation, for example, to switch from white letters on a dark background to vice-versa. Or you might want to use a graphic image as a background, such as your company logo. Such changes do not change the template, of course—they affect only the current presentation.

The following sections show how to change the color scheme and the background.

Choosing a Different Color Scheme

The slide color scheme is one part of the package that you get when you start with a template (or apply one from a design). Most templates come with at least a couple of alternate color schemes that use the same basic colors as one another, so you can switch from, say, a light background to a dark without having to re-choose all the colors manually. Most templates also provide a grayscale color scheme for black-and-white presentations. You also can create your own custom color schemes.

Hands On: Changing to a Different Color Scheme

Say you have a light-background color scheme in use, and you decide you would prefer a dark background. To try out the one provided with your template, follow these steps:

1. Choose Format, Slide Color Scheme. The Color Scheme dialog box opens (see Figure 6.4).
2. Click on the dark-background color scheme.
3. Click on the Apply To All button. The color scheme is applied to all slides in your presentation.

If you want, you can apply the different color scheme to only a single slide. Just make sure that slide is active before you start the above steps, and then click

Figure 6.4
Choose among the pre-set color schemes from here.

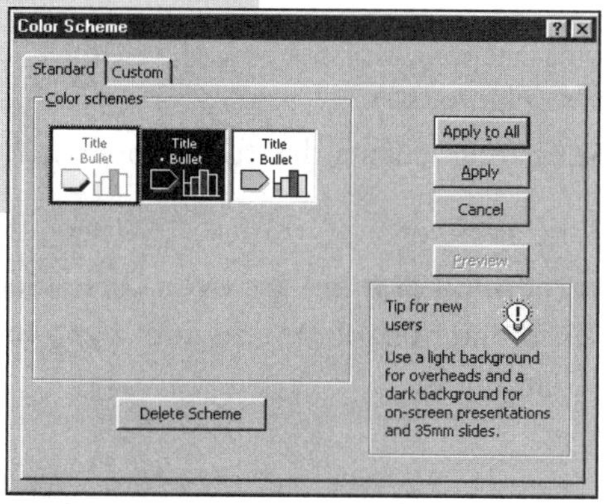

Note

Any changes you make to an individual slide override the template's settings. If you make changes on the Slide Master to all slides, any individual slides you previously changed won't be altered.

on Apply instead of Apply To All in step 3. This is usually not such a good idea, however, because it makes your presentation look inconsistent. Do it only if you have a good reason for wanting the individual slide to be different (for example, to make it stand out).

Tip

If you have a presentation that is really two presentations in one, and you want to dramatize that fact, make the first half of the presentation's slides with one color scheme and the second half with another. Just select the first half's slides in Slide Sorter view and then change the color scheme, clicking on the Apply button at the end.

Creating New Color Schemes

As you may have noticed in the preceding section, except for having a light or dark background, the color schemes that come pre-set with a template really aren't that different from one another. They all use the same basic colors in different arrangements. If you want something really different, you should try creating your own color schemes.

Follow these steps to set up a new color scheme:

1. Choose Format, Slide Color Scheme. The Color Scheme dialog box opens (refer to Figure 6.4).
2. Click on the existing scheme that most closely matches what you want.

Note

Don't worry if none of them are even close. For example, just click on the light background one if you have a light background in mind.

3. Click on the Custom tab. The Custom controls appear (see Figure 6.5).
4. Click on a color next to an element that you want to change. For example, click on the color next to Text and Lines to change the color of the lettering.
5. Click on the Change Color button. A Color dialog box opens for the element you selected. For example, Figure 6.6 shows the Text and Line Color dialog box.
6. Click on the hexagon that represents the color you want. A sample of it appears in the lower-right corner of the dialog box.

Tip

From step 6, you can click on the Custom tab in the Color dialog box to choose a color from a larger palette. However, the colors available on the Standard tab are so many and varied that most people never need to do this.

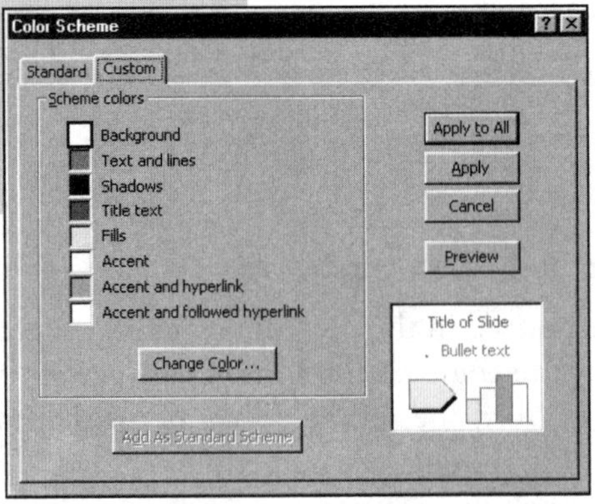

Figure 6.5 You can choose the color of each element from this tab.

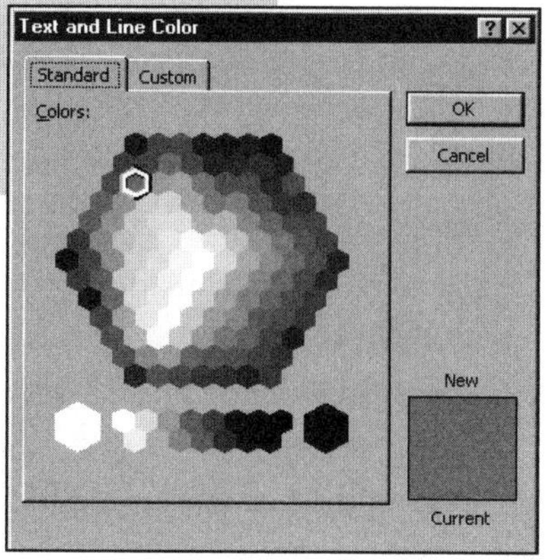

Figure 6.6 Choose from a large palette of available colors.

7. Click on OK. You return to the Color Scheme dialog box with the new color in place.
8. Repeat steps 4 through 7 to change other elements in the color scheme.

Tip

You can click on the Preview button if you want to see how your changes are shaping up without closing the dialog box. Just click on Preview and then drag the title bar of the dialog box to move the dialog box off to the side so you can see the slide underneath.

9. When you are finished, click on the Add As Standard Scheme button. This places your new scheme on the Standard tab.
10. Click on the Apply To All button to apply your new scheme to the presentation.

Changing the Slide Background

You changed the slide background color when you changed the slide color scheme in the preceding section. What more is there to it than that? Well, for people with simple tastes, there's nothing more. For these people, a background is merely a color. But for those of us who like a little more pizzazz, there's a lot more fun to be had.

You see, your background can be a plain color, as you've seen, but it also can be a gradient pattern that shifts from one color to another. It can be a graphic image like a logo or photo. It can be a pattern that looks like straw, wood, or marble. It can be all kinds of interesting things!

Here, in very general terms, is how to change a background:

1. Choose Format, Background. The Background dialog box appears.
2. Choose a different background from the Background Fill drop-down list.
   - Pick a color from the color scheme.
   - Choose More Colors to open a Colors dialog box (like the one in Figure 6.6) and pick from that.
   - Choose Fill Effects to open a dialog box of interesting effects you can use.
3. When you're done choosing the background, click on Apply To All.

You may be thinking "Those first two bullets in step 2 sound easy, but I'm not sure about that third one." And you're right—I haven't scratched the surface in the preceding steps when it comes to Fill Effects. But if you'll follow me in the upcoming Hands On sections, I'll give you a complete education in Fill Effects.

Creating a Gradient Background

If you've ever watched a sunset (and who hasn't?), you know how the red of the sun slowly fades into the blue/black of the evening sky. You may not have thought of it quite this way before, but that's a *gradient.* Whenever one color turns gradually into another one, it's called a gradient. (You know you've been working with PowerPoint too long when you find yourself thinking about opening up the sky's Background dialog box to change the color!)

Hands On: Creating a Sunset Gradient

Continue with the sunset motif. Follow these steps to create a two-color gradient from orange to dark blue as the background for your presentation.

1. Choose Format, Background. The Background dialog box appears.
2. Choose Fill Effects from the Background Fill drop-down list. The Fill Effects dialog box opens, with the Gradient tab already active.
3. In the Colors section, click on Two Colors. Two drop-down lists appear next to your selection, as shown in Figure 6.7.
4. Choose More Colors from the Color 1 drop-down list.
5. In the Colors dialog box that appears, click on a vibrant shade of orange and then click on OK to return to the Fill Effects dialog box.

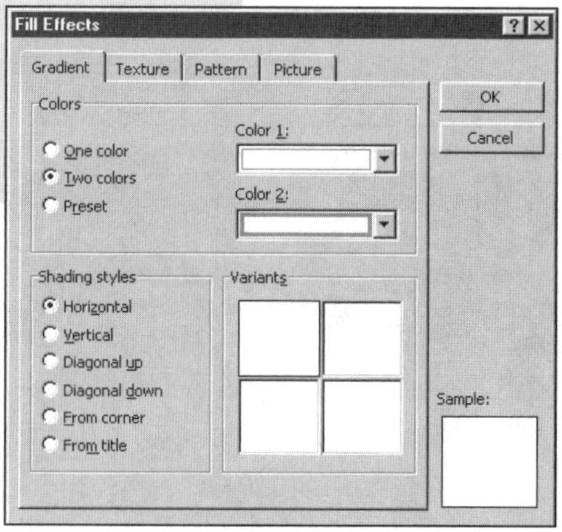

Figure 6.7 Set up your gradient fills here for your background.

6. Choose More Colors from the Color 2 drop-down list.
7. Click on a very dark blue and then click on OK to return to the Fill Effects dialog box again.
8. In the Shading Styles section, make sure the Horizontal radio button is selected.
9. In the Variants area (which shows the samples), click on the variant that has orange on the bottom and black on the top (see Figure 6.8).
10. Click on OK to return to the Background dialog box.
11. Click on Apply To All. Your background is applied to all the slides in your presentation. Figure 6.9 shows the finished result.

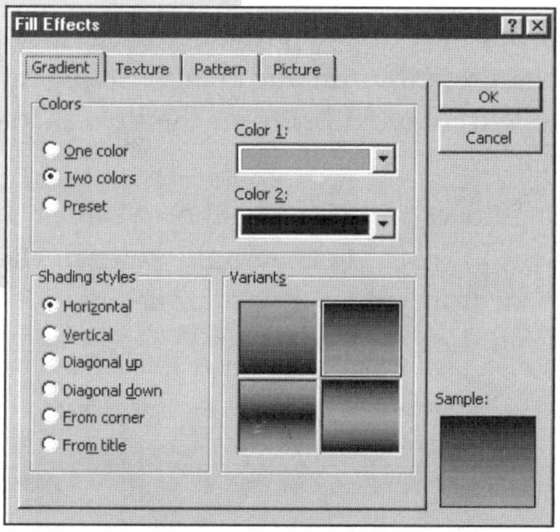

Figure 6.8 When you have the colors selected, the Variants area shows samples from which you can choose.

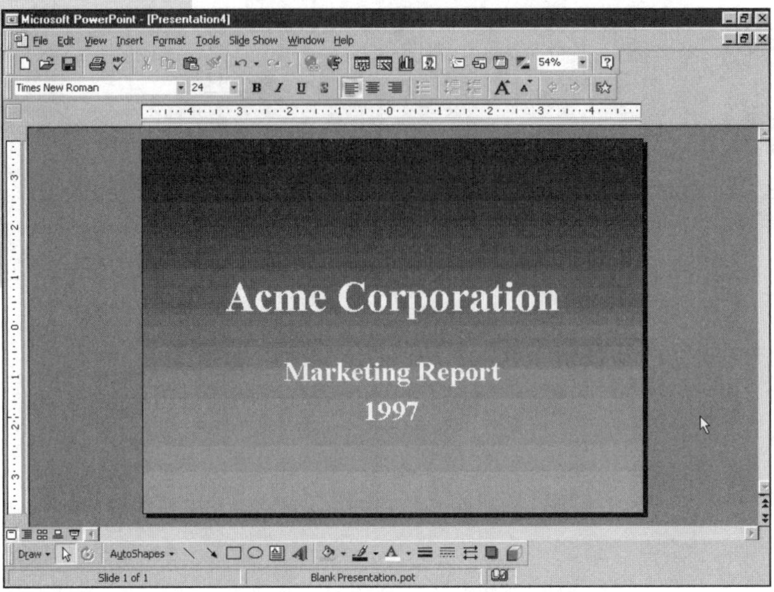

Figure 6.9 Here's my finished gradient that fades orange into blue. I made the letters yellow to make them stand out; you'll learn that in Chapter 7.

Besides the specific gradient that you just created, you can do some other interesting things on the Gradient tab:

- You can have a one-color gradient (that is, one color plus black or white) by clicking on the One Color button. Then, instead of the Color 1 and Color 2 drop-down lists, you get a single drop-down list plus a Light/Dark slider bar. Move it toward Dark to get varying degrees of black, or toward Light to get varying degrees of white.
- PowerPoint comes with many pre-designed gradients. Use them by clicking on the Preset button and then selecting one of the picturesque names (like Nightfall or Moss) from the Preset Colors drop-down list that appears.
- In the Shading Styles area you can choose one of the other orientations for the gradient to "run." For example, you can choose Diagonal Up to run the gradient from upper-left to lower-right, or From Title to have it radiate out from the center of the slide.

Applying a Textured Background

After the complexity of a gradient, textures are a snap to apply. A texture can make the background look like a familiar real-life material, like marble or wood. The result can be very impressive!

Hands On: Creating a Walnut Panel Background

Try applying the Walnut texture, to give your slide the look of a fine walnut panel.

1. Choose Format, Background. The Background dialog box appears.
2. Choose Fill Effects from the Background Fill drop-down list. The Fill Effects dialog box opens.
3. Click on the Texture tab. Samples of all the available textures appear on a scrollable list (see Figure 6.10).
4. Scroll down to the bottom of the textures list and click on Walnut (the darkest wood texture). The word "Walnut" appears below the list when it is selected.
5. Click on OK. The texture is applied to the slide, as shown in Figure 6.11.

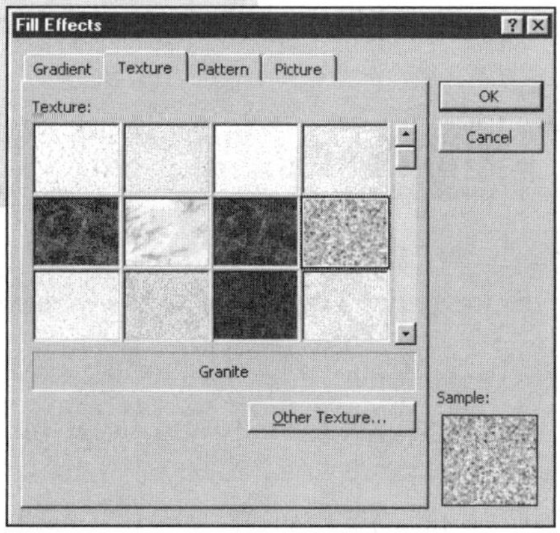

Figure 6.10 Choose from among many available textures.

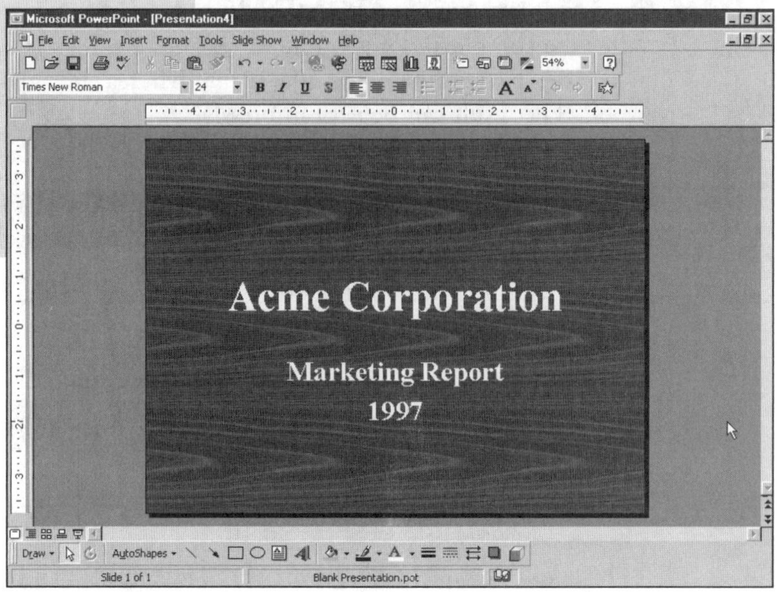

Figure 6.11 Here, the Walnut texture makes the title slide look like the letters are resting on a polished wood panel.

Applying a Patterned Background

Patterns are not as flashy as gradients or textures, but they have their place. A pattern, simply stated, is an arrangement of lines or shapes of one color over the background of another color. For example, a pinstripe suit has a pattern of gray or white lines over a black, blue, or gray background. You get the idea.

Hands On: Creating a Gray Pinstripe Pattern

Following along with that gray pinstripe motif, create a background with thin white lines over a medium gray background. Follow these steps:

1. Choose Format, Background. The Background dialog box appears.
2. Choose Fill Effects from the Background Fill drop-down list. The Fill Effects dialog box opens.
3. Click on the Pattern tab. The Pattern controls appear (see Figure 6.12).
4. Click on the white square in the Foreground drop-down list. White will be your stripe color.

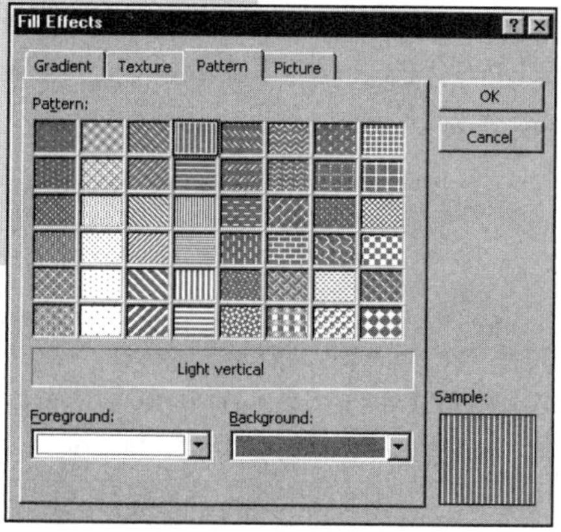

Figure 6.12 To use a pattern, pick the pattern and choose the foreground and background colors.

5. Click on a medium gray square in the Background drop-down list. If you do not see such a square, click on More Colors and choose a medium gray from the Colors dialog box that appears.
6. Back on the Patterns tab, click on the fourth pattern from the left in the top row, Light Vertical. Its name appears below the patterns when it's selected.
7. Click on OK. You return to the Background dialog box.
8. Click on Apply To All to apply the pattern to your presentation.

You may find, after seeing this result, that gray pinstripe gives you a headache when used for a slide background. There's no shame in that—just go back in and pick a different pattern. Try some of these on:

- For a pattern that looks like polka-dotted fabric (with little tiny dots), try the 5% pattern (the upper-left one) with bright yellow foreground and navy blue background.
- For a background of tiny bricks, choose Horizontal Brick as the pattern with a brick red as the background and black as the foreground. (Of course, you also could use the Brick texture instead.)
- You can create a red-and-white checked tablecloth look by using the Plaid pattern with a red foreground and white background.
- A vertical stripe that's easier on the eyes than the pinstripe you created is the Narrow Vertical pattern. Use two similar colors (like two shades of blue) for the foreground and background to add interest without making the audience's eyes hurt.

Note

Many people find that any pattern, no matter what colors or striping, is distracting as a background. You may decide not to use patterns at all for this purpose.

Using a Picture as a Background

Some people will tell you never to use a picture as a background for your presentation. Depending on the picture, it can make the information over it hard to read. Your audience may also get tired of seeing the same picture over and over in your presentation, on every single slide.

Used judiciously, a picture background can be a very nice touch. Three guidelines, though:

See Chapter 8 to learn how to insert a graphic on a slide or on the Slide Master.

- Make sure you have a good reason for using the particular graphic. Don't make the reader wonder why you chose it. If you can't locate the perfect image to use, don't use one.
- In most cases, you should apply the picture background to an individual slide. Even the best picture gets old and boring after the audience has seen it several times. An exception to this rule is some of the images designed especially for backgrounds. These work well appearing on every slide in the presentation because they are fairly unobtrusive. (You'll find them in Program Files\Microsoft Office\Clipart\Backgrounds.)
- If you want some control over where and how the image appears, place it as a graphic on the Slide Master. Don't make it a background. You can't control the image's size when it's used as a background.

Hands On: Using a Picture as a Background

Follow these steps to insert a background image that came with PowerPoint. You can use this same basic procedure with any image, including ones that you have scanned in.

1. Choose Format, Background. The Background dialog box appears.
2. Choose Fill Effects from the Background Fill drop-down list. The Fill Effects dialog box opens.

3. Click on the Picture tab. Initially the Picture tab doesn't have much on it; all the controls are greyed out. That's because you have not selected a picture yet.
4. Click on the Select Picture button. The Select Picture dialog box opens.
5. Navigate to the Program Files\Microsoft Office\Clipart\Backgrounds folder. You'll find some images there to practice with.
6. Click on Stained Glass on Side.
7. Click on OK. You return to the Picture tab, with the selected image displayed.
8. Click on OK to return to the Background dialog box.
9. Click on Apply To All to apply this image to all the slides. Figure 6.13 shows a slide with the Stained Glass on Side image in the background.

When you place an image as a background, you don't get to choose the proportions. It stretches the image to fit the slide background area. The image may become distorted to the point where you don't even recognize it. If image dimensions are important, try placing the image on the Slide Master as a graphic (see Chapter 8).

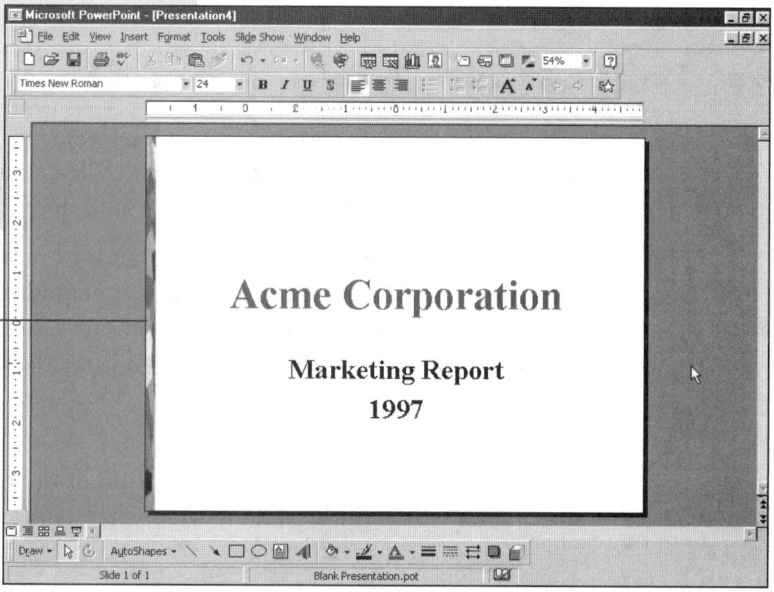

Figure 6.13 An image like this is unobtrusive enough to be used on all slides in the presentation.

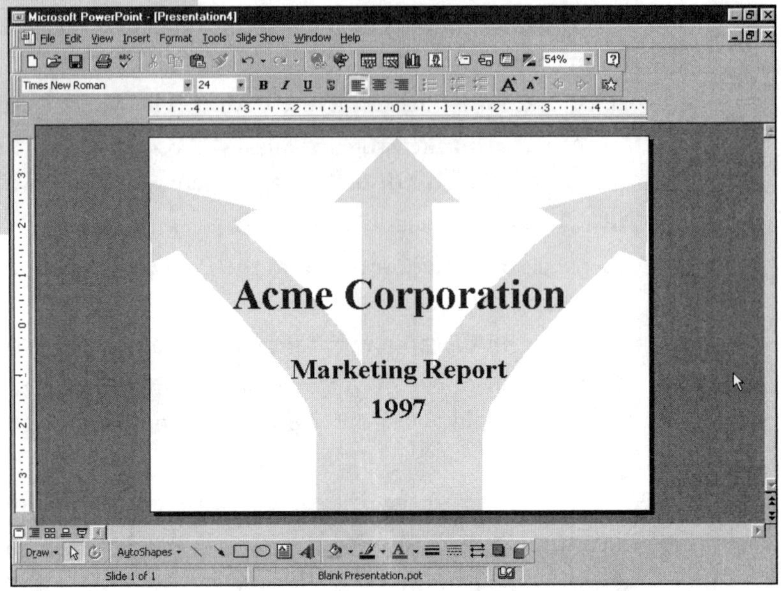

Figure 6.14
The arrows make a dramatic one-time effect, but would quickly lose their impact if repeated on every slide.

Not all images are appropriate for repeating on every slide, however. Figure 6.14 shows an image (taken from the Program Files\Microsoft Office\Clipart\Popular folder) that would become irritating very quickly if used over and over.

Changing Slide Size and Orientation

Normally, slides are proportioned so that that when you display them on a computer screen, they fill the entire screen. When you view them in Slide Show view, you see only the slides on-screen, and no border on any side.

However, on-screen shows are not the only kinds of presentations that people give. Occasionally you may need to build a presentation that will be printed on 35mm slides or 8.5 × 11 transparencies. In cases like that, you will want to resize the dimensions of the slides before you print them so there will not be lots of extra space with nothing in it, and so your slides will not be stretched or distorted when printed in the final format.

Size is pretty self-explanatory; it's the dimension of the finished product. Orientation refers to whether the slide is wider than it is tall (landscape) or vice versa (portrait). You cannot make these changes for an individual slide—the changes you make automatically affect the entire presentation.

Follow these steps to adjust the size and/or orientation for the type of final output you are planning:

1. Choose File, Page Setup. The Page Setup dialog box appears (see Figure 6.15).
2. Open the Slides Sized For drop-down list and choose the format that you will eventually give the presentation in:
   - *Onscreen show.* 10 × 7.5 inches, resized on the fly as needed to fill the monitor in use.
   - *Letter paper.* 10 × 7.5 inches. That's an 8.5 × 11 sheet of paper with one-half-inch margin on all sides.
   - *A4 paper.* 10.83 × 7.5 inches. A4 is an alternate paper size (210 × 297 mm) popular in European countries.
   - *35mm slides.* 11.25 × 7.5 inches. 35mm slides are wider than computer screens.
   - *Overhead.* 10 × 7.5 Overhead projection screens are often slightly more square than 35mm slides.
   - *Banner.* A specialty format, 8 inches wide by 1 inch tall. Good for banner graphics on Web pages.
   - *Custom.* Enter your own dimensions.
3. In the Slides area, click on Portrait or Landscape. The default is Landscape, and that's what you'll want the majority of the time.
4. In the Notes, Handouts, & Outline area, click on Portrait or Landscape. The default is Portrait, because these elements are usually printed taller than they are wide.
5. Click on OK.

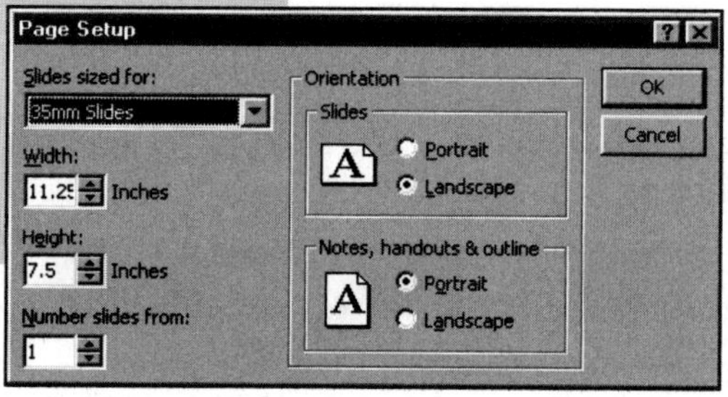

Figure 6.15 Use the Page Setup dialog box to change the slide dimensions.

Changing a Slide Layout

So far in this chapter, you mostly have learned about overall changes that affect the entire presentation (or least can potentially be applied that way). Now you will move from the general to the specific, and learn about changing individual slides.

You have seen how the slide's layout is controlled by the Slide Master. The slide title, bullet items, and so on fall in a certain spot based on the positions of the text boxes on the Slide Master. But within that broad framework, several layouts are available to choose from.

See Chapter 5 to recall how to add new slides to a presentation.

The available layouts are called AutoLayouts, and you saw them when you added new slides to the presentation (with the Insert, New Slide command). There are AutoLayouts for title slides, simple bullet list slides, slides with graphs, slides with organization charts, and so on. These make it very easy for you to build exactly the slides that you want.

After you add a slide, you may decide that it has the wrong AutoLayout applied. Or, you have tinkered with a slide, moving and deleting elements, until the slide is no longer recognizable as its original layout, and you want to reapply the original.

You can apply a different AutoLayout, or reapply the same one originally chosen, by following these steps:

1. Display the slide you want to change in Slide view.
2. Choose Format, Slide Layout or click on the Slide Layout button on the Standard toolbar. The Slide Layout dialog box appears (see Figure 6.16).
3. Click on the picture that best shows the layout you want.
4. Click on Reapply.

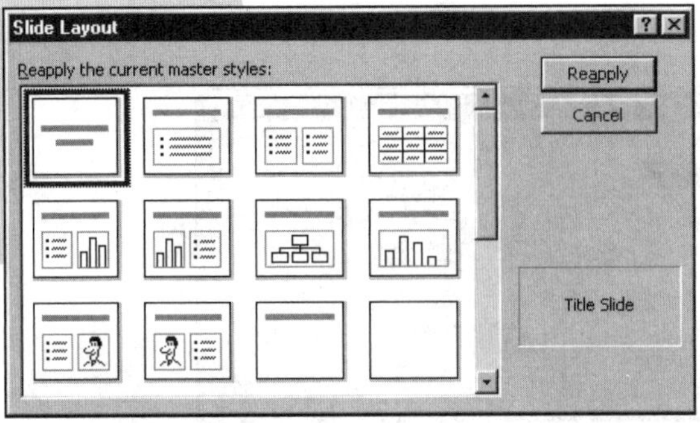

Figure 6.16 Choose a different AutoLayout from here if you want, or reapply the same one.

Reviewing the Presentation Text

Now that you have your basic text in place, take a few minutes to review it and make sure you haven't made any mistakes or introduced any errors that will make you cringe later when your slide is displayed eight feet tall on a wall during your presentation. In the following sections, you'll learn about some of PowerPoint's tools to help with this.

Checking Your Spelling

If you think a spelling check can't improve the look of your presentation, just think for a moment how ugly a blatant spelling error looks in huge type on a five-foot projection screen. Frightening, isn't it? If that image makes you nervous, it should. Spelling mistakes can creep past even literate people, and spring up where you least expect them, often at embarrassing moments.

Fortunately, like other Microsoft Office programs, PowerPoint comes with a powerful spelling program that can check your work for you at any time, minimizing the number of embarrassing spelling mistakes. The Office programs all use the same spelling checker, so if you are familiar with it in another Office program, you should be able to breeze through a spell check in PowerPoint with no problem.

Note

When PowerPoint marks a word as "misspelled," it really just means that the word is not in its dictionary. Many words, especially proper names, are perfectly okay to use and yet not in PowerPoint's dictionary, so don't believe PowerPoint against your own good judgment.

To begin the spelling check of your worksheet, click on the Spelling button on the Standard toolbar, or choose Tools, Spelling, or press F7. If you have no misspelled words, PowerPoint presents a dialog box telling you that your spell check is complete. Click on OK to close the dialog box.

On the other hand, if PowerPoint finds a misspelled word, as it did in Figure 6.17, you can choose from the following options:

- *Ignore.* Skips over this occurrence of the word.
- *Ignore All.* Skips over all occurrences of the word in this worksheet.

- *Suggestions.* Lists words that Excel thinks may be what you meant instead of the word you actually typed. Choose the correct one by clicking on it.
- *Change To.* Shows the word that you selected from the Suggestions list. If none of the words on the Suggestions list are right, you can type your own correction into this text box instead.
- *Change.* Changes the word in the cell to the word listed in the Change To text box. (Don't click on this button until you've put the correct word in the Change To text box.)
- *Change All.* Changes all occurrences of the word in the entire worksheet to the word listed in the Change To text box.
- *Add.* Adds the word to Excel's dictionary so that it will recognize it in the future.
- *AutoCorrect.* Adds the word to the AutoCorrect list so that if you misspell it the same way in the future, Excel automatically corrects it as you type.

When the spell check is over, PowerPoint displays a dialog box to that effect; click on OK.

Caution

Don't click on the AutoCorrect button for misspellings that you may sometimes want to change to some other word, or you may introduce embarrassing mistakes into your presentation. For example, if you often type "pian" instead of "pain," but sometimes you accidentally type "pian" instead of "piano," don't tell PowerPoint to always AutoCorrect to "pain," or you may find that PowerPoint has corrected your attempt at typing piano and made it a pain!

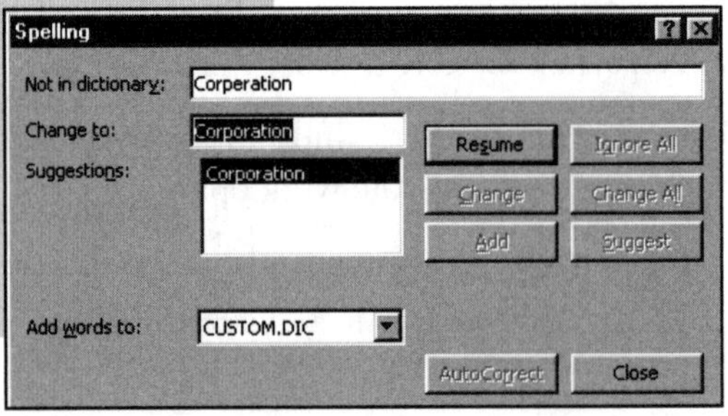

Figure 6.17 If PowerPoint finds a word that is not in its dictionary, this dialog box asks you what to do about it.

Using AutoCorrect to Prevent Common Mistakes

With AutoCorrect, PowerPoint can correct certain common misspellings automatically as you type. One way to put a word on this AutoCorrect list, as you saw, is to click on the AutoCorrect button in the spelling checker. Another way is to directly access the AutoCorrect feature.

To access AutoCorrect, choose Tools, AutoCorrect. The AutoCorrect dialog box appears, as shown in Figure 6.18.

At the top of the dialog box is a series of check boxes that helps you fine-tune some other corrections that AutoCorrect makes:

- *Correct TWo INitial Capitals.* If you accidentally hold down the Shift key too long and get two capital letters in a row, such as *MIcrosoft*, PowerPoint corrects this if you leave this check box marked.
- *Capitalize First Letter of Sentence.* Leave this check box marked to have PowerPoint capitalize the first word that comes after a sentence-ending punctuation mark, such as a period, or that occurs at the beginning of a paragraph.
- *Capitalize Names of Days.* Leave this check box marked to make sure the names of days, like Sunday, Monday, and so on, are capitalized.

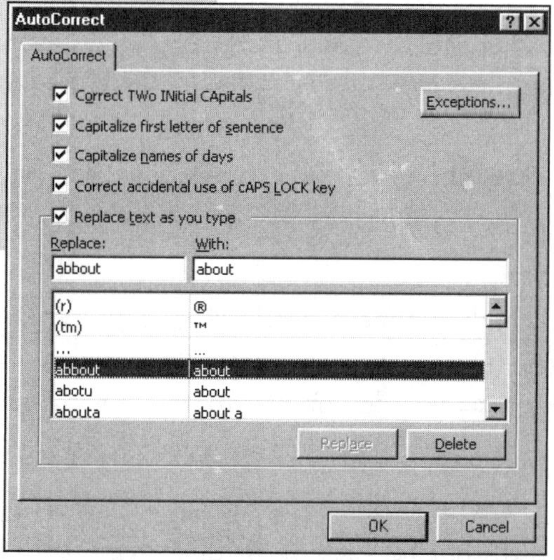

Figure 6.18 The AutoCorrect dialog box enables you to edit the list of AutoCorrections that PowerPoint makes.

- *Correct Accidental Use of cAPS LOCK key.* If you leave the Caps Lock on, PowerPoint can sometimes detect it and fix the problem. For example, if you had a sentence like "hE WAS GLAD TO SEE US", PowerPoint could conclude that the Caps Lock was inappropriately on and would turn it off for you.
- *Replace Text As You Type.* This check box enables the main portion of AutoCorrect: the word list. You must leave this check box on if you want AutoCorrect to correct the words on the list.

On the list in this dialog box, you'll see a number of word pairs. To the left is the common misspelling, and to the right is the word that PowerPoint substitutes in its place. Scroll through this list to get a feel for the corrections PowerPoint makes.

If PowerPoint insists on making a correction that you do not want, you can delete it from the list. Simply select it on the list and click on the Delete button. For example, my editors like me to code certain headings with (c) in front of them, so the first thing I do in any Office program is remove the AutoCorrect entry that specifies that (c) must be converted to a copyright symbol (©).

To add your own entries to the list, type the misspelling in the Replace text box and the correction in the With text box, and then click on the Add button.

When you are finished, click on OK to close the AutoCorrect dialog box.

Proofing with Style Checker

The Style Checker is like a spelling checker plus some extra benefits. You can run the spelling checker within it, and also get some advice on other aspects of your presentation, such as the attractiveness and grammar.

The Style Checker checks for three things:

- Spelling
- Visual clarity
- Case and ending punctuation

You can turn each of these on/off with a check box, so, for example, if you just did a spelling check, you do not have to bother with another one.

Check your presentation's style now by following these steps:

1. Choose Tools, Style Checker. The Style Checker dialog box appears, with a check box for each of the three items listed previously.
2. Deselect the check box for any item you don't want to check; then click on Start.

3. Respond to the dialog boxes as they appear.
   - If the Spelling Checker appears, respond to it as you learned in the preceding section.
   - If a style or ending punctuation error is found, as in Figure 6.19, respond to it by clicking on Ignore or Change as appropriate.
4. When you get through all the individual errors and inconsistencies, a summary dialog box appears, as shown in Figure 6.20, giving you some ideas for making your presentation better.
5. Make a note of the things listed that you want to change, and then click on OK. Unfortunately, you cannot print this list, and there is no way to save if, so you must jot down on paper anything you want to take a look at.

Figure 6.19 Here's a punctuation inconsistency that the style checker found.

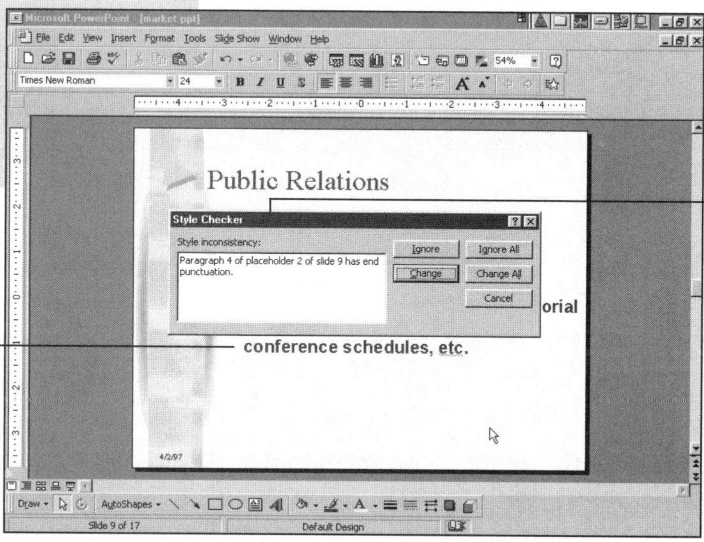

Drag the dialog box's title bar to see the slide being referenced.

In this case, I would click on Ignore because the end punctuation goes with "etc."

Figure 6.20 PowerPoint offers some suggestions, which you are free to take or reject.

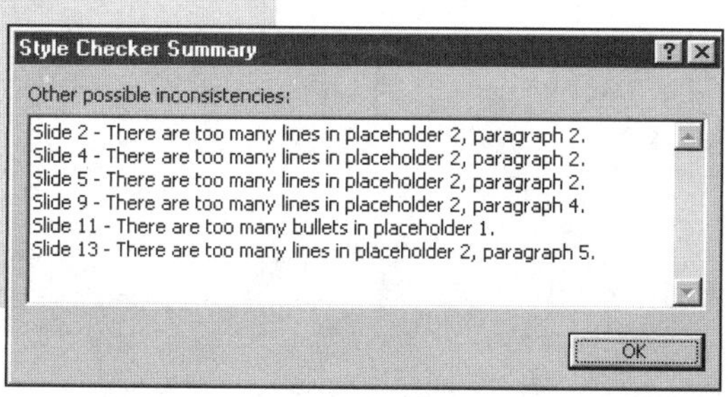

Tip

You can alter how the Style Checker works somewhat. In the initial Style Checker dialog box that you get when you choose Tools, Style Checker, click on the Options button. A dialog box full of options appears, from which you can fine-tune the style you want to enforce.

Summary

After completing this chapter, you should have some pretty sharp looking text. You may even have some fancy patterns and backgrounds. But text is only half the story; in the upcoming chapter, you'll learn how to work with graphics.

7

Formatting Text on a Slide

In This Chapter

- Creating Text Boxes
- Changing the Look of Your Text
- Making Global Font Changes
- Borders and Shading
- Multi-Column Lists
- Copying Formats with Format Painter

Just for the moment, put aside all the whiz-bang stuff that PowerPoint is famous for—the graphics, the animation, the built-in graphs and organization charts. Focus on one thing: text. In this chapter, you'll learn more than you ever thought possible about placing and arranging text on a PowerPoint slide.

Adding Text Boxes to Slides

In Chapter 5, you learned a very easy, important way of putting text on slides: typing it in Outline view. This is great if you have a lot of text you have to get onto a group of slides quickly, but it has one drawback: you can't decide for yourself how the text will be placed. The text just flows onto each slide in whatever way is set up in the Slide Master.

Chapter 5 covered adding new slides to a presentation.

If you want to craft a slide with text placement that exactly matches your specifications, the best way to do it is to add a text box to the slide in Slide view. This method, although not as fast as the Outline view method, gives you the most control over placement.

When you create new slides with most of the AutoLayouts from the New Slide dialog box, you get several text boxes pre-placed for you. That may not always be what you want. So in the following Hands On, you'll create a new, blank slide from scratch and then add a text box to it.

Hands On: Placing a Text Box on a Slide

1. In any presentation, switch to Slide view.
2. Click on the New Slide button on the toolbar. The New Slide dialog box appears.
3. Click on the totally blank AutoLayout, as shown in Figure 7.1. Click on OK. You get a new, blank slide.
4. On the Drawing toolbar, click on the Text Box button. (It looks like a white piece of paper.)
5. Move the mouse pointer onto the slide. The pointer looks like a vertical insertion point.

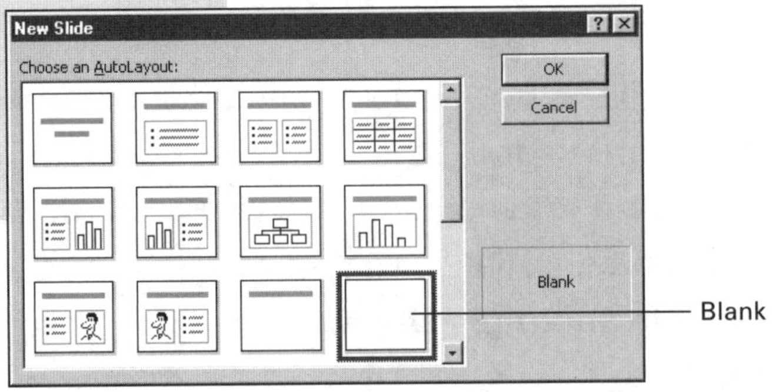

Figure 7.1 To create a slide with no pre-made text boxes, use the blank AutoLayout.

6. Do one of the following:
   A. Drag your mouse to draw a rectangular box to constrain the text. PowerPoint ignores the height of the box you draw but adheres to the width. The text box will expand vertically to hold your text, with words wrapping to the next line when they hit the box's right margin. (I recommend that you use this method.)
   B. Click on where you want the first word in the text box to start. The text box will expand as needed to hold your text, and will run off the edge of the slide if you type more than will fit.
7. Type your text. If you used B in step 6, you must press Enter when you want to start a new line. If you used A, new lines wrap automatically. Figure 7.2 shows some text; if you don't know what to type, type what you see here!
8. When you are finished, click outside the text box.

Changing Text Attributes

Okay, now that you have some text in a text box, what can you do with it? Lots of things. You can dress it up, dress it down, move it, recolor it—the possibilities are endless.

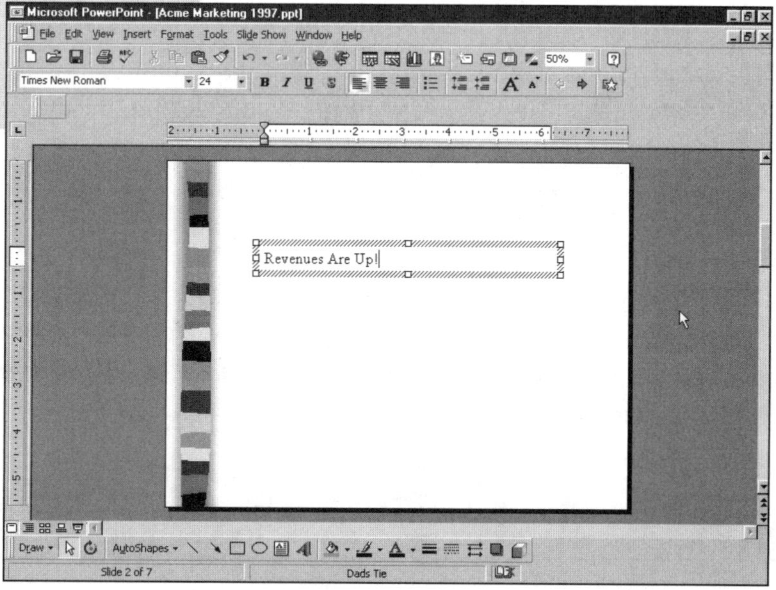

Figure 7.2 Type some sample text into a text box.

Note

You also can affect the text attributes by applying a different design template, but remember, in this chapter you are doing things manually, for maximum control.

Choosing a Different Font and Size

Microsoft Office 97 comes with lots of different fonts, and you may have acquired some other fonts from other programs too. A font is a typeface, a style of lettering. For example, compare the lettering in this book in the headings to the lettering in this line of text you're reading now. These are two different fonts.

About Fonts

Appearance-wise, there are two basic kinds of fonts: serif (those with little "tails" on each letter, like the little horizontal line at the bottom of "I" and "t", for example) and san-serif (those without tails). The headings in this book are san-serif and the regular paragraph text is serif.

Experts say that serif fonts are easier for people to read in big blocks because the "tails" make letter recognition easier. San-serif fonts are better for headings because they're eye-catching and clean-looking. The fonts chosen for this book were no accident! Some fonts of each kind you may have on your system include:

Arial

Courier

Times New Roman

In your presentations, try to use san-serif fonts for short lines of information or big headings. Use serif fonts when you're presenting a whole paragraph. But remember, be consistent with your usage! If the bullets on one slide are in a san-serif font, the bullets on the next slide should be too.

Besides changing the font, you also can change the size of the type. Almost all Windows fonts are TrueType fonts, so you can resize them to any size you want, from as small as 6 or 8 points to over 72 points. A point is 1/72 of an inch; it's a measurement of how tall the tallest letter in the character set is.

Hands On: Changing the Font to 36-Point Arial

Try changing fonts. Take the text you typed earlier in this chapter, and format it in 36-point Arial, using these steps:

1. Select the text by dragging your mouse across it.
2. Click on the Font drop-down arrow and scroll down the list until you see Arial (see Figure 7.3).
3. Click on Arial. The font changes.
4. Click on the Font Size drop-down arrow and scroll down the list until you see 36.
5. Click on 36. The letters change size.
6. Click away from the text to remove the selection and see your results.

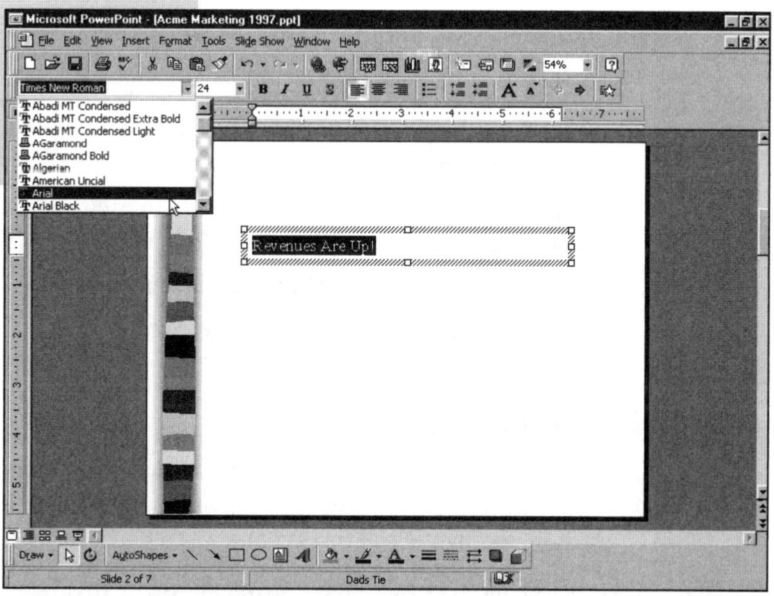

Figure 7.3
Change the font and font size with the drop-down lists on the toolbar.

Tip

Here's a quick way to increase or decrease the size of selected text: click on the Increase Font or Decrease Font button on the Formatting toolbar. These look like large and small capital A's, respectively, and they bump up or down the point size on selected text by one place on the size list. This is not always one point! If you open the Font Size drop-down list, you'll see that sometimes there is a larger jump between available sizes.

Making Global Font Changes with Replace Fonts

Say your coworker created a 40-slide presentation in which he used the Carnival font. But now you need to work with the presentation on your own computer, and you don't have that font! You need to change all instances of the Carnival font to a font you have.

Another reason you might want to replace a certain font is simply because you've changed your mind. It seemed like a good idea initially to use a script font for your headings, but now that you see the entire presentation, you realize that plain old Arial would have been a better choice.

In both cases, the easy way out of your situation is to use the Replace Fonts feature to replace all instances of one font with another instantly.

Follow these steps:

1. Select Format, Replace Fonts. The Replace Font dialog box opens.
2. Open the Replace drop-down list and choose the font to be replaced. Only the fonts currently in use in the presentation appear on this list.
3. Open the With drop-down list and choose the font to substitute for it. This list contains every available font on your system.
4. Click on the Replace button. Every instance is replaced.
5. Click on Close to close the dialog box.

Changing Text Color

Color really makes your text stand out! When you apply different designs, the text color changes, but you also can manually change the color of any text. Here's how to change the text color:

1. Select the text by dragging your mouse across it.
2. Open the Font Color pop-up list (on the Drawing toolbar, looks like a

capital A) by clicking on the arrow next to the button; choose a different color for your text, as shown in Figure 7.4.

Or, if you don't see the color you want, click on More Font Colors and choose a color from the Colors dialog box and click on OK.

3. Click away from the text to deselect it and see your result.

Color is more than just decoration—you also can use it to help convey your message. Here are some ideas:

- Different colors connote different emotions. Choose the colors that make your audience feel the way you want them to feel. For example, choose red lettering to indicate urgency, or green to say "all is well."

The colors that appear on the pop-up list are the other colors in the current color scheme. That's because PowerPoint assumes you want to stick with your current scheme, and not introduce any new colors that might potentially clash. Think carefully before you dismiss the colors in the color scheme in favor of something else—if you start using lots of "foreign" colors, your presentation will not look as cohesive and well-planned.

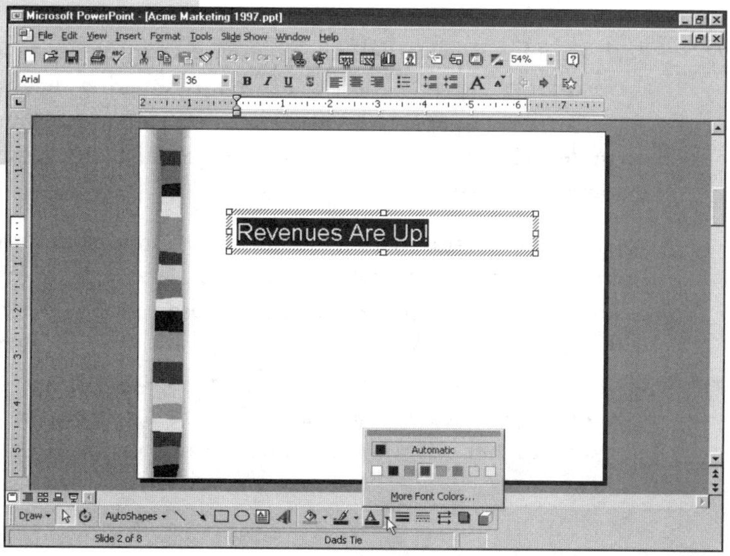

Figure 7.4
Change the text color from the Font Color pop-up list.

- If you are using a dark background, try yellow lettering instead of white. Yellow is a much warmer color that will make the audience feel more positive toward your message.
- If you are "building" from one slide to another, for example, showing a list that builds from one slide to the next, make all the bullets on the list that you are not discussing at the moment a neutral color, perhaps a darker or lighter shade of your background color. Then make the one line that you are referring to at the moment a bright, contrasting color.

Other Ways to Enhance Your Text

PowerPoint provides a few other ways to enhance your text. These are called *attributes* in PowerPoint, but you probably know them by their more common names: bold, italic, underline, and so on.

The easiest way to apply this kind of formatting is with the buttons on the Formatting toolbar. Just select the text and then click on the appropriate button:

B	Bold
I	Italic
U	Underline
S	Shadow

Each attribute is pretty self-explanatory except for Shadow. Shadow means that the text looks like it is "raised" off the page with a shadow behind it. You can apply attributes separately or in any combination. Figure 7.5 shows some examples. (I made Shadow very large because otherwise it's hard to see the shadow on-screen.)

You may have noticed that Figure 7.5 contains one other type of attribute: Emboss. *Embossing* makes the text look like it is "stamped" into the background, like one of those seals people use to mark the books in their library with their initials. When you use embossing, any text color you selected becomes void, because embossed text is colorless. I haven't talked about embossing yet because there is no button for it on the toolbar. You have to access it another way, through the Font dialog box.

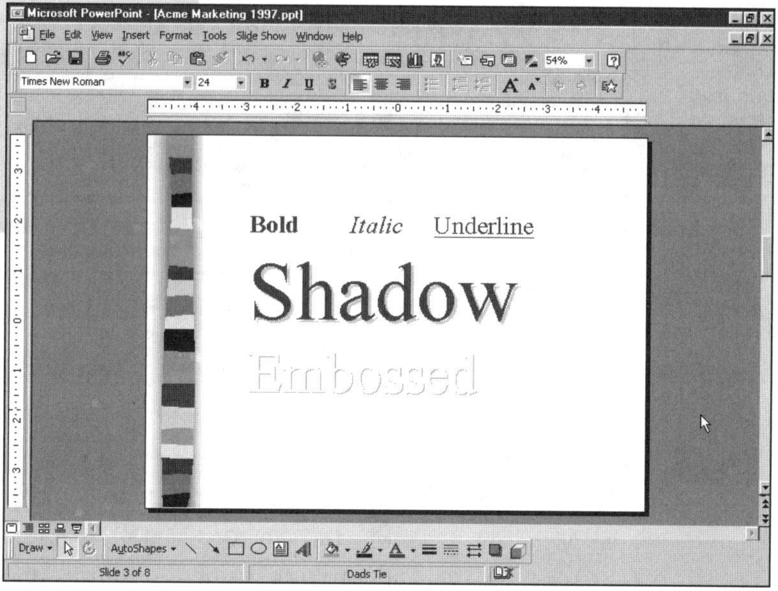

Figure 7.5 Bold, Italic, Underline, and Shadow attributes can all be applied directly from the toolbar.

The Font dialog box also enables you to apply superscript and subscript formatting to text. These rather specialized attributes enable you to offset certain letters above or below the rest, like these:

Subscript: $H_2 0$

Superscript: Footnote^1

> ***Note***
>
> **You can apply any of the text formatting that you've learned so far through the Font dialog box, although the ways you've learned earlier are easier.**

Hands On: Embossing Text

Follow these steps to apply embossing, or any other text formatting, from the Font dialog box:

1. Select the text by dragging your mouse across it.
2. Choose Format, Font. The Font dialog box appears (see Figure 7.6).

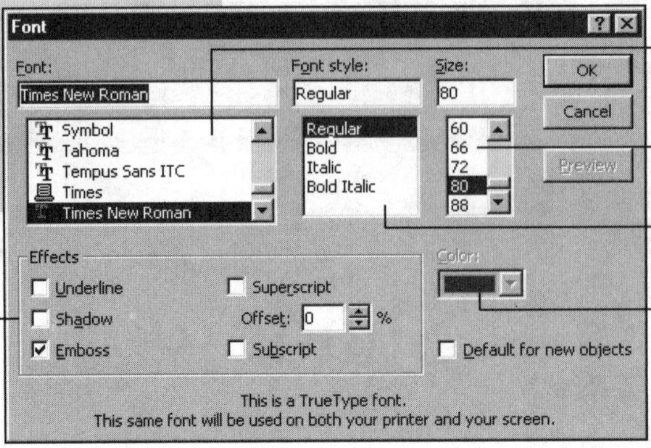

Figure 7.6 You can do all your character formatting from the Font dialog box.

3. To emboss, click on the Emboss check box to select it.
4. Make any other text formatting selections you want. You can change the font, size, and attributes using the controls shown in Figure 7.6.
5. When you are finished, click on OK to apply your changes.
6. Click away from your text to deselect it and see your results.

Changing Text Alignment

By default, text aligns to the left in your text boxes. That's fine for most situations, especially because you can move a text box around on the slide to place it where you want it. But sometimes you may want certain text to be centered or even right-aligned to give a certain look. For example, in Figure 7.7, the heading is centered and the last line of text is right-aligned.

Note

Alignment refers to the text's placement in its text box, not on the slide. The right-aligned text box in Figure 7.7 might appear centered overall on the slide if its box were moved to the left a few inches, but it would still be right-aligned within its box.

Figure 7.7 Some examples of text alignment.

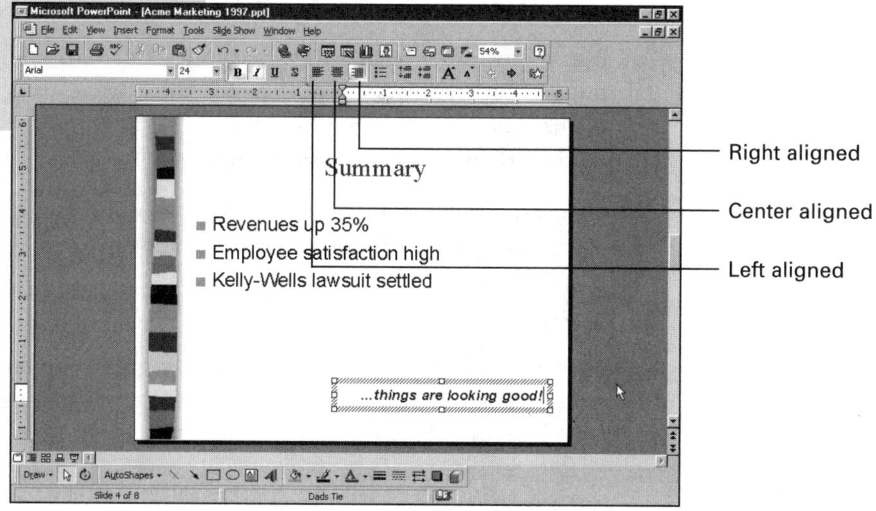

The easiest way to align text is with the text alignment buttons on the Formatting toolbar. Just select the text and click on the button you want. In fact, for a single paragraph, you don't even have to select it; just click to place the insertion point anywhere within it before clicking the button.

 Align Left

 Center

 Align Right

There is a fourth alignment option, Justify, that does not come up very often in a PowerPoint presentation. If a paragraph has more than one line to it, this alignment option aligns all lines except the last one with both the right and left edges of the text box. It ignores the last line of the paragraph, so if the paragraph has only one line, it is essentially the same as Left alignment. Justify looks good for large paragraphs, but is of limited usefulness for the brief bullet points that are the hallmark of most slides. To just Justify, select Format, Alignment, Justify. (You also can set the other alignments from this menu, but you seldom will want to because the toolbar buttons are faster and easier.)

Adjusting Line Spacing

You might have noticed as you were typing text into your text box that when you press Enter, you start a new paragraph. By default, PowerPoint leaves a blank line between paragraphs, and single-spaces all paragraphs. You can change this if you want, though. For example:

- Within a bullet list, you might want to eliminate the extra line between paragraphs so your bullet items will appear to be closer together.
- If you want to make a large paragraph easier to read, you might add extra space between the lines.
- If you need more space between paragraphs, you could add it with the line spacing controls rather than trying to press Enter more times for extra Returns between paragraphs.

To adjust line and paragraph spacing, you use the Line Spacing dialog box. Use the following Hands On to try it out.

Hands On: Changing Line and Paragraph Spacing

1. Start a blank slide in your presentation, and type the following paragraphs on it:

   Revenues are up 50%, but expenses have also risen, resulting in a net decrease in profitability of 12%.

   To offset this decrease, Acme Corporation plans to implement a cost-cutting initiative in FY-98 that will trim waste from the operating budget.
2. Select the text you just typed.
3. Choose Format, Line Spacing. The Line Spacing dialog box appears (see Figure 7.8).
4. To increase the spacing between lines, enter **1.2** in the Line Spacing text box. (The default is 1.0.)
5. To increase the spacing between paragraphs, enter **1** in the Before Paragraph text box. (The default is 0.5).
6. Click on OK to close the dialog box.
7. Click away from the text to deselect it.

The result appears in Figure 7.9; your slide should look similar (although you might have a different template applied).

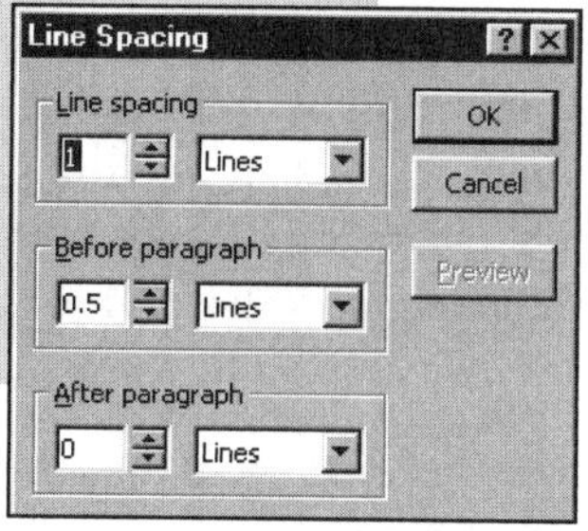

Figure 7.8 Use the Line Spacing dialog box to change the space between lines and paragraphs.

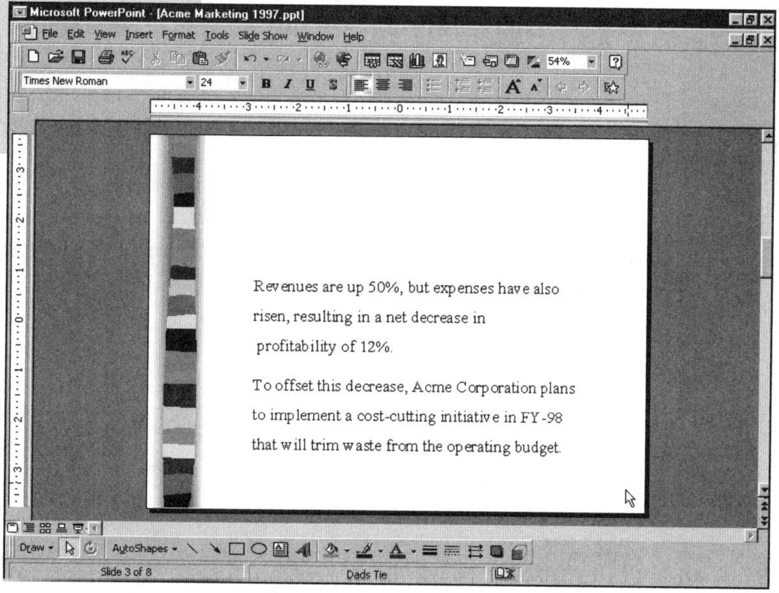

Figure 7.9 The result of adjusting the line spacing on the sample.

You may have wondered about some of the other controls in the Line Spacing dialog box. First, what about the drop-down lists to the right of each text box, that say "Lines" by default? These enable you to choose the unit of measurement, either Points or Lines. Remember, a point is 1/72 of an inch, so if you choose Points, you'll get a precise measurement. Lines, the default, is flexible. It's calculated as a percentage of the tallest font used in that paragraph. For example, if the largest font in the paragraph is 16-point, and you have Line Spacing set to 1.5, the actual line spacing you'll get is 24-points (16 times 1.5).

The other thing you may have wondered is why there is both a Before and After control. That's so you can specify the extra space between paragraphs as being either before or after each paragraph. In general, you should use one or the other of these, not both. If you enter both a Before and After value, you may get more space than you intended. For example, if you set Before and After both to 1 line, you'll get one line of space before paragraph #1, but two lines of space between subsequent paragraphs—one line for after the initial paragraph and one for below the paragraph that follows it.

Adding Colors and Lines

You'll draw rectangles and other shapes in Chapter 8.

Lines and colors (sometimes called "borders" and "shading") can really dress up your text boxes. They provide sort of a pseudo-graphics effect without the hassle of creating a separate rectangle. You can place a line around a text box to make it stand out on its own. Colors (background shading) are useful within text boxes to further make the text stand out. Figure 7.10 shows an example.

There are two distinctly different ways of adding lines and background colors to your text box. One is to use a dialog box, and the other is to rely on the tools of the Drawing toolbar. Ordinarily in PowerPoint, the toolbar methods are easiest, but in this case that's open for debate because the dialog box method lets you apply both lines and colors in the same place, whereas with the toolbar you have to use separate tools for them. In the following Hands On, I'll walk you through an exploration of both methods, so you can choose what works best for you for real-life work.

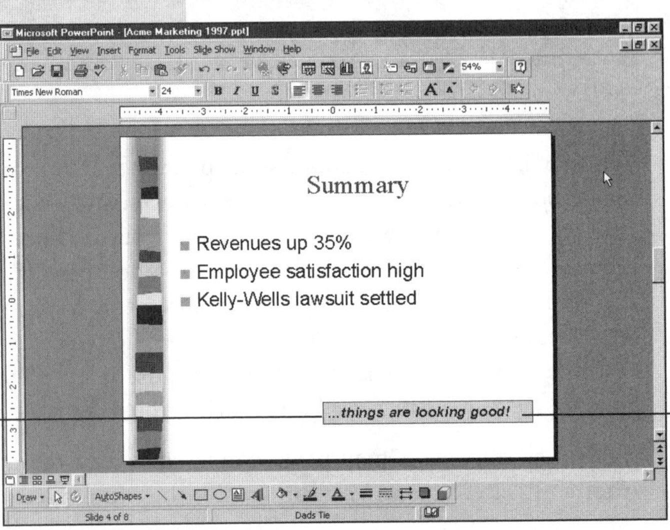

Figure 7.10
Use lines and colors with your text to make it stand out.

Hands On: Applying Lines and Colors to a Text Box

1. Click inside the text box you want to work with.
2. Choose Format, Colors and Lines. The Format Text Box dialog box appears with the Colors and Lines tab displayed (see Figure 7.11).
3. In the Fill area, open the Color drop-down list and choose a background color for the text box. For this example, pick a light blue. Just like with slide backgrounds, you can choose More Colors or Fill Effects for extra choices.
4. In the Line area, open the Color drop-down list and choose a color for the border outside the text box. For this example, pick red.
5. Open the Dashed drop-down list and choose a line dash style. For this example, pick the third one from the top of the list.

Note

The Fill area's Color drop-down list also has a choice called Background. This sets the background of the text box to "clear" so that it reflects whatever background color the slide has. This is the default.

Also notice the Semitransparent check box. This applies the chosen color but makes it semi-see-through so that you can see part of the slide behind it.

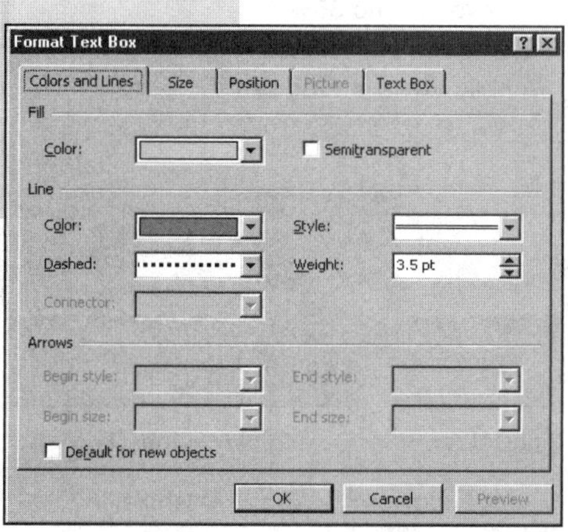

Figure 7.11 From this dialog box tab, you can change both lines and colors.

6. Open the Style drop-down list and pick a line style. For this example, pick the first double line on the list (the one that says 3 pt next to it).
7. The Weight field adjusts itself automatically to the Style that you chose, but you can change it. For this example, click on the up increment arrow next to the Weight field until the Weight reads 3.5 pt.
8. Click on OK. The dialog box closes and you see your result. Ugh! Pretty awful, eh? So let's use the Drawing toolbar controls to change it.
9. Click on the down arrow next to the Fill Color button on the Drawing toolbar. A shortcut menu of color choices appears (see Figure 7.12).
10. You have fewer color choices here than you did in the dialog box, so click on More Fill Colors to see more. The by-now-familiar Colors dialog box appears.
11. Click on a bright orange, and click on OK. The dialog box closes and your text box background changes to orange.
12. Click on the down arrow next to the Line Color button on the Drawing toolbar. (It's the button directly to the right of the Fill Color one you just used.) A shortcut menu appears.

Figure 7.12 Open the Fill Color button's menu by clicking on its arrow.

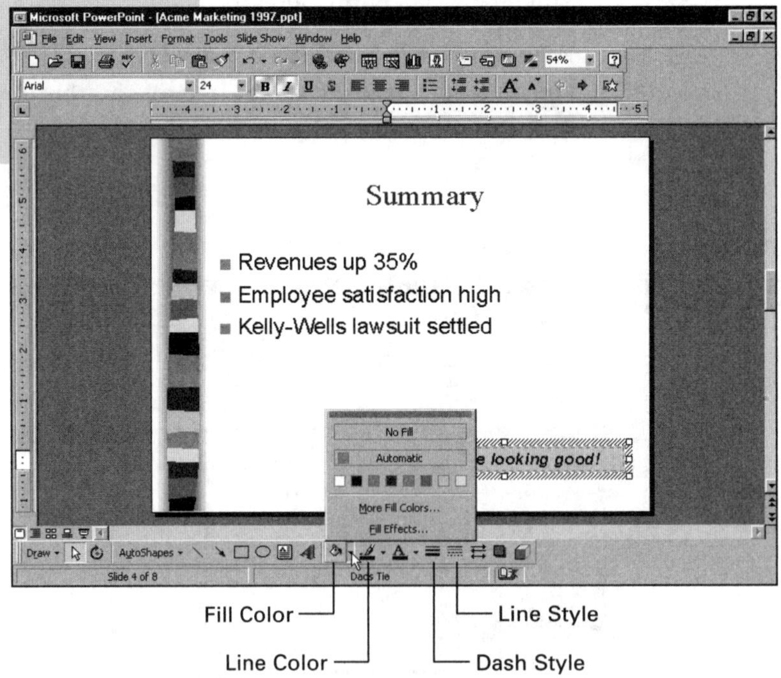

13. Go for basic black this time. Click on a black square. Your text box line color changes to black.
14. Click on the Line Style button. A pop-up list of line styles appears.
15. Click on a plain thin line.
16. Click on the Dash Style button. A pop-up list of dash styles appears.
17. Click on a solid line.

When you have finished all these steps, your text box should have an orange background and a plain, thin, solid black line around it. Although this may not be exactly what you had in mind for your own presentation, you now know where all the controls are located, and can fix up your text boxes the way you want them.

Moving and Resizing a Text Box

A text box is an object, the same as anything else on your slide. (I'll say this many times in the book because it's an important concept: everything on a slide is an object. Everything.) And all objects are moved and resized in the same way—by dragging with the mouse.

You might want to move a text box to reposition it on the slide without changing its dimensions. To do so, just follow these steps:

1. Point the mouse pointer at the border of the text box, but away from the handles (those little squares in the corners and on each side). The mouse pointer turns into a four-headed arrow, as shown in Figure 7.13.
2. Hold down the left mouse button and drag the text box to a different location on the slide.
3. Release the mouse button.

If you want to move a text box from one slide to another, use the Cut and Paste buttons on the toolbar.

To resize an object, you drag it by one of its handles. Depending on what dimension you want to change, you grab different handles: use the corners to resize both height and width at once, or one of the side handles to do only one dimension at a time. You might want to resize a text box, for example, to change its margins.

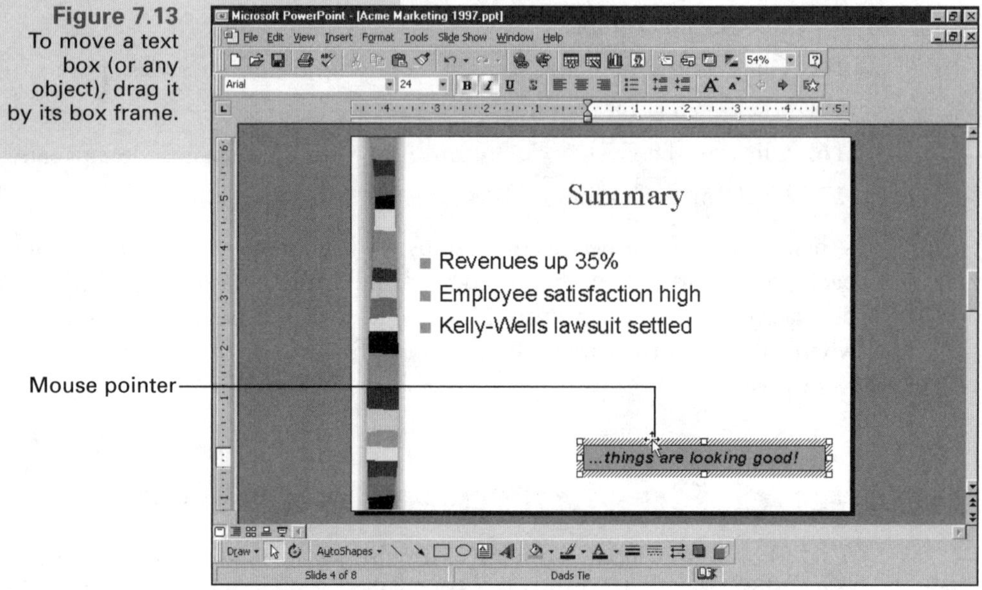

Figure 7.13 To move a text box (or any object), drag it by its box frame.

Tip

If you wanted to place two bullet lists side-by-side, you could create two text boxes and resize them so that they fit next to one another.

Resize a text box with these steps:

1. Position the mouse pointer over a handle. The mouse pointer turns into a double-headed arrow, indicating the directions you can drag (see Figure 7.14).
2. Hold down the left mouse button and drag the text box to a new size.
3. Release the mouse button.

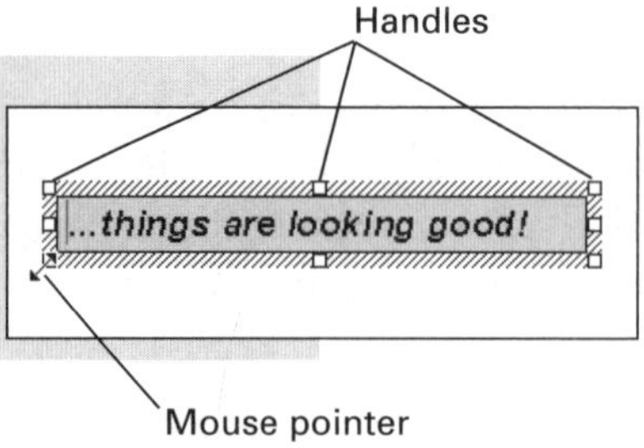

Figure 7.14 To resize a text box (or any object), drag it by its handles.

Setting Tabs

If you have worked in a word processor before, you are probably familiar with tabs. You set them and then press the Tab key to move the insertion point to them quickly. Each text box has its own tab settings in PowerPoint, and you set them, as you do in Microsoft Word, with the ruler.

Note

Unlike in Word, tab settings apply to the entire text box as a whole in PowerPoint, not to individual paragraphs.

In the following Hands On, I'll show you the Tab features that PowerPoint has to offer.

Hands On: Setting Tabs

1. Click inside the text box you want to set tabs for.
2. Notice the ruler at the top of the screen. Its white area matches the boundaries of the text box.
3. Click on the ruler where you want to place your tab. A little L appears, showing that you've just placed a left tab stop. (See Figure 7.15.)

You also can have centered, right-aligned, or decimal-aligned tabs. So continue the steps to place some of those:

4. Click on the Tab Type button at the far left of the ruler (see Figure 7.15). Its symbol changes to an upside-down T, indicating a center tab.
5. Click again on the ruler (at a different spot). A center tab is placed.
6. Click again on the Tab Type button. The backwards L you see stands for a right tab. Place one of these on your ruler.
7. Now click once again on the Tab Type button. The center tab symbol with a period that you see is a decimal tab symbol. With this tab type, columns align with the decimal point in the text. This is good for columns of numbers.
8. Click again on the Tab Type button. You're back to the left tab. The types cycle through like that each time you click.

Figure 7.15
Click on the ruler to place tab stops on it.

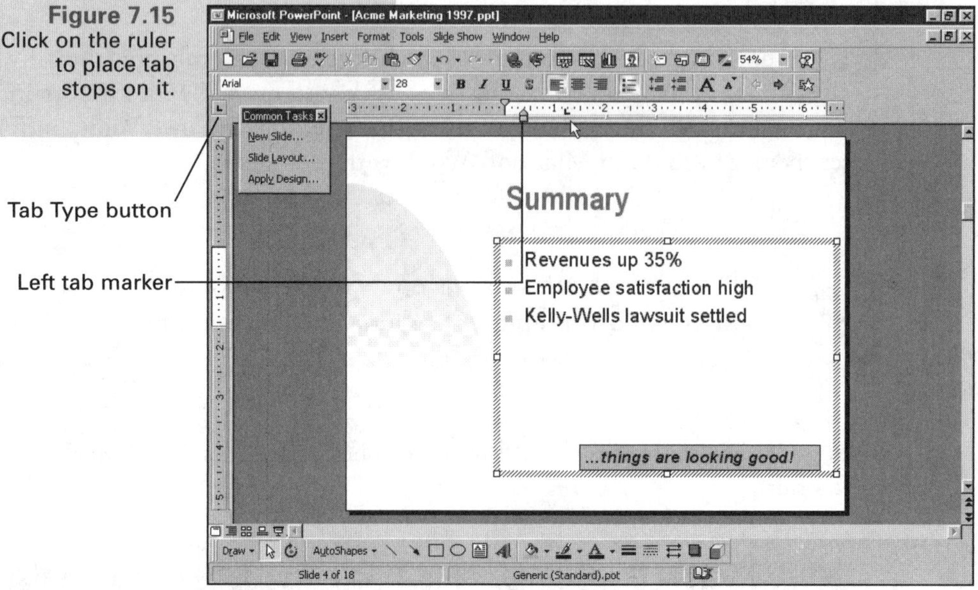

9. To remove a tab from the ruler, drag it away from the ruler with your mouse. Do this for all your tabs. (You were just practicing.)

Changing Text Box Indents

You may have noticed on the ruler that there were little gray triangles at the left end. These are indent markers; they show how far from the edge of the text box the actual text will start. They're askew in Figure 7.14 because I've got a bullet list, and the first line in a bullet paragraph is indented less than subsequent lines (to account for the bullet). In text boxes without bullets or numbered lists, the triangles align with one another by default.

You can drag these triangles to change the indentation.

- Drag the top triangle to change the first line indent.
- Drag the bottom triangle to change the subsequent line indent.
- Drag the rectangle beneath the bottom triangle to change both triangles at once.

The paragraph indents, like tabs, apply to the entire text box. You can't have two paragraphs with two different indent settings in the same text box. If you want this, you'll have to create a new text box to hold the second bit of text separately.

An exception to this is multi-level bullet lists. These are allowed in a single text box, as you'll see in the next section.

Working With Bullet Lists

Creating a bullet list in a text box is easy. Just follow these steps:

1. Click in the text box where you want the bullet list to start.
2. Click on the Bullet button on the Formatting toolbar. A bullet character appears in front of that line.
3. Type your text, and press Enter. The next line automatically has the same bullet too.
4. To finish up the bullet list, press Enter to move to a new line and then click on the Bullet button again to turn the feature off.

You also can turn existing text into a bullet list; just select the text (all of it) and then click on the Bullet button on the toolbar.

Creating Lists Within Lists

Sometimes you may need lists-within-list, or multiple-level bullet lists. To create a list within a list like the one in Figure 7.16:

1. Press Enter to start a new line.
2. Press Tab to indent the new line to the next level. Each time you press Tab, you move in another level and the bullet character changes.
3. Type the text, and press Enter. The new line has the highest level bullet character by default, no matter what the previous line's level.
4. Press Tab as many times as needed for the new line.
5. Repeat steps 3 and 4 as needed to complete the list.

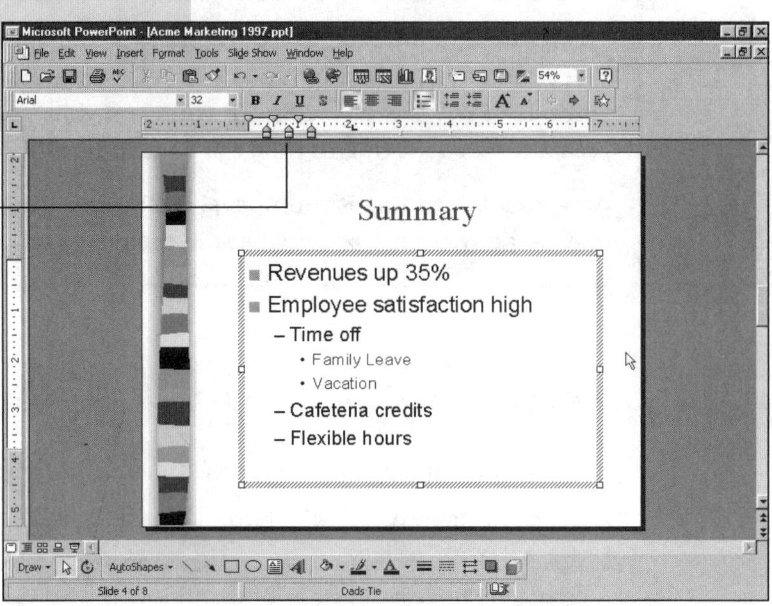

Figure 7.16 This bullet list has three levels.

Changing the Bullet Character

You may have noticed in the preceding section that the bullet character changed each time you tabbed to create a new list level. PowerPoint does that to help keep you from getting the levels confused. But did you know that you also can choose the bullet character yourself?

You can choose from a wide variety of bullet characters, from simple dots and blocks to check marks, happy faces, and more. You can change the bullet for an individual paragraph, for all paragraphs on the slide, or for the entire presentation. It's all in what you select:

- To change a single paragraph, click in that paragraph before you make the change.
- To change all the bullets on the slide, select all of the text before you make the change.
- To change the entire presentation's bullets, make the change on the Slide Master.

Now try a simple bullet change, just one paragraph. You can tackle the rest on your own later if you learn the basics now.

Hands On: Changing a Bullet Character

1. Click in a paragraph that has a bullet in front of it.
2. Choose Format, Bullet. The Bullet dialog box opens (Figure 7.17).
3. Open the Bullets From drop-down list and choose the font from which you want to take the bullet. For this example, choose Monotype Sorts.
4. Click on various characters to magnify them, so you can see what's available. When you find one that you like, leave it selected.
5. Open the Color drop-down list and choose the color you want for the bullet. As usual, you can click on More Colors for a Color dialog box if you don't like the colors that appear. For this example, pick a dark blue or black.
6. Change the size of the bullet in relation to the text. For this example, let's make it big by changing the size to 120.
7. Click on OK. You see your new bullet on the slide.

Some fonts, such as Monotype Sorts, have bullet characters that look like circled numbers: 1, 2, 3, 4, and so on. You can apply these to individual paragraphs to create a really unique looking numbered list.

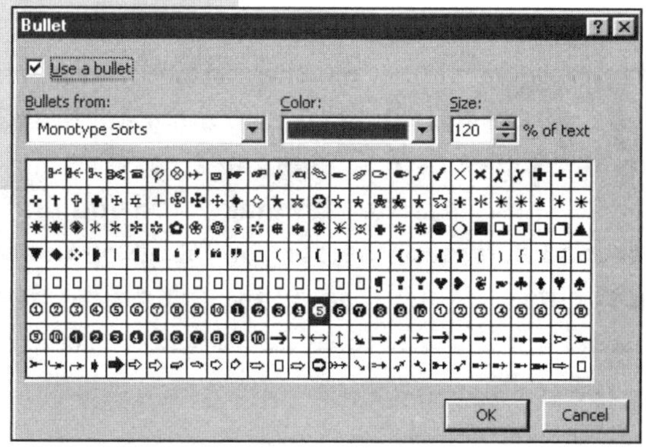

Figure 7.17 You can choose any character from any font for your bullet.

Using Format Painter to Copy Formats

Once you get some text formatted just the way you like it, it's an easy affair to copy that formatting to some other text. This is such a great time saver! Let's say that it takes you six steps to format a particular paragraph the way you want it, with a special font, size, color, and so on. You can use the Format Painter to transfer that format to another paragraph without having to go through those six steps again.

Use the following Hands On to try it out.

Hands On: Copying Formatting

1. Create two paragraphs in a text box on a slide. (You can use some text you have already created earlier in this chapter if you want.)
2. Format one paragraph with 16-point Arial font, italic, and red.
3. Select that paragraph by dragging across it with the mouse.
4. Click on the Format Painter button on the Standard toolbar (looks like a paintbrush).
5. Drag the mouse across the second paragraph. All of the first paragraph's formatting is automatically applied.

Pretty handy, eh? You can use this to copy almost any type of formatting you want.

When you go to select the second paragraph in step 5, make sure you don't click before you drag across it. Clicking cancels the paint job prematurely. And make sure you drag across the entire second paragraph before you let up on the mouse button, or some of the paragraph won't get formatted.

Summary

In this chapter, you learned how to place text boxes on your slides and to enhance the text with different colors, fonts, and sizes. You also learned how to move boxes, set tabs, and copy formats.

8

Placing Graphics on a Slide

In This Chapter

- **Choosing and Inserting Clip Art**
- **Downloading Graphics from the Internet**
- **Cropping and Editing Pictures**
- **Changing a Picture's Colors**
- **Drawing Shapes and Lines on a Slide**

In Chapter 7, you learned about text; the flip side of that is graphics. You can use PowerPoint's pre-drawn clip art, import photos and other images, and even draw your own artwork in PowerPoint. In this chapter, you'll learn to do all of those things.

Using the Clip Gallery

Everyone has heard the phrase "Don't reinvent the wheel." If something has already been done, take advantage of that fact! That's the principle behind clip art. PowerPoint's creators have supplied you with hundreds of common images that you can use royalty-free in your work, without having to draw your own.

Try it out now with the following Hands On procedure.

Hands On: Importing ClipArt from the Clip Gallery

1. In Slide view, display the slide on which you want to place the clip art.
2. Click on the Insert Clip Art button on the Standard toolbar. (It looks like a portrait of a man.) The Microsoft Clip Gallery 3.0 opens, shown in Figure 8.1.
3. Click on the Gestures category in the left panel. Previews of the available shapes appear.
4. Click on the picture of clapping hands (or any other picture that you like).
5. Click on the Insert button. The Clip Gallery closes and the image appears on your slide. Don't worry if it's huge; you'll learn to resize it later in this chapter.

If you are eager to resize the image now, just hold down the Shift key and drag one of its corner handles to make it smaller, just as you resized the text box in Chapter 7.

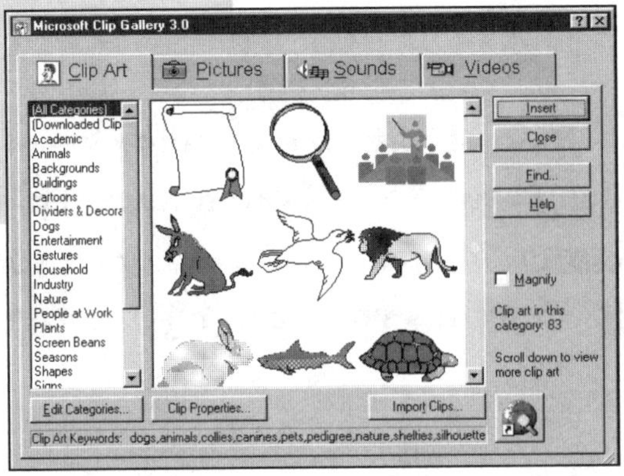

Figure 8.1 You can browse and choose from hundreds of images with the Clip Gallery.

If you get a message like `Cannot Insert Picture`, perhaps the Clip Gallery cannot find the file. The images that appear in Clip Gallery are taken from a kind of "table of contents" of the graphic files. If this table of contents gets out of sync with what's really on your computer, you may see images in the Clip Gallery that in reality have been deleted or moved. Simply select a different image if this happens.

There's a lot more that you can do with the Clip Gallery than the simple image import that you just saw in the Hands On. Go back in and take a look. Click on the Insert Clip Art button again to reopen the Clip Gallery.

First, notice the categories in the left panel. By default, All Categories is selected, which means that you see all the images in the right panel, bar none. If you are looking for a specific image theme or type, you can click on a category, as you did in the Hands On, to narrow it down.

Notice also the Magnify check box. If you mark this box, when you click on a clip to select it, the clip is displayed in large format, so you can have a better look at it. Some people find this helpful; others think it's irritating. It's your choice.

Chapter 12 covers sounds and video.

You may have noticed the three other tabs in the Clip Gallery: Pictures, Sounds, and Videos. These are simply different kinds of clips, but Clip Gallery handles them all the same. Click on a different tab to see the Clip Gallery for that type of object, and insert them into your slide in exactly the same way that you did the clip art. If you don't have anything on these tabs, try putting your Office 97 of PowerPoint 97 CD-ROM in your CD-ROM drive, and then exiting and reentering the Clip Gallery. The CD-ROM contains extra clips of all types, as you'll learn later in this chapter.

Organizing Your Clips

You can create your own categories and organize the clips into them. This works not only with clip art categories, but also sounds, videos, and pictures categories. To modify the categories in use in your Clip Gallery, you click on the Edit Categories button. This opens the Edit Category List dialog box, in which you can add, delete, and rename categories (see Figure 8.2).

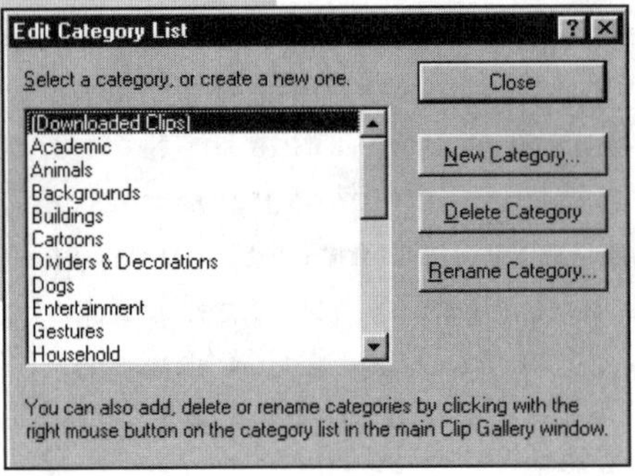

Figure 8.2 You can change your categories here to reflect the way you actually use the clips.

For example, suppose you want to rename the Academic category to "School". You would do the following from the Edit Category List dialog box:

1. Click on the Academic category.
2. Click on the Rename Category button.
3. Type **School** in the New Category Name dialog box.
4. Click on OK.

To delete a category, just click on it and click on the Delete Category button.

Don't delete a category unless you are sure you don't want to use it. Deleted categories can't be restored, and if you recreate the category with the same name, it won't have any clip art assigned to it and you will have to manually reassign each clip to that category.

You can add a new category by clicking the New Category button. You're prompted for a name; type it and click on OK. That's it! The new category appears on the list. However, of course, it doesn't have any clips assigned to it yet. You need to do that with the Clip Properties.

That leads us to a related topic: choosing which clips are assigned to which categories. You assign categories independently for each clip, so this can be a rather lengthy process. However, if you use clip art extensively, and have added lots of additional clip art into the system, it may be worth it for you to set this up.

Note

Some clips' properties are "locked" and you can't make changes to them, but others can be changed. (Generally, the clips that came with your original installation are locked and the ones you download or acquire from other sources are unlocked. You'll learn how to download more clips later in this chapter.) When you open the Clip Properties for a clip, if you see a picture of a lock at the top of the dialog box, it means that clip's properties are locked.

To change a clip's categories, select the clip and then click on the Clip Properties button to open a Clip Properties dialog box where you can reassign the clip's categories that it falls in. If the clip is locked, you'll see a picture of a lock at the top of the dialog box and all the controls will be non-working. If you don't see the lock, you can select or deselect the check box for each category as desired, as shown in Figure 8.3. Each clip also has keywords, which appear in a text box above the list of categories. Keywords are used when you search for a particular image. You can change them to any words that you might commonly use when you were looking for the image.

Figure 8.3
You can set the properties for some clips; other clips are read only, which means you can display this information but not change it.

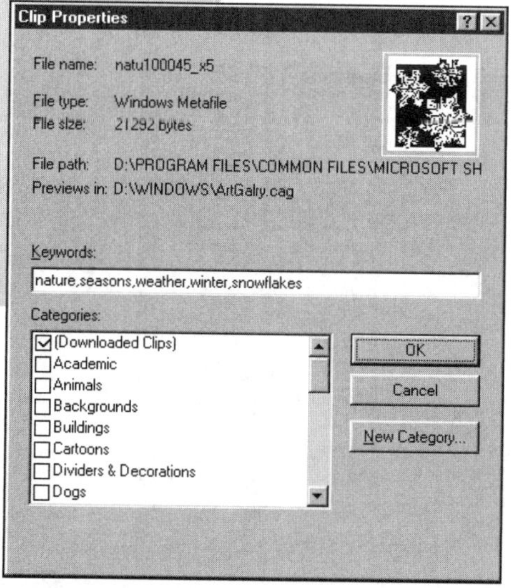

Finding Clips

If you have a lot of clips in your gallery, you'll appreciate the ability to search by keyword. (You learned about keywords in the preceding section.) Some clip art has preassigned keywords that cannot be changed; other clips let you change and add keywords.

Hands On: Finding All Clips with a Common Keyword

Say you were looking for clip art for a presentation with teamwork theme. You could search for all clips that had "teamwork" as the keyword using these steps:

1. From the Clip Gallery, click on the Find button. The Find Clip dialog box opens.
2. Select the phrase [**All Keywords**] in the Keywords text box, and press the Delete key to remove it.
3. Type **Teamwork** in the Keywords text box (see Figure 8.4).

If you have searched for the same keyword in the past, open the Keyword text box's drop-down list. The word may still be there for you to select.

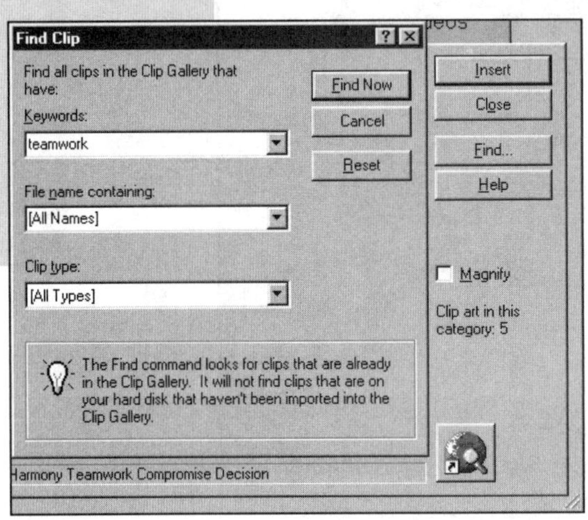

Figure 8.4 You can search for clips by name, type, and keyword, but in this example you're searching by keyword.

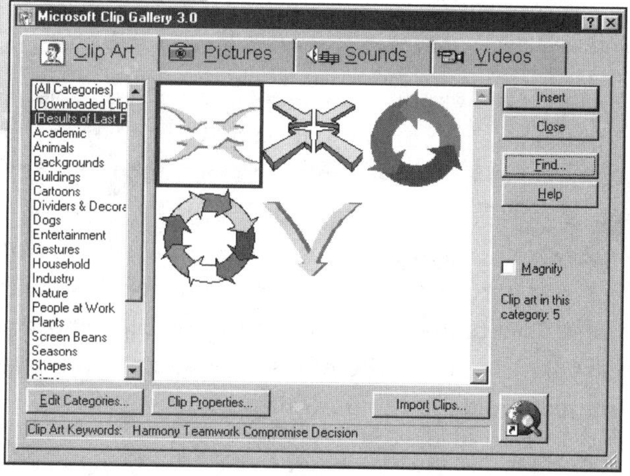

Figure 8.5 Only the clips that match the criteria appear.

4. Click on the Find Now button. The Clip Gallery reappears, with a new category showing called Results of Last Find. In that category, all the clips that had the keyword "teamwork" appear, as shown in Figure 8.5.

Working with Pictures

What's the difference between a Picture and Clip Art? From an end-result standpoint, very little. They're just different file formats. The Clip Gallery keeps them separate because there are some differences in the things you can do to modify the two types of images, as you'll learn later in this chapter.

Examples of pictures might be images that you have scanned, such as your company logo or a photo of your CEO, or images that you have downloaded or acquired. Typical picture formats include PCX (PC Paintbrush), BMP (Windows bitmap), GIF (Graphics-Exchange Format), and JPG (Joint Photographic Experts Group).

Although PowerPoint comes with an impressive collection of clip art, it offers very little in the way of pictures. That's because typically pictures are more personalized, and you will have your own to use rather than using a library of "stock photos."

Say you have scanned in a picture that you want to include in your Clip Gallery. Use the following Hands On to add that image.

Understanding Image Types

So what's the big difference between clip art and pictures? Well, it's all in the image type. Clip art is a "vector" image type, which means that in its purest form, it's nothing but a bunch of math formulas. Remember in geometry classes where you would take an algebraic equation and plot it on a grid? Well, if you plotted enough lines and curves on a grid, you would come up with a clip art image. This math basis is what makes clip art resizable. When you resize the clip, PowerPoint just changes the math formula to redraw a perfect image in the new size.

In contrast, a picture is a "bitmap" image. It's made up of a bunch of pixels set to different colors. Remember those Light Brite toys? If you didn't have one, you probably wanted one. There was a grid of little holes, and you pushed colored pegs into the holes in patterns to form pictures. Basically, that's how a picture is formed. There's this really tiny grid, and each square has a color assigned to it. (If the square isn't part of the image, it has a background color like white.) This makes for a rich-looking, often photographic-quality picture. However, when you resize a bitmap, distortions may occur, because these kind of images are not really made to be resized.

Hands On: Adding a Picture to the Clip Gallery

1. In the Clip Gallery, click on the Pictures tab.

Tip

By the way, this procedure also works for adding more clip art to the Clip Art tab too; just click on the Clip Art tab instead of Pictures in step 1. It also works for sounds and videos.

2. Click on the Import Clips button. The Add Pictures to Clip Gallery dialog box appears (see Figure 8.6).
3. Navigate to the drive and folder containing the picture you want to add.

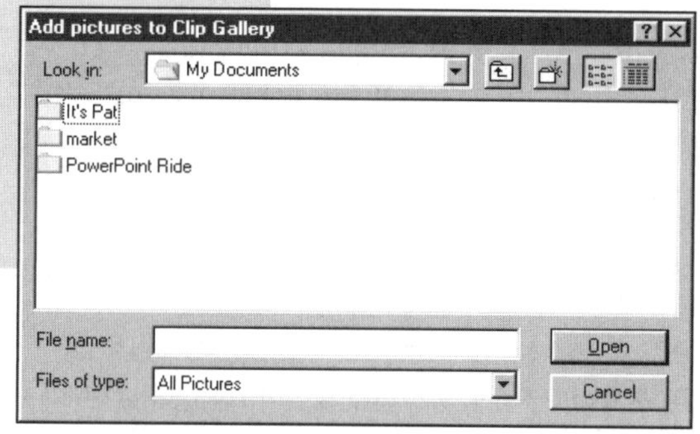

Figure 8.6 You can use this dialog box to locate and select more images to add to your Clip Gallery.

See Chapter 3 if you don't remember how to navigate drives and folders.

4. Click on the picture name and then click on Open. A Properties dialog box appears for the image (see Figure 8.7).
5. Type any keywords you want to use in the Keywords text box. Separate words with a comma and space.
6. In the Categories list, click to mark the check box for every category that this clip should appear in.
7. Click on OK. The clip now appears on the Pictures tab of the Clip Gallery.

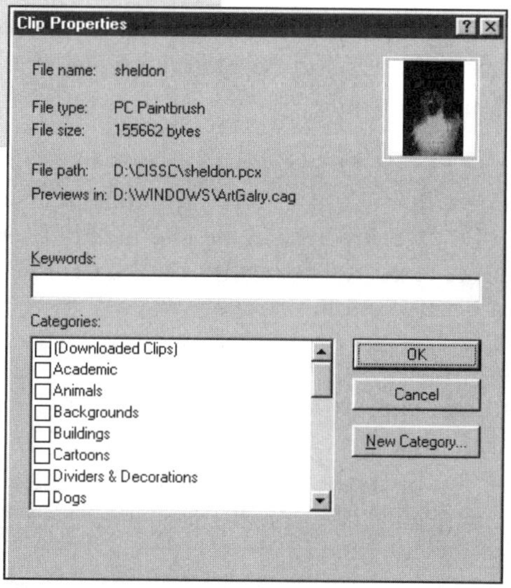

Figure 8.7 Assign keywords and categories to your clip here.

Getting More Clips

PowerPoint comes with a nice basic collection of clip art, but you may want more choices. There are two ways to get more clip art:

- From the Office 97 (or PowerPoint 97) CD-ROM
- From the Microsoft Web site

You may want to get clip art from *both* places, for maximum variety!

Don't stop with this book in your quest for more clip art! Clips are available from many other Web sites on the Internet, and from other programs you may already have on your computer, such as WordPerfect, CorelDraw, Lotus 1-2-3, and so on. Almost all programs come with clip art these days. You also can purchase clip art collections wherever software is sold.

Getting Clips from the CD-ROM

There are over 3,000 additional pieces of clip art on the CD-ROM, organized into several types (based on who developed the images):

- *Microsoft Additional Clip Art.* This is more images of the same type that you have already. It comes from Microsoft.
- *Screen Beans.* These clips are made by a company called A Bit Better. They are more of those little shadow outline characters that you may have seen in the Clip Gallery.
- *Instant Icons.* A company called Centermark provides these images, which are fancy borders and decorative images that look very professional, not "cartooney."

You can open up PowerPoint Central to read more about each of these art types and see previews of them. However, in the interests of expediency, I'm going to show you the fast way to pull these images off the CD-ROM in this chapter, and PowerPoint Central simply isn't the quickest way.

Getting the additional clip art from the CD-ROM is very easy, almost automatic. Just make sure that the Office or PowerPoint CD-ROM is in your CD-ROM drive before you open the Clip Gallery. If the CD-ROM is available, the Clip Gallery automatically includes all clips from the CD-ROM in its search.

Tip

To transfer a lot of extra clip art to your hard disk, so you won't need the CD-ROM to access it, rerun the Setup program (see Appendix A) and choose to install the Additional Clip Art collection.

Getting Clips from the Internet

What? You say you *still* don't have enough to choose from? Well then, you can visit the Microsoft Web site and see what kind of clips are there for the taking. Microsoft maintains a large Web site, where all PowerPoint users can download clips of all types for special uses. For example, Microsoft might place special-interest clip art on the Web site that might appeal only to a small percentage of their users. That way, only the people who need that clip art have to mess with it. Or they might provide brand-new clip art (or sounds, or pictures, or videos) that was not available when they released the original product.

Note

To access the Web site, you have to have an Internet connection. If you don't have one, you can sign up with Microsoft's own MSN (the Microsoft Network) by double-clicking the Microsoft Network icon on your Windows 95 desktop and following the prompts.

Follow these steps to acquire more clips from the Web site.

1. Start your Internet connection if it is not already started. (If you connect through your company's LAN, the connection is probably always "on".)
2. In PowerPoint, open the Clip Gallery if it is not already open.
3. Click on the Internet button in the Clip Gallery (the globe with the magnifying glass). Your Web browser opens and displays the Clip Gallery Live page. (You may have to click on OK in an information dialog box before the browser opens.)
4. Click on the Accept button to go on. The clip search controls appear (see Figure 8.8).

Figure 8.8 You can get additional clips from the Clip Gallery Live.

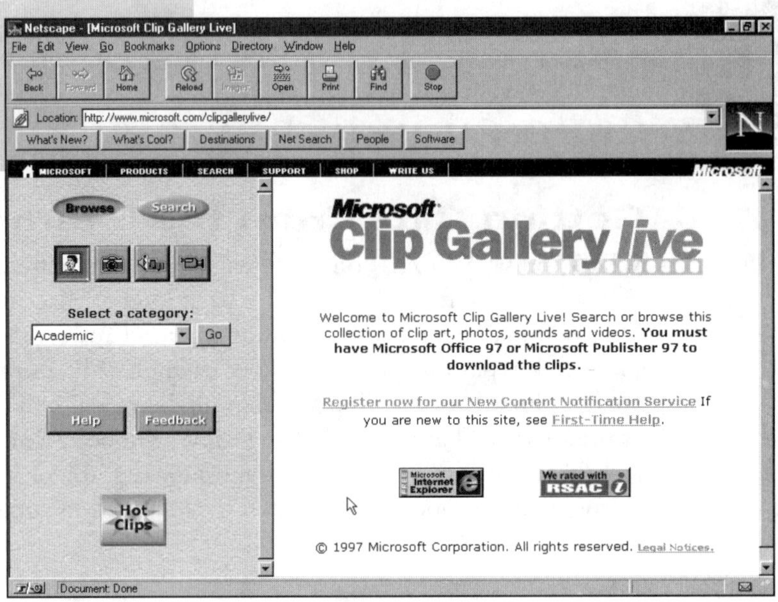

5. Click on the button for the type of clip that you want:

 Clip art

 Picture

 Sound

 Video

6. Open the drop-down list below the buttons and choose a category. For example, the Business category might contain some images you can use.
7. Click on the Go button. The available clips in that category appear in the right pane (see Figure 8.9).
8. Click on the underlined link for a clip that you want. The clip is automatically transferred to your Clip Gallery.
9. Get additional clips as desired, changing the type and category if needed. When you are finished, close your Web browser and terminate your Internet connection.

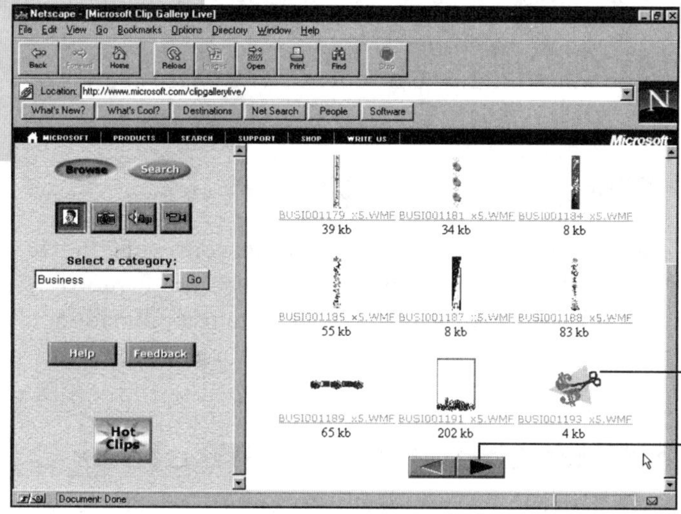

Figure 8.9 The right pane shows you miniatures of the available clips.

After you have downloaded the clips you want, you may want to recategorize them, as you learned earlier in this chapter. By default, all clips that you download have their properties unlocked, so you can categorize them any way you want.

Importing a Graphic from a File

So far in this chapter, you've looked only at the Clip Gallery, because that's the easiest way to work with clips (images, sounds, and video) in your presentation. However, if there is one particular image that you want to place in your presentation, and it's not in the Clip Gallery (perhaps it's on a floppy disk that someone gave you, or on your hard disk), it seems like an awful lot of trouble to add the image to the Clip Gallery just so you can use it in your presentation.

See Chapter 3 if you don't remember how to navigate drives and folders.

That's where importing a graphic from a file comes in handy. With this method, you bypass the Clip Gallery, and thereby bypass the step of having to add the image to it.

To import a graphic from a file, follow these steps:

1. Display the slide on which you want to place the image.
2. Choose Insert, Picture, From File. The Insert Picture dialog box appears.

3. Navigate to the drive and folder containing the image.
4. Click on the image.
5. Click on the Insert button. The image appears on your slide.

Editing Clips and Pictures

Well, now you have your image on your slide, but it probably doesn't look exactly like you want it to. That's because it probably needs to be cropped, resized, recolored, reshaped, or some combination of those things. Never fear—in this section you'll learn to do all those things.

Understanding the Picture Toolbar

Whenever the active object is a picture or some clip art, the Picture toolbar appears. It's a floating toolbar (although you can easily drag it to the top or bottom of the screen to "dock" it), and it contains tools that you can use to edit the image. (You can look ahead to Figure 8.10 if you want to see how it looks on-screen.) Table 8.1 shows the tools it contains. I'll refer you to these tools where appropriate in the upcoming sections.

Moving and Resizing an Image

Images are like any other object on a slide, in that you can move and resize them freely. You do it just like any other object:

- To move the image, point at the center of the image (any area except the handles) and drag the image where you want it.
- To resize an image in one dimension, drag one of the side handles.
- To resize an image in both dimensions, drag one of the corner handles.
- To resize an image and keep its proportions, hold down the Shift key as you drag one of the corner handles.

For example, in Figure 8.10, I am resizing the image by dragging its corner. Notice that the mouse pointer turns into a double-headed arrow when you rest the mouse pointer over a handle. When you are moving, in contrast, the mouse pointer becomes a four-headed arrow.

Table 8.1 The Picture Toolbar

Button	Name	Purpose
	Insert Picture from File	Opens the Insert Picture from File dialog box so you can add another picture to the slide.
	Image Control	Switches between grayscale, black and white, color, and watermark image modes.
	More Contrast	Increases the difference between the lights and darks.
	Less Contrast	Decreases the difference between the lights and darks.
	More Brightness	Makes colors in the picture brighter.
	Less Brightness	Makes colors in the picture darker.
	Crop	Changes the mouse pointer to a cropping tool, which you can exclude parts of the image.
	Line Style	Changes the thickness/style of the border surrounding the clip.
	Recolor Picture	Opens the Recolor Picture dialog box.
	Format Picture	Opens the Format Picture dialog box.
	Set Transparent Color	Enables you to set one color of the image as "see-through" (not available for all images).
	Reset Picture	Restores the pictures original settings that it had when you first placed it on the slide.

Figure 8.10
Resize an image by dragging one of its handles.

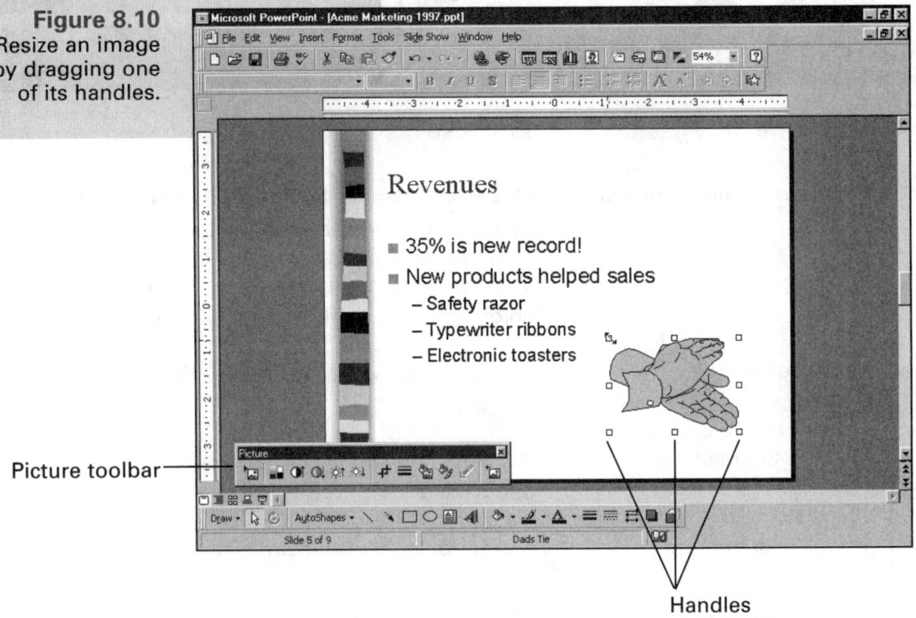

Switching Between Image Modes

Most images can be displayed in any of four modes:

- *Automatic.* This is usually color if it is a color image. It's the image's default appearance, and is best for color presentations.
- *Grayscale.* This is a gray-shaded version of the original image, with shades of gray substituted for each color. This works well for presentations that must be given in one color (such as a presentation given with transparencies printed on a black-and-white printer).
- *Black and white.* The entire image consists of black and white. There is no shading. Any colors are "rounded" to either black or white—that is, light colors become white and dark colors become black. This can result in a loss of image quality.
- *Watermark.* This is a light background image of the original, suitable for placement behind text. Its effect is subtle.

Figure 8.11 shows an image in each of the four modes. (You can't tell much difference between Automatic and Grayscale since this is not a color book, but you'll immediately see the difference on your own screen.

Figure 8.11 Use the Image Control button to switch between these four modes.

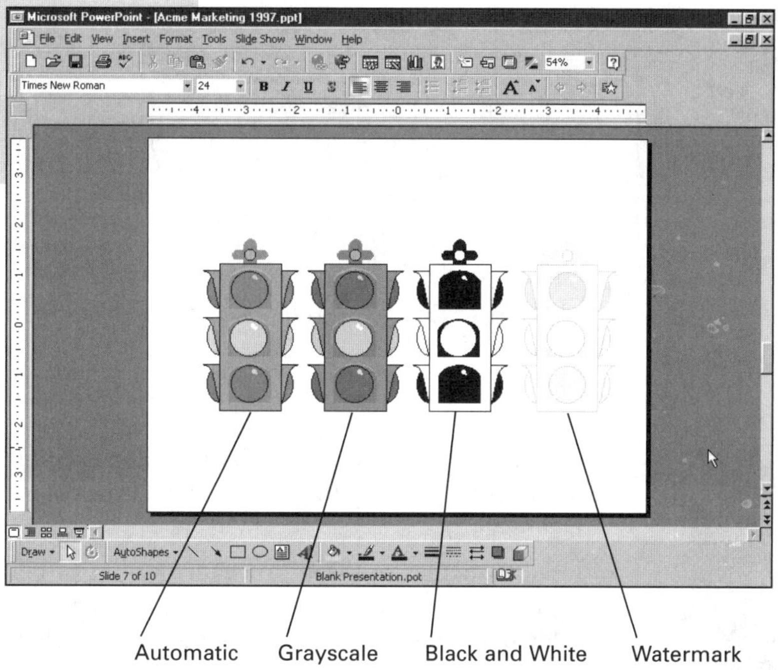

To switch between modes, just click on the Image Control button on the Picture toolbar. A pop-up list presents the four choices I just told you about; just click on the one you want.

Changing an Image's Colors

There are lots of things you can do to modify an image's coloring. Some basic ones are:

- To increase or decrease the image's contrast, click on the More Contrast or Less Contrast buttons on the Picture toolbar.
- To increase or decrease the image's brightness, click on the More Brightness or Less Brightness buttons on the Picture toolbar.

In addition to subtly modifying the colors with these buttons, you can dramatically alter them with the Recolor Picture dialog box. Follow these steps to recolor a picture that way:

1. Select the image that you want to modify. The Picture toolbar appears.

Figure 8.12
You can change any or all of the colors used in the picture.

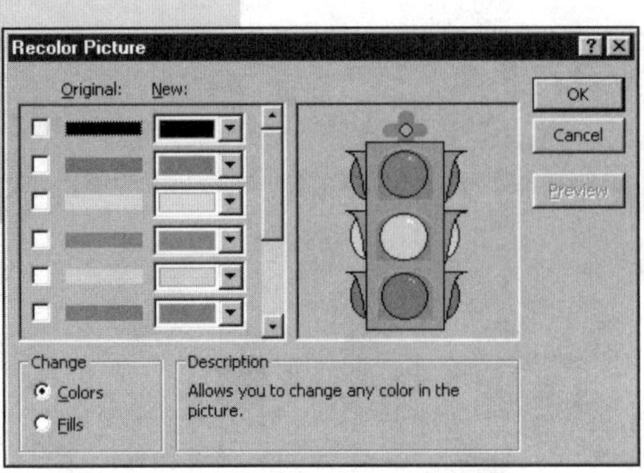

You worked extensively with the Colors dialog box when you were changing text colors in Chapter 7 and background colors in Chapter 6.

2. Click on the Recolor Picture button. The Recolor Picture dialog box appears showing the picture and all the colors used in it (see Figure 8.12).
3. Decide whether you want to change Colors or Fills, and click on the appropriate option button in the bottom left corner of the dialog box. (Not all pictures will have both choices available.)

   Colors. Enables you to change any color in the image, whether it's a line, a fill, or a background. If this is available, I recommend you go with this, as it gives maximum flexibility.

   Fills. Enables you to change only the fill colors. Some pictures only have this choice available.
4. Scroll through the list of colors in the left pane until you see the color you want to change.
5. Open the New drop-down list next to that color, and choose a new color. If you don't see the color you want, click on More Colors and select the new color from the Colors dialog box that appears.
6. Repeat steps 4 and 5 for each color you want to change.
7. Click on OK when you're finished changing colors.

Note

If you decide to go back to the original color in any case, just deselect the check box next to the color. (The check box became selected in the first place when you chose the new color.)

Setting a Transparent Color

The Transparent Color feature is really cool, but not all pictures support it. It's available for bitmap images ("pictures" in the Clip Gallery lingo) that do not already have transparency settings and for some, but not all, clip art. For example, suppose you have a scanned picture of your CEO and you want to make the background transparent so it looks like the CEO's head is sitting right on the slide. This feature could help you out with that.

Note

Some clip art already has the background color set to transparent, which is why it won't work with this Set Transparent Color feature.

If Set Transparent Color is available for the active picture, its button is available on the Picture toolbar. Otherwise the button is grayed out. To set a transparent color:

1. Make the picture active by clicking on it.
2. Click on the Set Transparent Color button on the Picture toolbar.
3. On the picture, click the mouse pointer on the color that you want to make transparent.

That's all there is to it! If the results are not what you wanted, click on the Undo button on the Standard toolbar or press Ctrl+Z to undo.

Adding a Background to the Image

As I said in the preceding section, some clip art has a background color of "transparent," which means it shows through to the slide beneath it. You can set the background color to a real color, so it won't show through, or you can change an existing background color to something different. For example, suppose you have some clip art of a sun. You can change its appearance dramatically by coloring its background to a bright, sky blue from its original transparent background.

Note

As with many other color and image choices, the background is an aesthetic choice that you need to make on a case-by-case basis according to your own good taste and the statement you are trying to make with the image.

You set a background for an image in exactly the same way you do for a text box (see Chapter 7). Follow these steps to set a background for the image:

1. Click on the image to select it.
2. Click on the down arrow next to the Fill button on the Drawing toolbar. A shortcut menu opens.
3. Click on the color you want, or if you don't see it, click on More Colors and choose a color from the Colors dialog box.
4. If you went the Colors dialog box route, click on the color you want and then click on OK (see Figure 8.13).

You also can put custom backgrounds behind an image, like patterns, textures, and so on. Refer to Chapter 7 for details.

Tip

If you want some color behind the image but you also want the slide beneath it to show through, mark the Semitransparent check box in the Colors dialog box.

Putting a Border Around the Image

See Chapter 7 for more about placing borders around objects.

A border around an image helps to delineate where the image begins and ends. This is not always what you want—there are times when the image should blend gracefully into the rest of the slide. But when you need to make the image stand apart, a border is an excellent aid.

To add a border to your image, use the Line Style button on either the Picture or the Drawing toolbar. (Both are identical.) Just click on the image, and then click on the Line Style button and choose a line style from the pop-up list.

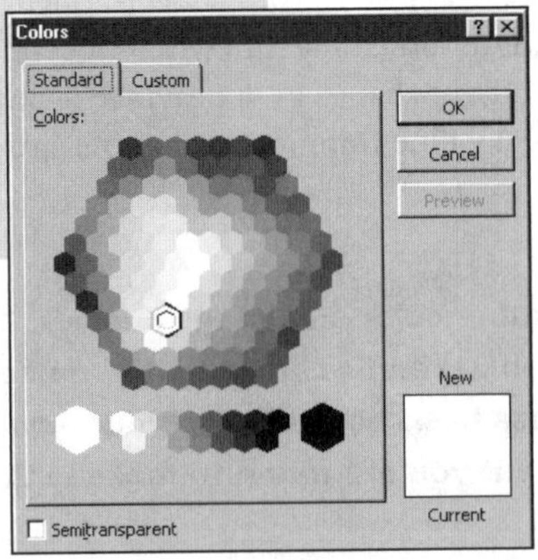

Figure 8.13 Choose a background color that will apply to the image box.

The default border is black, but you can choose another color (after you have created the border, that is) by clicking the picture and then selecting a line color from the Drawing toolbar's Line Color pop-up list.

Cropping an Image

Cropping is for those times when you want only a piece of an image, not the whole thing. For example, you might have a full head-to-toe picture of your CEO, but all you want on your slide is a head shot. You can crop out the rest of his or her body with the cropping tool.

To use the cropping tool, follow these steps:

1. Select the image to be cropped.
2. Click on the Crop tool on the Picture toolbar. Your mouse pointer changes to a cropping tool.
3. Position the mouse pointer over a side handle on the image frame, on the side where you want to cut some of the image off.
4. Drag the handle inward toward the center of the image until only the part of the image that you want to keep is within the dotted box (see Figure 8.14).

Figure 8.14 When cropping an image, a dotted box shows what will remain in the final image.

5. Release the mouse button. Your image is cropped.
6. Repeat steps 3 through 5 for each side you want to crop.

Format Picture: Your One-Stop Formatting Destination

All of the picture formatting and editing things that you've done so far also can be done in one big dialog box: Format Picture. You can either click on the Format Picture button on the Picture toolbar or right-click on the image and choose Format Picture from the shortcut menu to open it.

The Format Picture dialog box contains five tabs:

- *Colors and Lines.* Here you choose the colors for the picture's lines and background fill.
- *Size.* You can set a specific size for the image here instead of resizing with the mouse.
- *Position.* You can set a specific position on the slide for the image instead of moving it with the mouse.
- *Picture.* On this tab you can set cropping, image mode, and recoloring, instead of the respective tools you've learned about so far in this chapter.
- *Text Box.* This tab is unavailable because the image is not a text box.

I'm not going to spend a lot of time looking at this dialog box because, frankly, there are easier ways to do everything that it does, as you've seen. The only time that this dialog box is helpful is when you want to enter a precise numeric measurement for a sizing, scaling, or positioning setting.

Drawing Your Own Graphics

If you are an artist, or if you just need a few simple shapes, you may be able to draw what you need with the Drawing toolbar. This is the same Drawing toolbar that's available in all Office products, so if you have used it in Word or Excel, you have a head-start in learning.

Drawing Simple Shapes and Lines

There are two types of drawing tools on the Drawing toolbar: tools that draw shapes, and tools that manipulate shapes. Since you can't manipulate a shape before you've drawn it, look at the drawing tools first:

Line

Arrow

Rectangle

Oval

The procedure is basically the same for all these tools, although it may take you a bit of practice to master them:

1. Display the slide on which you want to draw.
2. Click on the drawing tool you want.
3. Point the mouse pointer where you want the line or shape to begin.
4. Hold down the mouse button and drag to where you want the line or shape to end.
5. Release the mouse button to view the finished line or shape.

If you double-click instead of click in step 2, you can repeat the procedure from step 3 to draw more of the same shape. Otherwise you must go back to step 2 each time.

Placing AutoShapes on the Slide

AutoShapes are pre-drawn shapes that function just like the lines and boxes that you draw. They're great for people who want shapes like arrows and starbursts but aren't coordinated enough to draw them (or simply don't have the time to waste). To use an AutoShape, follow these steps:

1. Display the slide on which you want to place the AutoShape.
2. Click on the AutoShape button on the Drawing toolbar. A menu pops up listing categories of shapes.

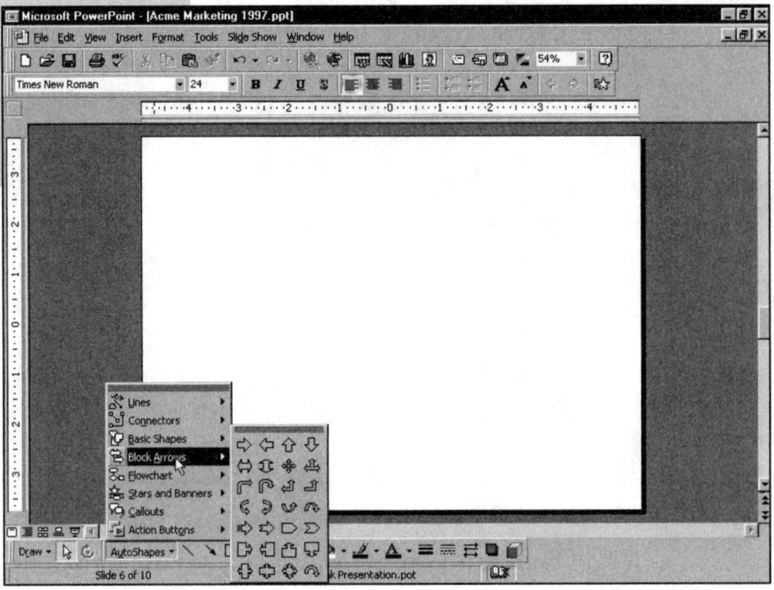

Figure 8.15 Choose the category of AutoShape you want and then the shape itself.

3. Point your mouse at the category you want (for example, Block Arrows). A menu of the available shapes in that category appears (see Figure 8.15).
4. Click on the shape you want. Your mouse pointer turns into a crosshair.
5. Drag on the slide to draw a box where you want the shape to appear. When you release the mouse button, the shape appears on your slide.

Manipulating Lines and Shapes

Remember, everything on a slide is an object, and you manipulate all objects in roughly the same way. Consequently, a lot of the basics for working with the lines and shapes you draw are the same as working with clips (which you learned about at the beginning of this chapter). For example, to move a line or shape, simply click on it to select it, and then position the mouse pointer over it so that your pointer becomes a four-headed arrow. Then drag the line or shape to its new position.

Resizing a line or shape is the same as resizing a clip too: just point to one of the line or shape's selection handles and drag it to change the line or shape.

Copying and Deleting Drawn Objects

You can copy lines and shapes the same way that you copy anything else in PowerPoint:

1. Select the object.
2. Choose Edit, Copy, click on the Copy button on the toolbar, or press Ctrl+C.
3. Select where you want it to go.
4. Choose Edit, Paste, click on the Paste button, or press Ctrl+V.

Deleting is just what you'd expect too: select the object and then press the Delete key.

Rotating and Flipping Drawn Objects

Suppose you've drawn an arrow that points up with the AutoShape feature, but you want it to point down. No problem—just flip it. To flip a drawn object:

1. Select the drawing.
2. Click on the Draw button on the Drawing toolbar. A menu appears.
3. Point to Rotate or Flip on that menu. Another submenu appears.
4. Choose Flip Vertical or Flip Horizontal, depending on what you're after. (To turn the arrow upside down, I'll choose Flip Vertical.)

As you saw while you had the menu open, the Rotate or Flip submenu also has commands for Rotate Right and Rotate Left. You can use these to rotate your shape 90 degrees.

If you want to control the precise amount of rotation, use the Free Rotate feature:

1. Choose Draw, Rotate or Flip, Free Rotate, or just click on the Free Rotate button on the Drawing toolbar. The selection handles around the shape turn into green circles.
2. Position the mouse pointer over one of those circles, so that the mouse pointer turns into a circular arrow. Then drag that selection handle to rotate the shape to the exact position you want (see Figure 8.16).
3. Click anywhere away from the shape to finish.

Figure 8.16
Drag the round green selection handles to rotate the shape.

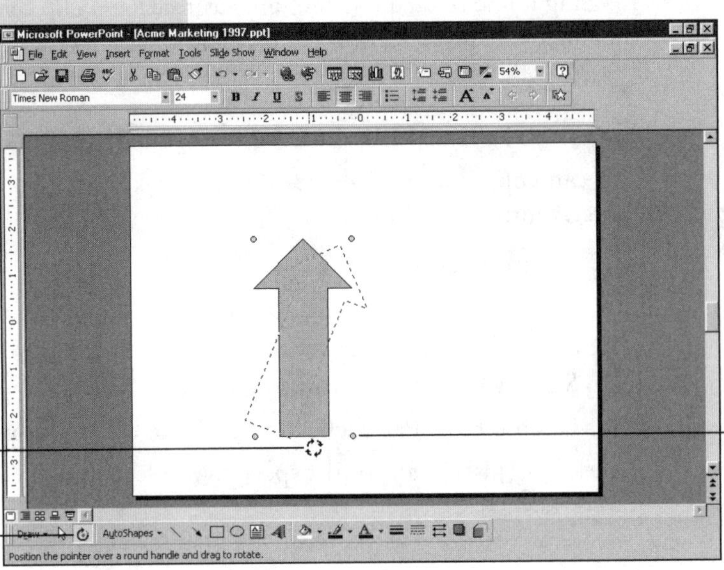

Modifying a Drawn Object

Many of the tools on the Drawing toolbar that you've been using the for last several chapters are also applicable for drawn objects:

Fill Color. Open the drop-down list to choose a fill color, and then click on the button to apply the color to the selected shape. (Does not work with lines).

Line Color. Open the drop-down list to choose a line color, and then click on the button to apply the color to the line or shape. (If working with a shape, it changes the outline color around the shape.)

Line Style. Select the line or shape, and then open this drop-down list and select the line thickness to use. If applied to a shape, it changes the border around the shape.

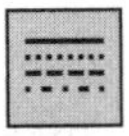

Dash Style. Select the line or shape, and then open this drop-down list and select the line style (dotted, dashed, etc.) If applied to a shape, it changes the border.

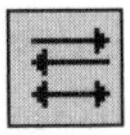

Arrow Style. Select the line, and then open this drop-down list and select the type of arrow to use (including None to remove an arrow). Doesn't work with shapes.

Shadow. Select the shape, and then click on this button to open a list of shadow types. Click on the one you want to apply it. Doesn't work with lines.

3D. Select the shape, and then click on this button to open a list of 3D types. Click on the one you want to apply it. Doesn't work with lines. This is especially cool with rectangles; it makes them into boxes.

You can access all the controls from the Drawing toolbar in a more formal form, with more precise controls, by right-clicking on the shape or line and then choosing Format AutoShape from the shortcut menu. (It doesn't matter whether you actually created it with the AutoShape button or not; PowerPoint considers all shapes and lines AutoShapes once they're drawn.)

Making Fancy Text with WordArt

All of the Office programs (including PowerPoint) come with an "applet" (a mini-application) called WordArt that helps you make interesting-looking text. You can take a standard line of text and bend it, squeeze it, twist it into a form that will make your reader pay attention. Figure 8.17 shows some WordArt text.

Figure 8.17 Here are some examples of what WordArt can do.

Caution

Be careful not to overuse WordArt. Used sparingly, it adds interest to your text, but used frequently it can become jarring and annoying to the reader.

You can create a piece of WordArt easily using some standard settings, and then refine it later to be exactly what you want. Follow these steps to create some WordArt:

1. Display the slide where you want to place the WordArt.
2. Click on the Insert WordArt button on the Drawing toolbar (the one with the crooked A on it). The WordArt Gallery dialog box appears (see Figure 8.18).
3. Select one of the gallery designs for your WordArt. If there isn't one that's exactly what you want, pick something similar; you can modify it later.
4. Click on OK. The Edit WordArt Text dialog box appears (see Figure 8.19).
5. Type the text you want in the Text box. (You can make multiple lines by pressing Enter at the end of a line.)

Note

Don't type too long a phrase for WordArt. WordArt looks best with short words or phrases. More than three words is too much and doesn't look very good.

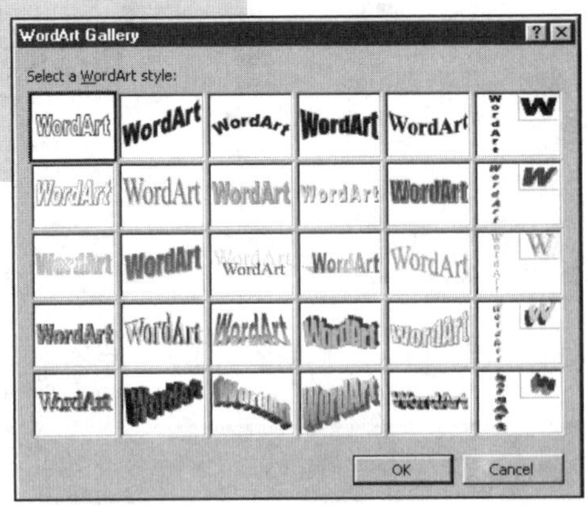

Figure 8.18
Choose a design from the WordArt Gallery.

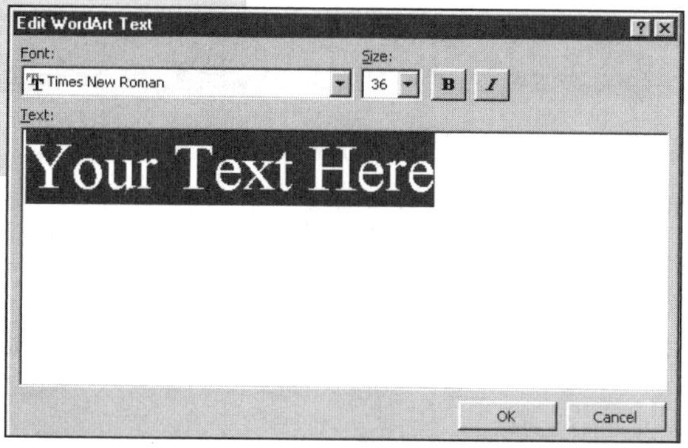

Figure 8.19 Type the text you want to use in your WordArt.

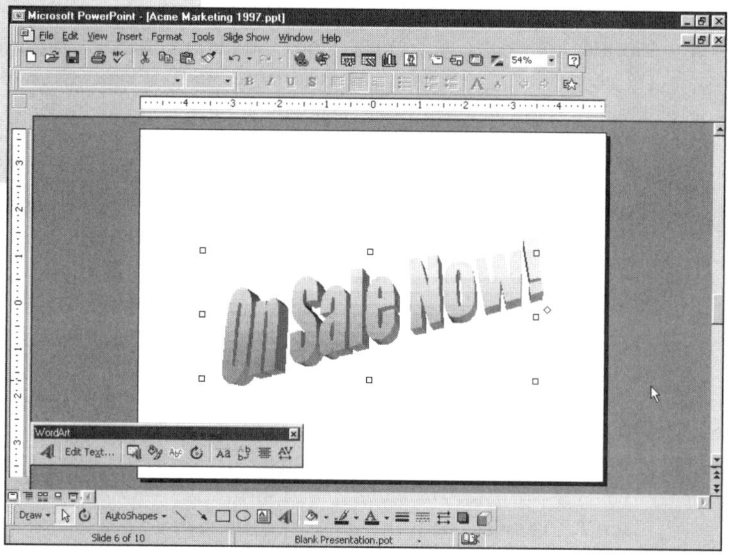

Figure 8.20 The finished WordArt appears in the slide, along with the WordArt toolbar.

6. Click on OK when you're done typing. The finished WordArt appears on your slide (see Figure 8.20).

If the WordArt toolbar does not appear, right-click on the WordArt image and choose Show WordArt Toolbar from the shortcut menu that appears.

Editing Your WordArt

WordArt has its own toolbar, made especially to help you make changes to your WordArt objects. It appears automatically when you create a piece of WordArt (refer to Figure 8.20). Table 8.2 explains what these buttons are for.

Table 8.2 WordArt Toolbar buttons

Button	Name	Purpose
	Insert WordArt	Opens the WordArt Gallery dialog box for a new WordArt object.
Edit Text...	WordArt Edit Text	Reopens the Edit WordArt Text dialog box (refer to Figure 8.19).
	WordArt Gallery	Reopens the WordArt Gallery dialog box for the existing WordArt object.
	Format WordArt	Opens the Format WordArt dialog box, where you can change the lines and colors used. (The tabbed sections are the same as the ones in the Format Picture dialog box.)
	WordArt Shape	Opens a pop-up array of shapes you can choose to have your WordArt conform to.
	Free Rotate	Enables you to rotate the WordArt (works the same way as the Free Rotate tool on the Drawing toolbar).
	WordArt Same Letter	Makes all the letters the same height Heights.
	WordArt Vertical Text	Toggles between vertical and horizontal text orientation.
	WordArt Alignment	Opens a shortcut menu of text alignments (centered, left aligned, and so on).
	WordArt Character Spacing	Changes the spacing between letters.

To edit a piece of WordArt, double-click on it. This displays the WordArt toolbar (if it isn't visible already) and the Edit WordArt Text dialog box. When you are done making changes to the WordArt, click outside it to deselect it. Like any other drawn object, you can drag it around on the slide to reposition it, or resize it using the selection handles in the corners.

Summary

In this chapter, you learned the ins and outs of graphics in PowerPoint: how to import them, manipulate them, and even create your own from scratch. In the next chapter, you'll build on the knowledge from this and the preceding chapter to learn more things you can do with objects on a slide.

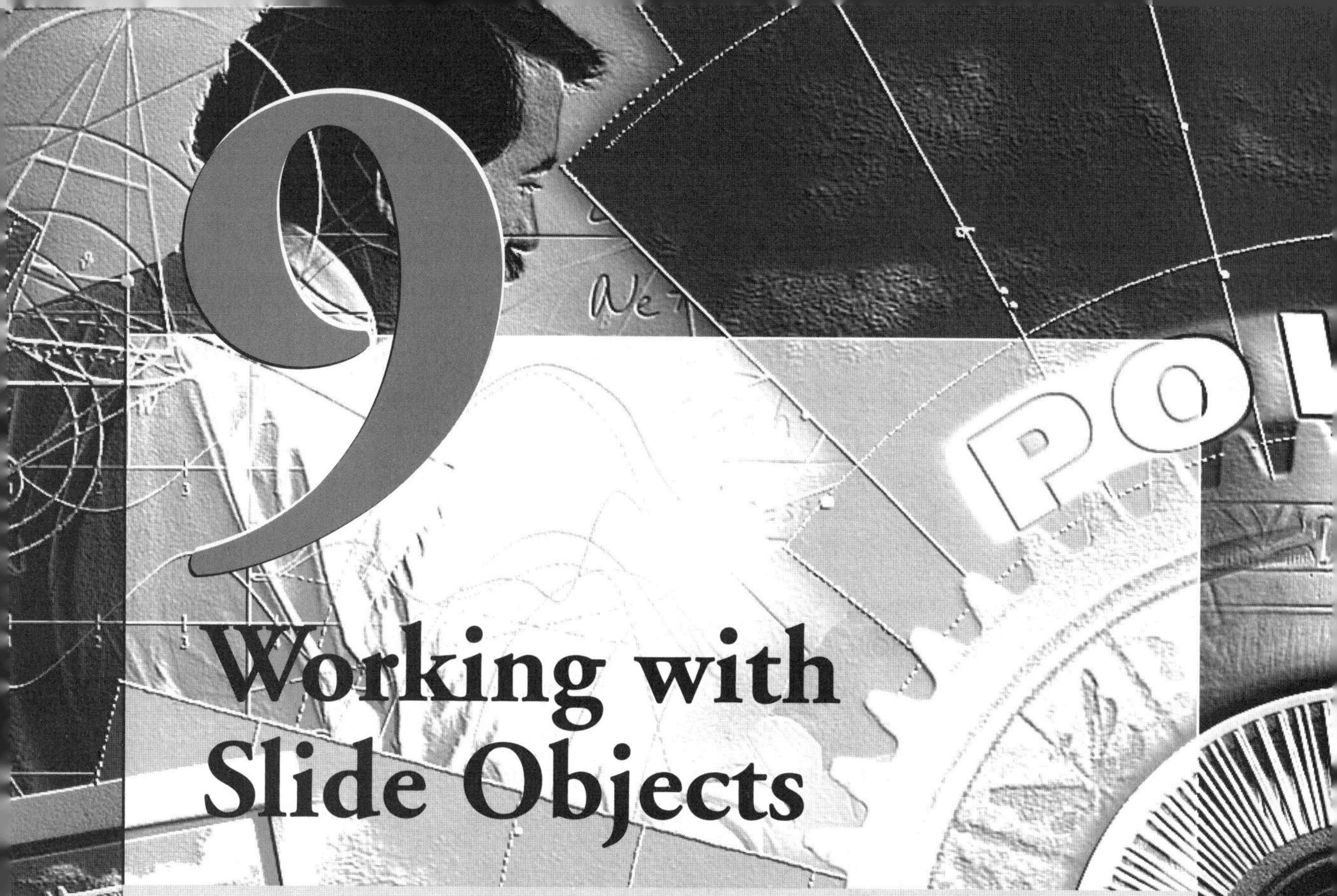

9

Working with Slide Objects

In This Chapter

- The Properties All Objects Share
- Multiple Objects and Layers
- Grouping and Ungrouping
- Adding Effects to Objects
- Copying Another Object's Formatting

Well, in the preceding two chapters, you learned about two types of objects: text and graphics. This chapter is a collection of information about objects in general. Unless I specifically note otherwise, everything you'll learn in this chapter applies both to text and graphic objects, as well as such specialized objects as graphs, sound and video files, and organizational charts that you'll learn about later in the book.

Refresher: Everything Is an Object!

Everything on a slide is an object. Have you internalized this fact yet? I hope so. That means that everything on a slide sits in its own box, and each box can be moved and sized independently. In the last two chapters, you saw that text sits in a box, and so do graphics. Here's a fairly comprehensive list of things that can be objects on slides, and the chapters in which you learn about them:

- Text boxes (Chapter 7)
- Imported pictures (Chapter 8)
- WordArt (Chapter 8)
- Lines and shapes you draw with the Drawing toolbar (Chapter 8)
- Clip art (Chapter 8)
- Charts that plot data graphically (Chapter 10)
- Organizational charts (Chapter 11)
- Imported objects from other programs (Chapter 12)
- Sound file icons (Chapter 13)
- Video clips (Chapter 13)
- CD audio tracks (Chapter 13)
- Hyperlinks (Chapter 15)

Selecting Objects

No matter what type of object you're dealing with, you select it in the same way: just click on it with the mouse. Handles appear around it (white squares), as shown in Figure 9.1.

You have learned about selecting single objects already, in earlier chapters, but now go one step further and select multiple objects. For example, suppose you have several shapes that you've drawn, and you want to select them as a group so you can move them. Try out the following Hands On to do just that.

Note

When one object is selected, you can shift the selection to other objects on the slide by pressing Tab. Each time you press Tab (or Shift+Tab to go backward) a different object is selected.

Figure 9.1
All objects show handles when they are selected.

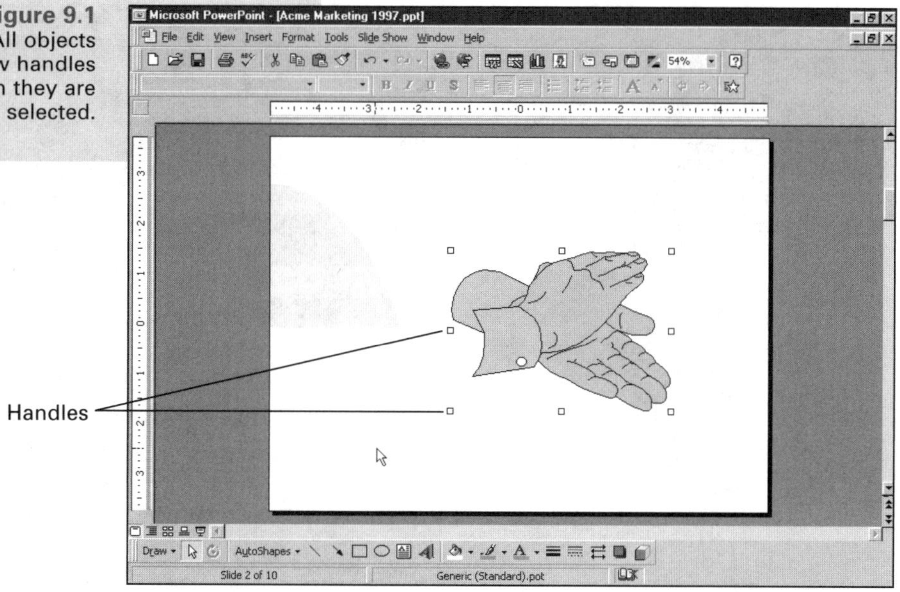

You learned to draw shapes in Chapter 8.

Hands On: Selecting Multiple Objects

1. Start with a new, blank slide. (Click on the New Slide button, click on the blank AutoLayout, and click on OK.)
2. Draw several shapes on the slide using the Drawing toolbar.
3. With your mouse pointer, drag a box that completely encompasses all the shapes, as shown in Figure 9.2.
4. Release the mouse button. All the objects that fell into that box are selected (see Figure 9.3).
5. Click away from the objects to deselect them. Now you can learn another way to select objects.
6. Click on the first object you want to select.
7. Hold down the Ctrl key and click on another object. It becomes selected too.
8. Keep holding down Ctrl and clicking on objects until you have selected all the objects that you want.
9. Release the Ctrl key.
10. Click away from the objects to deselect them.

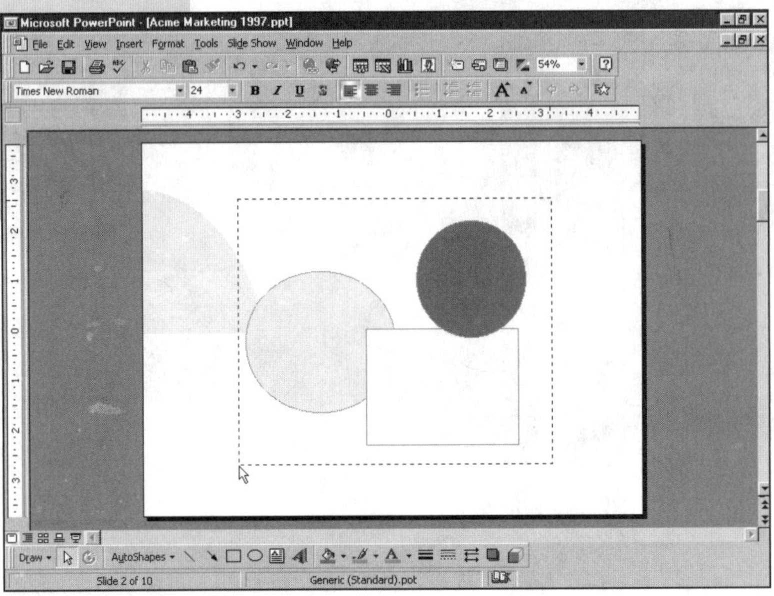

Figure 9.2 Hold down the mouse button and drag a box that includes all the shapes you want to select.

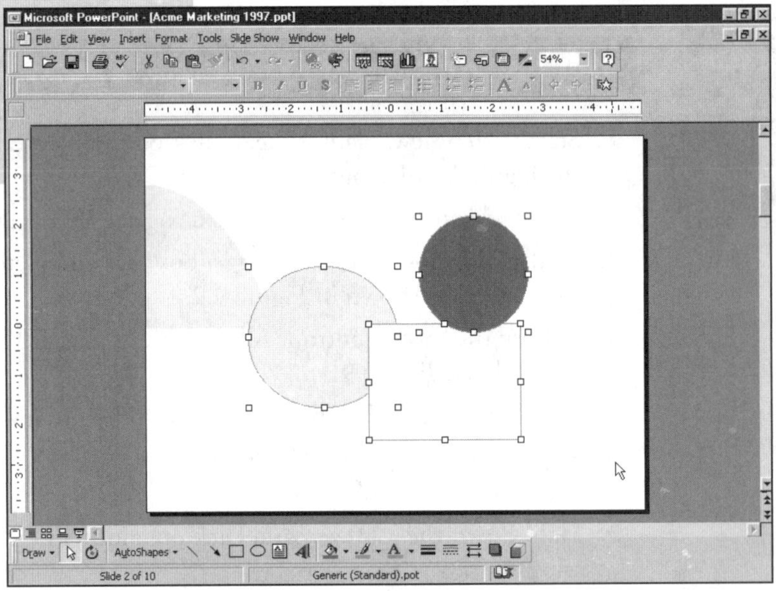

Figure 9.3 All selected shapes have their own selection handles.

Don't delete these shapes yet; you'll use them in another Hands On procedure in this chapter.

Moving, Resizing, and Copying Objects

This information may be a review for you if you followed along with the last two chapters. But go over it one more time, because it's such important stuff. All objects can be moved, resized, and copied using the same procedures.

Resizing an Object

You have already learned how to resize text and graphic boxes in earlier chapters, and other objects work the same way. Just drag one of the object's handles. To resize both dimensions at once, drag a corner handle. To maintain the object's perspective (the ratio of height to width), hold down the Shift key as you resize.

Moving an Object

Objects are not stationary—you can move them anywhere you want. There are two ways to move an object, depending on where you want to move it:

- To move an object on a slide, drag it with the mouse. Just position the mouse pointer over any part of the object except a handle, so that the mouse pointer changes to a 4-headed arrow, and then drag the object to a new location.
- To move an object to a different slide, use the Cut command. Just select the object and then press Ctrl+X or click on the Cut button on the toolbar. Then view the destination slide and press Ctrl+V or click on the Paste button on the toolbar.

Copying an Object

There are many reasons why you might need to copy an object. You might want to copy an object to repeat on several slides in a series. Or, you might want to copy some text many times on the same slide, for an unusual visual effect, as in Figure 9.4.

Note

If you want an object to appear at the same spot on every slide in the presentation, add the object to the Slide Master rather than trying to copy it onto every slide.

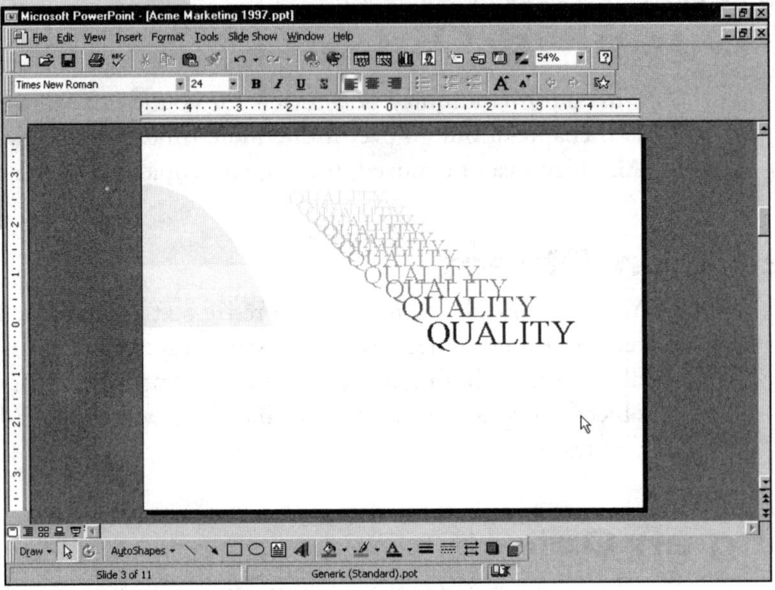

Figure 9.4 Copying this text box and formatting the text in different ways produced this graphical effect.

To copy an object, follow these steps:

1. Select the object(s) that you want to copy.
2. Press Ctrl+C or click on the Copy button on the Standard toolbar.
3. If you want the object(s) to be copied to a different slide, display that slide.
4. Press Ctrl+V or click on the Paste button on the Standard toolbar.

If you copy onto the same slide, the copy appears slightly below and to the right of the original. Pasted copies are selected by default, so you are ready to reposition them as needed.

Working with Object Layers

As you can see from the overlapping shapes in Figures 9.1 through 9.3, objects can be placed on top of one another. This can be really handy, because it means you can stack a text box over a shape, or a piece of clip art over a graph, or anything else you want.

Note

If you stack one object over the other, the top object covers up the one underneath unless you have the top object's background set to None. To do that, right-click on the object and select Format from the shortcut menu that appears. (The actual name of the Format command varies with the type of object; it might be Format Text Box, for example.) Then on the Colors and Lines tab, open the Color drop-down list and choose No Fill.

When you have a stack of objects, you need a way of reordering them in the stack so that the appropriate object is on top. By default, objects "stack" in the order that you create them, but that is not always the order that you want. That's why PowerPoint provides an Order command that enables you to rearrange the order of stacked objects.

Use the following Hands On to explore the Order command with the shapes you drew earlier in the chapter.

Hands On: Rearranging Objects in a Stack

1. Move all of your shapes into a single stack on the slide. (Drag them where you want them.)
2. Click on the top object in the stack.
3. Open the Draw menu on the Drawing toolbar.
4. Point to Order. A submenu appears (see Figure 9.5).
5. Choose Send to Back. The top object is now at the bottom of the stack.
6. Click on the object that is now at the top of the stack.
7. Open the Draw menu again, then select Order, Send Backward. The top object moves down one spot in the pile.
8. Experiment with the commands on the Order menu until you are confident with all of them.

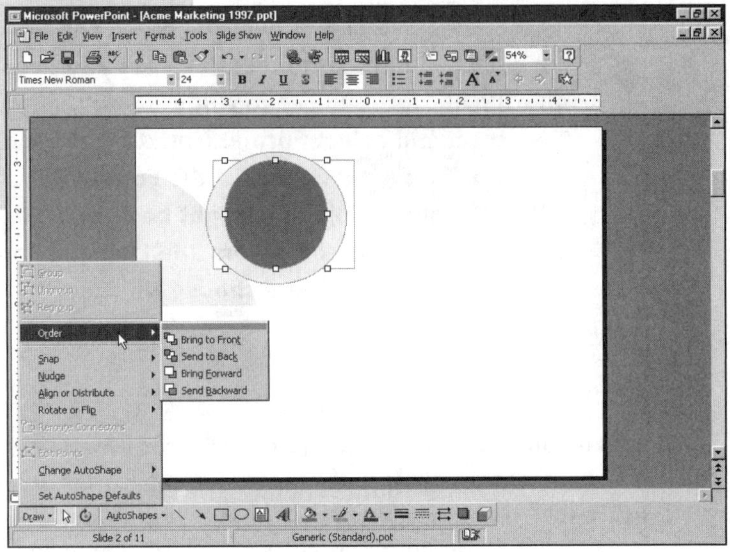

Figure 9.5 Use the Order submenu's commands to rearrange objects in a stack.

Grouping and Ungrouping

Earlier in this chapter you saw how to select multiple objects at once and work with them as a unit. For example, you might want to select several shapes together that together form a picture.

If these objects are always going to be considered a single unit, you can save yourself some time by grouping them together. When you group two or more objects, those objects become a single object for the purposes of moving and resizing. You can always ungroup them later if you need to work with the objects separately.

In the following Hands On, you'll group your stack of shapes from the preceding section.

Hands On: Grouping Objects

1. Select all the objects that will be grouped together. (Remember, drag a box around the whole cluster to select them all at once.)
2. Open the Draw menu on the Drawing toolbar and choose Group. The objects are now a single object. You can tell because there is only one object frame, with one set of handles, around them now.

3. To ungroup, normally you have to select the object to ungroup first. However, in this case the object is still selected from step 2, so you don't need to do anything to reselect.
4. Select Draw, Ungroup. The objects are once again separate.

Framing an Object

You may want to place a *border*, or frame, around an object to accentuate it. Many beginners make the mistake of placing a drawn rectangle around an object when they want a border around it (a frame). This works, but it is terribly inefficient. Because the rectangle and the object it frames are two separate objects, they move separately, so when you resize or move the object, the rectangle has to be moved and resized separately. (Sure, you could group them, but that would be still another step.)

A much easier way to put a frame around an object is to simply turn on the object's Line attribute. For drawn shapes, the line clings to the shape itself and it looks like someone has taken a pencil and outlined the shape. For text and graphic boxes, the line runs around the outer edge of the object frame, in the same area as the selection handles appear. Figure 9.6 shows some examples of lines around various types of objects.

Figure 9.6 Different object types use frames differently.

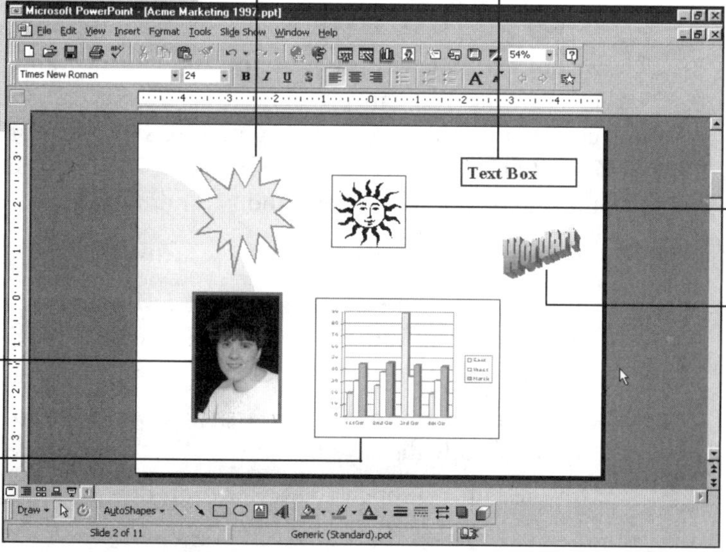

To frame an object, follow these steps:

1. Right-click on the object and choose Format from the shortcut menu. The command varies depending on the object type (for example, Format AutoShape or Format Text Box).
2. In the Format box that appears, click on the Colors and Lines tab if it is not already displayed.
3. In the Line area, open the Color drop-down list and choose a line color.
4. If you want the line to be dashed rather than solid, open the Dashed drop-down list and choose a dash style. (The default is a solid line.)
5. Open the Style drop-down list and choose a line style.
6. If you want to change the weight of the line, open the Weight drop-down list and choose a different weight. (Different styles have different default weights.)
7. Click on OK. The frame appears around the object.

Adding Effects to Objects

Once you have an object on the slide, you may want to dress it up with a background or another special effect. In the following sections, you'll learn about some of your options.

Adding a Decorative Fill

Here's another review session, as you have learned about background fills in earlier chapters. You can place any background color or texture behind any object, not just the text and graphic boxes you've worked with in previous chapters. (The only exception is WordArt; when you add a fill to WordArt it fills the letters, not the background behind them.)

To add a fill to any object, follow these steps:

1. Right-click on the object and choose Format from the shortcut menu. The command varies depending on the object type (for example, Format AutoShape or Format Text Box).
2. In the Format box that appears, click on the Colors and Lines tab if it is not already displayed.
3. In the Fill area, open the Color drop-down list (see Figure 9.7).

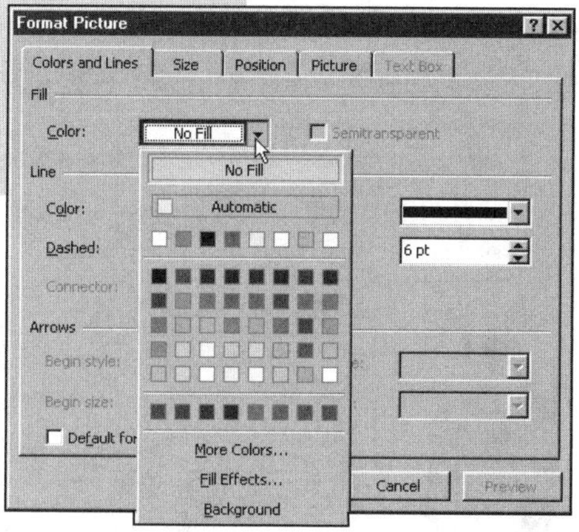

Figure 9.7 You can choose among many background types.

For more information about background colors and textures, see Chapters 7 and 8.

4. Choose a color, or choose one of the following:

   No Fill. Sets the background to transparent.

   Automatic. Allows the slide color scheme to decide the color.

   More Colors. Opens a Colors dialog box where you can choose from a full spectrum of colors.

   Fill Effects. Opens the Fill Effects dialog box, where you can choose all sorts of interesting textures and patterns for the fill.

   Background. Sets the color of the background to the same as the slide's background.

5. Click on OK. The background is applied to the object.

Note

Choosing Background is different from choosing No Fill, which makes the object's background transparent. If you choose Background, the object has an opaque background that matches the slide's background. If you change the slide's background, the color in the object box changes too.

Adding Shadows

In Chapter 8, you learned about applying effects to drawn objects. But did you know that you can apply effects to any object? Figure 9.8 shows shadows applied to the variety of objects you saw earlier.

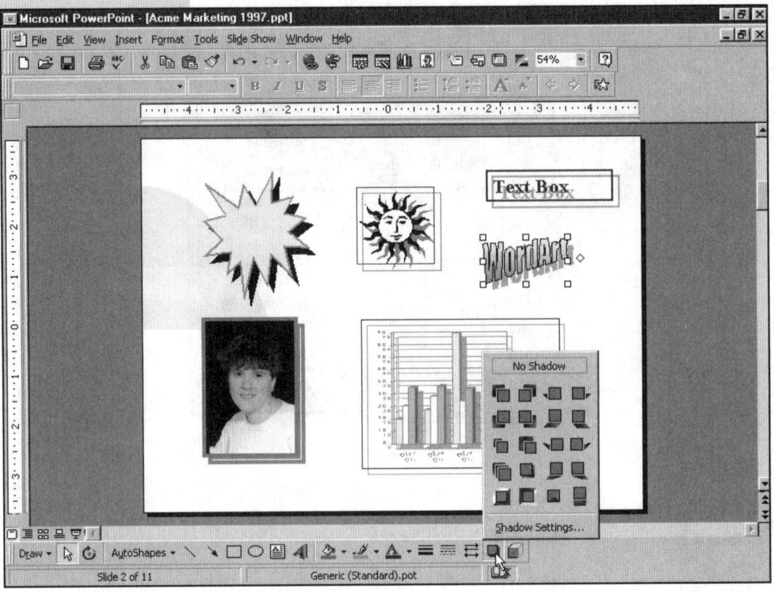

Figure 9.8 Almost any object can have a shadow.

As you can see in Figure 9.8, different object types use the shadow differently.

- WordArt and AutoShapes apply the shadow directly to the object. The shadow clings to the actual object.
- Other objects apply the shadow both to the frame itself and to what's in the frame if the background fill is set to No Fill. (You can see this with the text box and the graph in Figure 9.8).
- If an object has a background fill (even if it is the same as the color of the slide), the shadow applies only to the outer frame of the object. You can see this in the clip art and the photo in Figure 9.8.

To apply a shadow to an object, follow these steps:

1. Click on the object.
2. Click on the Shadow button on the Drawing toolbar. A shortcut menu appears (see Figure 9.9).
3. Click on the button for the type of shadow. Or, to turn a shadow off, choose No Shadow.

Besides the simple buttons on the Shadow shortcut menu, there are several more sophisticated shadow controls. To see them, choose Shadow Settings from the shortcut menu. A Shadow Settings toolbar appears containing controls that help you fine-tune the shadow. See Table 9.1 for an explanation of them.

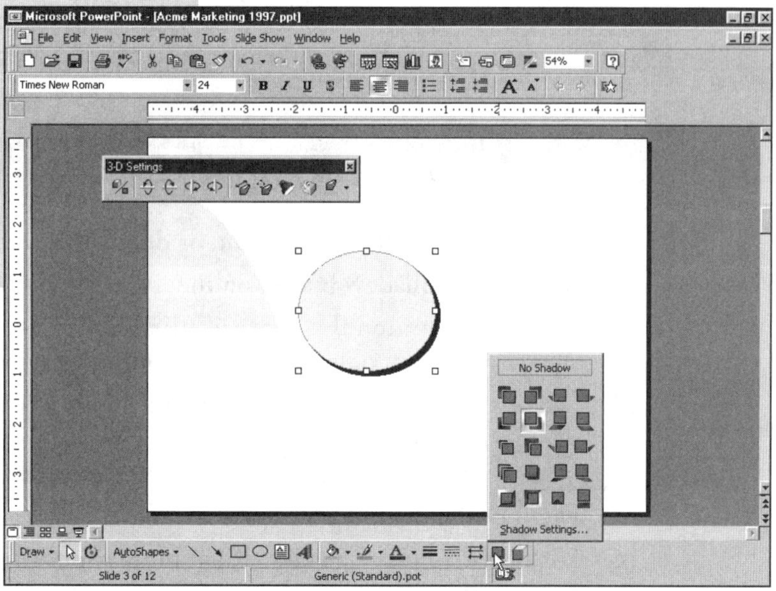

Figure 9.9
The buttons on this shortcut menu show different types of shadows you can apply.

Table 9.1 Buttons on the Shadow Settings toolbar

Button	Name	Description
	Shadow On/Off	Toggles the shadow on and off
	Nudge Shadow Up	Moves the shadow up slightly
	Nudge Shadow Down	Moves the shadow down slightly
	Nudge Shadow Left	Moves the shadow to the left slightly
	Nudge Shadow Right	Moves the shadow to the right slightly
	Shadow Color	Opens a drop-down list where you can select a different color for the shadow

Once you get a basic shadow applied to an object, the Nudge buttons on the Shadow Settings toolbar can help you increase or decrease the height and width of the shadow. Try the following Hands On exercise to fine-tune a shadow.

Hands On: Working with Shadows

1. Select a shape that you've drawn, or draw a new one.
2. Click on the Shadow button on the Drawing toolbar.
3. Click on the button that looks like a shadow appearing in the lower-right corner of an object. Your object now has a basic shadow.
4. Click on the Shadow button again and click on Shadow Settings. The Shadow Settings toolbar appears.
5. Click on the Nudge Shadow Down button four times to increase the length of the shadow.
6. Click on the Nudge Shadow Right button four times to increase the width of the shadow.
7. Click away from the shape to deselect it. Notice how this makes your object look further from the slide? Mine is shown in Figure 9.10.
8. Click on the shape again to reselect it.

Figure 9.10 A simple lower-right corner shadow makes the object look further away.

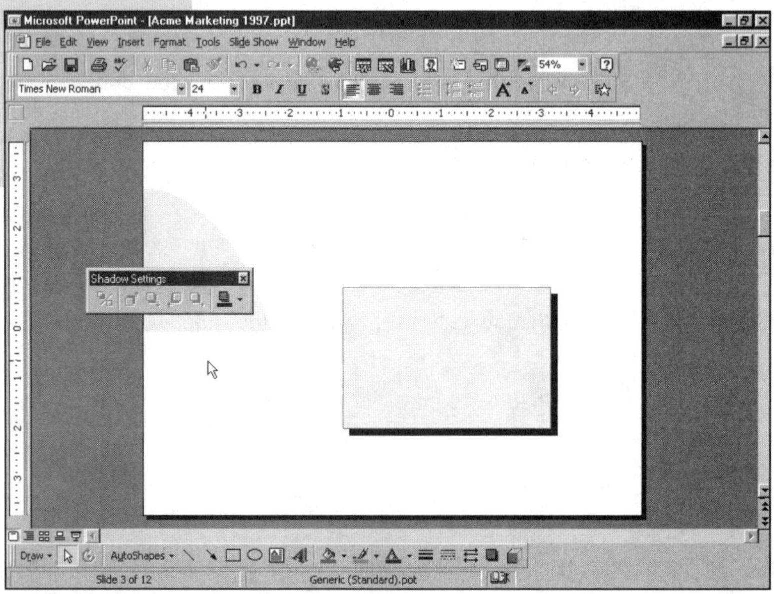

Colors that are lighter than the slide background do not look good as shadows.

9. Open the Shadow Color drop-down list on the Shadow Settings toolbar and choose a lighter color for the shadow.

Adding 3-D Effects to an Object

3-D effects make an object look like it has "sides," like it's ready to jump off the page. You saw 3-D at work with your WordArt in Chapter 8, but it also works with most other objects too.

To apply a 3-D effect to an object, follow these steps:

1. Click on the object.
2. Click on the 3-D button on the Drawing toolbar. A shortcut menu appears (see Figure 9.11).
3. Click on the button for the type of 3-D effect you want. Or, to turn the 3-D effect off, choose No 3-D.

Figure 9.11 Choose the 3-D appearance that you want from this shortcut menu.

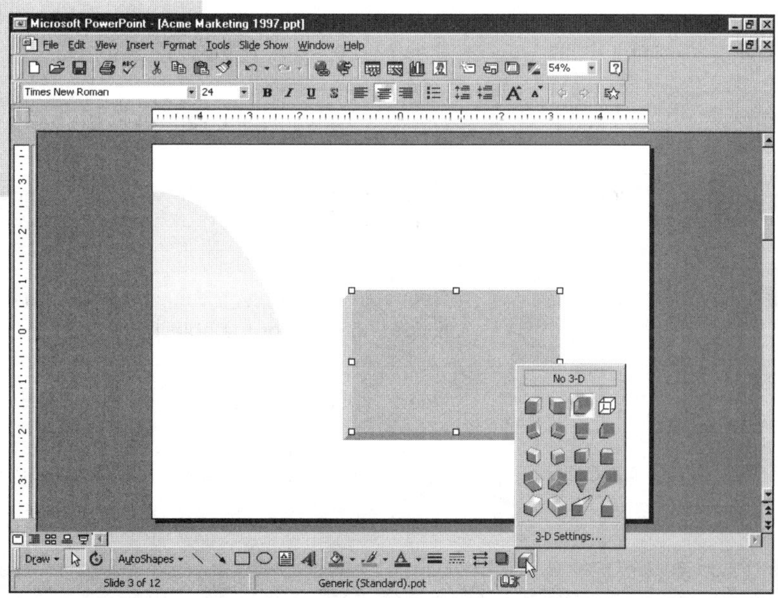

Note

You cannot apply both a shadow and a 3-D effect to the same object. When you apply one, the other disappears.

There is also a special toolbar for 3-D effects, which you can display by choosing 3-D Settings from the shortcut menu in Figure 9.11. Table 9.2 describes the buttons on the toolbar.

Table 9.2 Buttons on the 3-D Settings toolbar

Button	Name	Description
	3-D On/Off	Toggles the 3-D effect on and off
	Tilt Down	Rotates the shape down slightly
	Tilt Up	Rotates the shape up slightly
	Tilt Left	Rotates the shape to the left slightly
	Tilt Right	Rotates the shape to the right slightly
	Depth	Opens a list where you can select the depth of the 3-D effect
	Direction	Opens a list where you can select the direction of the 3-D effect
	Lighting	Opens a list where you can choose where the "light" is coming from for the object shading
	Surface	Opens a list of surface types for the object
	3-D Color	Opens a list of colors for the 3-D sides of the object

In the following Hands On, try out these 3-D controls on one of your drawn shapes. You can use 3-D effects with any kind of object, but they are usually the most dramatic and look the best on drawn objects.

Hands On: Applying 3-D Effects to an Object

In the following steps, you'll use the Drawing toolbar and the 3-D effects to create what looks like a round piece of wood.

1. On a blank slide, draw a circle. (Use the Oval tool on the Drawing toolbar.)
2. Click on the 3-D button on the Drawing toolbar.
3. Click on the button that looks like a 3-D box starting at the front and running to the top and left. Your object now has a basic 3-D effect, as shown in Figure 9.12.
4. Click on the 3-D button again and click on 3-D Settings. The 3-D Settings toolbar appears.
5. Click on the Tilt Down button repeatedly until it becomes grayed out. This rotates the shape, as shown in Figure 9.13. (When you do this later on your own you also can use the Tilt Up, Tilt Left, and/or Tilt Right buttons.)

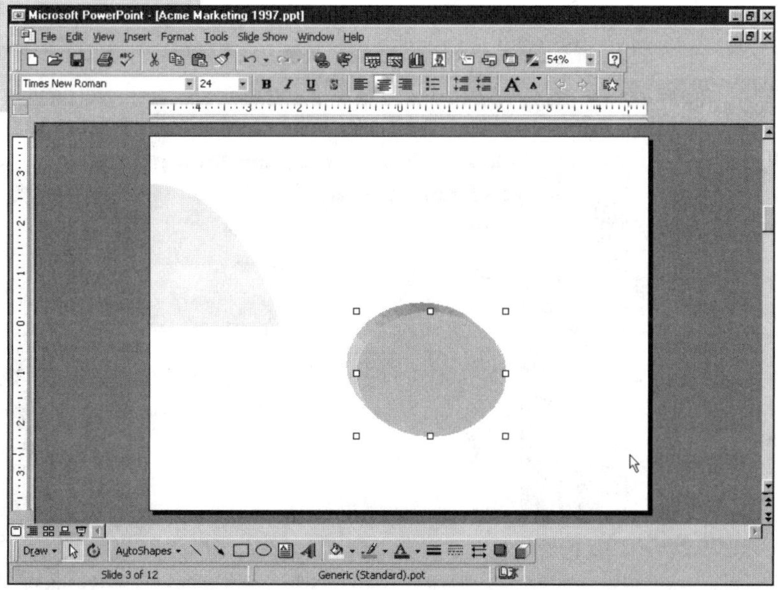

Figure 9.12 Your basic 3-D shape is created.

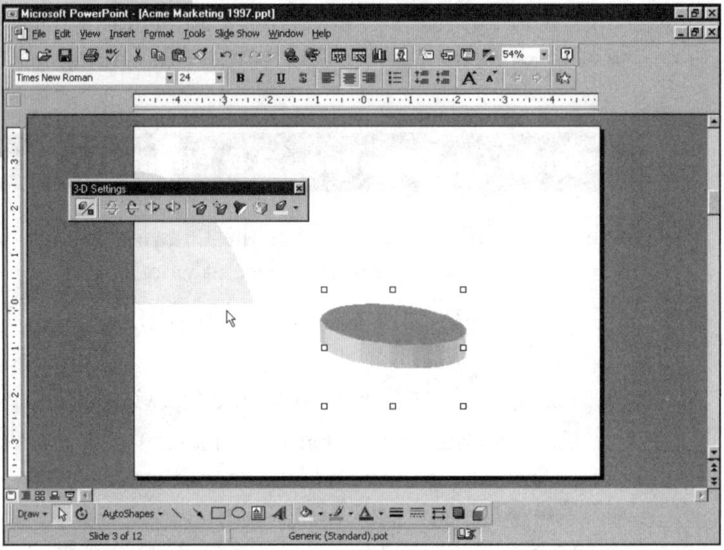

Figure 9.13 I tilted the shape until it looks almost like a platform.

6. Click on the Depth button, and then click on 144 pt. This makes the 3-D portion of the shape much taller.
7. Click on the Direction button and choose the middle direction icon in the bottom row. Now your shape's 3-D effect is facing straight toward you, as shown in Figure 9.14.

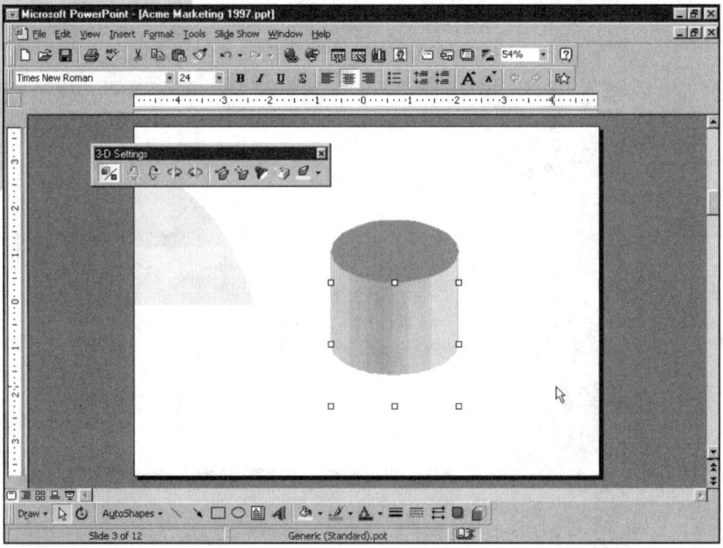

Figure 9.14 The "platform" is much taller now and it's facing straight forward.

8. Click on the Lighting button, and click on the lamp in the upper-right corner.
9. Click on the Lighting button again, and click on Normal.
10. Now add a texture to the front (now the top) of the shape. In the Drawing toolbar, open the Fill Color drop-down list and choose Fill Effects.
11. Click on the Texture tab, and choose Oak.
12. Click on OK. Now the flat part of the shape has an oak veneer. Notice that the 3-D portion of the shape is untouched by the texture.
13. Back on the 3-D Settings toolbar, open the Shadow Color drop-down list and click on More 3-D Colors.
14. Click on the Standard tab, and click on a light peach color.
15. Click on OK. Now the shading in the 3-D portion matches the oak veneer, as shown in Figure 9.15.

Copying Another Object's Formatting

You're going to love this feature! All of the Microsoft Office products come with a feature called Format Painter that helps you copy the formatting from one object to another. This saves you the trouble of repeating multiple steps.

Figure 9.15 Here's the finished product—a cylinder that looks like wood.

For example, you could apply the 3-D formatting that you did in the preceding hands-on to another shape. (Format Painter works with all kinds of objects, including text, but because you've already got a drawn shape on the screen from the last example, go ahead and use it.)

Follow these steps to copy formatting:

1. Create the new object that is going to receive the formatting, if it isn't already created. For example, you could draw a square or another circle to try it out with the shape you ended up with in the preceding steps.
2. Select the object that already contains the correct formatting.
3. Click on the Format Painter button on the Standard toolbar. (It looks like a paint brush).
4. Click on the object to receive the formatting. The formatting is immediately applied. That's it!

To make the Format Painter stay activated to paint more than one object, double-click on it.

Summary

In this chapter, you learned some of the finer points of working with objects. Combined with the information you learned in Chapters 7 and 8, you are now ready to go out there and conquer the wide world of PowerPoint objects!

10

Placing Charts on a Slide

In This Chapter

- Inserting a Chart into Your Presentation
- Changing the Numbers on the Datasheet
- Modifying the Data Series
- Changing the Chart Type
- Adding Legends and Data Tables
- Dressing up the Chart's Appearance

Often when you're giving a presentation, it's to explain some number-crunching that you or someone else has done. Charts work great for explaining numbers. They're colorful and visual, and they keep your audience's eyes from glazing over with endless rows and columns of numbers. In this chapter, you'll learn how to create charts in PowerPoint.

Introducing Microsoft Graph

Microsoft Graph is a mini-program that's built into PowerPoint. You may have worked with it in other Office applications, like Word; if so, this section will be easy for you to cruise through. It helps you create good-looking charts.

To start it up:

1. In Slide view, display the slide that you want to put the chart upon.
2. Click on the Insert Chart button on the Standard toolbar. A sample chart appears on your slide, and a datasheet and a lot of new toolbar buttons appear (see Figure 10.1).

Note

Yes, I know, the program is called Microsoft Graph, not Microsoft Chart, but Microsoft has always been somewhat fuzzy on whether they're going to call the darned things charts or graphs.)

Tip

If you choose an AutoLayout from the New Slide dialog box that has a chart on it, you can double-click that chart icon on the slide to open Microsoft Graph.

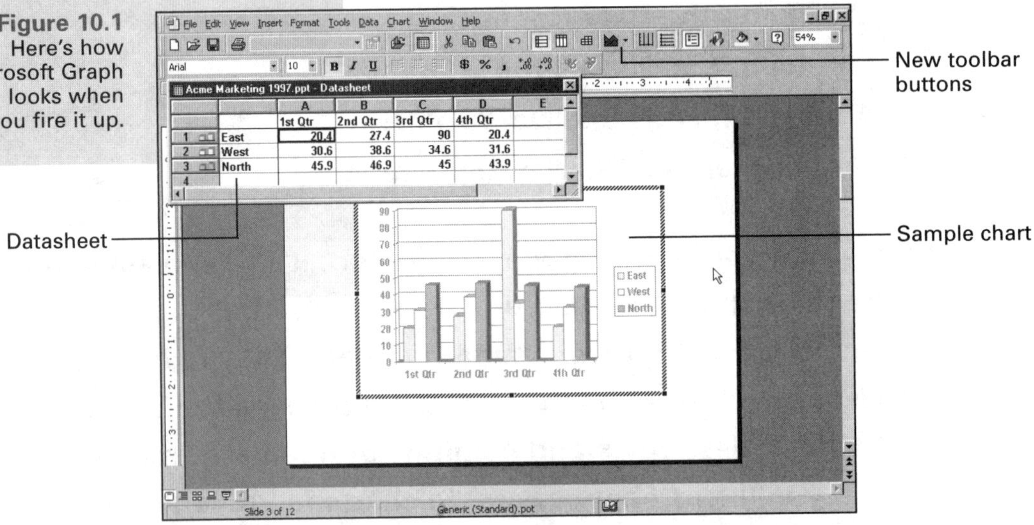

Figure 10.1 Here's how Microsoft Graph looks when you fire it up.

Data is arranged in *series*; in Figure 10.1, the quarters are the series (1st, 2nd, and so on). Notice how these translate into the chart. The row and column headings determine the labels on the chart's bars.

Just jump right in! The first thing you need to do is change the data on the datasheet to match what you want to display on your chart. Go ahead and work on your own on this, or if you don't have any data handy, use the following Hands On to create some sample data that you can use in the examples in the rest of the chapter.

Hands On: Modifying the Datasheet

1. Replace the regions with real people's names. On the datasheet, click on the word East, and type **Mary**.
2. Click on the word West, and type **Bob**.
3. Click on the word North and type **Jeff**.
4. Add another person. Click in the cell under **Jeff**, type **Roy**.
5. Now delete a column. Click on the letter D, highlighting the entire D column, and press the Delete key.
6. Replace the headings 1st Qtr, 2nd Qtr, and 3rd Qtr with the words **January**, **February**, and **March.**
7. Time to assign our own numbers. In Mary's row, enter **35**, **42**, and **32**, replacing the numbers that are there.
8. In Bob's row, enter **26**, **22**, and **28**, replacing the numbers that are there.
9. In Jeff's row, enter **30**, **38**, and **30**, replacing the numbers that are there.
10. In Roy's row, enter **22**, **28**, and **24**. (You're not replacing anything because Roy is new.)

Notice that as you make changes to the datasheet, the chart behind it changes too. If you entered the numbers exactly as directed in these steps, your screen should look like Figure 10.2.

Note

When Microsoft Graph is running, the datasheet is usually displayed. If you need to modify the datasheet later but don't see it, click on the View Datasheet button, pointed out in Figure 10.2.

Figure 10.2
Congratulations, you've just created a chart!

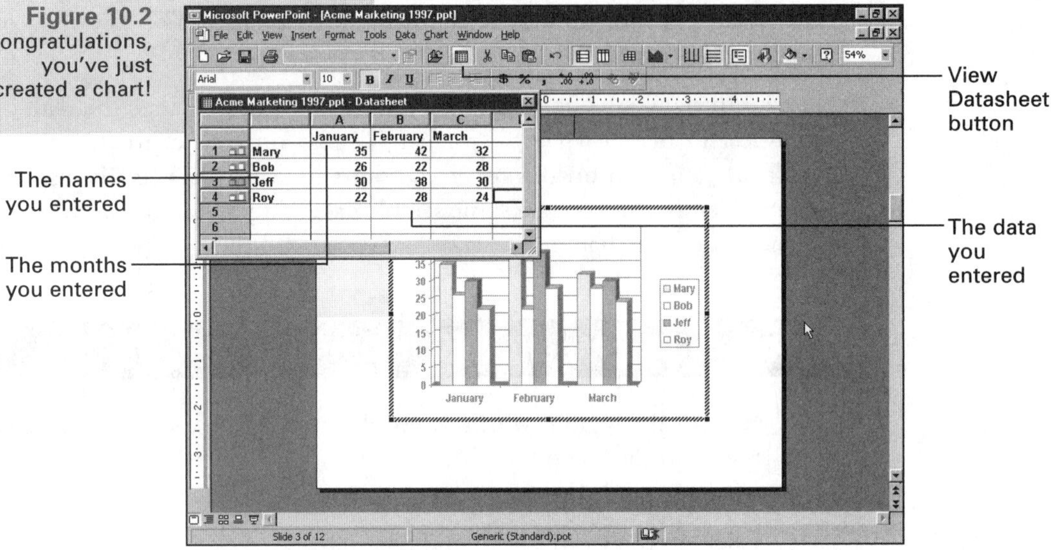

You can add or delete rows and columns just by typing in them or deleting what's there. Use as many or as few as you need to convey your information.

Switching Between the Presentation and Microsoft Graph

Chapter 9 discussed moving and resizing objects.

If you need to get back to the main presentation, just click on the slide outside of the chart frame. Boom, you're back, and your old toolbars return as usual. The data sheet goes away, and your chart is just another object on the slide. You can click on the chart to select it, and then move it or resize it like any other object.

To edit the chart some more, double-click on it to reopen Microsoft Graph.

Changing the Chart Type

You're not stuck with the default column chart shown in Figure 10.2; there are lots of chart types to choose from. Not all of them will be appropriate for your data, of course, but you may be surprised at the different spin on the message that a different chart type presents.

Tip

Many chart types are offered in 2-D or 3-D models. You choose which look is most appropriate for your presentation. Try to be consistent, though. It looks nicer to stick with all 2-D or all 3-D rather than mixing the types in a presentation.

Here are some of the chart types offered:

- *Bar and Column charts.* You already saw this kind in Figure 10.2. You can have them running vertically, as shown there (column), or horizontally (bar).
- *Area and surface charts.* These convey the same information as vertical bar charts, but the area between the bars is filled in.
- *Line charts.* Again, these convey the same information as bar charts, but instead of the bars, a line or ribbon runs where the tops of the bars would be.
- *3-D Cones, Cylinders, and Pyramids.* These are just like bar charts except the bars have different, more interesting shapes.
- *Pie and Doughnut charts.* These are very different; they show how various parts relate to the whole rather than showcasing individual values.
- *Bubble and Scatter charts.* These show each bit of data as a point (or a bubble) on a grid. These are useful for spotting trends among lots of data points.
- *Radar chart.* This is a special-purpose chart that plots points on axes radiating out from a center point. Most business presenters never use it.

Figures 10.3 through 10.5 show some examples of these chart types.

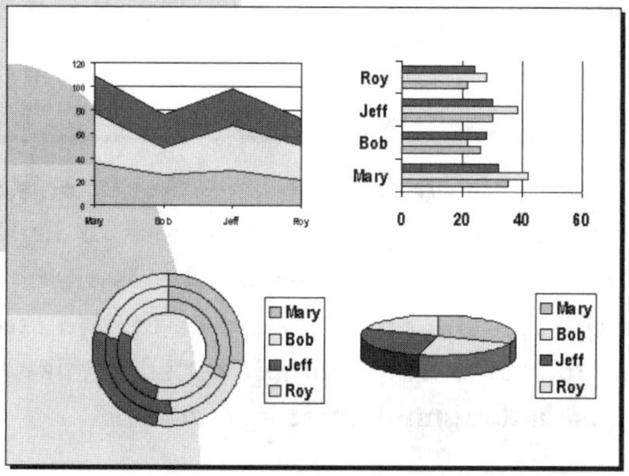

Figure 10.3 (Clockwise from upper-left) Area chart, Bar chart, 3-D Pie chart, and Doughnut chart.

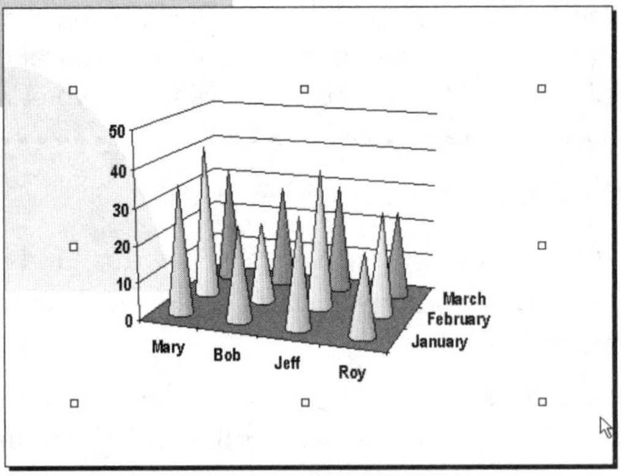

Figure 10.4
A Cone chart.

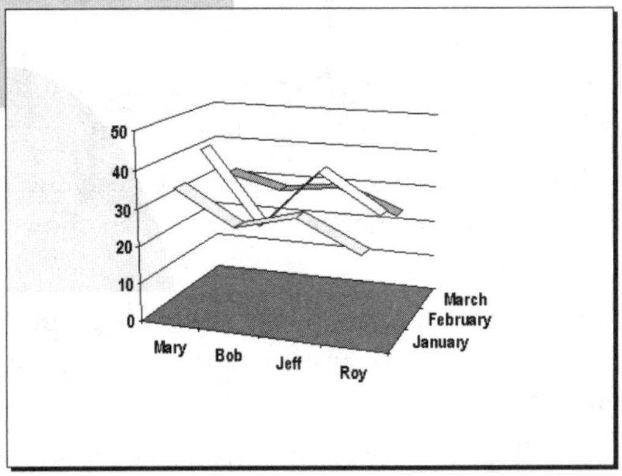

Figure 10.5
A 3-D Line chart.

To change the chart type, follow these steps:

1. If you are not already in Microsoft Graph (with the Microsoft Graph toolbar buttons showing), double-click on the chart.
2. Open the Chart Type drop-down list and click on a different chart type (see Figure 10.6).

Pie charts take only one data series—that is, only one row or one column. Notice that the pie chart in Figure 10.3 shows data for only one month, the first one. Be careful when switching from any other chart to a pie that you do not lose data that you need. If you need to keep all your data from multiple series but like the pie chart message, use a doughnut chart instead.

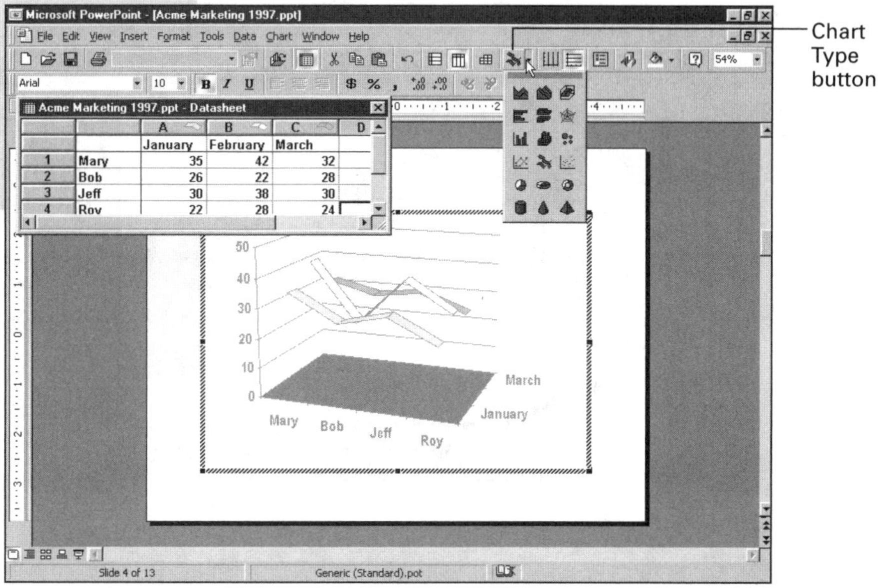

Figure 10.6 The easiest way to change the chart type is to choose a chart type from the toolbar.

Plotting Data in Rows Versus Columns

By default, the rows of the datasheet form the data series. In the figures that you've seen so far, the people's names are the series. But if you want, you can switch that around, so, for example, the months would be the series. Figures 10.7 and 10.8 show the same chart plotted both ways, so you can see the difference.

To switch back and forth between using rows and columns, click on the By Row or By Column buttons on the Standard toolbar.

Note

What does it mean when I say something is "the series"? Take a look at Figures 10.7 and 10.8. Notice that there is a legend next to each chart that shows what each color (or shade of gray) represents. Each of those colors, and the label associated with it, is a series. The other variable (the one that is not the series) is plotted on the chart's horizontal (x) axis.

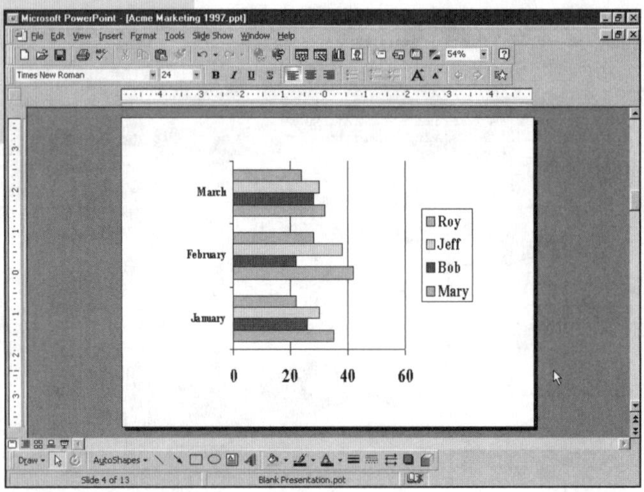

Figure 10.7 The data series are the people's names.

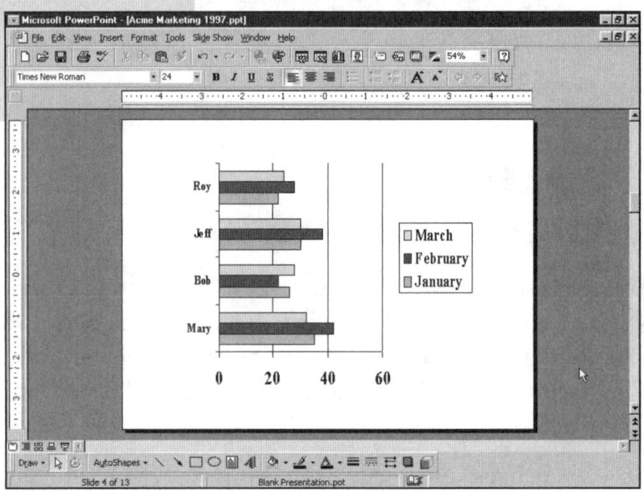

Figure 10.8 The data series are the months.

So why would you care about this? Because a chart carries very different messages when arranged by rows versus by columns. For example, take a look at Figure 10.7. This chart compares the performance of the people against one another for each month. The message here is competition—which person did the best? Contrast this to Figure 10.8, in which the series are the months. Here, you're invited to compare one month to another. The overriding message here is time—which was each person's best month? It's easy to see how the exact same data can convey very different messages; make sure that you pick the arrangement that tells the story you want to tell.

Data Tables and Legends

Sometimes the chart tells the full story that you want to tell, but other times the audience may benefit from seeing the actual numbers that the chart is built from. In those cases, it's good to include the data table with the chart.

To do so, click on the Data Table button in Microsoft Graph. Figure 10.9 shows a chart with its data table displayed.

You can do the same thing for the legend, which is like a data table with no data! A legend just lists the data series in use and shows a little colored block that indicates which colored bars or shapes represent that series. You've seen these in some of the charts you've looked at earlier in this chapter.

To turn on/off the legend, just click on the Legend button on the toolbar (refer to Figure 10.9).

Note

Sometimes Microsoft Graph doesn't do a very good job of sizing the fonts in the data table appropriately. If the data table's fonts look too big, you can adjust them. Just right-click on the data table and choose Format Data Table. Then on the Fonts tab of the dialog box that appears, choose a different font size.

Figure 10.9 Sometimes the data table can help your audience understand the chart better.

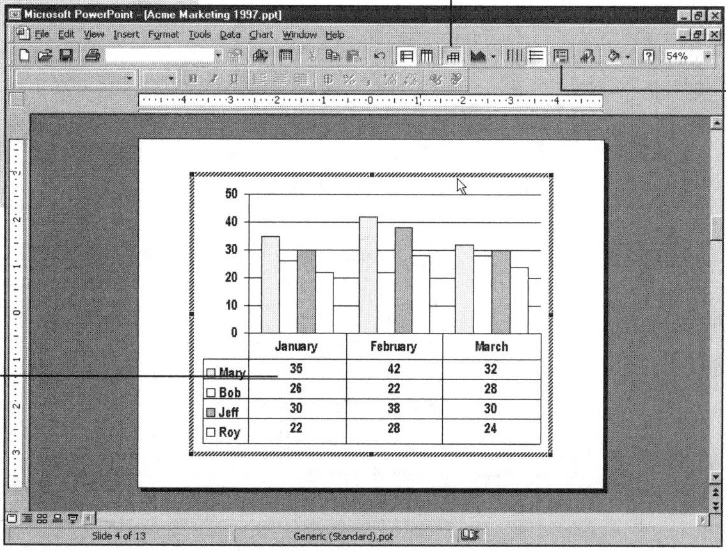

Tip

If you use a data table, you don't need a legend. It's redundant. So turn off the legend if your chart includes a data table.

Understanding the Parts of a Chart

Before I start talking about what you can do to the parts of a chart, you need to know what those parts are. Up until now it hasn't been a big deal—the chart pretty much hung together as a whole. But if you need to change, for example, the y axis, you had better find out where that is exactly.

Figure 10.10 shows the parts of a typical chart.

A few of these items deserve some extra explanation:

- The walls are the areas behind the chart. They may or may not include gridlines. (They do in Figure 10.10). You can color the walls or make them transparent.
- The plot area is the inner frame of the whole chart picture. It contains the chart itself.
- The chart area is the outer frame. It contains the plot area as well as the legend and data table if either of these are used.

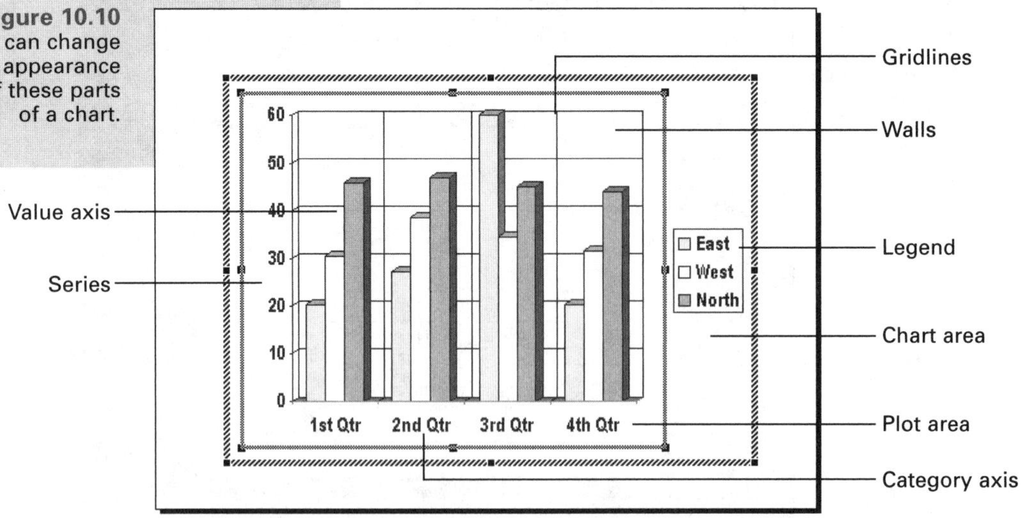

Figure 10.10
You can change the appearance of these parts of a chart.

- The Category axis is usually the horizontal, or x axis. It lists the categories that the series are plotted against.
- The Value axis is usually the vertical, or y axis. It shows the numbers that the bars (or whatever) reach up to.

The important thing to note about each of these elements is that you can format it! To format any chart element, right-click on that element and choose Format from the shortcut menu that appears. The actual name of the command varies depending on what it is; if you right-click on the legend, it'll be Format Legend, for example. A Format dialog box appears, with all kinds of settings appropriate for that element. You'll see some of these showcased in upcoming sections in this chapter, but keep in mind that this right-click trick works for everything.

Working with Titles

Look at titles next. You can add a title to the chart itself to let your audience know what they're looking at. There are two ways to go about this: one is to put the title on the slide on which the chart sits, and the other is to add the title directly to the chart frame. There is no right or wrong way—it just depends on the look that you're after. By default, Microsoft Graph assumes that the title is already on the slide, so it doesn't include a title.

Besides the chart title, there are other titles you can work with on a chart. Each axis can have a title too (such as "Quarters" and "Sales in Thousands" in Figure 10.11.)

Figure 10.11 Here are some titles you can add to your chart.

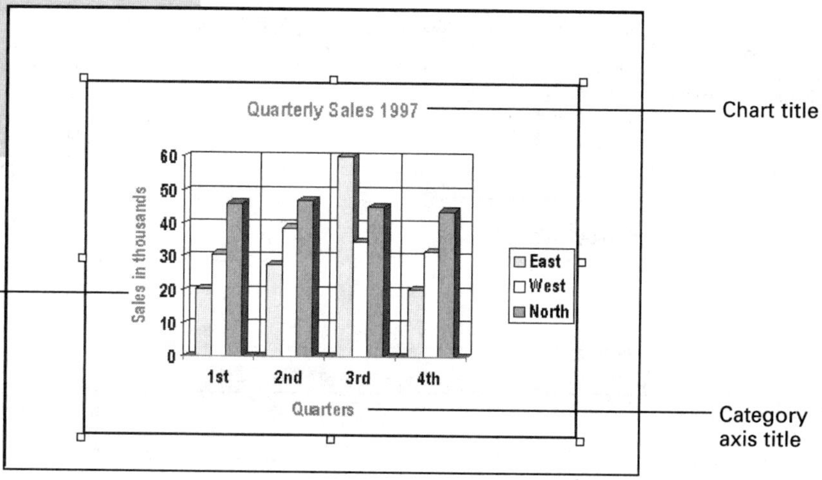

Hands On: Adding a Title

If you need to add or modify a title (either an axis title or one for the entire chart), follow these steps:

1. While editing the slide in Microsoft Graph, right-click on the chart area. (If you aren't sure where that is, point to the blank space just inside the chart frame. A ScreenTip should say "Chart Area." If it doesn't, move the mouse to try a different spot.)
2. Choose Chart Options from the shortcut menu that appears. The Chart Options dialog box opens.
3. Click on the Titles tab if it is not displayed already.
4. Enter the titles you want in the text boxes provided (see Figure 10.12). For example, to enter a chart title, type one in the Chart Title text box.
5. Click on OK.

Caution

When you add titles, you take away from the available space for the plot area in the chart frame. The chart in the plot area will appear smaller after you add titles, because Microsoft Graph shrinks it so that it, along with the added titles, all fit in the chart frame.

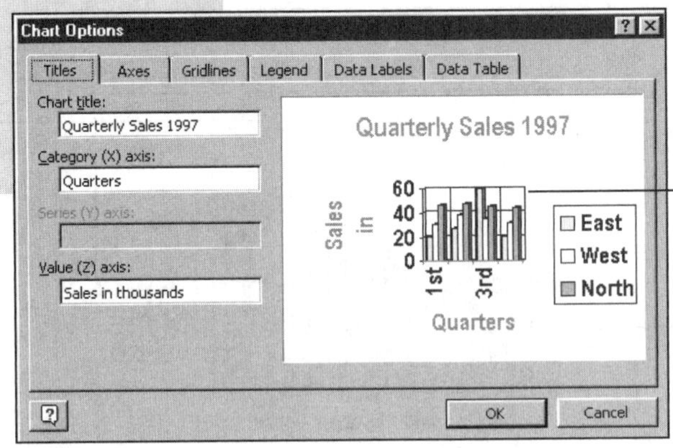

Figure 10.12 Create chart titles from the Chart Options dialog box.

Formatting a Title

Refer to Chapters 7 and 8 for more information about object backgrounds.

Once you have a title on your chart, the formatting fun begins. Right-click on the title you want to format, and choose Format Chart Title (or whatever kind of title it is) from the shortcut menu. A Format dialog box opens with that title type's name (for example, the Format Chart Title dialog box shown in Figure 10.13).

The first tab is Patterns. In the Area part of this tab, you can set a background for a chart title the same as for any other object.

You also can set border around the title. The default is None, which means the border frame blends in invisibly with the background on which it's placed. But if you prefer, you can place any color or thickness of border around it.

Follow these steps:

1. From the Patterns tab of the Format Chart Title dialog box, click on the Custom button in the Border area.
2. Open the Style drop-down list and choose a line style (solid or broken in any of a variety of ways).
3. Open the Color drop-down list and choose a line color.
4. Open the Weight drop-down list and choose a line weight (in other words, a thickness).

Before you click on OK to close the dialog box, look at the other two tabs to make sure there aren't any more changes you want to make.

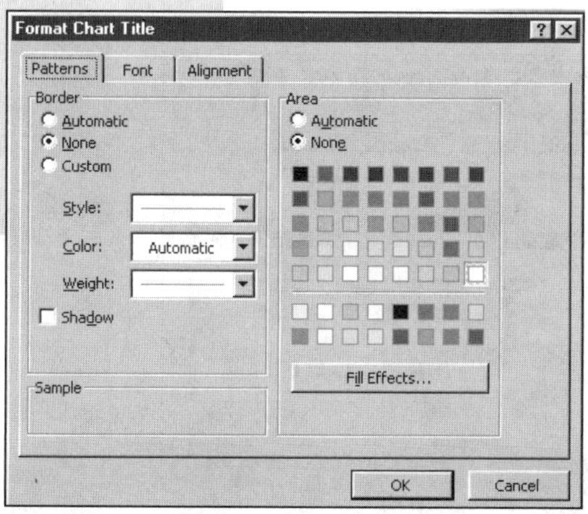

Figure 10.13 The Format Chart Title dialog box lists all the formatting you can do to a chart title.

See Chapter 7 for help using the Font controls.

The next tab is Font (see Figure 10.14). It works exactly the same as the Font controls you have worked with in regular text boxes. Just choose a font, font size, and any attributes. The only thing that's different is that there is an AutoScale check box at the bottom of the dialog box. Leave this marked; if you later resize the Chart Area, the font for the title will adjust itself in proportion as long as this stays marked.

Tip

It's a good idea to make the chart title big—the biggest text on the chart. That way it gets noticed.

Tip

Don't forget the Formatting toolbar controls. You can still use them to change the font and font size, even when you're working on a chart in Microsoft Graph. You may find them to be quicker and easier than the Font tab of the Format Chart Title dialog box.

Text alignment was covered in Chapter 7.

The final tab in the Format Chart Title dialog box is the Alignment tab (see Figure 10.15). You choose Left, Right, or Center for Horizontal alignment and Top, Center, or Bottom for Vertical, just like aligning a text in a text box. However, alignment is a moot point with a title, because it is aligned only within its own frame, not within the whole chart area. And since its frame is exactly as big as it needs to be to hold the text, there is nowhere for the text to go in any direction. Therefore, no matter what alignment you choose, the text will look the same.

Figure 10.14 These Font controls work the same as font controls you have used earlier, but they govern only the title you selected.

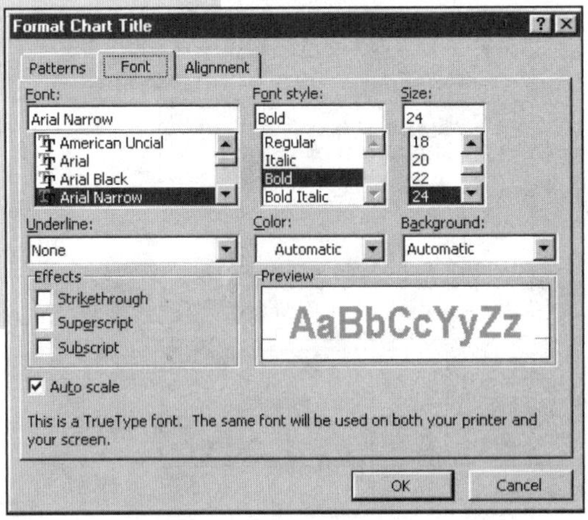

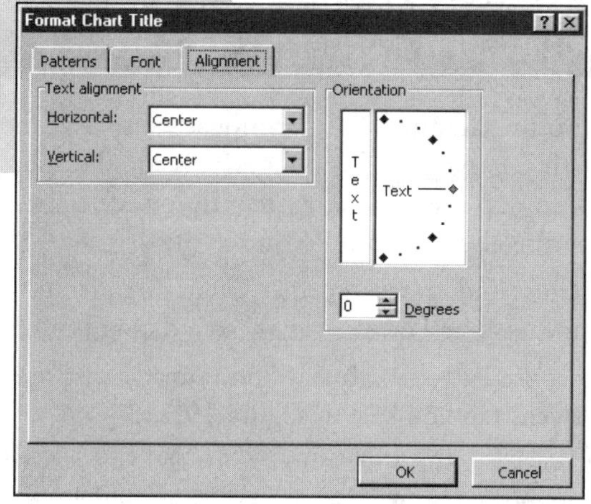

Figure 10.15 Set the alignment for the title within its frame.

Now is a good time to check out the Orientation controls on the Alignment tab. This comes in very handy in running text vertically along a vertical axis, like you saw in Figure 10.11.

By default, all text starts out formatted horizontally, at 0 degrees of tilt. But it doesn't have to stay that way; you can rotate it to any number of degrees of tilt, from 1 to 359. (360 is a full circle, so 360 is the same as 0.) To do this, just enter a number of degrees in the Degrees text box, or drag the red diamond in the Orientation panel to a different position (refer to Figure 10.15). Figure 10.11 showed the sample chart with some rotated text along the Value axis.

Remember, titles are separate elements from the plot area. That means you can drag their frames to reposition them anywhere within the chart area.

Formatting the Chart Area

Our next task is to format the big picture: the chart area. The chart area is the whole big frame that the chart and all its accouterments are contained within (the legend, the data series, the title, and so on.)

The chart area controls two important things: the background of the chart frame and the default font in the chart frame. To try your hand at changing these, complete the following Hands On.

Hands On: Adding a Colored Background and Border to a Chart

1. In Microsoft Graph, point the mouse pointer at the area outside the legend (if you have one), or slightly inside the chart frame. A ScreenTip should pop up saying Chart Area. If you see something different, move your mouse elsewhere until you see that.
2. Right-click, and choose Format Chart Area from the shortcut menu that appears. The Format Chart Area dialog box appears.
3. Click on the Patterns tab if it's not already displayed. It looks just like the Patterns tab you saw in Figure 10.12.
4. Add a border around the outside. In the Border area, click on Custom. Then open the Color drop-down list and click on a black square.
5. Open the Width drop-down list and choose one of the widest bars.
6. Now put a colored background in. In the Area section, click on a pale yellow.

Tip

You can click on Fill Effects to apply a texture or pattern to the chart background, just as you can with a slide or object background.

You learned about changing fonts in Chapter 7.

7. Click on the Font tab. This controls the default font for the entire chart. (This looks just like the controls in Figure 10.13.) If you do not specify otherwise (in upcoming sections in this chapter), all text in the chart will have the font chosen here.
8. Make the default font 18-point. Choose 18 from the Size list.
9. Click on OK to close the dialog box.

Changing How the Axes Appear

Every time I see the word "axes" I think of the axes that chop down trees, but in Microsoft Graph, "axes" is the plural of axis, and an *axis* is a side of your chart containing the measurements that your data is plotted against. For example, in the chart you've been working with in the last few sections, the Category (x) axis contains the quarters (1st, 2nd, 3rd, and 4th) and the Value (y) axis contains dollar amounts (0 through 60).

There are a number of things you can do to an axis. The option with the biggest potential impact on the chart is changing the scale. For example, take a look at the chart in Figure 10.16. The bars are so close to one another in

Figure 10.16 This chart doesn't show the differences between values very well.

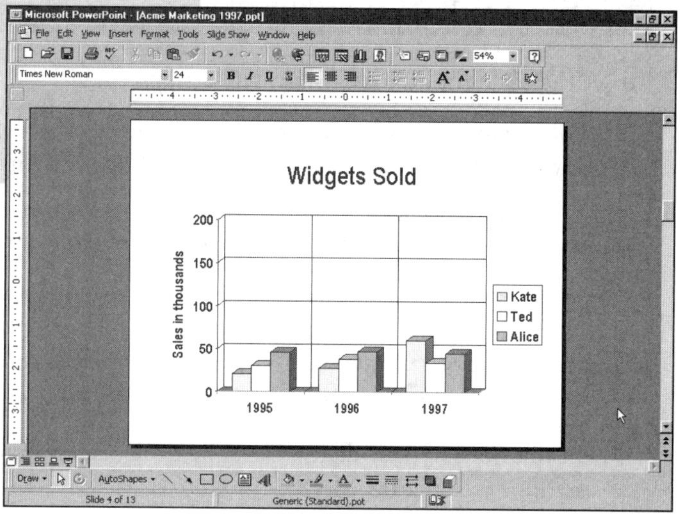

Figure 10.17 A change to the Value axis scale makes the differences easier to see.

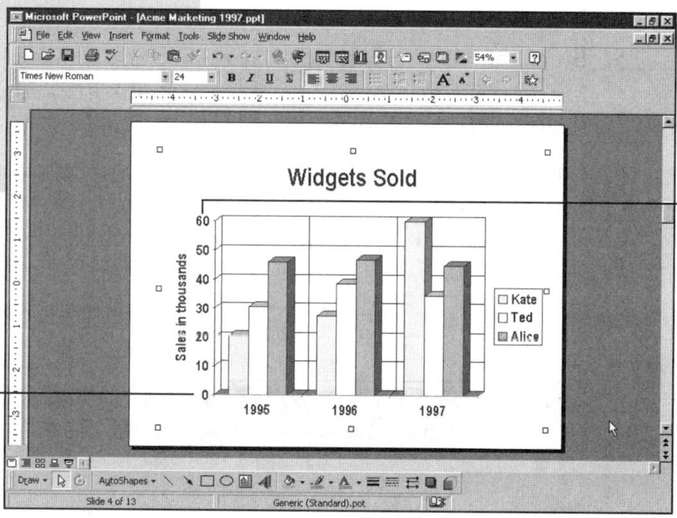

. . . and ends at 60.

Scale now starts at 0 . . .

value that it is difficult to see the difference between them. Compare it to the same chart in Figure 10.17 with an adjusted scale. Since the scale is smaller, the differences are more dramatic.

You will probably never run into a case as dramatic as Figure 10.16, because Microsoft Graph has an Auto setting for the scale that's on by default. However, you may sometimes want to override it for a special effect.

Hands On: Setting an Axis Scale

To set the scale for an axis, follow these steps:

1. Point your mouse at the axis to be scaled (probably the vertical axis), and wait for a ScreenTip to pop up telling you you're pointing at the right spot.
2. Right-click, and choose Format Axis from the shortcut menu.

Tip

You can double-click on one of the axis labels (for example, any of the numbers along the Value axis in Figure 10.16) to open the Format Axis dialog box quickly.

3. In the Format Axis dialog box, click the Scale tab to display the scale settings (see Figure 10.18).
4. Enter the number you want at the bottom (or left) end of the axis in the Minimum text box, or leave its check box marked to have Microsoft Graph calculate it automatically.
5. Enter the number you want at the top (or right) end of the axis in the Maximum text box, or leave its check box marked to have Microsoft Graph calculate it automatically.
6. Enter the units you want counted off on the scale in the Major Unit text box, or leave its check box marked to have Microsoft Graph calculate it automatically. (For example, in Figure 10.17 the major unit is 10).

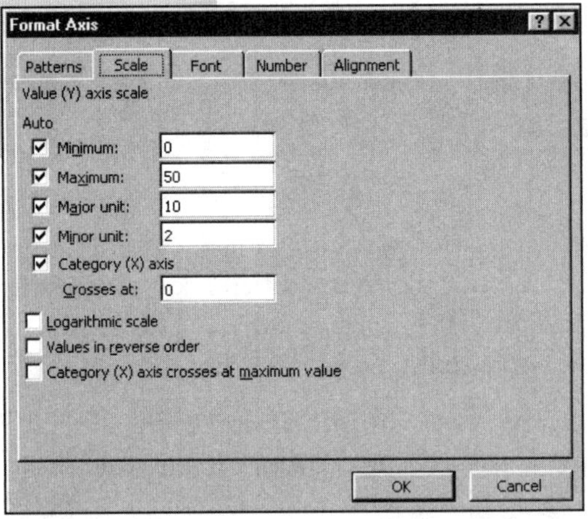

Figure 10.18 Set your scale numbers on the Scale tab.

7. (Optional) If you want to show a minor unit between the major ones, enter it in the Minor Unit text box, or leave its check box marked to have Microsoft Graph calculate it automatically.

Tip

Most charts look better without minor units shown. Minor units can make a chart look too cluttered. Microsoft Graph can determine whether a minor unit would be useful or not, and omit it when appropriate, if you leave the Minor Unit check box marked.

8. If you want a specific number at the floor other than the number you entered under Minimum, enter it in the Crosses At text box. (This is rarely done; usually the floor shows the minimum value.)
9. If you want any of the following special features, select their check boxes:
   - *Logarithmic Scale.* Rarely used by ordinary folks, this check box recalculates the Minimum, Maximum, Major Units, and Minor Units according to a power of 10 for the value axis based on the range of data. (If that explanation doesn't make any sense to you, you're not the target audience for this feature.)
   - *Values in Reverse Order.* This check box turns the scale backwards so the greater values are at the bottom or left.
   - *Floor (XY Plane) Crosses at Minimum Value.* This sets the Crosses At text box's value to the smallest value represented on the chart. For example, if the shortest bar on the chart were $10,100, the minimum value on the scale would be $10,100 and that bar would have no height.

Caution

Each of these check boxes recalculates the numbers in the Minimum, Maximum, Major Units, and Minor Units text boxes. Don't select them after you have entered specific values for any of these if you want to keep those entered values.

10. Click on OK when you're done, and take a look at the results in your chart.

As you may have noticed in the Format Axis dialog box, there are several other tabs that contain settings you can change for your axis. Many of these controls are ones that you have seen earlier in the book, so you should be familiar with them:

- *Patterns.* You can set text and background colors and patterns the same as you can any other part of the chart.
- *Font.* Changing the font used to display axis labels is the same as changing any other font.
- *Number.* You can change how the numbers on your Value axis appear. (If you have used Excel before, you'll recognize these; if not, they're easy to understand.)
- *Alignment.* Just like the titles on the chart, the axis labels can be aligned.

Formatting the Legend

With a multi-series chart, the value of the legend is obvious—it tells you what colors represent which series. Without it, your reader wouldn't know what the various bars or lines meant.

You can do all the same formatting things to a legend that you can do to other chart elements you've seen so far. Just right-click on the legend and choose Format Legend from the shortcut menu, and then use the tabs in the Format Legend dialog box to do any of these things to it:

- *Change the background.* Use the Area controls on the Patterns tab.
- *Change the border around the legend.* Use the Border controls on the Patterns tab.
- *Change the font, font size, and attributes.* Use the controls on the Font tab.
- Change the placement of the legend in relation to the chart. These controls are on the Placement tab.

The only thing that's tricky here at all is that the Placement tab controls do not mean the same thing as Alignment does for other elements. For other elements, Alignment refers to the text's alignment within its frame. But Placement is something different. It refers to the placement of the frame in relation to the plot area. You select between Bottom, Corner (upper-right corner), Top, Right, or Left.

You also can drag the legend's frame around to manually place it wherever you want it. Move it as you learned to move objects around in Chapter 9.

Data Labels

Data labels aren't appropriate for every chart. In fact, so far you haven't used any of them at all in our sample charts! Data labels announce the value, percentage, series, and so on for a bar, slice, or other value marker. The best place to use them is on a pie chart, since there's a fairly large expanse of area for each slice. Series and Percentage data labels are shown in Figure 10.19.

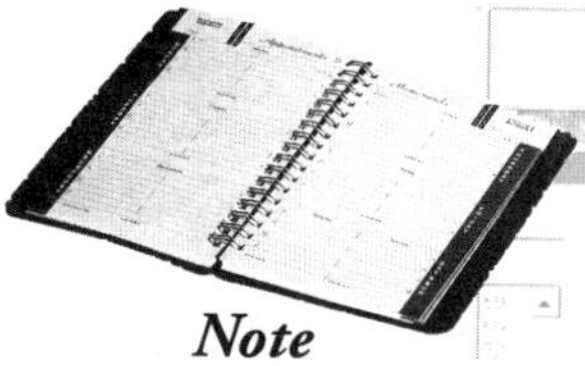

Notice that Figure 10.19 doesn't contain a legend. It doesn't need to because the data labels are conveying the legend information in this case.

To add data labels to your chart, follow these steps:

1. Right-click on the chart area and choose Chart Options from the shortcut menu.

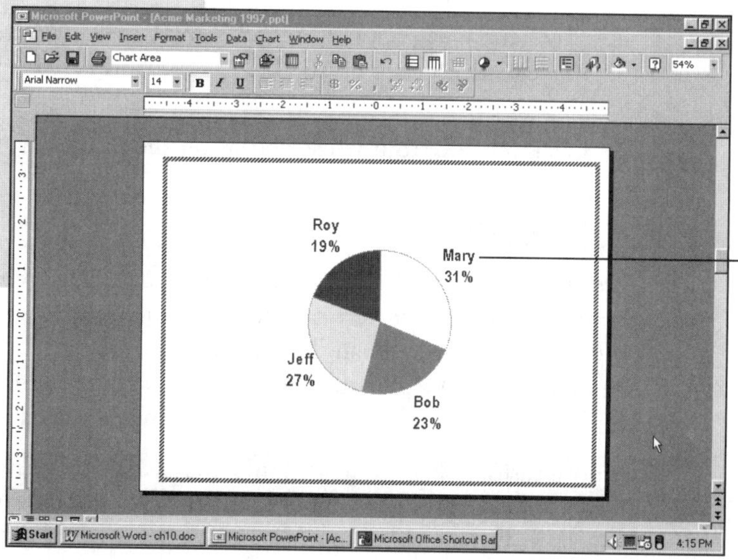

Figure 10.19 For some types of charts, data labels can help make the meaning more clear.

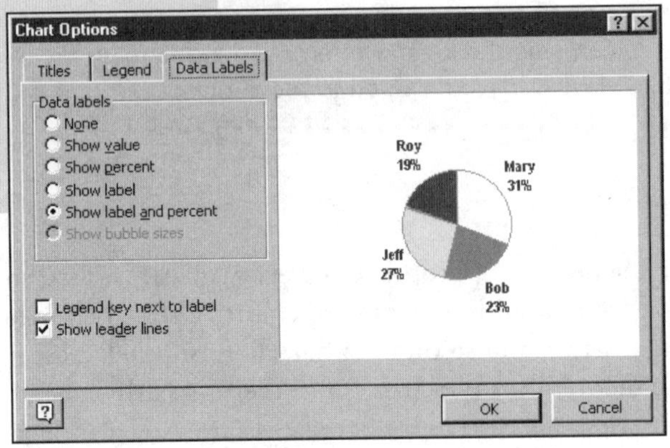

Figure 10.20 Choose what type of labels you want to appear on your chart.

2. Click on the Data Labels tab (see Figure 10.20).
3. Click on the option button for the kind of labels you want:
   - *None.* No labels (the default).
   - *Show Value.* Shows the actual value from the cell that the chart takes its information from.
   - *Show Percent.* Shows what percentage of the whole each series represents.
   - *Show Label.* Shows the label from the legend next to the series.
   - *Show Label and Percent.* A combination of Show Percent and Show Label. (This is what you see in Figure 10.19.)
4. If you are using Show Label or Show Label and Percent, you don't need the legend, so click on the Legend tab and deselect the Show Legend check box.
5. Click on OK. Your labels appear on the chart.

Gridlines and Walls

Gridlines help the readers' eyes follow across the page. Gridlines are related to the axes. You have both vertical and horizontal gridlines available for your use. *Walls* are nothing more than the space between the gridlines formatted in a different color than the plot area. Set the Walls area to None, and good-bye walls. (Don't you wish tearing down walls were always that easy?)

In most cases, the default gridlines that Microsoft Graph adds work well. However, sometimes you might want to make the lines thicker or a different color, or turn them off altogether.

Displaying or Hiding Gridlines

To change which gridlines are displayed, you can just click on the Category Axis Gridlines and Value Axis Gridlines buttons on the Microsoft Graph toolbar. Or, for more control, follow these steps:

1. Right-click on the chart area and choose Chart Options.
2. Click on the Gridlines tab (see Figure 10.21).
3. Select or deselect the check boxes to turn on/off the gridlines.
   - *Category Axis.* These are not normally used, but if you want them, select either Major or Minor or both.
   - *Value Axis.* Normally just Major gridlines are shown here, but if you want to see minor ones too, select the Minor check box.
4. (Optional) To make the walls and gridlines 2-D on the 3-D chart, select the 2-D Walls and Gridlines check box.
5. Click on OK.

Formatting Gridlines

You can format gridlines the same way you format other objects on a chart. Just right-click on a gridline and select Format Gridline. Any changes you make affect all gridlines of that type (for example, all horizontal Major ones).

When you open the Format Gridlines dialog box, you see two tabs. One is for Scale, which is the same as the Scale settings for the axis that that gridline touches. Any changes made in one place will be reflected in the other.

Figure 10.21 You can turn on/off selected gridlines here.

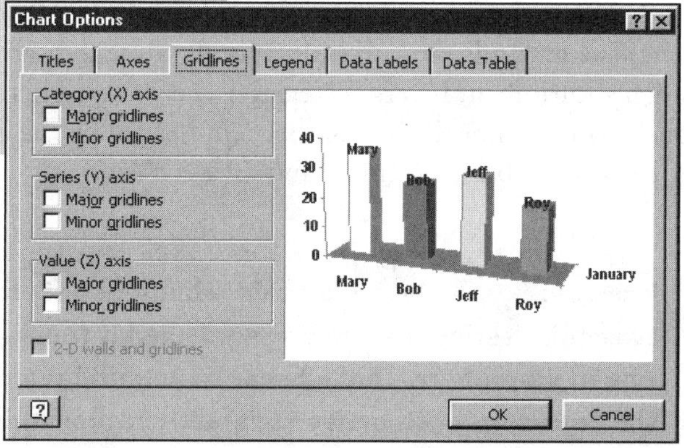

The other tab is Patterns, and the controls there are the same as the controls you saw earlier for changing other chart parts. The only difference is that the None option is grayed out. That's because you can't turn gridlines off from here. You must use the procedure outlined in the preceding section.

Formatting the Data Series

Now comes the fun part. You get to change the colors of the bars, lines, or slices, move them around, and otherwise tinker.

To format a data series, just right-click on the bar, slice, or whatever, and choose Format Data Series from the shortcut menu. Then, depending on what type of chart you've got, you will see different tabs with which you can modify the series' appearance.

Note

You can format either the data series (all bars, slices, or whatever in the series) or the individual data point. When you right-click on the data point, if it says Format Data Series, that's what you'll get. If you want to format the individual data point instead, double-click on that data point and then try right-clicking again. The menu option should now read Format Data Point. Most of what you'll learn in the upcoming sections applies equally to either data series or data points.

Series Patterns and Colors

The first stop is the Patterns tab. This is just like the Patterns tab you worked with for backgrounds, and the controls all work the same way. There is only one small addition: an Invert If Negative check box. This swaps the foreground and background colors if the number represented by the data series is negative. It applies to pies, bars, columns, and areas.

Note

The colors you choose on this tab apply only to the particular series that you right-clicked if there is more than one in your chart. That's because you will want to select the colors for each series separately rather than having them all be the same color.

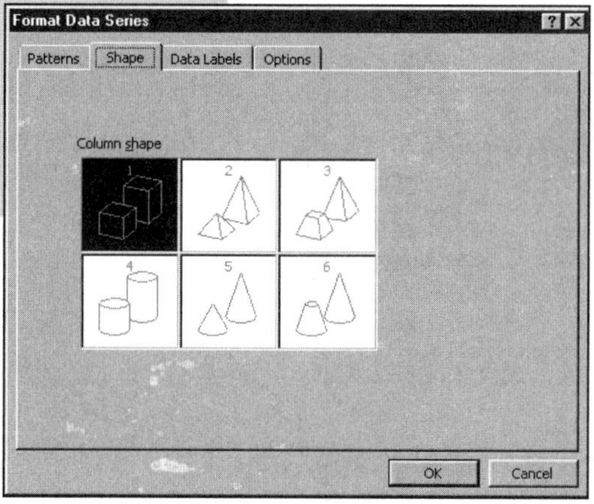

Figure 10.22 On the Shape tab, you can choose among several bar or column shapes.

Shape

On the Shape tab, you get to choose what shape your bars or columns will be (see Figure 10.22). Why settle for an ordinary bar? Have some fun with these.

Data Labels

The Data Labels tab contains the same basic controls as the Data Labels tab you worked with in the Chart Options dialog box, except these controls apply only to the selected data series. You could use these, for example, to add data labels only for the series that you want to spotlight.

Options

The Options tab is different for different chart types. It contains options specific to that type. For example, Figure 10.23 shows the options for a Column chart. You can set the gap between bars and the overall chart depth. Figure 10.24 shows the options for a Pie chart. Here you can set the angle of the first slice, effectively rotating the slices so that any slice is at any position you want. Other chart types have other options you can explore on your own.

Caution

There is also a Vary Colors By Slice check box on the Options tab for pie charts. Leave this checked! If you deselect it, all the slices will be the same color, and you won't be able to tell them apart, even with a legend.

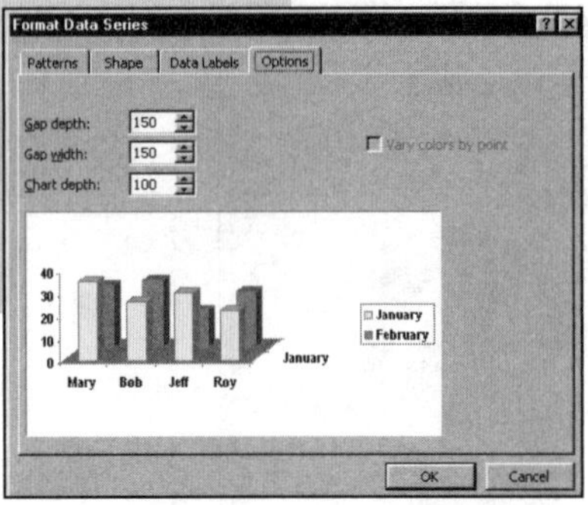

Figure 10.23 The Options tab for column and bar charts enables you to set the gaps between bars.

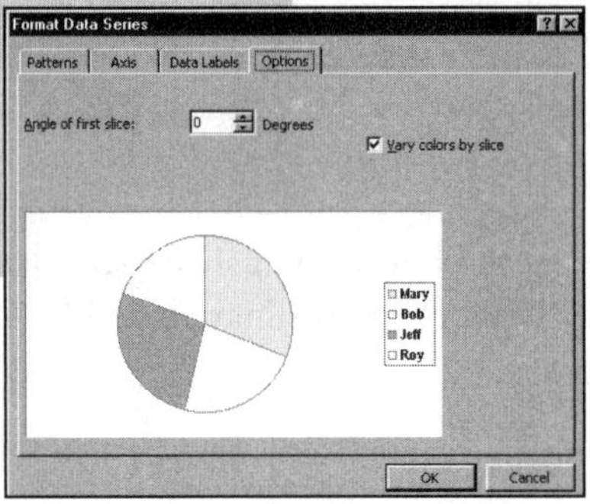

Figure 10.24 The Options tab for pie charts enables you to specify the angle of the first slice.

Rotating Pie Slices: A Real-World Example

A few years back, I was administering a program in which I had to provide monthly reports showing a breakdown of the percentage of users in certain categories. I used a pie chart for this, but there were several categories, and the pie slices were rather thin. The labels often got cut off or ran into each other like this:

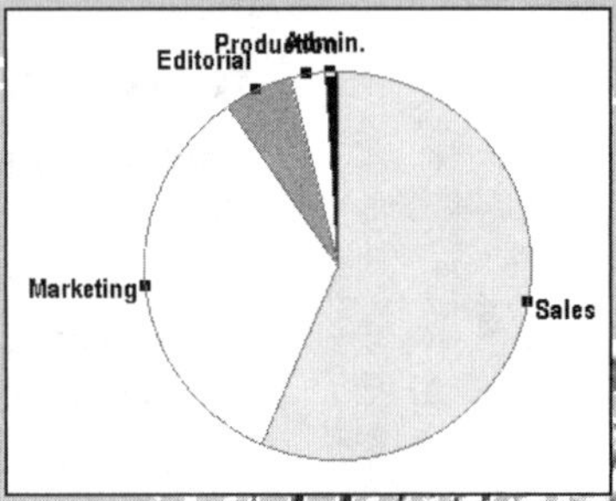

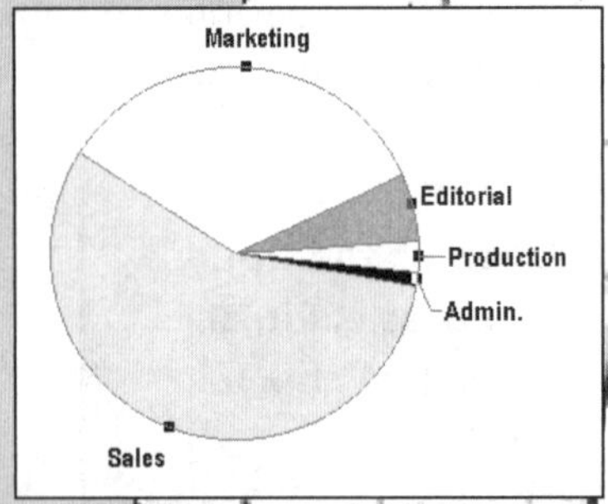

I solved the problem by adjusting the Angle of First Slice until the pie rotated enough that the thinner slices were on the sides, where there was more room for their labels.

Changing the 3-D View

This feature is a little bit advanced, but can be a real lifesaver when you have a 3-D chart that needs some tweaking.

Not all of Microsoft Graph's charts turn out perfectly the first time. Microsoft Graph can't anticipate how your data is going to look in a chart, so sometimes in a 3-D chart some of the data bars or lines are obscured by other, taller ones in front of them. For example, in Figure 10.25, the back row's value for January isn't visible because the middle row is too tall. Modifying the 3-D settings makes the chart appear at a different angle, bringing into view the obscured data point.

To change the 3-D view, follow these steps:

1. Right-click on the chart area, plot area, or walls and choose 3-D View from the shortcut menu.
2. In the 3-D View dialog box, shown in Figure 10.26, click on the buttons to change the view, and then click on Apply to try out the settings (drag the title bar of the dialog box to move it out of the way as needed):
   - Use the Elevation buttons to tilt the view up and down.
   - Use the Rotation buttons to rotate the chart. When you rotate a chart so much that the walls will be in the way, the walls move to the opposite side. (Convenient, eh?)

Figure 10.25
This chart could benefit from some 3-D setting changes to make the back row more readable.

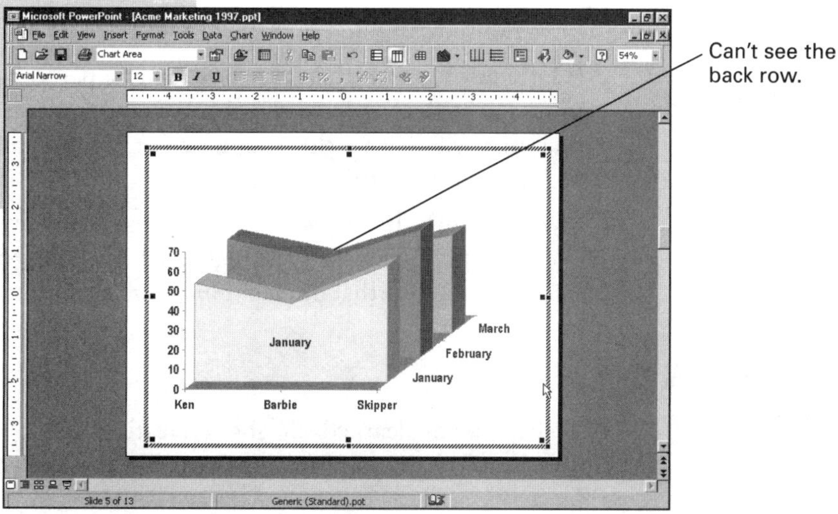

Figure 10.26
Use these 3-D tools to adjust the view of a 3-D chart.

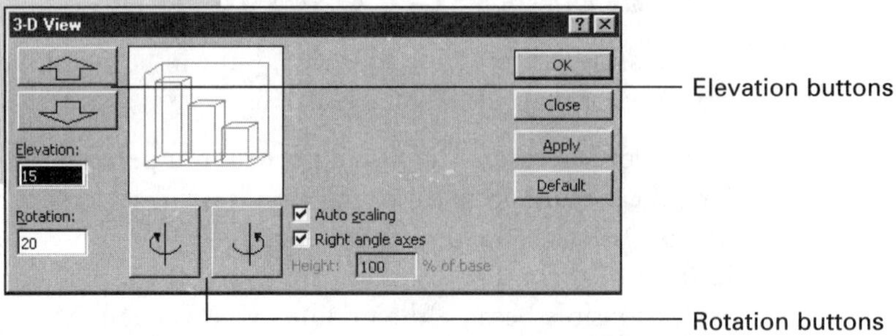

Figure 10.27
Now each series is completely visible, thanks to some 3-D adjustments.

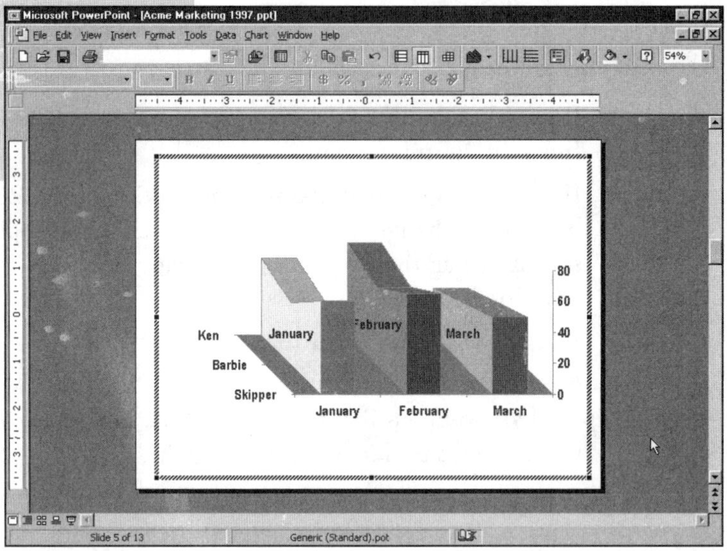

3. (Optional) In the Height text box, enter a percentage of the base width to represent the height of the chart. The default is 100; a setting of less than that will make a short, squat chart; a setting of more than that will make a taller, thinner chart.
4. When you are satisfied with your settings, and have tested them out by clicking Apply, click on OK. Figure 10.27 shows the chart from Figure 10.25 adjusted so that all data points are visible.

Summary

In this chapter you learned all about creating and formatting charts with Microsoft Graph. Now you can add charts like these to your presentation with confidence.

11

Placing an Organization Chart on a Slide

In This Chapter

- Placing an Organization Chart on a Slide
- Editing the Chart Structure
- Changing the Chart Style
- Changing Lines and Colors

If you have ever struggled to create an organization chart by hand, or by using circles, rectangles, and lines in a drawing program, you know how frustrating it can be. Org charts are complicated pieces of artwork. Luckily for you, PowerPoint comes with Microsoft Organization Chart, a little program that can whip one out for you in no time.

Introducing MS Organization Chart

Microsoft Organization Chart, like WordArt and the Drawing toolbar tools, is a mini application (sometimes called an *applet*) that comes with PowerPoint (and the Microsoft Office suite). It provides an easy way to create simple or even complex organization charts, with consistent boxes and lines that match up perfectly.

Starting an Org Chart

The best way to see what Microsoft Organization Chart does is to dive right in and start playing with it. Follow these steps to start it up:

1. Display the slide on which you want to place the organization chart. A blank slide or one with only a title text box works best.
2. Choose Insert, Picture, Organization Chart. The program opens, with a sample chart, as shown in Figure 11.1.

If you start a new slide from the New Slide dialog box using the AutoLayout with an organization chart on it, you can double-click on the icon on the resulting slide to open Microsoft Organization Chart quickly.

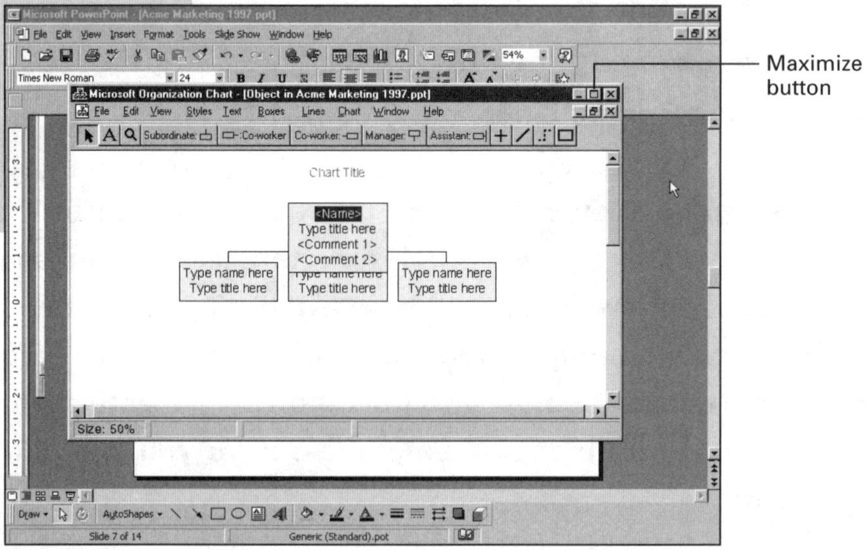

Figure 11.1 Microsoft Organization Chart shows a sample chart to which you can add your own personnel.

What Can You Convey with Org Charts?

You might think that, if you are not going to show any personnel information in your presentation, you have no use for Microsoft Organization Chart. That might not be true. You also can use the program to do these things:

- Simple flow charts of processes
- Time progressions of how various versions of a product have evolved
- Diagrams of how the parts that comprise your product are assembled or fit together

Obviously, Microsoft Organization Chart is not going to be as powerful for these tasks as it is for diagramming personnel—what it's designed for. But it is certainly more help than drawing these objects yourself with the rudimentary shapes on the Drawing toolbar.

If you get an error message when you try to run Organization Chart, you may not have installed the Organization Chart component. Rerun the Setup program (see Appendix A) and make sure you select Organization Chart from the list of components.

You may want to maximize the window (click on the Maximize button) so you have the largest possible work area.

Tip

You can change the default chart specs by choosing Edit, Options and selecting a different option button in the dialog box that appears.

Typing Names into the Chart

The first <Name> field in the topmost box of the chart is already highlighted when you start up the program, so all you have to do is type the first name and press Enter. From there, you work through the other fields in the box and then proceed to the next box.

Hands On: Filling in the Names

Follow these steps, using the names and titles in Figure 11.2.

1. Type the name of the top person in the org chart, and press Enter. The <Title> line below it becomes highlighted.
2. Type that person's title and press Enter. The <Comment 1> line below it becomes highlighted.
3. (Optional) Type a comment if you want. If you have more than one comment, press Enter again and type in the second <Comment> line as well.
4. When you are finished with that box, press Esc.
5. Click on the next box you want to type in.

Note

You can use names from your own organization if you prefer, but I'll be referring to these names throughout the chapter when directing you to make changes, so sticking with the names from my example chart might be easier for you.

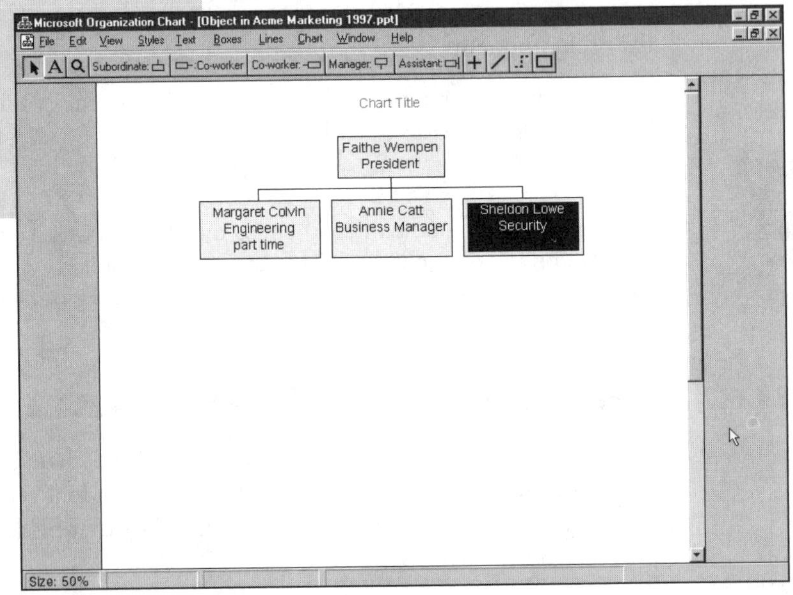

Figure 11.2 To follow along with the examples in this chapter, duplicate this org chart.

6. Start typing the name that goes there. When you begin typing, the box changes to have the same fields (<Name>, <Title>, <Comment 1>, and <Comment 2> as the preceding box.
7. Repeat steps 1 through 4 for that box. Then click on the next box and keep repeating until you have filled in all the boxes.

Note

Notice in Figure 11.2 that the box on the left uses one of the Comment fields. Because of that, it is three lines long rather than two like the others. But because Microsoft Organization Chart likes to keep everything tidy, it increases the size of the other boxes in the same row to match. That's why the center and right boxes have a blank line in them.

Editing the Chart Structure

The basic organization chart can be used exactly as-is, but how often do organizations have exactly the default number of boxes? Not often. That's why the program includes tools for creating different box types and different arrangements, as you'll learn in the following sections.

Adding and Deleting Boxes

At some point in the preceding Hands On, you probably thought, 'Wait a minute, there aren't the right number of boxes in the right places!' The org chart that you start out with is just a template, and you can add and delete boxes as needed. (You also can move boxes around, as you'll learn in the section following this one.)

To add boxes, you need to understand a little bit about the types of boxes available. When you are adding a box, you are adding it *in relation to* an existing box on the chart. No boxes can be added as independent entities, unconnected to the rest. With that in mind, a new box can have one of four relationships to an existing box:

The new box reports to the existing box.

The new box is of the same level and has the same manager as the existing box.

The existing box reports to the new box.

The new box is an assistant to the existing box. (Some organizations differentiate between an assistant and a subordinate; others classify assistants as subordinates.)

Try it out now in the following Hands On.

Hands On: Adding People to the Chart

1. Start with the one-boss-three-employees default chart you created earlier in this chapter.
2. First you will add another employee. Click on the Subordinate button on the toolbar.
3. Click on the President box (the top one). A new box appears.
4. In that new box, enter **Jane Washburne** as the name and **Photographer** as the title. Press Esc when done.
5. Now add another employee, using a different method. Click on the second (rightmost) Co-Worker button.

Note

There are two coworker buttons, a left and a right one. You choose which you want depending on where you want the new box to be placed in relation to the existing one: to the left or to the right.

6. Now click on the Jane Washburne box, the one you just added. Another new box appears.

Note

Note that steps 3 and 6 did the exact same thing, although they used different buttons. That's because the box placement depends on what box you selected. In step 3, you added a subordinate to the president, which is the same as a coworker to the photographer.

7. In the new box, type **Missy Colvin** as the name and **Operations** as the title. Press [Esc] when finished.

Note

When you added that last box, the screen may have scrolled off to the left. Drag the horizontal scroll bar to bring everything back into view if needed.

8. Want to appoint a CEO who the President reports to? Click on the Manager button.
9. Click on the President box. A new box appears above it.
10. In that box, type **Lois Adams** for the name and **Chief Executive Officer** as the title. Press [Esc] when finished.
11. Now give that hard-working president an assistant. Click on the Assistant button.
12. Click on the President box. A new box appears next to it.
13. For the assistant name, type **Ashley King**. This time don't bother with a title; just press [Esc] after you've typed the name. (Titles are not mandatory.)
14. Finally, give some employees to the Business Manager. Click on the Subordinate button, and then click on the Business Manager box. Repeat that process three times.
15. Enter the following names in the subordinate boxes you just created: **Molly Hopper**, **Jeff Phillips**, and **Janet Bailey**. Don't enter titles.

When you're finished, your chart should look just like the one shown in Figure 11.3.

Moving and Deleting Boxes

When moving things around on an org chart, relationships are everything. You may have worked with programs in the past where you could click on a box and drag it where you wanted it, but Microsoft Organization Chart does not work quite like that. Instead, you cut and paste to move, as shown in the following Hands On.

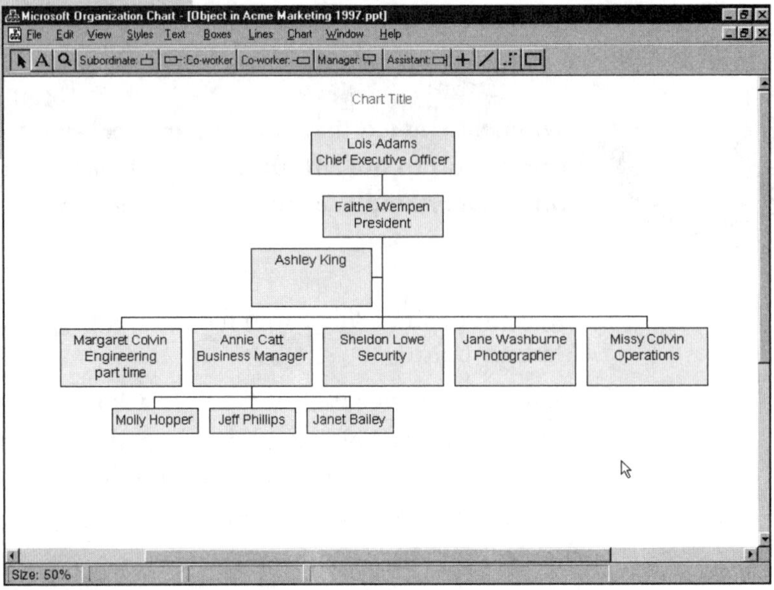

Figure 11.3 Follow the steps carefully to produce this chart.

Hands On: Moving Boxes in the Chart

Follow these steps to simulate a reorganization within our sample company!

1. The CEO got canned, and the President became the CEO. So delete the CEO box. Click on it and press the Delete key.
2. Click on the President box and edit the title to read Chief Executive Officer.
3. Ashley King, the assistant, now reports to Missy Colvin. So click on Ashley King's box and press Ctrl+X to cut it from its present location.

You also can use the Cut and Paste toolbar buttons or the commands on the Edit menu, but for this kind of work, I find the shortcut key methods shown in these steps much faster.

4. Click on Missy Colvin to select that box, and then press Ctrl+V to paste.
5. The photographer, Jane Washburne, now reports to Missy Colvin as well. So click on Jane Washburne and press Ctrl+X, then click on Missy Colvin and press Ctrl+V.

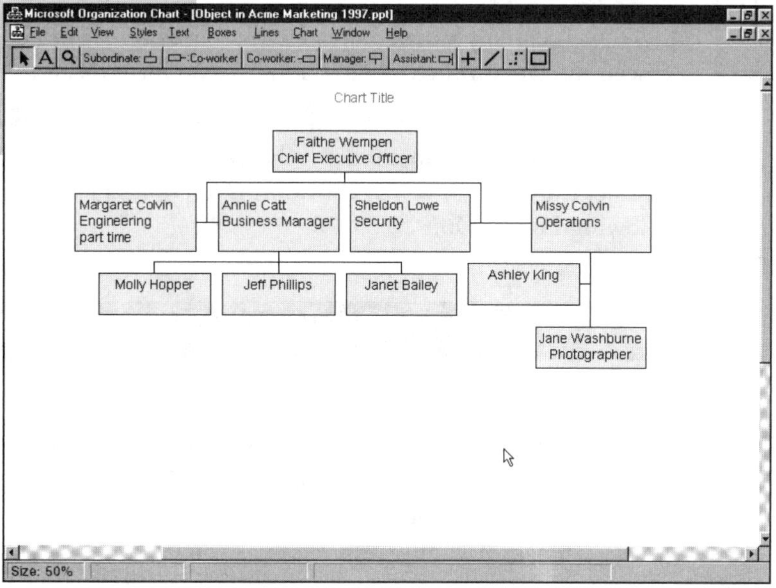

Figure 11.4 The result of the company's recent reorganization.

When you're finished, it should look like Figure 11.4.

Working with Multiple Boxes

If you have a lot of moving around to do, you may want to move more than one box at once. It can certainly save you some time. To do so, you must select multiple boxes before you do the cut-and-paste operation.

There are several ways to select, depending on what your goal is:

- To select more than one box manually, click on the first box, then hold down the Shift key while you click on other boxes.
- To select all of a certain type of box (for example, all manager, which would be everyone who has at least one person reporting to them), choose Edit, Select, and then a category (for example, All Managers).
- To select certain levels of the chart (for example, in Figure 11.4 there are three levels), choose Edit, Select Levels. In the dialog box that appears, indicate which levels you want selected (for example, two through three) and click on OK.

Changing the Chart Style

There are many ways to arrange the boxes on an org chart, and so far you've seen just one of them. You're about to be introduced to some others, though.

Open the Styles menu. See all the little pictures of organization styles? These are what you have to choose from. But before you can apply one, you have to select the boxes to which you want it to apply. That's what you'll do in the following Hands On:

Hands On: Changing the Subordinate Style

1. Select the boxes of the people who report to Annie Catt, Business Manager. You can click on them with the Shift key held down to do so.
2. Open the Styles menu and click on the middle button in the top row of buttons. The subordinates change to appear stacked vertically, as shown in Figure 11.5.
3. Now arrange the second-level folks vertically. Select the four boxes in the middle row.
4. Open the Styles menu and click on the right button in the top row. The chart changes to the arrangement shown in Figure 11.6.

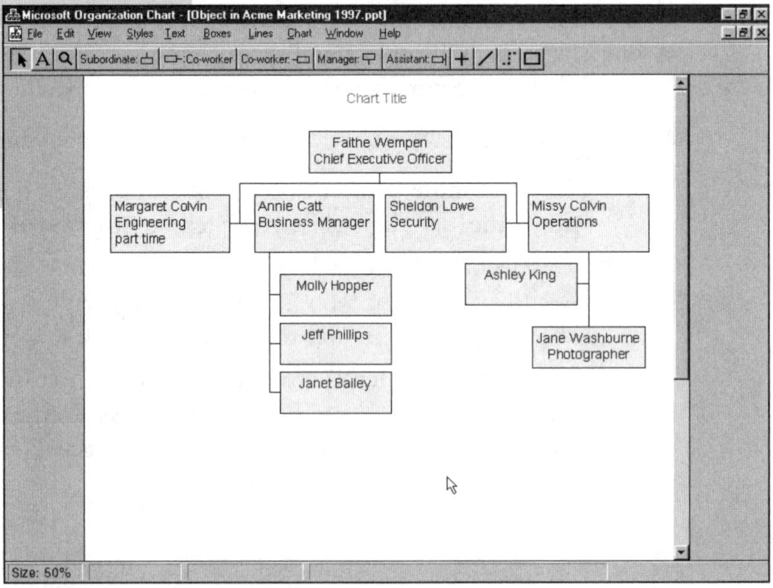

Figure 11.5
This subordinate arrangement takes up less space and is easy to understand.

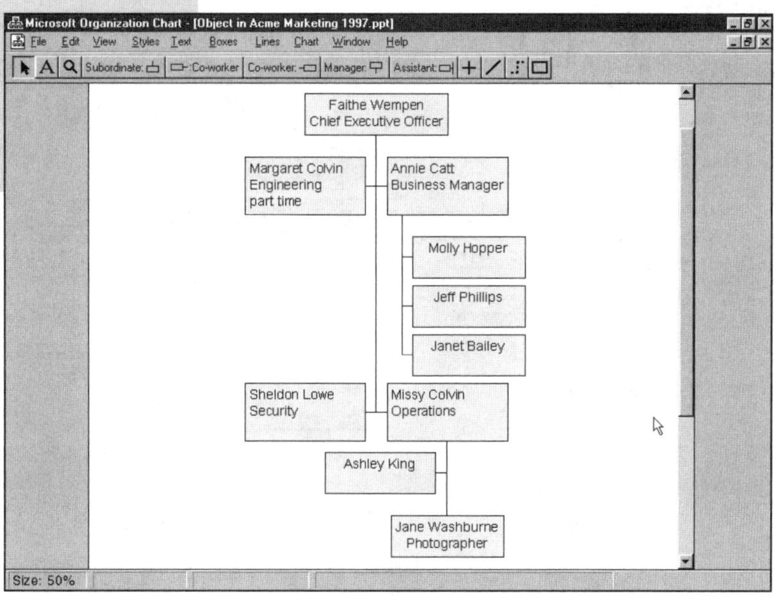

Figure 11.6 For large charts, a vertical arrangement like this might work well.

Adding Titles and Explanations

You may have noticed at the top of the org chart are the words "Chart Title." Obviously you don't want that for the actual title, so click on those words to move the insertion point there, and then drag across the entire phrase to select it; then type your new title.

You also can add more text boxes that aren't connected to the rest of the org chart, for subtitles, for example, or explanations. Follow these steps:

1. Click on the Enter Text button on the toolbar (looks like an A).
2. Click anywhere in the work area to position the insertion point.
3. Type your text. Press Enter to start a new line when needed.
4. When you are finished, click anywhere away from the text. The text appears floating on the chart, as shown in Figure 11.7.

When you add text in this way, it becomes an object on the organization chart. When you click on it, black selection handles appear around it. You can drag it around on the org chart the same as you drag objects around on your PowerPoint slides. The chart title is slightly different, in that it's fixed in place; you can't drag it around.

Figure 11.7 This descriptive text is not attached to any box.

Text

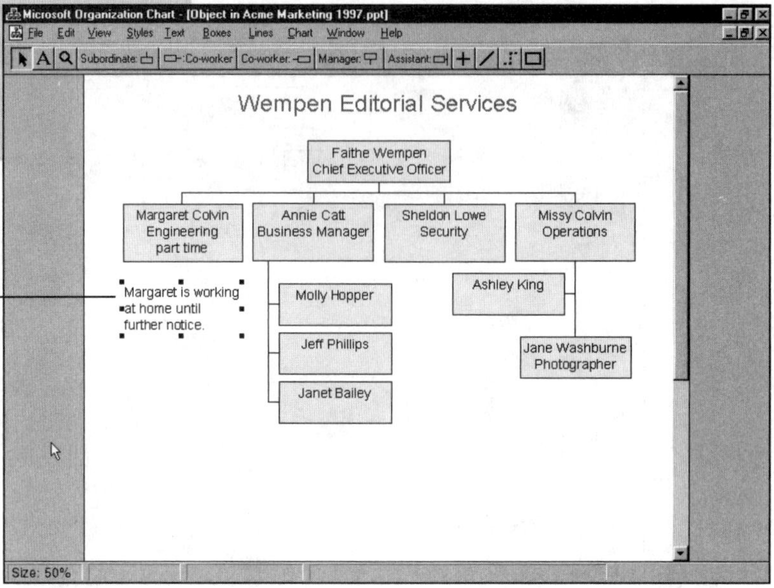

Adding More Lines

If you need to add more reporting lines to the chart, for example, some dotted lines for shared reporting, you'll want to use Microsoft Organization Chart's drawing tools. These are a little different from PowerPoint's drawing tools, in that they consist only of lines and a rectangle. Click on the one you want, and then drag on the chart to draw.

If you do not see these buttons on your toolbar, choose View, Show Draw Tools to make them appear.

Click on this button and then drag on the chart to draw a vertical or horizontal line. This line is not tied to any particular box, so you can put it anywhere.

Click on this button and then drag to create a straight line going in any direction. It need not be completely vertical or horizontal.

Click on this button and then drag to create a reporting line between two boxes. You have to start the line at the edge of one box and end it at another; otherwise you get an error message.

Click on this button to draw a rectangle that's decorative rather than to hold org chart data.

Changing the Org Chart's Appearance

After you have finalized the chart's structure, you may want to dress it up by changing the appearance of the boxes, lines, and text. You'll learn about the features that enable this in the following sections.

Formatting Chart Text

Just like the text on your PowerPoint slides, you can format the text in your organization chart. For example, you might want to make the text in the boxes smaller so you can fit a more complicated chart onto a single slide.

Note

When you change the size of the font in a box, it changes it only for that selected box (or boxes). However, because all boxes of the same level must be the same size, if the box has had to expand to accommodate larger text, all the boxes of that level in your chart get bigger too.

To change the font and/or font size used in a text box, follow these steps:

1. Select the box(es) you want to format.
2. Open the Text menu and choose Font. A Font dialog box appears, as shown in Figure 11.8. Its controls should be very familiar, since they are the same controls you've used to format text in earlier chapters.
3. Choose a different font if desired from the Font list.
4. Choose a different size if desired from the Size list.

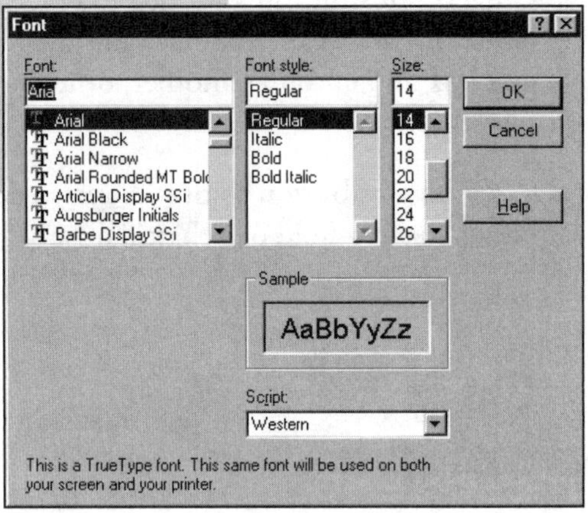

Figure 11.8 Use the Font dialog box to modify the look of the text.

5. Apply any special formatting you want, like Bold or Italic, from the Font Style list.
6. Click on OK. Your changes are applied to the selected boxes.

See Chapter 7 for more about text formatting.

You can format the descriptive text on your slide (the title and any other text you added in the preceding section). Just highlight it and then jump into the above procedure at step 2.

Text also can be aligned differently in the boxes. The default is Center, which usually looks the best. But if you ever need to change the alignment, just select the box(es) and then open the Text menu and click on Left or Right.

Changing Box Appearance

By default, the boxes pick up colors from the presentation's color scheme. But you can make them any color you want, or even transparent.

Hands On: Formatting Chart Boxes

Follow these steps to change the appearance of certain boxes on the chart:

1. Select the box(es) you want to format. For example, suppose you want to change all the managers' boxes to a yellow background. You could select Edit, Select, All Managers to highlight them.

2. Open the Boxes menu and choose Color. A very simple Color dialog box appears, with just an assortment of colors in it.
3. Click on the color you want (for example, yellow) and click on OK. (The gray raised button in the bottom right corner sets it to transparent.)
4. With those same boxes still selected, open the Boxes menu again and point to Shadow. A submenu of the various shadow types appears.
5. Click on the second shadow on the left (a 3-D shadow). It is applied to the selected boxes.
6. Now change the line around the boxes. Open the Boxes menu once again.
7. Point to Border Style, and then click on the left border in the third row (see Figure 11.9).
8. Open the Boxes menu again, and choose Border Color. A dialog box appears showing available colors.
9. Click on a red square, and click on OK.

As a result of this formatting, the managers' boxes really stand out.

Figure 11.9
Choose a border style from the drop-down list.

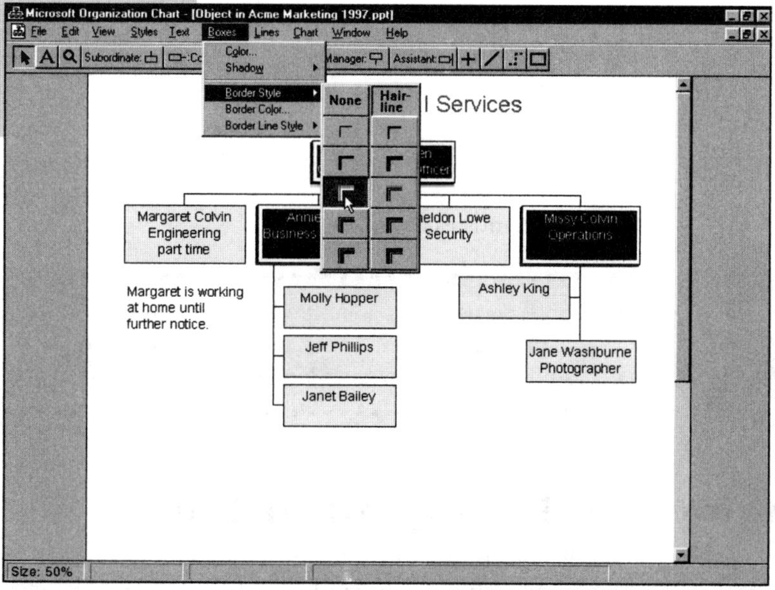

Changing the Lines

Lines in Microsoft Organization Chart refers to the lines that connect one box to another. These are drawn automatically for you, but you can change their thickness, color, and style (solid, dotted, or dashed).

Tip

In organization charts, dotted lines are usually used to indicate something that is shared or that is only partly the case. For example, an employee might report mainly to one boss but have "dotted line reporting" to another one. That means that although the second boss does not have responsibility for the employee, he or she may sometimes assign work or provide guidance. See the section that follows this one for information about adding additional lines like that.

You might want to change certain lines to emphasize them; for example, you could make the lines that denote the main organization bolder than those that show a satellite office.

To select a line, click on it. To select more than one line, hold down the Shift key while you click on multiple lines. It's kind of hard to tell when a line is selected; it looks somewhat fuzzy or dotted when selected, but you may have to squint to see it.

Once the line(s) are selected, open the Lines menu and choose a command. Here's what you'll find:

- *Thickness.* Choose a different line thickness, or hairline (very thin) or None.
- *Style.* Choose from solid, dotted, or dashed.
- *Color.* This command opens a dialog box of colors, the same as for boxes and text.

Tip

None might be useful as a line thickness if you want to create two separate parts of the same chart. You could set the line that joins the two parts to None, effectively removing it, so the parts look separate.

Changing the Background Color

Like all objects, an organization chart can have a colored background. Your choices are somewhat more limited for an organization chart than for most objects—you can't use textures or patterns. However, there are a wide variety of colors to choose from.

To set the background color, choose Chart, Background Color. A Color dialog box appears (with nothing but swatches of colors in it, like before). Click on the color you want and click on OK.

Saving the Chart and Returning to PowerPoint

When you've finished your organization chart, you need to exit the Microsoft Organization Chart program and return to PowerPoint, taking your chart with you. Follow these steps to do so:

1. Choose File, Exit and Return to {**presentation name**}. A dialog box appears asking you if you want to update the copy of the org chart on the slide.
2. Click on Yes. You're back in PowerPoint, and your finished chart appears on the slide, as shown in Figure 11.10.

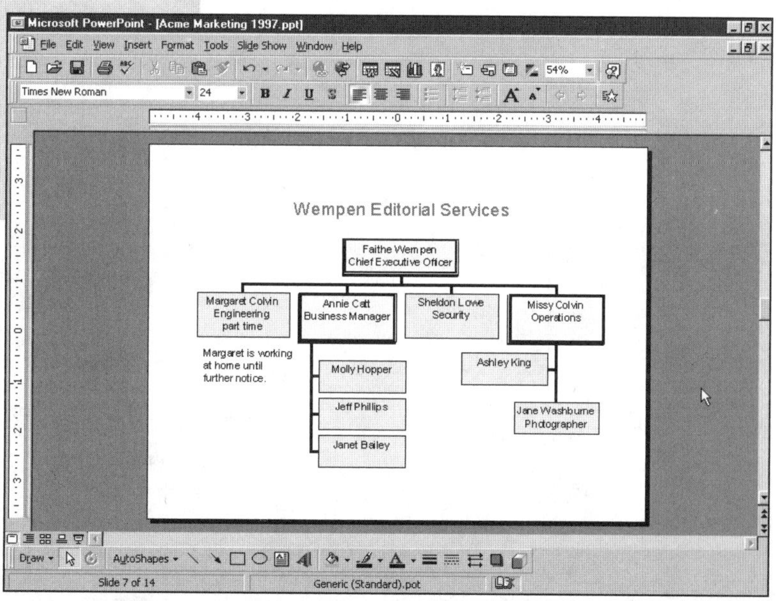

Figure 11.10 Here's the chart you've been working on, in its new home on the PowerPoint slide.

From the slide, you can move and resize the org chart like any other object. Try right-clicking on it, too, and see what options are available on its shortcut menu. If you want to return to editing the chart, double-click on it to reopen Microsoft Organization Chart.

Tip

If there is an org chart that you want to save independently of the presentation, for example, to use in many other presentations, choose File, Save Copy As in Microsoft Organization Chart, before you return to PowerPoint. A dialog box appears where you can save the chart under its own name. You can then place it in any presentation.

Summary

In this chapter, you learned how to create, edit, and format organization charts that you can use in your presentations. Organization charts can be very useful in certain presentations for conveying information about an organization or process. In the upcoming chapter, you'll learn how to incorporate data from other programs like Excel and Word into your presentation.

12

OLE: Exchanging Data with Other Programs

In This Chapter

- Borrowing Slides from Other Presentations
- Importing Objects
- Linking and Embedding Objects

Your PowerPoint presentation may work great as a stand-alone, but it might be even better with elements that other programs or other presentations can provide. Whether you want to borrow some slides from another PowerPoint presentation or link up a totally foreign object, you'll learn how to get it done in this chapter.

Importing Slides from Other PowerPoint Presentations

If you give multiple presentations, one of the great time-savers is to reuse some of the same slides. Some people even create an entire presentation that consists of nothing but boilerplate slides they use over and over again; then they borrow slides from that presentation when creating each unique new presentation for various situations.

In Chapter 4, you learned how to create templates containing slides that you use over and over, and then start new presentations based on that template. This accomplishes the same ultimate goal as importing slides from other presentations: saving time by creating fewer new slides.

Don't forget, you can create templates that let you start a new presentation with a base set of slides already in place; see Chapter 4.

When should you import slides instead of using a template containing premade slides? Each method has its own uses:

- If you frequently create presentations that use the same basic set of slides, it might be worth your time to create a template to use each time.
- If you want to reuse a few slides (or even lots of slides) on a one-time basis, it's easier to import them from another presentation than to go to the trouble of creating a template.
- If you want to create a presentation file that's a "library" of slides you frequently reuse, it's best to save it as a file—not a template—and import the slides you need.

If you decide that importing is what you need, use the following Hands On.

Hands On: Importing Slides

For this exercise, you should have at least two presentation files saved on your hard disk. If you don't, save your current presentation under a different name, so you at least have two different files, even if they are the same. That way you'll have a file to import from. In real life, of course, you would import from a file that contained different slides than what you already have in your presentation.

1. Open the presentation into which you want to import slides.
2. Choose Insert, Slides from Files. The Slide Finder dialog box opens. Initially, most of its controls are grayed out; don't worry about that.

3. If you happen to know the complete name and path for the presentation file from which you want to take slides, enter it in the File text box. Otherwise click on Browse and use the Insert Slides from Files dialog box to locate it; then click on Open.
4. Click on the Display button. The slides from the presentation appear in the preview area, as shown in Figure 12.1.
5. Click on each slide you want to import. Use the horizontal scroll bar to move to the next three slides as needed. When you click on a slide, a dark box appears around it, indicating it's selected.

Tip

If you want to insert all the slides from the presentation, you don't have to select any of them. Instead of steps 5 and 6, just click on the Insert All button.

Note

In the Slide Finder dialog box, you can select multiple slides without having to hold down Shift or Ctrl or anything like that.

6. When you have selected all the slides you want, click on the Insert button.
7. Click on the Close button to close the dialog box.

Figure 12.1 You can choose from the slides in the selected presentation from here.

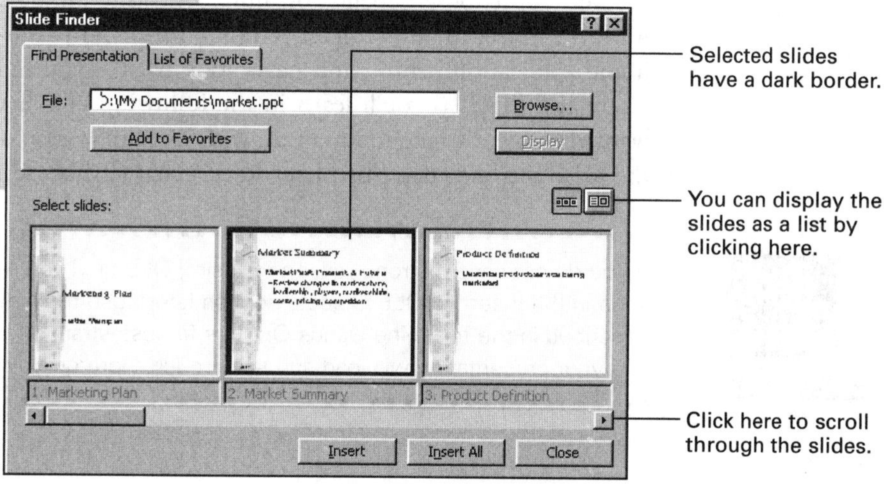

Notice that your imported slides immediately take on the appearance of the other slides in their new home. That's because when you import a slide, it takes on the properties of the Slide Master.

Importing Objects from Other Programs

I know, I know, I told you that all objects are basically alike in PowerPoint. And that's pretty much true, once the objects actually get into your presentation. But placing an object in your presentation can depend on what kind of object it is.

You have already seen in earlier chapters how to import objects from some of the mini-programs that come with PowerPoint, such as WordArt (Chapter 8), Microsoft Graph (Chapter 10), and Microsoft Organization Chart (Chapter 11). These are easy; you just choose the desired object type from the Insert menu in PowerPoint and away you go. Graphics, as you saw in Chapter 8, are similarly easy, no matter what program they come from.

However, there are a host of other objects that don't fall into any of these categories, any of which might be useful occasionally in a presentation. They might include text from a word processor, a slide from a different presentation program (such as Harvard Graphics or Lotus Freelance), a chart from Lotus 1-2-3 or Microsoft Excel, or any of many other objects. With these objects, you have to be a little sneaky in bringing them in.

There are two ways to bring in "foreign objects" to your presentation. The method you choose depends on how you want the object to behave. If you want the object to be a "full citizen" of your presentation—that is, to leave its home application behind and never look back—you can do a simple Cut or Copy and Paste, as you'll learn in the following Hands On. However, if you want the object to maintain a link with its native application, you should use the OLE methods described later in this chapter instead.

Tip

If you do not have a strong reason for using OLE (and you'll read about those reasons in the Inserting OLE Objects section later), use the simpler method described in the following Hands On. It is far less strain on your computer's brain, and your presentation will load and save much more quickly and with less fuss.

Hands On: Importing an Object from a Different Program

To copy an object from another program and use it in PowerPoint, follow these steps:

1. Open both PowerPoint and the application that contains the object to be copied.
2. Switch to the other application, and select the object.
3. Choose Edit, Copy or press Ctrl+C. The object is copied to the Windows Clipboard.
4. Switch to PowerPoint. You can close the other application if you want to, or leave it open (your choice).
5. Display the slide on which the object should be placed.
6. Choose Edit, Paste or press Ctrl+V.

Tip

There are lots of ways to copy and paste—the Edit menu commands, the toolbar buttons, the shortcut keys, and so on. Personally, I never use anything but the shortcut keys anymore. They're simply the fastest, easiest method, once you memorize them.

Inserting OLE Objects

OLE (Object Linking and Embedding) enables Windows applications that use it to share information easily. For example, you might create a chart in Excel that shows the month's revenue, and link it to your PowerPoint presentation. Then every time you opened that presentation, it would check to see if the chart had been updated, and if it had, it would pull in the most recent version. Pretty cool, eh?

And even though the name OLE is a little scary (ranks right up there with SQL, in my book!), the concept is very elementary, and anyone can understand and use it.

You already understand the term "object" in the PowerPoint sense, and the term is very similar to that in this case. An object is any bit of data (or a whole file) that you want to link to another document.

OLE links can slow down the loading of your presentation file significantly, and can make your presentation editing feel sluggish. Therefore, you should add OLE links as the last step of creating the presentation. Adding more memory (RAM) to your computer can help alleviate the problem.

Then there's linking and embedding. These are separate but related:

- *Linking* creates a link between the original file and the spot in your presentation, so that the spot in your presentation always has the most current version of the file.
- *Embedding* creates a new object in your presentation, or edits an existing one, in its native application without leaving PowerPoint.

Embedding by itself doesn't maintain a link to any data file. It just inserts a copy into your document, like the regular copy command. However, it does maintain a link to the application that created it, so you can double-click on the embedded object to open that program. Conversely, linking by itself doesn't embed.

Some objects can be both linked and embedded; others are only one or the other. Linked objects must already exist independently of the PowerPoint presentation, because they are referred to by name in the link. The instructions to the computer might be "Go out and find Sales.xls and bring me the most recent version of what's in cells A1 through C8." Embedded objects can be created on-the-fly right in PowerPoint. Don't worry if you don't fully understand this yet; it will become clearer.

OLE isn't suitable for every task. If you want to use an object (like an Excel chart or a picture from your graphics program) that will not be changing, it's best to simply import it through normal means. Reserve OLE for objects that will be changing and that you will always need the most recent version of.

Here are some ideas for when OLE might be useful:

- If you have to give the same presentation every month that shows the monthly sales statistics, link to your Excel worksheet where you track them during the month. Your presentation will always contain the most current data.
- If you want to draw a picture in Paint (a program that comes with Windows 95) or some other graphic program, embed the picture in

PowerPoint. That way you don't have to open Paint (or the other program) separately every time you want to work on the picture while you're fine-tuning your presentation. You can just double-click on the picture in PowerPoint to open Paint.

- If you know that a coworker is still finalizing a chart or drawing, link to his or her working file on the network. Then whenever changes are made to it, your copy will be updated too. (Beware, however, that once you take your presentation away from the computer that has network access, you will no longer be able to update the item.)

Creating Links and Embedding

There are several ways to link and/or embed, depending on the object that you want to place and how you want to place it. Use the appropriate Hands On steps for your situation.

Hands On: Linking and/or Embedding a Part of a File

To and/or embed link a part of a file into PowerPoint, you use the Edit, Paste Special command. It's similar to the regular Paste command (Ctrl+V) but with some differences.

When you paste an object with the regular Paste command, the object plops down into PowerPoint with no memory of where it came from. When you use Paste Special, it retains its memory about things like its original file name and location, the application that created it, and where it used to live within its original file. This extra information makes it possible for the object to be linked and/or embedded in PowerPoint.

1. In its native application (for example, Excel), copy the object to the Clipboard by selecting it and choosing Edit, Copy.
2. Switch to PowerPoint and open the presentation you want to paste it in.
3. View the slide that you want to paste it on.
4. Choose Edit, Paste Special. The Paste Special dialog box opens (see Figure 12.2).
5. Click on the Paste Link option button if you want to link (with or without embedding), or the Paste option button if you only want to embed.

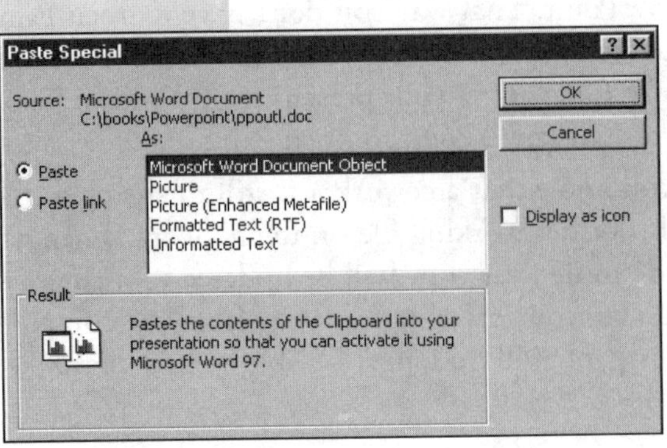

Figure 12.2 Use the Paste Special dialog box to control the linking and/or embedding.

Note

If the Paste Link button is grayed out, you probably have not saved the source file, so the source file has no name. Go back to the original application and save your work.

6. Choose the format you want to use from the As list. The formats change depending on the object type and whether you chose Paste or Paste Link step 5, but you might see some of these:
   - *Object.* Any type that ends with the word "object" is an OLE-capable format that enables embedding. Choose this if you want to both link and embed the object.
   - *Formatted Text (RTF).* This data type formats text as it is formatted in the original file. For example, if the text is formatted as underlined and bold, it is pasted as underlined and bold. This format does not support embedding.
   - *Unformatted Text.* This is the same as formatted text except it doesn't retain any formatting. It is not embedded.
   - *Picture.* The object comes in as a Windows metafile picture. It is not embedded.
   - *Device Independent Bitmap.* The object is comes in as a bitmap picture, like a Windows Paint image. It is not embedded.
7. If you want the pasted object to appear as an icon instead of as itself, click on the Display As Icon check box. This is useful for pasting sounds and video clips because you can plan them later. This check box is grayed out if the object type you chose in Step 5 does not support it.
8. Click on OK. The object is placed in your presentation.

For more information about using sounds and videos in presentations, see Chapter 13.

Hands On: Embedding an Entire File (With or Without Linking)

If you want to place an entire file from another program into PowerPoint, you use the Insert, Object command. This is handier than the preceding procedure because you do not have to start the application that the file is coming from in order to do it.

Note

When you are working with whole, named files, as this procedure is, you cannot avoid embedding. You can either embed only or you can both embed and link. I can't imagine why you would want to avoid embedding, however, as it is harmless and can be very helpful.

1. Open the PowerPoint presentation and display the slide on which you want to place the object.
2. Choose Insert, Object. The Object dialog box appears.
3. Click on the Create from File button. The controls change, as shown in Figure 12.3.
4. Click on the Browse button and use the Browse dialog box to locate the file. (It works the same as the Save and Open dialog boxes.) Then click on OK to accept the file name.
5. If you want the file to be linked as well as embedded, click on the Link check box to select it.
6. Click on OK.

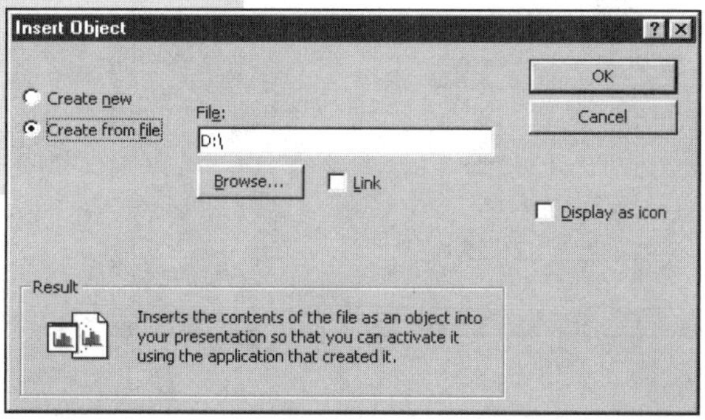

Figure 12.3 The Insert Object dialog box helps you import and link an entire file.

Hands On: Creating a New Embedded Object

So far you've looked at fragments of saved files and entire saved files. But what if you don't have any file yet, and need to create one? Use these steps:

1. Open the PowerPoint presentation and display the slide where you want to put the new embedded object.
2. Choose Insert, Object. The Object dialog box appears.
3. Click on the Create New button. A list of available object types appears (see Figure 12.4).
4. Click on the object type you want (for example, Paintbrush Picture) and click on OK. The application opens.
5. Create the object using that program's controls.
6. When you are finished working with the object, click anywhere on the slide outside of that object's frame. Your PowerPoint controls return to normal, and the object floats on the slide.
7. Resize and reposition the object as needed.

Note

Because you are creating a file here that doesn't have a name or a saved location separate from the PowerPoint presentation, you can't link it to anything; embedding is your only option.

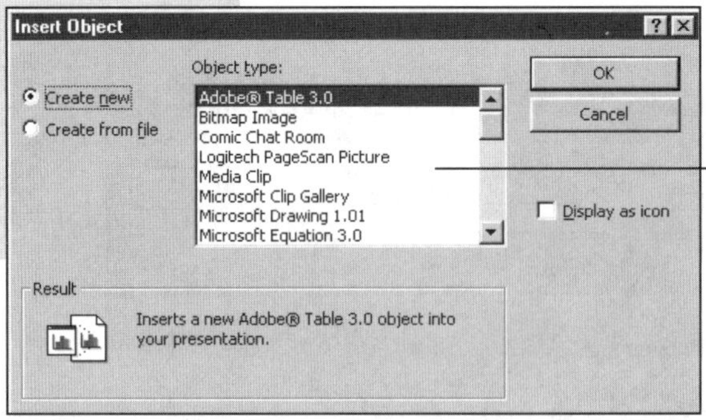

Figure 12.4 You can create a new object with any program that Windows 95 is aware of on your system.

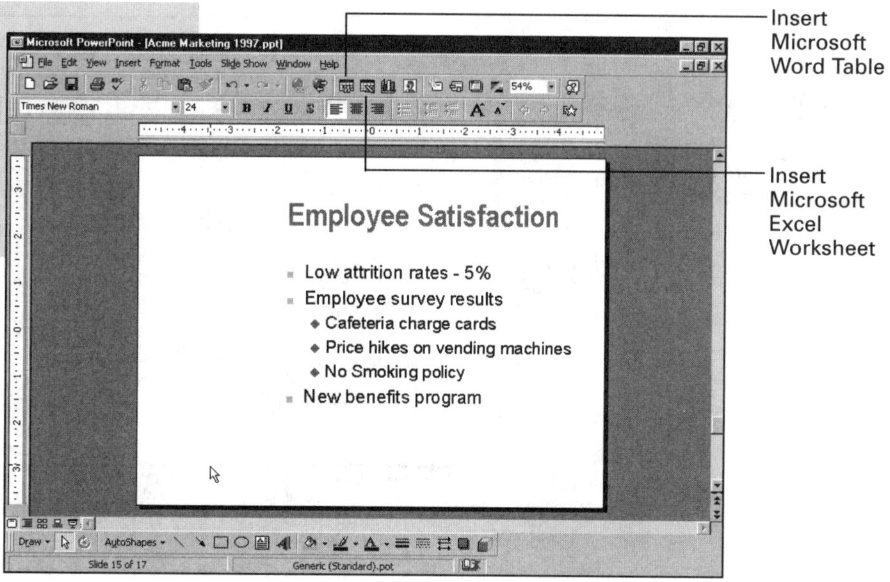

Figure 12.5 These two buttons offer shortcuts for embedding Word tables and Excel worksheets.

Tip

If you want to embed a new Word table or Excel worksheet, click on the Insert Microsoft Word Table or Insert Microsoft Excel Worksheet button on the Standard toolbar (see Figure 12.5). These buttons provide a shortcut to starting those kinds of embedded objects.

Editing Linked or Embedded Objects

Editing an embedded object is where the benefit of embedding really shows. You don't have to remember the name and location of any other files—you just double-click on the object and its original application starts, enabling you to edit the object.

Follow these steps to edit any embedded object, linked or not:

1. Open the PowerPoint presentation containing the embedded object, and display the slide that it's on.
2. Double-click on the object or choose Edit, Object.
3. Edit the object. Depending on the object, its native application may appear in a separate window or its controls may seem "built into" PowerPoint, as Paint is in Figure 12.6.

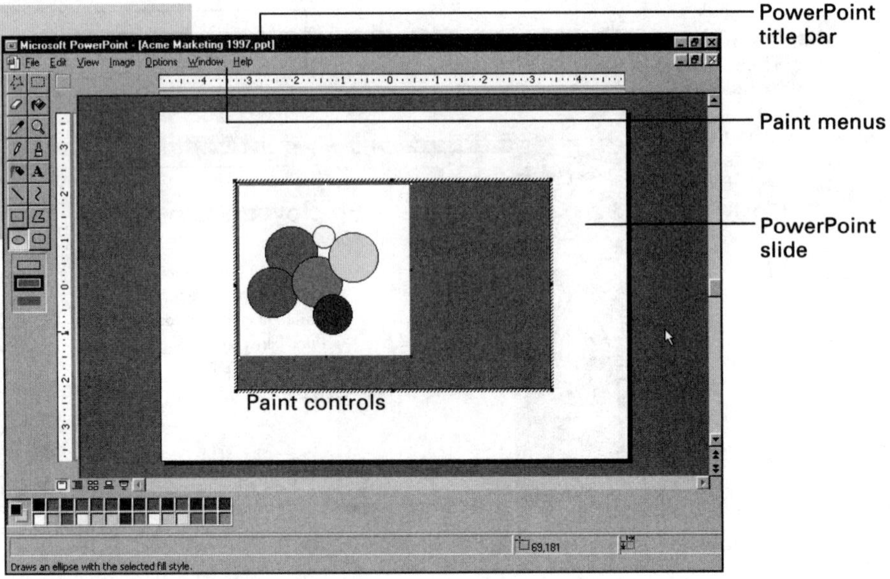

Figure 12.6 Some applications, like Paint, merge with PowerPoint; others are independent.

4. Return to PowerPoint in one of these ways:

   If the embedded object is not linked to a saved file, simply click on the slide behind the object to return to PowerPoint's controls.

   If the embedded object is linked, open the File menu and choose Exit in the object's native application. When you're asked to save your changes, click on Yes.

You also can edit a linked object directly in its original application, independently from PowerPoint. Just close PowerPoint (if it's open) and open the original application. Do your editing, and save your work. When you reopen your PowerPoint presentation, the object will reflect the changes.

Changing the Link Update Settings

Links can be updated manually or automatically. Automatically is the default; that means that the link is updated every time the PowerPoint file that contains it is opened. You may want to set a link to update manually, however, especially if you have lots of links or a slow computer. If the links don't have to all update when you open the file, the file will load faster.

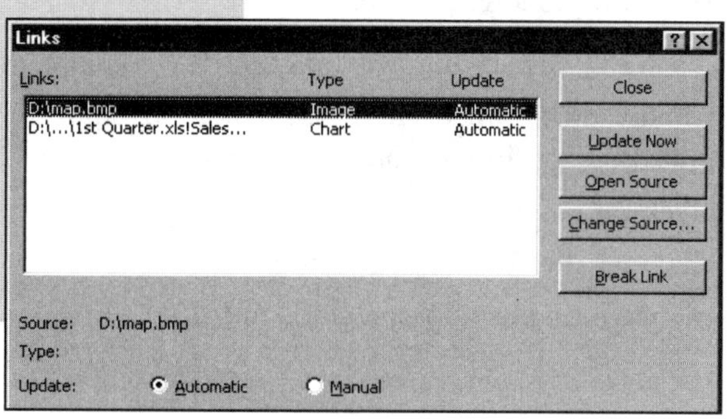

Figure 12.7 Manage all your presentation's links from this one handy location. Here I have two links: a chart and a graphic.

To set a link to manual update, follow these steps:

1. Open the PowerPoint presentation that contains the linked objects.
2. Choose Edit, Links. The Links dialog box appears, showing all the linked objects in your document (see Figure 12.7).
3. Click on the link to update.
4. Change the update setting by clicking Manual.
5. Update the link by clicking Update Now.
6. If you want to change any other links, repeat steps 3 through 5.
7. Click on OK to close the dialog box.
8. Choose File, Save to save the presentation changes (including the changes to the link settings.)

When a link is set to manual, you have to open the Links dialog box and click on Update Now, or right-click on the object and choose Update Link, every time you want to update that link.

Breaking a Link

When you break a link, the object remains in your presentation, but it becomes an ordinary object, just like any picture or other object you might have imported. You can't double-click on it to edit it anymore, and it doesn't update when the source changes.

To break a link, follow these steps:

1. Open the PowerPoint presentation that contains the linked objects.
2. Choose Edit, Links. The Links dialog box appears, showing all the linked objects in your document (refer to Figure 12.7).
3. Click on the link to break.
4. Click on the Break Link button.
5. If a warning box appears, click on OK.

Summary

In this chapter, I talked about "foreign objects," but not the scary kind (like alien spacecraft or things you get in your eye) but the useful kind—the kind that can enhance your presentation. You learned how to import slides, to copy objects, and to harness the power of OLE.

PART III

Creating a Presentation that Moves

13

Adding Sounds and Videos to Your Presentations

In This Chapter

- Inserting Sound and Video Clips
- Inserting a Sound or Video from a File
- Choosing the Right Sounds and Videos
- Setting When and How a Sound or Video Will Play
- Displaying or Hiding a Sound Icon
- Setting the Size of a Video Clip Window

There's a new buzzword in town: *multimedia*. Literally, it means "multiple media," but most people know it as something that includes not only still pictures but also sounds and moving video clips, and perhaps animation too. In this chapter, you'll learn how easy it is to place sounds and videos on your slides, and how to control them to "go off" at the right times.

Why Use Sound and Video?

There are lots of good reasons to incorporate sounds and video clips into your presentation, and only a few reasons not to. Here are some ideas for using sounds and videos:

- You can assign a recognizable sound (such as a beep) to each slide, so that your audience hears a beep each time the slide changes. This can signal the audience to look up and read the new slide.
- You can record a message (sound or video) from a CEO or other important person who couldn't be with you to give a live presentation.
- You can punctuate important points with sounds, or use sounds to add humorous touches.
- You can demonstrate how a product works with a video; this is much more effective than simply showing a picture of the product.

Sounds great, eh? But sounds and videos are not always appropriate. Here are some situations where you want to avoid them:

- If you are trying to pack a lot of information into a short presentation time, avoid sounds and videos, as they take up time playing.
- If your presentation is delivering very serious news, avoid "fun" background and transition sounds.
- If the computer you are using to show the presentation isn't very powerful, avoid video clips, as they may play jerkily or with poor audio and/or video quality.

Inserting Clips: The Clip Gallery Revisited

Refer to Chapter 8 for detailed information about the Clip Gallery.

In Chapter 8, I introduced you to the Clip Gallery, an organizer that helps you place several kinds of objects on your slides: clip art, pictures, sounds, and video. You learned about pictures and clip art in Chapter 8, and I promised you more information on the sounds and videos later. Well, here it is.

Sound and video clips work exactly the same way as static visuals (clip art and sounds) as far as placing them on your slides goes. The Clip Gallery has all the same controls for them, and you organize your sound and video clips the same way. The differences come in how you can set up your sounds and videos after

If you don't have any clips on your Sounds tab, turn back to Chapter 8 to learn how to get some from the Microsoft Office CD and/or the Microsoft Web site.

they're placed on the slides. Because sounds and videos are "dynamic," that is, they do something, rather than just sitting there, you have to set some additional controls to tell how and when you want them activated.

Just so you don't have to turn back to Chapter 8 to get the scoop, I've included the following Hands On to remind you how to use the Clip Gallery.

Hands On: Placing a Sound Clip on a Slide

Follow these steps to place a sound clip on your slide.

1. Display the slide onto which you want to place the sound clip.
2. Choose Insert, Movies and Sounds, Sound from Gallery. The Clip Gallery opens, with the Sounds tab selected, as shown in Figure 13.1.
3. Click on the sound you want to insert. If you are not sure which one you want, click on one and then click on the Play button to hear it.

Tip

Some speakers take a second to "warm up" after being idle. If you play a sound but hear nothing, try clicking on Play again a few times.

4. Click on the Insert button. The sound's icon appears on your slide (see Figure 13.2). You'll learn how to hide the icon later in this chapter.
5. Test the sound by double-clicking on the icon on the slide. The sound should play.

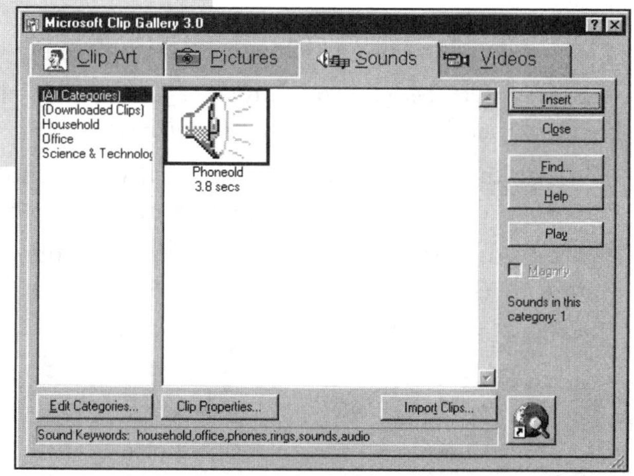

Figure 13.1 Use the Clip Gallery to choose the sound you want.

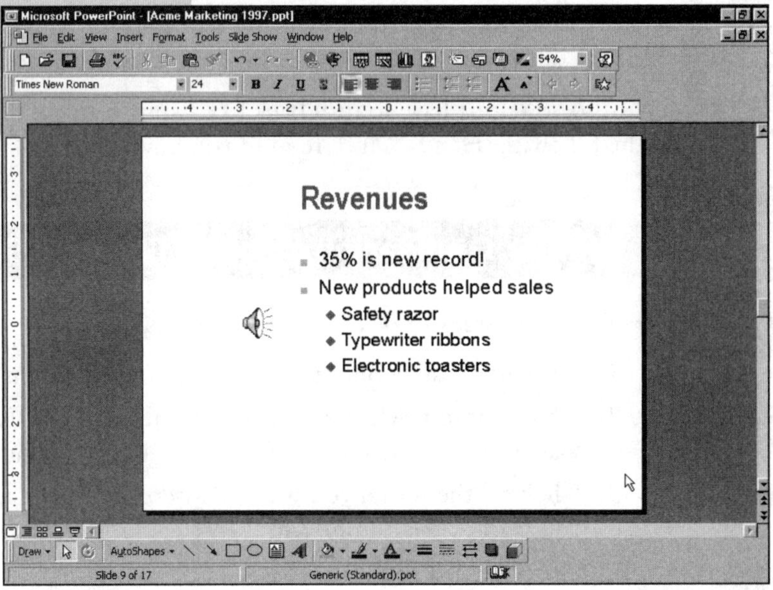

Figure 13.2 Here's what a sound icon looks like on a slide.

Hands On: Placing a Video Clip on a Slide

In PowerPoint, video clips are called *movies*. This may well seem odd to you, because in the Clip Gallery, they are called videos. No matter—it's all the same thing.

Inserting a video clip on a slide is almost exactly the same as inserting a sound clip:

1. Display the slide onto which you want to place the video clip.
2. Choose Insert, Movies and Sounds, Movie from Gallery. The Clip Gallery opens, with the Videos tab selected.
3. Click on the video you want to insert. If you are not sure which one you want, click on one and then click on the Play button to see it.
4. Click on the Insert button. The first frame of the video appears on your slide (see Figure 13.3).
5. Test the video by double-clicking on it. The video should play.

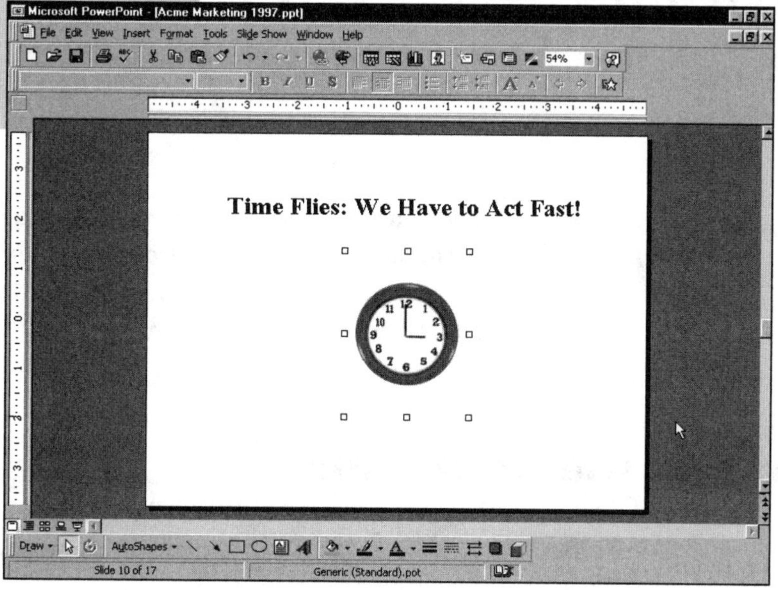

Figure 13.3 Here's a simple video clip placed on a slide.

Inserting Sounds and Videos from Files

Just like with pictures, you can insert sounds and videos directly into the slide, rather than going through the Clip Gallery, if you prefer. This method works well for clips that you have acquired from other sources (perhaps a coworker has given you a video clip on a diskette, for example), because these will not show up automatically in the Clip Gallery. Of course, you could add them to the Clip Gallery using the Import Clips button (which you learned about in Chapter 8), but that's an unnecessary step if you are going to use this clip only once.

To insert a sound or video from a file, follow these steps:

1. Display the slide on which you want to place the sound or video.
2. Choose Insert, Movies and Sounds, and then click on either Movie from File or Sound from File. A dialog box opens where you can browse for the file.
3. Choose the file you want and click on the Insert button. The clip appears on your slide.

Controlling Your Sounds

Placing a sound icon on a slide is cool, but it's only the tip of the iceberg in terms of PowerPoint's abilities. You can control exactly when the sound should play, assign it to an object, set timing for it, and more.

Note

If you want to assign sounds to certain events in your presentation, such as the switch from one slide to another, you set that up through animation and transition effects, which you'll learn about in the next chapter.

When Will the Sound Play?

By default when you place a sound on a slide, it plays when you click on its icon. But you can also make it play whenever the mouse pointer moves over the icon, without clicking.

Note

You can associate a sound with a particular object, for example, and make that sound play whenever the object appears. You'll learn to do that in Chapter 14, when you learn about object animation.

To change between "mouse click" and "mouse over" for the sound icon, follow these steps:

1. Right-click on the sound icon and choose Action Settings. The Action Settings dialog box appears (see Figure 13.4). All the controls are grayed out except Object Action.
2. On the Mouse Click tab, if you want the sound to play when someone clicks on the icon, leave the Object Action set to Play. Otherwise open that drop-down list and choose None.
3. Click on the Mouse Over tab. The same controls appear, but they refer to what happens when the mouse is over the icon.
4. If you want the sound to play when someone moves the mouse over the icon, choose Play from the Object Action drop-down list. Otherwise leave it set to None.
5. Click on OK.

Turn to Chapter 14 to learn about animation settings.

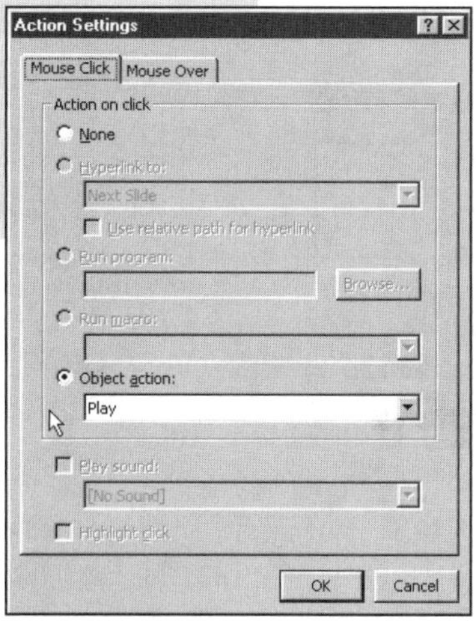

Figure 13.4 Use the Action Settings dialog box to set up when the sound icon will activate.

Note

You can also specify animation settings for the sound icon, because, after all, it is an object like any other. Animation settings enable you to specify when the sound icon appears on the slide and when it plays.

Assigning a Sound to a Slide Transition

You can have sounds associated with a particular slide's coming or going, so that every time that slide appears, a certain sound plays. When you do that, there is no sound icon; instead, the slide itself becomes the sound icon. The sound will play every time that slide appears.

Here's how:

1. Switch to Slide Sorter view.
2. Click on the slide you want to assign the sound to.
3. Choose Slide Show, Slide Transition. The Slide Transition dialog box appears.
4. Open the Sound drop-down list and choose the sound you want, or choose Other Sound and browse for it (see Figure 13.5).
5. Click on Apply.
6. Use Slide Show view to check your work.

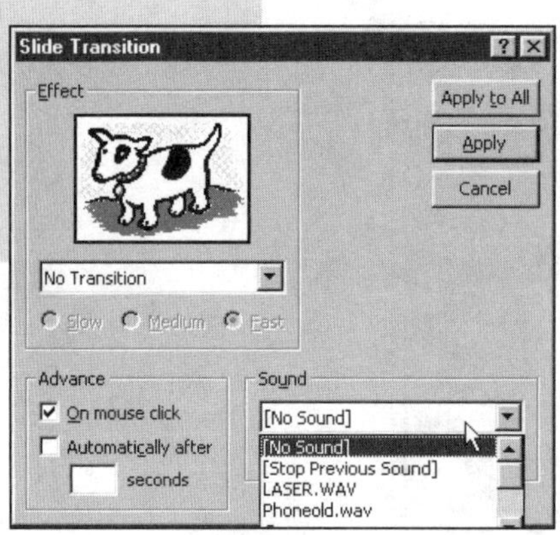

Figure 13.5 Choose a sound from the drop-down list in the Slide Transition dialog box.

Assigning a Sound to an Object

As you've seen, sounds can be objects on a slide or they can be attached to the slide transition. But you can also assign sounds to individual objects on the slide. To assign a sound to an object, you don't need to insert the sound separately (as you learned to do earlier in this chapter). Instead, you follow the steps in the following Hands On:

Hands On: Attaching a Sound to an Object

1. Display any slide that has a title on it. (Probably most, if not all, of your slides meet this criterion.)
2. Right-click on the title. A menu appears.
3. Choose Custom Animation from the menu. The Custom Animation dialog box opens.
4. Open the Entry Animation and Sound drop-down list and choose Appear (see Figure 13.6).
5. Right below the Entry Animation and Sound drop-down list, where it says No Sound, open that drop-down list.
6. If you see the sound you want on the list, click on it. Otherwise click on Other Sound, use the Add Sound dialog box to locate the sound, and click on OK.
7. Click on the Timing tab (see Figure 13.7).
8. Click on the Automatically button.
9. Type the number of seconds you want to wait between the time that

You'll learn about the fancier animation settings in Chapter 14.

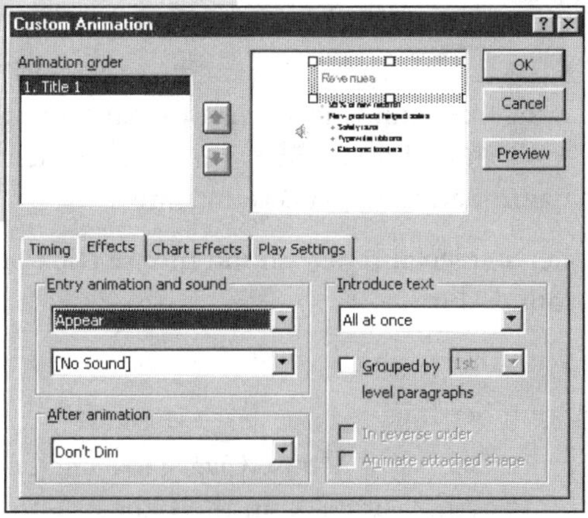

Figure 13.6 Use the Custom Animation dialog box to assign a sound to an object.

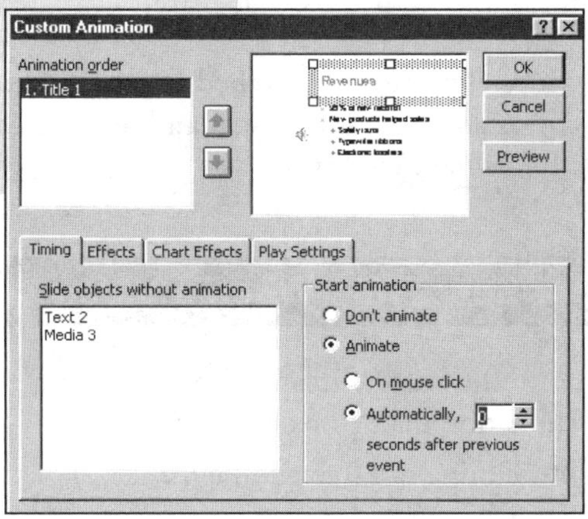

Figure 13.7 On the Timing tab, you specify when the sound should play.

the object appears and the time that the sound plays. (The default is 0, which means they happen simultaneously.)

10. Click on OK.
11. Use Slide Show view to check out the new sound and make sure it works the way you envisioned.

Note

To use Slide Show view, just click on the Slide Show button at the bottom left corner of the screen and then use the Page up and Page Down keys to move from slide to slide. You'll find more information about testing your slide show in Chapter 16.

Controlling Your Video Clips

Video clips are a lot like sounds in terms of what you can do with them. You can specify that they should play when you point at them or click on them, or make them play automatically at a certain time.

To specify whether a video clip plays upon mouse click or mouse point, do the same as with a sound clip:

1. Right-click on the video clip.
2. Choose Action Settings.
3. On the Mouse Click and Mouse Over tabs, click on the None button if you want no action, or click on the Object Action button if you want it to play.
4. Click on OK.

Unlike sounds, video clips can't be attached to other objects. However, you can treat the video clip as an object unto itself, and set up custom animation for it, as shown in the following Hands On.

Hands On: Specifying When a Video Clip Will Play

1. Right-click on the video clip and choose Custom Animation. The Custom Animation dialog box appears.
2. Click on the Timing tab (refer to Figure 13.7).
3. Click on the Animate button.
4. In the Automatically box, specify how many seconds after the slide appears the video should start playing. (The default is 0.)
5. Click on the Play Settings tab (see Figure 13.8).
6. In the While Playing section, choose what you want the rest of the slide show to do while the video plays: Pause Slide Show or Continue Slide Show.
7. Click on the More Options button. The Play Options dialog box appears (see Figure 13.9).
8. If you want the clip to play continuously, select the Loop Until Stopped check box.

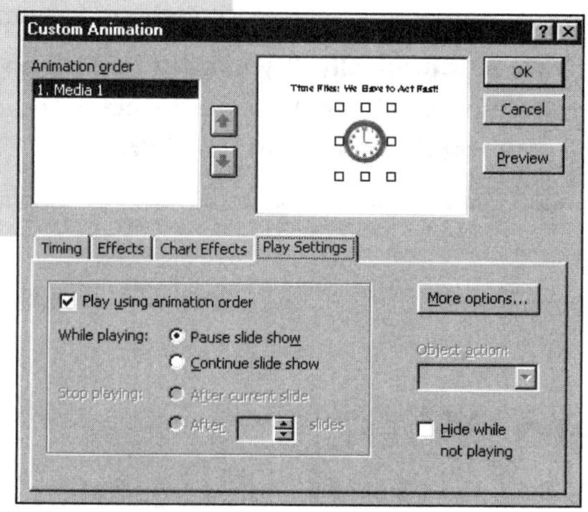

Figure 13.8 The Play Settings tab contains settings to fine-tune how your video performs.

Figure 13.9 Special settings for videos appear in this box.

Note

The Rewind Movie When Done Playing check box returns the video clip display to the first frame of the video when it finishes playing. If you leave this check box cleared, the last frame of the video remains when it's done. However, if you reactivate the video clip, it still starts over from the beginning, even if you didn't choose to rewind it.

9. Click on OK to close the Play Options dialog box.
10. (Optional) If you want to hide the video clip when it's not playing, select the Hide While Not Playing check box.

Don't hide the video while not playing if you don't have it set to activate automatically. If you have to click on it to activate it, but you can't see it unless it's activated, you may be hard-pressed to find it on the slide.

11. Click on OK.

What Else Can You Do with Sounds and Videos?

Video clips, other than the fact that they move when you activate them, are much like still pictures. You can format them the same as you learned to format pictures in Chapter 8. Just right-click on the video clip and choose Format Picture. You can also format a sound icon as if it were an ordinary picture too.

As you'll see in Chapter 14, you can also attach sounds to slide transitions (that is, the movement from one slide to the next in a presentation).

Summary

In this short but important chapter, you learned how to insert and control sounds and videos in your presentation. Stay tuned for even more information in the following chapter about making your presentation come alive with animation and other movement.

14

Making Motion: Slide Transitions and Animations

In This Chapter

- Transitions Between One Slide and Another
- Animating the Objects on a Slide
- Building Self-Running Presentations

Transitions and animations make the difference between *your* presentation—the state-of-the-art one—and your competitor's version shown on an old-fashioned slide projector. These little wisps of color and motion make your audience feel like you've gone the extra mile to make your show exciting and entertaining.

What are Transitions?

Transitions are how you get from Slide A to Slide B. Back in the old slide projector days, there was only one transition: the old slide got pushed out and the new slide plunked into place. But with a computerized presentation, you can choose from all kinds of fun transitions, including wipes, blinds, drives, and much more.

The looks of the individual transitions are hard to explain on paper; it's best if you view them on-screen to understand what each one is. You'll have an opportunity to do just that in the following Hands On.

In Chapter 13, you learned how to attach a sound to a transition using the Sound drop-down list shown in Figure 14.2.

Hands On: Trying Out Transitions

1. Switch to Slide Sorter view. Notice the Slide Sorter toolbar; it contains the controls you'll use to set transitions (see Figure 14.1).
2. Click on the Slide Transition button on the Slide Sorter toolbar (on the far left). The Slide Transition dialog box opens (see Figure 14.2).
3. Open the Effect drop-down list and choose one of the effects.
4. Click on the picture above the drop-down list to see the effect. If you miss it, click on the picture again.

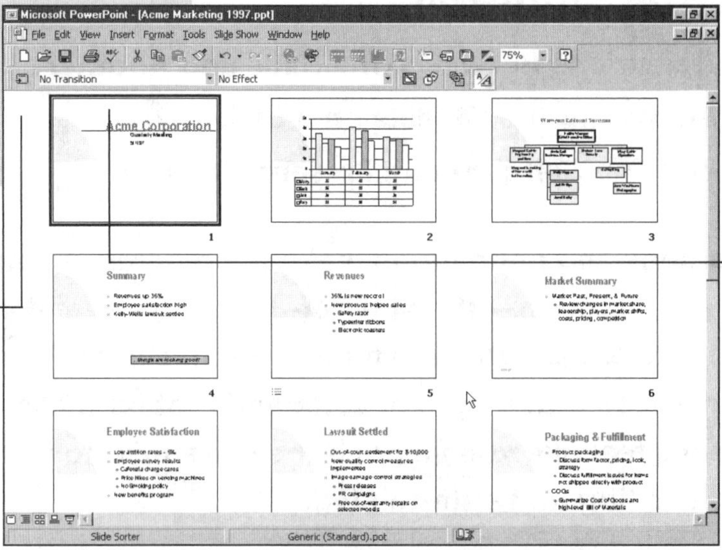

Figure 14.1 The easiest way to set transitions is in Slide Sorter view with the toolbar controls.

Click here to open the Slide Transition dialog box.

Slide Transition Effects drop-down list

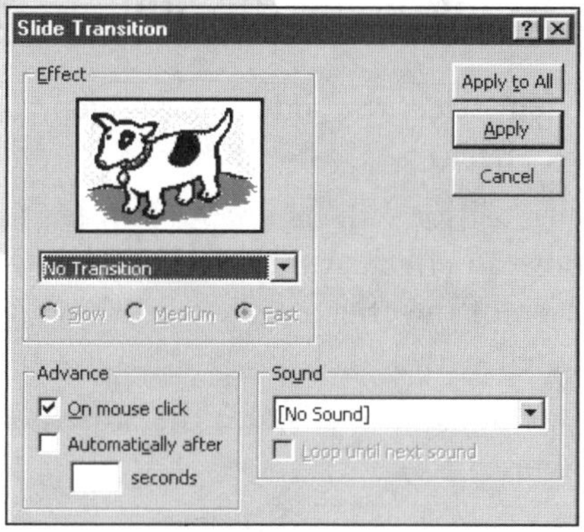

Figure 14.2 Use this dialog box to experiment with the available transitions.

5. Click on the Slow, Medium, or Fast option button and try the effect again to see the difference in speed.
6. Repeat steps 3 through 5, trying out all the effects, until you are familiar with them.
7. Click on Cancel. You're just practicing; you don't need to choose an effect now.

You've just learned one way to choose a transition effect for a slide. The Slide Transition dialog box offers full control over your transitions. To assign a transition to a slide, you would just select the slide and then open the dialog box and choose a transition.

Note

Later in this chapter, you'll learn how to make the transitions happen automatically, in a self-running presentation.

However, there is an easier way to set transitions, and that's with the Slide Transition Effects drop-down list. The disadvantage to it is that you can't set the speed (slow, medium, or fast) from there, but the advantage is that it's really quick and easy. Use the following Hands On to set the transitions for some slides with it.

Hands On: Setting Slide Transitions

1. In Slide Sorter view, select the slide(s) for which you want to assign a certain transition effect.
2. Open the Slide Transition Effects drop-down list on the Slide Sorter toolbar and choose an effect. A little rectangle with an arrow under it appears below each of the affected slides to show that there is a transition associated with it.
3. To try out a slide's transition, click on the aforementioned little rectangle (see Figure 14.3).

Note

If there is a sound attached to the slide transition (see Chapter 13), it will play when you try out the transition (step 3 above). However, if a sound is attached to a particular object on the slide, the sound will not play when testing the transition. It will play only in Slide Show view.

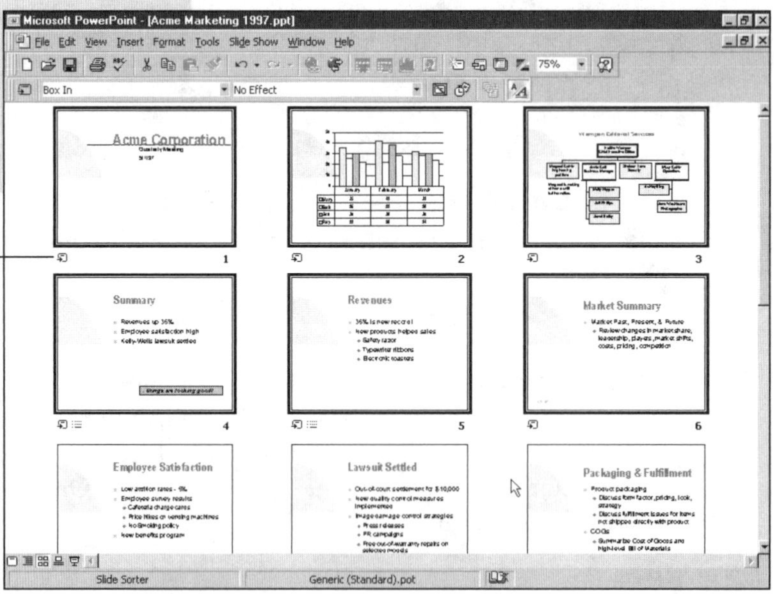

Click here to view the slide's transition effects.

Figure 14.3
Slides that have transitions assigned show a special icon below them.

What are Animations?

If transitions are the big picture, then animations are the close-up view. Transitions are actions that happen to move from one slide to another, and animations are actions that happen to move the focus from one object on a single to slide to another object on that same slide.

For example, suppose you have a slide that contains a bullet list of three items. You could show all three bullets at once, but wouldn't it be more interesting to have each bullet point "fly in" one at a time? That's easy to do with animations. Here are some other things you can do with animations:

- Dim each bullet point when the next one comes into view, so you are, in effect, highlighting the current one.
- Animate parts of a Microsoft Graph chart so that the data appears one series at a time.
- Make certain objects flash and then disappear.
- Rearrange the order in which objects make their appearance on the slide—for example, you could make the bullet points appear from bottom to top.
- Set certain objects to appear a specified length of time after the previous object, or upon a mouse click.

Using Preset Animation

The easiest animation to assign is preset animation. This kind of animation is applied only to text, and it can be applied only in an all-or-nothing way to a slide. If you have more than one text box on the slide, you can't pick which text box it applies to—they all get it.

You can assign preset animation from Slide Sorter view. You may have noticed the other drop-down list to the right of the Slide Transition Effects one, and wondered what it does. That's the Text Preset Animation drop-down list, and you can choose one of the dozens of preset text animations from it.

See Chapter 7 if you've forgotten how to create a bulleted list on a slide.

Try it out with the following Hands On.

Hands On: Applying Preset Text Animation

1. In Slide Sorter view, select a slide that has a bulleted list on it. If you don't have such a slide in your presentation, create one.

2. Open the Text Preset Animation drop-down list and choose an animation. (Try Fly from Bottom.)
3. Click on the Slide Show button. Your selected slide appears in Slide Show view.
4. Click the mouse. Some text appears.
5. Keep clicking the mouse until all the text from that slide appears. Isn't that cool?
6. Press Esc to return to Slide Sorter view.

Using Custom Animation

Custom animation is harder to set up, but much more powerful than the presets. With custom animation, you can animate each object on your slide separately, set animation timings, animate the elements on a chart, and more. Try it out!

Note

Custom animation is set up from Slide view, not Slide Sorter view. In Slide Sorter view, the Custom Animation command is not available. That's because custom animation must be set up separately for each slide individually.

Hands On: Custom Animating A Slide

1. In Slide view, display the slide you want to set custom animation for. To follow along with the examples, you may want to pick a slide that has a title and several bullet items, as well as some other element like a graphic or text box.
2. Click on the Animation Effects button on the toolbar (looks like a star). The Animation Effects toolbar opens, shown in Figure 14.4. You don't have to open this every time, but I wanted you to see it.
3. On the Animation Effects toolbar, the top two buttons are Animate Title and Animate Slide Text. You can use them to turn on/off the animation for these objects. Keep these in mind for later use.
4. Click on the last button on that toolbar, Custom Animation. (If you didn't have the toolbar open, you would want to choose Slide Show, Custom Animation to open it instead.) The Custom Animation dialog box appears (see Figure 14.5).

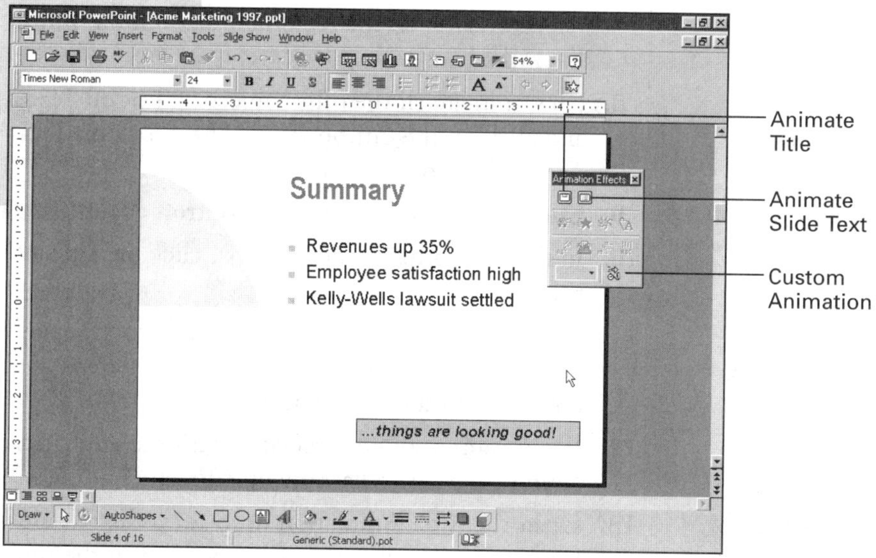

Figure 14.4 The Animation Effects toolbar contains buttons that can help you with your animation.

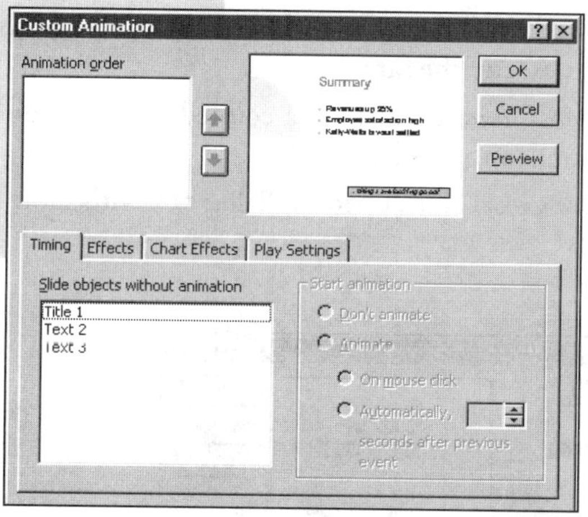

Figure 14.5 You'll use the Custom Animation dialog box to animate the individual objects on the slide.

5. Animate the title first. Click on Title 1 on the list of objects. The title becomes selected in the sample at the top.
6. Click on the Animate option button.
7. Choose one of the following for the title:
   - To have the title wait to appear until you click the mouse, leave the On Mouse Click button selected.

- To have the title appear a certain number of seconds after the last event, click on the Automatically option button and enter a number on the box.

8. Now animate all the other objects. Click on Text 2 in the object list, and click on the button for it. Then click on Text 3 and click on the Animate option button for it too.
9. Click on the Effects tab. The controls change, as shown in Figure 14.6.
10. In the Animation Order list box, click on Title 1. You'll start with the title.
11. In the Entry Animation and Sound section, open the first drop-down list and choose an effect. To try out the effect, click on the Preview button and watch the sample area.
12. If you want a sound associated with the animation, choose it from the Sound drop-down list (the one directly under the effects).
13. Open the After Animation drop-down list. These controls set what happens to the object after its moment in the spotlight is over. Make your selection from the available choices:
    - *Don't Dim.* This is the default. It basically means that the object stays exactly the same.
    - *Colored squares.* Click on a colored square if you want the object to change to that color.
    - *More Colors.* This opens a dialog box with more color choices.

For more information about sounds, see Chapter 13.

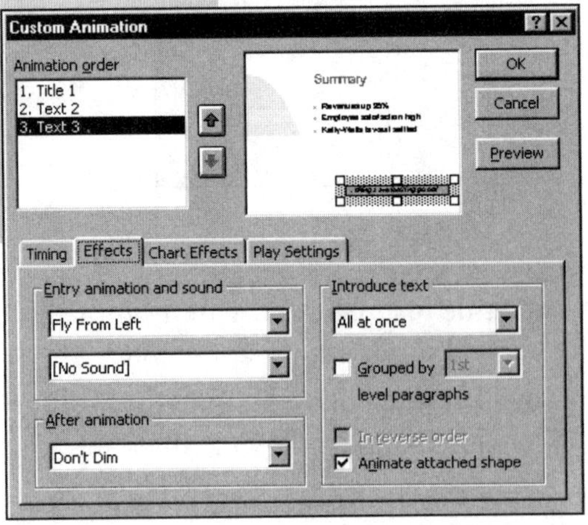

Figure 14.6 Use this tab to choose what effects are associated with each animated object.

- *Hide After Animation.* The object disappears entirely after its animation.
- *Hide on Mouse Click.* The object disappears entirely when you click the mouse.

Tip

I usually leave the slide title set to Don't Dim. You want to be able to see the title on the slide while everything else is going on.

14. Now click on Text 2 on the Animation Order list, or whichever one is your text box containing the bullets.
15. Set an animation effect (and sound if desired) for this object. I'm going to choose Fly from Bottom.
16. For the bullets, set them to dim after each one. Open the After Animation drop-down list and click on a shade that's lighter than the regular bullet text.
17. With a bullet list, or any text box with multiple paragraphs, you get some extra controls. Open the Introduce Text drop-down list and take a look at your options there
18. As you can see, you can introduce text All at Once, By Word, or By Letter. For this example, stick with All At Once, so click away from the drop-down list to close it without making a change.
19. If you would like the paragraphs animated separately (a really cool effect), leave the Grouped By check box marked. For our example, leave it.

Tip

If you have multiple outline levels on the slide (such as a list within a list) you can animate by the lower-level lists by choosing 2nd or 3rd or such from the Grouped By drop-down list.

20. For our example, leave the In Reverse Order check box alone. For future reference, though, this would animate the paragraphs in the object in bottom-to-top order rather than top-to-bottom.
21. And now finish up by clicking on Text 3 or whatever your last object on the slide is called, and setting an animation effect for it. Your choice.

Note

If you have a shape that contains text, like a colored text box, the Animate Shape check box becomes available. By default it's checked; that means the entire object is animated as a single unit. If you deselect that check box, the colored box background (or whatever) is fixed on the slide and only the text inside it is animated.

22. Use the Up and Down arrow buttons next to the Animation Order text box to rearrange the objects' order to the order in which you want them to play.
23. Click on the Preview button to try it all out. If it doesn't look like you expected, adjust the settings.
24. Click on OK. Your slide has been successfully animated!

What about the other two tabs: Chart Effects and Play Settings? There are not applicable unless the slide contains a chart or a playable object (a sound or a video). You learned how to animate sounds and videos in Chapter 13; charts are covered in the following section.

Animating a Chart

This falls into the "somewhat advanced" category, but is well worth your time because it can impress the heck out of your audience. When you have a chart created with Microsoft Graph, you can animate the individual elements on the chart to fly in (or whatever) separately.

Note

You cannot do this with a chart that's an imported object, like an Excel chart. Such charts can only be animated as a whole, single object, like any other graphic object.

Here's how to set it up:

1. Display the slide containing the chart and click once on it to select it. Don't double-click, or you'll open Microsoft Graph.

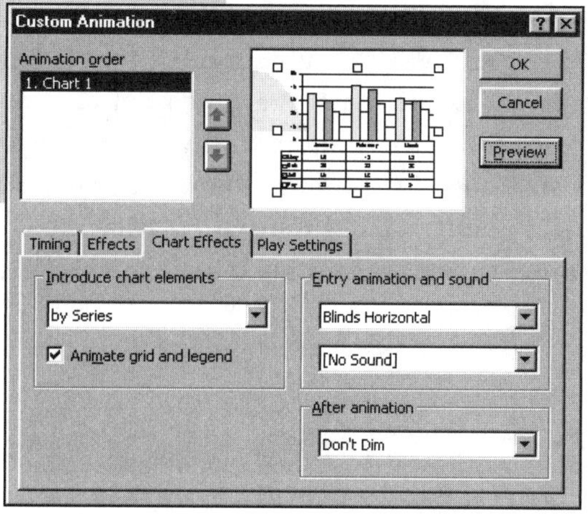

Figure 14.7
On this tab you can animate parts of a chart created in Microsoft Graph.

2. Choose Slide Show, Custom Animation. The Custom Animation dialog box opens, with the Chart Effects tab displayed (see Figure 14.7).
3. Open the Introduce Chart Elements drop-down list and choose one of the following:
   - *All at Once.* Brings in all parts of the chart at once; it's the equivalent to the "Off" setting.
   - *By Category.* Chart elements appear by whatever is on the X axis. For example, if the X axis contains months, all the bars for the first month will appear, then all the second, and so on.
   - *By Series.* Chart elements appear by whatever is in the legend. For example, if the legend contains salespeople names, all the bars for the first salesperson will appear, then the next one, and so on.
   - *By Element in Series.* Like By Series except that each bar in each series appears separately.
   - *By Element in Category.* Like By Category except that each bar in each category appears separately.
4. In the Entry Animation and Sound area, choose an entry animation effect (and optionally a sound), the same as you learned to do for regular objects earlier in the chapter. The same effect will apply to all the elements of the chart.
5. Click on the Preview button to try out the animation. When you are satisfied, click on OK.

Note

The After Animation check box is not quite what you would expect here. You would think that it would change the color of or hide each chart element as it appears, but that's not the case. It refers to the chart as a whole, and is applicable only if there are other elements on the slide besides the chart and if they come after the chart in animation order. I recommend leaving this setting alone.

Building Self-Running Presentations

As you put together your transitions and animations, you may have noticed that there is always an Automatically setting where you can specify a certain number of seconds that should pass before something happens by itself. Because of this capability, you can build presentations that don't require a leader to keep clicking the mouse or pressing a keyboard key to move them forward. These are called *self-running.*

A self-running presentation, in its simplest form, is nothing more than a presentation with all the slide transitions set to happen automatically. You can use it in any number of ways:

- You can set up a kiosk. This is good for conveying information that lots of people need. For example you could set up a presentation showing the meeting times and rooms and have it endlessly repeat on a monitor in the lobby of your convention hall.
- If your slides don't tie specifically to certain points in your presentation, you might set them up to cycle through automatically behind you as you give your speech.
- You can distribute a self-running presentation over an intranet or on a diskette for users to view at their own convenience.

It can get more complicated, of course; you can add recorded narration or a soundtrack, set up a special kiosk security features that prevent unsupervised viewers from stopping the show, and so on. I'll explain a little bit about these items as you go in the remainder of this chapter.

Rehearsing Timings

If you are going to set up your slides to run automatically behind you while you speak, you will need to set the timings fairly precisely so that the right slide will appear during the right part of your speech. Because this is rather tricky, and because it can fail if you get behind (for example, by answering an audience member's question), many people avoid this type of setup. However, when it does work, it works great and looks very professional.

The key is to rehearse your presentation ahead of time so that you know exactly how many seconds each slide should be on-screen. PowerPoint offers a special feature to let you do just that.

Tip

If you are going to record narration for the slides, skip to the Recording Narration section later in this chapter. You can set your timings and your narration at the same time, saving a step.

1. Get all your notes ready, as if you were going to give the presentation now. Be prepared with what you'll say.
2. Choose Slide Show, Rehearse Timings. You switch to Slide Show view and a Rehearse Timings dialog box appears to help you keep track of how long you're spending on each slide (see Figure 14.8).

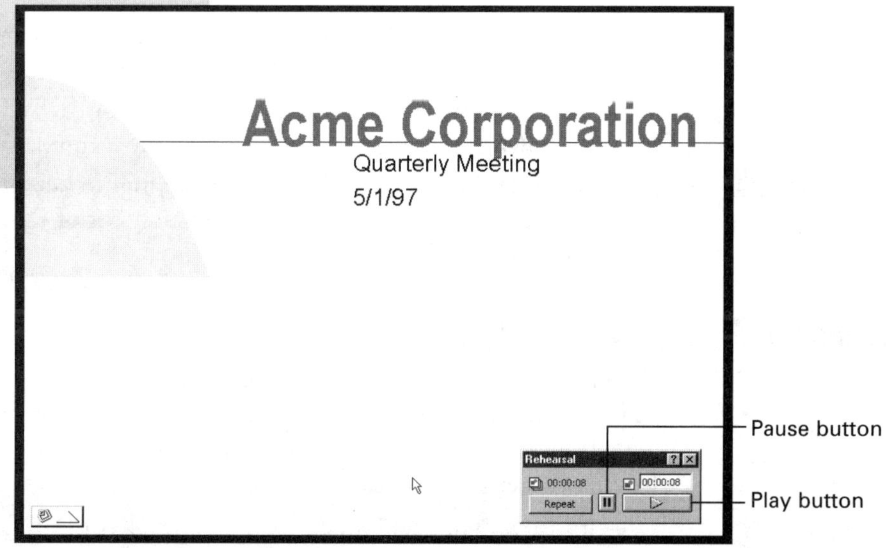

Figure 14.8 The clock is running while you're rehearsing timings!

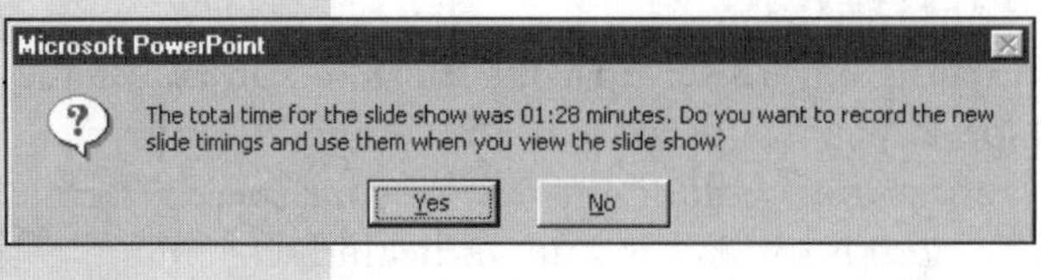

Figure 14.9 This box tells you the total amount of time the presentation took and asks you if you want to save the settings.

Tip

If you get sidetracked from your timing rehearsal, just click on the Pause button to stop the clock. Then click on the Play button again to resume when you're ready to get back to it.

3. Speaking in your normal voice, start giving the presentation. When you are ready to move to the next slide, click on the Play button or press the Page Down key.
4. Continue giving your presentation until you reach the end. As you go, notice the two counters in the Rehearsal dialog box. The left one shows the total presentation time, and the right one shows the time you've spent so far on this slide.
5. When you reach the last slide, you see a message like the one in Figure 14.9. Click on Yes.
6. Then another dialog box asks if you want to review the timings in Slide Sorter view. Click on Yes.
7. In Slide Sorter view, the amount of time for each slide appears below it, as shown in Figure 14.10. Check out these times.
8. If a time doesn't seem right for a slide, right-click on it and choose Slide Transitions, and set a different number of seconds in the dialog box that appears.

Recording Narration

If you aren't going to be there to speak to your audience while the presentation slides are running, you can do the next-best thing: record narration, so that the audience hears your recorded voice while watching. This is fairly simple to do, but it assumes two things:

- That you have the proper equipment needed to record your voice (sound card and microphone)

Figure 14.10 Each slide's timing appears below it. When you rehearsed the timings, you set each slide to advance automatically.

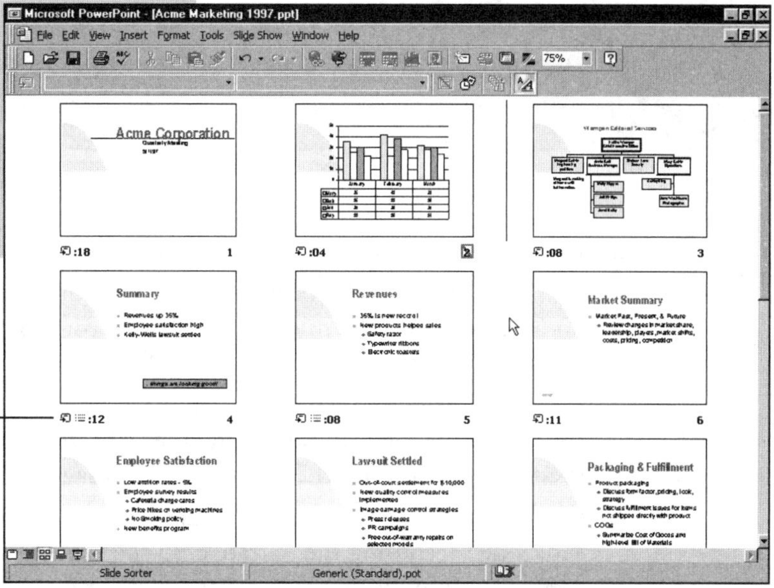

Slide timing

- That everyone viewing your presentation has the proper equipment to hear it (sound card and speakers)

If you're sure about both of those, follow these steps to make your recording.

1. Choose Slide Show, Record Narration. The Record Narration dialog box appears (see Figure 14.11).
2. The default quality is Radio. It's a moderate quality. The other qualities are CD (high) and Telephone (low) If you want a higher quality, click on Settings and choose a different quality. Otherwise just go on to step 3.

Figure 14.11 Here's your opportunity to change the recording settings before you start.

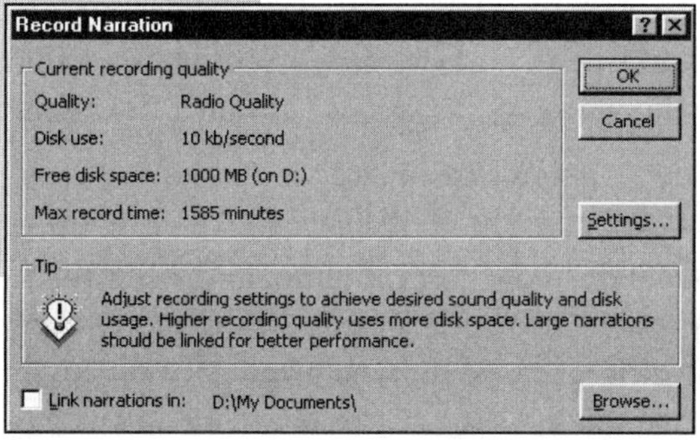

Note

The higher the quality you choose, the more space it takes on your disk. If disk space is an issue, use Telephone quality.

3. Make sure you have your microphone handy, and then click on OK. The slide presentation begins and you are recording.
4. Speak clearly into the microphone. When you are ready to advance to the next slide, click on the mouse button.
5. Continue through the presentation, narrating each slide. When you are finished, a message appears saying that narrations have been saved with the slides and asking whether you want to save the timings.
6. Click on Yes. The timings reflect the amount of time you spent on each slide when recording the narrative, so they should be accurate. Another message appears asking if you want to go into Slide Sorter view.
7. Click on Yes.
8. Click on the Slide Show View button to try out the slide show with the narration.

Caution

Your recorded narration will override any sounds that you have assigned to play at the same time that the narration is going on.

Self-Running Security

When you leave a computer unattended in a public place, you never know what mischief people are going to do to it. At the very least, someone will probably try to stop the presentation. Here are some things you can do to prevent tampering when you leave a self-running presentation unattended:

You'll learn about hyperlink buttons in Chapter 15.

- Hide the computer, keyboard, and mouse under a table or cloth, and put just the monitor on display.
- Choose Slide Show, Set Up Show, and select the Browsed at a Kiosk (full screen) button. This turns off the shortcut menu in slide view. The mouse can still move on-screen and click on any hyperlink buttons you've set up, but no one can access the menu system.

- Save the presentation as a PowerPoint Show (choose File, Save As) and then give the presentation using the PowerPoint Viewer program rather than PowerPoint itself.

Installing and Using the PowerPoint Viewer

If you want to run the presentation using the PowerPoint viewer, you have to install it first. Follow these steps to retrieve it from the CD-ROM and show a presentation:

1. Copy the viewer (Ppview32.exe) from the installation CD-ROM to your hard disk. Look for it in the \ValuPack or \Office folder on the CD-ROM.
2. In Windows Explorer, locate the file on your hard disk and double-click on it.
3. Locate and select the presentation file to show, then select any other options you want.
4. Click on Show.

Tip

You can show one or more presentations from the play list. In the Viewer, enter the file name of the document that shows the play list, and then click on Show. A play list can be created in any word processing program (like Word). Just create a new, blank document. Type the file name of the presentation(s), each on a separate line. Then save the document as a text file with an .lst extension in the same folder as the presentation(s) to which it refers.

Summary

In this chapter, you learned the value of motion in a presentation. You now can give each slide a grand entrance, and animate the individual elements on a slide! At this point, you may be ready to call your presentation good and start working on your handouts and rehearsal. If so, skip ahead to Chapter 16. The next chapter, Chapter 15, can help if you are planning to include hyperlinks in the presentation or present it on the Internet.

15

Hyperlinks for the Internet and Beyond

In This Chapter

- Introducing the Internet Templates
- Adding Hyperlinks to a Presentation
- Placing Action Buttons
- Saving in HTML Format
- Distributing a Presentation Over the Internet

Like the other programs in the Microsoft Office 97 suite, PowerPoint comes with some powerful features that help you work with the Internet. In this chapter, you'll check out PowerPoint's Internet potential and also experiment with some hyperlinks in other contexts too.

What are Hyperlinks?

Let's start out by answering this basic question. In its simplest form, a hyperlink is something that you click on that moves you somewhere else. You've seen hyperlinks in action in PowerPoint's Help system; you clicked on buttons and underlined words and it displayed different topics. Figure 15.1 shows some hyperlinks in the Help system.

The term hyperlink has been popularized by the Internet. On the Internet, a hyperlink is usually an underlined bit of text on a Web page. You click on the underlined text and a different Web page displays. You can hop all over the world jumping from link to link! Figure 15.2 shows a Web page with some hyperlinks.

Figure 15.2 shows a very fancy and complex page, in which there are not only text hyperlinks (the underlined words) but also graphics that you can click on. The graphics serve two purposes: they're interesting in themselves, and when you click on them, you hyperlink to another page.

How does PowerPoint fit into all of this? Well, you can add hyperlinks to your presentation slides, just like Web designers add them to Web pages. The hyperlinks in your presentation will work even if your presentation never goes anywhere near the Internet. Remember, as you saw from the Help system, hyperlinks can be completely self-contained within a system. Your hyperlinks can merely jump the reader from page to page in the presentation. Or, if you want to get fancier, you can include hyperlinks to Web locations. (In Internet-speak, Web locations are called Uniform Resource Locators, or URLs.)

Figure 15.1 PowerPoint's Help feature is built on a powerful hyperlink system.

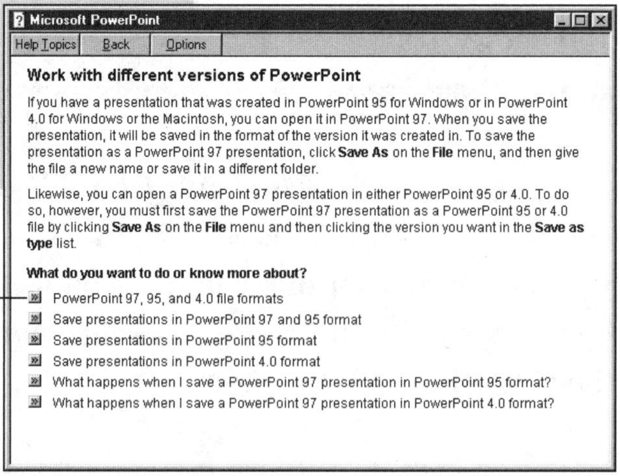

Hyperlink

Figure 15.2
Here is a Web browser program displaying a Web page with hyperlinks on it.

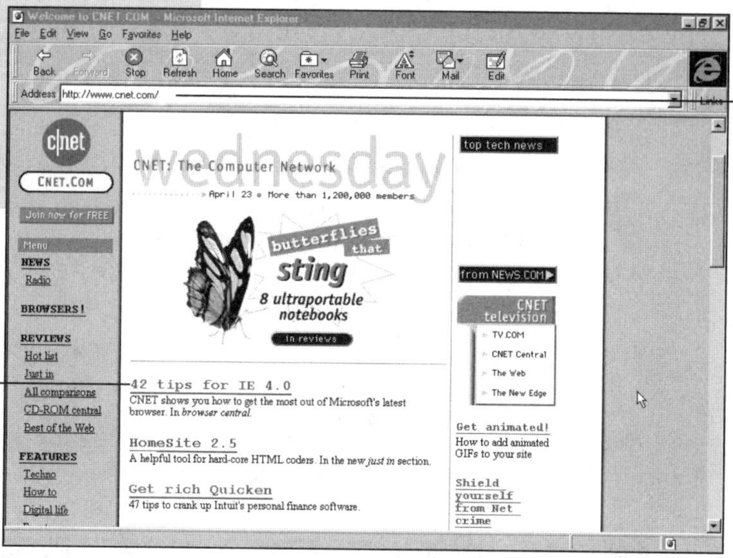

Using Online Templates and Pre-Made Hyperlinks

You have probably noticed as you used PowerPoint's presentation templates that there are two versions of most of them: Standard and Online. So far in this book, you have used only the standard models. What's the difference? The online ones have hyperlinks on the Slide Master that will enable your audience to click on links to navigate from slide to slide. These links are internal to the presentation, and don't really have anything to do with the Internet.

So why is the template called "online" if there's no special Internet capability in it? The answer is that the term "online" is being used very broadly and loosely to mean a user sitting down at a computer and interacting with your presentation, instead of the user sitting passively in a chair while you control

Note

There is nothing magical about an online template; it simply has some of the hyperlink-creation work done ahead of time for you. You can create the exact same effect with a Standard template by manually adding the hyperlinks yourself, as you'll learn later in this chapter.

the presentation flow in front of him. In that sense, Microsoft probably should have called these Interactive templates instead of Online!

Here are some situations where online templates are a good choice:

- Presentations you will distribute on a disk to the audience members, so they can each watch it on their own PCs.
- Presentations that will be posted at an Internet site or on your LAN for the audience to download or copy and run.
- Kiosk presentations where you are providing a mouse for the audience to interact with the presentation.
- Any other presentation that will not have a live speaker who is controlling the slides.

The best way to understand what these special online versions offer is to take a look at one, in the following Hands On.

Hands On: Exploring an Online Template

1. Choose File, New and click on the Presentations tab.
2. Double-click on Generic (Online). This looks like the same old generic template . . . but wait! What's that stuff at the bottom of the screen?
3. Choose View, Master, Slide Master. The presentation's Slide Master appears (see Figure 15.3). Here's where you can really see what special elements are offered in the template.
4. Click on the right-pointing arrow on the Slide Master to select it.
5. Just to prove that the arrow is just an objet, drag it around on the screen to reposition it, and then delete it by pressing the Delete key. Press Ctrl+Z to undo the deletion; you were just testing.
6. Now let's check out the left arrow. To see what link lies behind it, click on it and then choose Insert, Hyperlink. The Action Settings dialog box appears (see Figure 15.4).
7. Notice that the Hyperlink To button is selected and its drop-down list reads Previous Slide.
8. Open the drop-down list and examine some of the other choices. There are a lot of them, eh?
9. When you're done looking, click away from the list to close it without selecting. Then click on Cancel.
10. Now click on the words Jump to First Page at the bottom of the slide, and choose Insert, Hyperlink again to see what's behind those words.

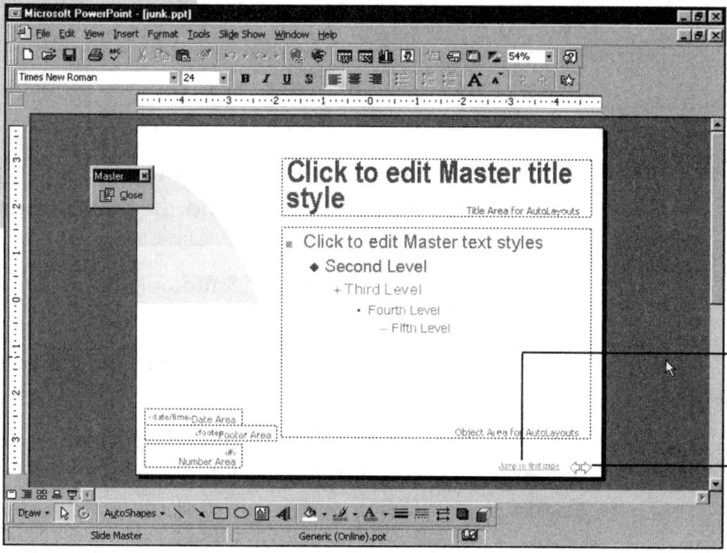

Figure 15.3 The Slide Master holds the special elements that make the presentation suitable for online use.

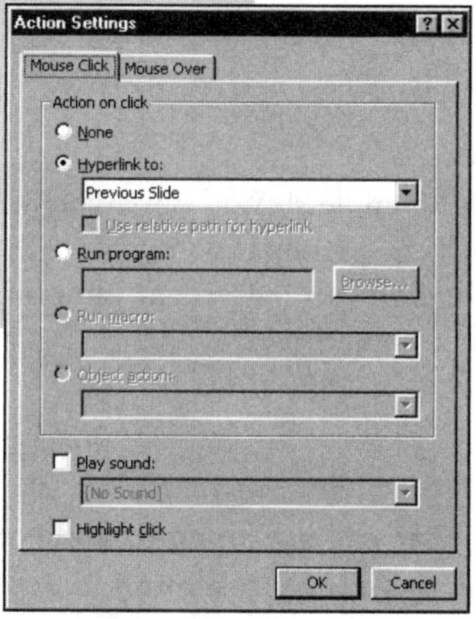

Figure 15.4 This is the same Action Settings dialog box you encountered with sounds and videos, but now you're using it for hyperlinks.

11. Notice that it says it's hyperlinking to the first slide. Then click on OK.
12. Click on the floating Close button to leave the Slide Master.

You have looked at only one online presentation template here, but they are all similar. They all offer hyperlinks and/or buttons at the bottom of the Slide Master, and that's the only difference between them and their standard counterparts.

Adding Hyperlinks to a Presentation

Now that you've seen some hyperlinks and hyperlink buttons in a presentation, it's time to get busy creating your own. You can probably think of many ways that hyperlinks can be useful in your presentation:

- To move forward and back through the slides in a kiosk situation where you have hidden the keyboard and the audience must rely on the mouse to move around.
- To provide an easy way for the audience to jump back to a Table of Contents slide at any time.
- To allow the audience to skip a portion of the presentation that they have no interest in.
- To jump to a specific slide for more information about a topic. For example, you could hide the slides that contained the extra information, so they weren't part of the regular slide show, and provide access to them through special hyperlinks on certain slides.
- To open a Web browser and display a Web page at a certain point in the presentation.
- To open a file in another program at a certain point in the presentation, such as an Access database or Excel spreadsheet.
- To jump to a different PowerPoint presentation at a certain point.

See Chapter 16 to learn how to hide slides.

The possibilities are almost endless! Without hyperlinks, your audience is stuck with moving through the presentation one slide at a time in the original order, but with hyperlinks, you can have them jumping all over the place to meet their individual interests precisely.

Note

Standard or online? If you are going to add Forward and Backward buttons to your presentation, it might be worth it to start out with the online version of the template, or to apply an online design to your existing presentation. But if you aren't going to be using hyperlinks for those purposes, you might as well start out with a standard template. In the following sections, I'll assume you're starting with a standard.

Hands On: Adding Navigation Buttons

Let's start with the presentation you've been working on throughout the book, and add some navigation buttons to the Slide Master to help your audience move from one slide to another. When you finish this exercise, you will have created the same buttons that you get automatically when you start with an online template. But don't think that this is a waste of time! By creating them yourself here, you're learning, and you'll be able to create different buttons on your own later.

1. Open the Slide Master in your presentation by choosing View, Master, Slide Master. The Slide Master appears.
2. If you have any objects at the bottom right corner of the screen, move them elsewhere on the slide or delete them. For example, in Figure 15.5, I've got a Number Area and Footer Area that may interfere. In my presentation these elements are not critical, so I'm going to delete them, but I could move them over to the left if I needed to keep them.
3. Choose Slide Show, Action Buttons. A submenu appears showing the various kinds of action buttons you can add.
4. Position the mouse pointer over different ones and see what name pops up for it. When you've examined all of them, click on the Back or Previous one (the left-pointing arrow). The mouse pointer changes to a cross hair.

Figure 15.5 Identify any objects that are in the way, and move or delete them.

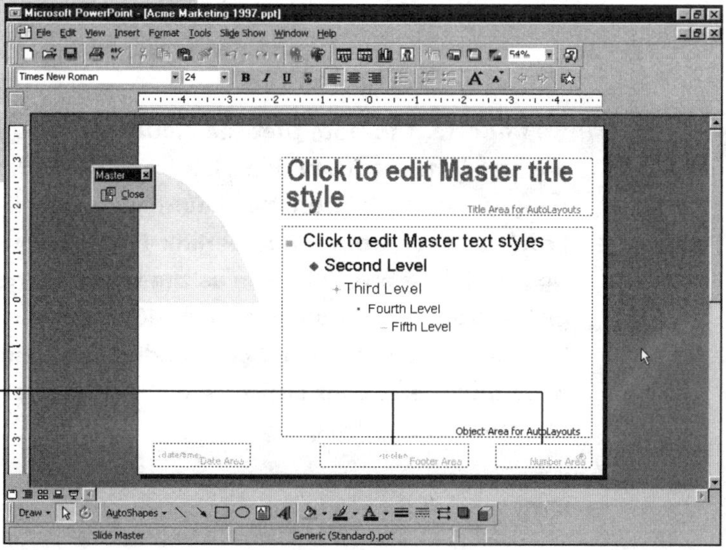

I want to put my navigation buttons here, so I'll delete these.

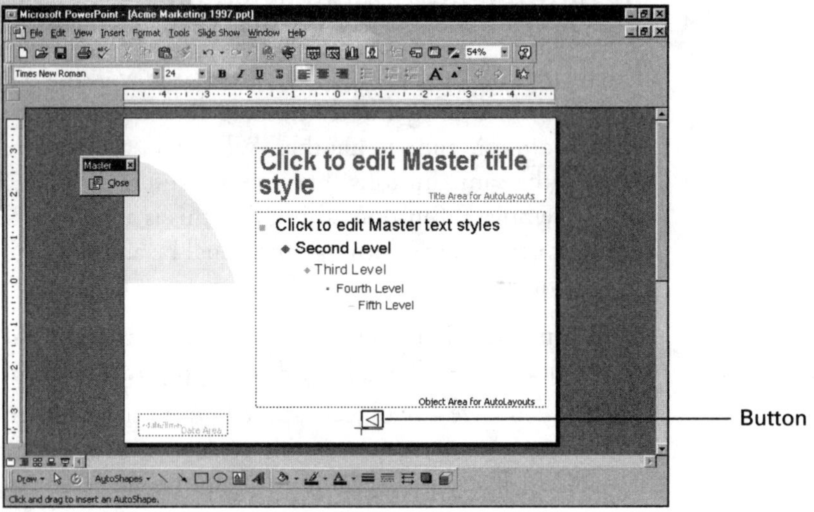

Figure 15.6 You can draw your buttons any size, but it looks better if you keep them small like this.

5. On the slide, drag to draw the button the shape and size that you want it. For this example, try to draw the button exactly square, at the bottom of the screen, small enough that it fits below the main text box. You can hold down the Shift key to force the button to be a perfect square. Figure 15.6 shows an example.
6. When you release the mouse button, the Action Settings dialog box opens, so you can assign an action to the button. Make sure that the Hyperlink To option button is selected.

Note

It's important to note that the pictures on the action buttons are just pictures. They don't have any tie with the hyperlink assigned to the button. You could just as easily choose Previous Slide from the Hyperlink To drop-down list for the right-pointing arrow button as the left-pointing one. The pictures are merely suggestions. However, if you assign a hyperlink to a button and your audience expects a different hyperlink there, your audience will get frustrated and not pay attention to your message.

7. Make sure that Previous Slide appears in the Hyperlink To drop-down list. If it doesn't, open the list and choose that.
8. Click on OK. Your button is now ready to go.
9. Now add the following other buttons to the bottom of your slide:

 Next Slide

 Beginning of Presentation

 End of Presentation

10. Resize the buttons if needed by dragging their handles. When you are finished, they should look like Figure 15.7.
11. Now let's test the buttons. Click on the floating Close button to leave the Slide Master.
12. Switch to Slide Show view.
13. Click on the buttons and see where it takes you! When you are finished experimenting, confident that the buttons are working, press Esc to return to PowerPoint.

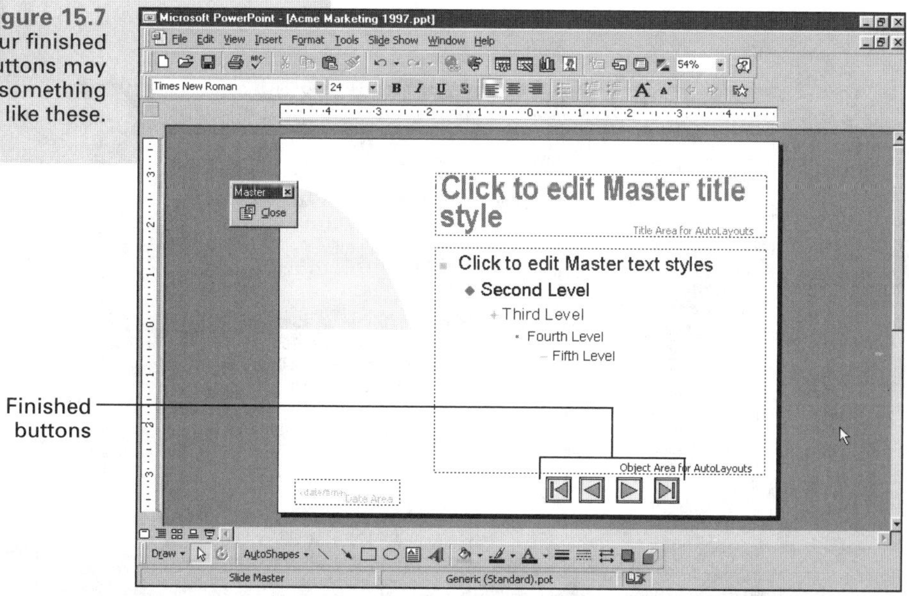

Figure 15.7 Your finished buttons may look something like these.

Hands On: Linking to an Individual Slide

So far, the buttons you've set up make your presentation function like a cassette tape player. You can go forward or backward, or move fast-forward or fast-reverse to the beginning or end. But wouldn't it be cool to have the presentation work like a CD player, where you can select individual tracks (slides) to see? You can do this by assigning particular slides to the hyperlinks.

1. Just for this exercise, create a new slide in your presentation, and copy the text from Figure 15.8 onto it. This is our "Information" slide that you're going to link to.
2. Now hide the slide so it doesn't appear in the regular presentation. To do so, choose Slide Show, Hide Slide.
3. Still working with the hidden slide, place the Return action button on the slide. It looks like the arrow making the U-turn. Accept the default setting in the Action Settings box. This button will help the audience return to the presentation after you view the hidden slide.
4. Now switch another slide in the presentation, still in Slide view. You'll add a hyperlink to our hidden slide on it.
5. Choose Slide Show, Action Buttons, and click on the button that looks like a small i with a circle around it.

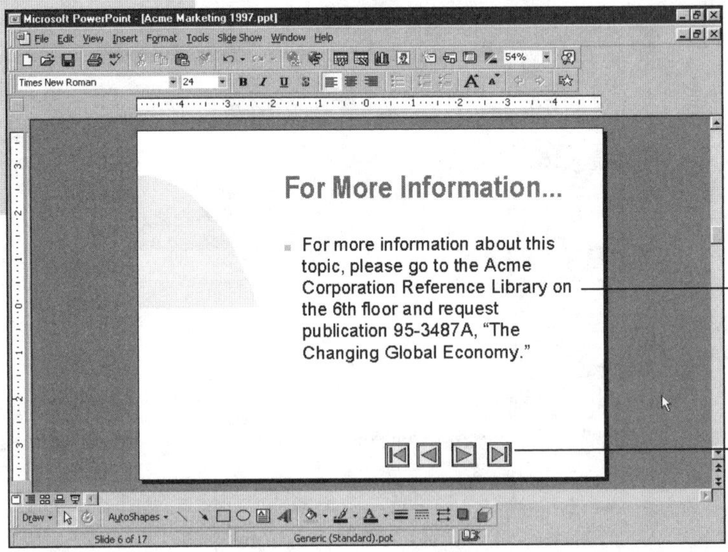

Copy this text.

These were already there; you added them to the Slide Master earlier.

Figure 15.8 Create this slide in your presentation to follow along with this Hands On exercise.

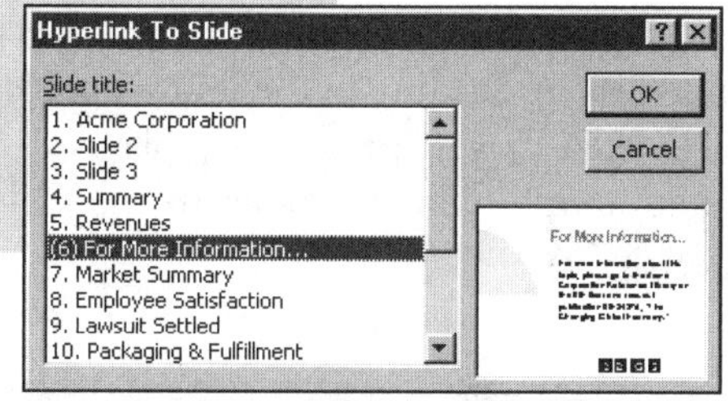

Figure 15.9 You can choose to hyperlink to any slide in the presentation.

6. Drag to place the button on the slide. The Action Settings dialog box appears.
7. Click on the Hyperlink To button.
8. Open the Hyperlink To drop-down list and choose Slide. The Hyperlink to Slide dialog box appears (see Figure 15.9).
9. Click on the For More Information slide. Its number appears in parentheses because it's hidden.
10. Click on OK, then OK again to close the dialog boxes.
11. Switch to Slide Show view and try out the button. It should jump to the hidden slide when you click on it.

Hands On: Hyperlinking to a Sound File

You can assign any hyperlink to any action button. Some of the buttons you saw on the Action Buttons submenu are appropriate for navigation (and as you saw some of them already have a default hyperlink assigned!), while some are more appropriate for playing sounds or videos. Let's create a button on a slide that plays a sound.

1. View a slide in Slide view that you want to place a button on.
2. Choose Slide Show, Action Buttons and click on the button that looks like a speaker.
3. Drag to place the button on the slide. The Action Settings dialog box appears.
4. Click on the Play Sound check box.
5. Open the Play Sound drop-down list and choose the sound you want.
6. Click on OK.

You learned how to assign sounds in Chapter 13.

There is no "play video" check box in the Action Settings dialog box, so you have to have to run a program that plays videos in order to attach a video to this button. You can use the procedure in the following Hands On to run Windows' own Mplayer (Media Player) program to play videos. Or, you can take the easier way out and simply add the video to the slide, as you learned in Chapter 13.

Hands On: Hyperlinking to a Different Program's Files

Now let's create a button that opens a document. You can use this same procedure to open any file from any outside program.

Tip

Before you start this, you need to know the complete name and path of the file you want to open, so use Windows Explorer to nail down that information first. You'll be asked to fill in the name and path, and you won't have an opportunity to browse for it.

1. Choose Slide Show, Action Buttons and click on the button that looks like a piece of paper.
2. Place that button on the slide. The Action Settings dialog box appears.
3. Click on the Hyperlink To option button.
4. Open the Hyperlink To drop-down list and choose Other File. The Hyperlink to Other File dialog box opens.
5. Locate the program you want to run. For example, if you want to hyperlink to a Word document, you may find it in the My Documents folder or the Windows\Personal folder, unless you stored it elsewhere.
6. When you find the file to open, select it and click on OK to return to the Action Settings dialog box.
7. Click on OK again.
8. Switch to Slide Show view and try out your button.

> **Refer to Chapter 4 to learn how to change folders and navigate your hard disk through Browse boxes like this.**

If you want a particular application to open without any specific file, instead of using Hyperlink To, use the Run Program option in the Action Settings dialog box. It enables you to select a program rather than a file to open.

You should be careful about allowing the audience access to other applications on your hard disk if they are going to be running the show unattended on your computer. Some programs have security holes that are not apparent. For example, in most Microsoft Office programs you can delete files from any dialog box that allows you to choose files for opening.

If the audience is going to be viewing the presentation on their own computers, make sure that the file and application that you link to will be available for them on their own machines.

Hands On: Hyperlinking to a Different Slide Show

If you have several small slide shows set up, you might want to enable your audience to jump to a particular show by clicking on certain buttons. This can help you tailor the show to the audience's self-described interests on the fly. I've saved this one for last because there really isn't a good pre-designed button to link to another show, so you have to set up a different kind of hyperlink: one that contains text. Follow these steps:

1. On the slide where you want the link, type the text that should describe the presentation(s) being linked to. For example, Figure 15.10 shows a sample menu of links I have typed in. At this point, it's just text; there aren't any links.
2. Select the text that you want to be the link. (For example, in Figure 15.10, I'll select Buy a Widget.)
3. Choose Slide Show, Action Settings. The by-now-familiar Action settings dialog box opens.
4. Click on the Hyperlink To option button.
5. Open the Hyperlink To drop-down list and click on Other PowerPoint Presentation.
6. Select the presentation from the dialog box that appears, and click on OK. The Hyperlink to Slide dialog box opens. (This is the same as the one you saw in Figure 15.9.)

Figure 15.10
Here's a sample menu I've created for my audience to select the show they want to see.

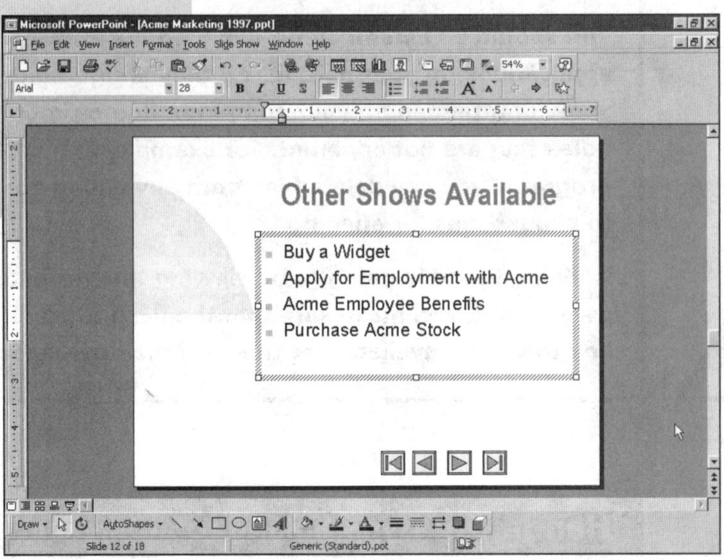

7. Click on the slide that you want to start with (usually the first one to show the whole presentation) and click on OK.
8. Click on OK again to close the Action Settings dialog box. The text is now underlined and a different color, indicating that it's a hyperlink, as shown in Figure 15.11.

Figure 15.11
Hyperlinked text is underlined.

Hyperlink

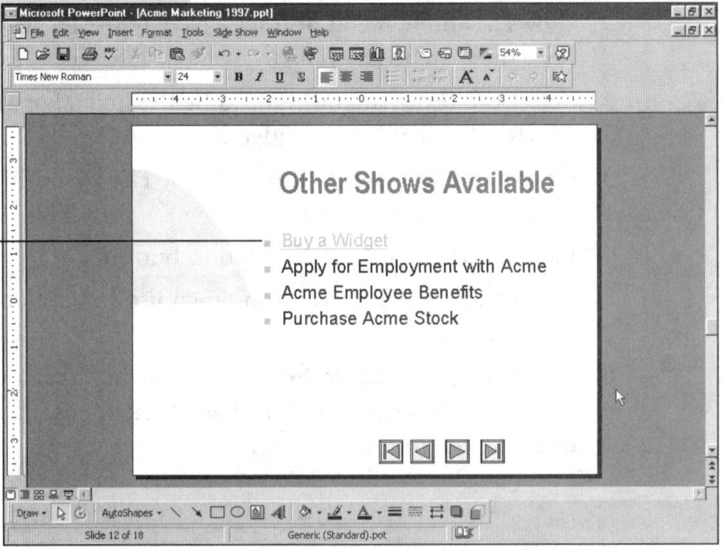

9. Do the same thing for each of your other paragraphs until all your hyperlinks to other presentations have been set up.
10. Go into Slide Show view and test out your links.

Hands On: Adding an Internet URL as a Hyperlink

Well, you probably started out this chapter thinking that Internet URLs were the only thing you could hyperlink, and I haven't even discussed them yet! As you can see, hyperlinking goes much deeper than just Internet addresses. Still, Internet addresses can be useful to hyperlink to in presentations, so you need to take a look at that.

1. Create a button or select text in any of the ways you have learned in the preceding Hands On sections. You can add a URL hyperlink to either.
2. If the button or text's Action Settings dialog box is not open, choose Slide Show, Action Settings.
3. If the Hyperlink To button is not selected, click on it.
4. Open the Hyperlink To drop-down list and choose URL. The Hyperlink to URL dialog box appears.
5. Type the URL in that text box and click on OK. (If you want one to practice on, try http://www.iquest.net/~fwempen.)
6. Click on OK to close the Action Settings dialog box.
7. Switch to Slide Show view and try out the link. Your Web browser opens when you click on the link, and if you are connected to the Internet, the linked page displays. (You may need to activate your Internet connection before it will work.)

Planning Where Your Show Will Run

Take a moment now that you know about your hyperlinking options to think about how your presentation will actually be presented. The conclusions you reach will help you plan the format that your presentation needs to take.

If your presentation is going to run on your company's LAN or local intranet, consider saving the file in PowerPoint Show format and distributing the PowerPoint Viewer program to everyone through the network. Then make your hyperlinks refer to files or presentations on the network server that everyone has access to.

See Chapter 14 for information about saving in the PowerPoint Show format.

If you are going to save your presentation on a disk and distribute it that way, again you would want to include the PowerPoint Viewer and save it in PowerPoint Show format, but you would want to confine your hyperlinks to just what's on that disk.

If you are planning to post your presentation on the Internet (that is, for worldwide distribution), you have a couple of options.

- You can assume that everyone either has PowerPoint or the PowerPoint viewer already, or needs to get it. This approach may seem rather arrogant, and it may cut down on the number of people who see your presentation. Many people will not be willing to spend the time needed to download and configure a viewer. However, this method keeps all your animations and multimedia effects intact. Your audience will see exactly the presentation you created.
- You can save the presentation in HTML format. HTML is the Internet's native language, and everyone browsing the Web has an HTML reader, so no additional viewers will be required. This makes your presentation very convenient for the audience to view. However, it also reduces your presentation to a stripped down set of static slides, without the extras and pizzazz.

We would all like to live in a world where the former method would be a success, but realistically, your presentation stands more of a chance for worldwide distribution if you save it in HTML format. You'll learn to do that in the following section.

Tip

PowerPoint is not a very good program to create your entire Web site in. There are much better programs, like Microsoft FrontPage or even Microsoft Word. In this chapter I'm assuming that you want to publish a particular presentation to your Internet site to provide information that supplements the rest of your Web site, not substitutes for it.

Saving your Presentation in HTML Format

PowerPoint comes with a wizard for saving in HTML format, so the whole process is very easy with not much fuss or confusion. Follow these steps to convert your presentation to HTML format and get it ready to go.

1. First of all, make sure your presentation is completely done, exactly the way you want it.
2. Choose File, Save as HTML. The Save As HTML Wizard opens.
3. Click on the Next button. You're asked to choose between a new or existing layout. If you haven't done this before, there aren't any existing ones, so leave New Layout selected and click on Next.
4. Choose the page style you want (see Figure 15.12). The top choice is without frames, and the bottom choice is with them. Click on Next to continue.

Frames are an HTML feature that shows multiple windows at a time. Not all Web browsers support this feature. If you use the frames, your presentation's outline will appear at the left side of the screen at all times and your users will be able to jump to the slides from there. This is very cool! But by using frames, you may be making it impossible for some potential audience members to see your presentation.

The best way is to create two separate versions and give your audience a choice between them on the Web page that you call the presentation from.

5. Next you're prompted to choose a graphic type. Choose one of these and click on Next:
   - *GIF.* This is a simple graphic format that all browsers recognize.
   - *JPEG.* This is a slightly more complicated format. You can set compression ratios for it for smaller images (with some quality loss) if size is an issue. (The larger the size, the longer it will take in download time before your audience can see it.)

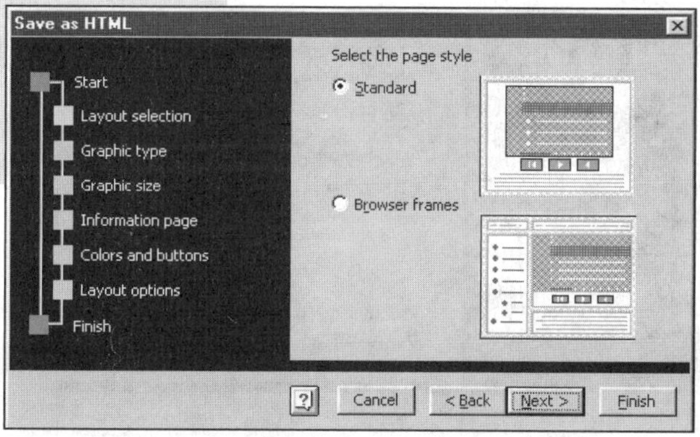

Figure 15.12 Choose the layout that you want: framed or frameless.

- *PowerPoint Animation.* This format preserves your object animations in the presentation, but forces your audience to download a plug-in for their browsers. Not recommended unless your presentation loses its meaning without the animations.

6. Next you're asked what size of screen to optimize the presentation for. Make your selection and click on Next.

Note

Monitor size is a toughie, because the "common" size is in flux these days. Everyone uses at least 640 × 480, but many people use 800 × 600. 800 × 600 gives a better looking presentation but some users may not be able to view it. 640 × 480 looks a bit chunky, but ensures wider acceptance. Don't consider higher resolutions than 800 × 600 unless you are distributing the presentation to an extremely select group that you are sure can support that resolution.

7. Next you're asked to fill in information for the information page, as shown in Figure 15.13. Enter the appropriate information in the blanks.
8. There are two check boxes on this screen. Select them if needed, and then click on Next.
   - *Download original presentation.* This automatically adds an on-screen button that will enable the audience to download the original presentation. This is useful if some but not all audience members have PowerPoint themselves. It enables the ones who do have

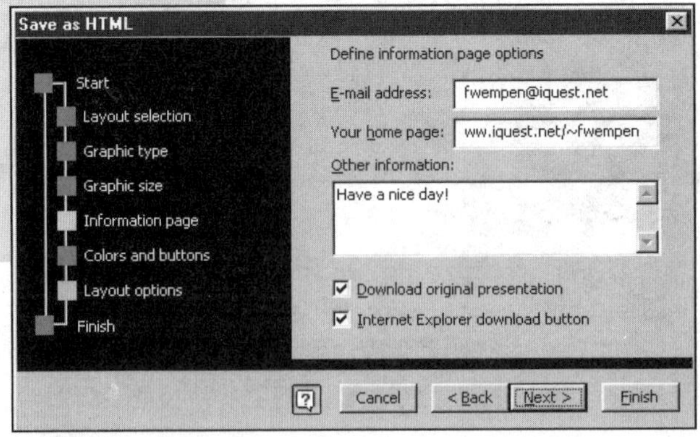

Figure 15.13 This information will appear in the presentation so the audience can contact you for more information.

PowerPoint to see the presentation in all its original glory, while those who don't have it can view the HTML version.

- *Internet Explorer download button.* This places a button on the presentation that the audience can click on to download Microsoft's Internet Explorer browser for free. Depending on how you look at it, this is either a great convenience you're providing for your audience or a bunch of free advertising for Microsoft.

9. Next you get to choose the colors that will appear in the HTML version of the presentation, as shown in Figure 15.14. Start by choosing between Use Browser Colors and Custom Colors.

   Use Browser Colors makes your presentation take on the default colors set up in each person's browser.

   Custom Colors forces the browser to display the presentation using your chosen colors. This gives you more control over the presentation experience that the audience will have.

10. If you chose Custom Colors in step 9, click on one of the "Change. . ." buttons and choose the color you want. Do this for each of the buttons (for example, Change Background, Change Text, etc.) Click on Next when you're done.

11. Next is the layout options. Choose a button style, as shown in Figure 15.15, and then click on Next.

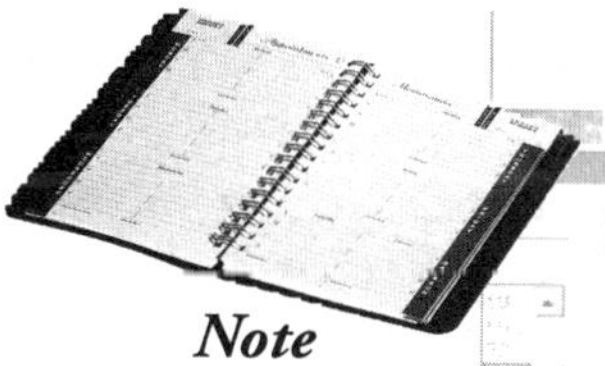

Note

Because you've created navigation buttons of your own earlier in this chapter, you probably understand perfectly what these navigation buttons in Figure 15.15 are for. Your audience will need them to move from one slide to the next.

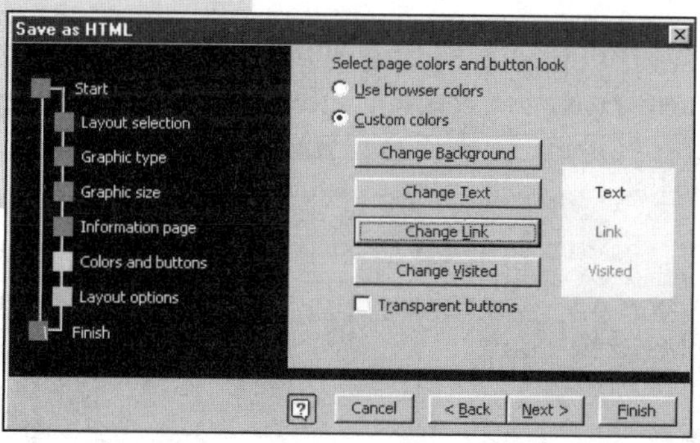

Figure 15.14 Choose custom colors or allow the browser to use its own.

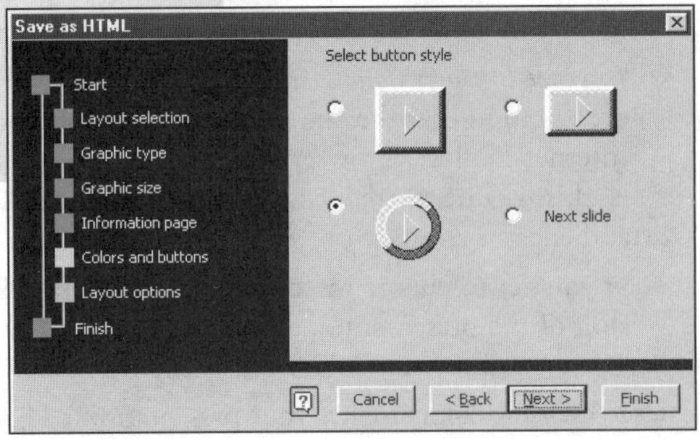

Figure 15.15 Pick the style of button that you want for slide navigation.

See Chapter 16 for information about creating notes.

12. If you chose a framed layout, you see a check box called Include Slide Notes in Pages. This gives you an option of having any notes that you've assigned to a slide appear in a separate frame under the slide. If you want this, click on the check box; otherwise just click on Next to move on.
13. Next you're asked where you want to create the HTML folder. Each slide is saved as a separate HTML file, and they're organized together in a new folder with the name of the presentation. Enter the location where you want the folder, and click on Next.

Tip

If you want to save the HTML folder directly to your Internet server, click on the Browse button in step 13. In the Browse dialog box that appears, open the Look In drop-down list and choose Internet Locations. You will be guided through the process of choosing an Internet location. Click on OK after you've chosen it. Then you don't have to worry about copying the presentation files to your Internet server later.

14. Click on Finish. A Save as HTML dialog box appears asking if you want to save these settings. (Remember back in step 3 you could choose existing settings?) If you want to save the settings, type a name and click on Save. Otherwise click on Don't Save.
15. Wait while PowerPoint exports the presentation to HTML format.
16. When you see the message that the presentation has been saved as HTML, click on OK.

Publishing Your Presentation on the Internet

Saving your presentation in HTML format is only half the battle. Now you have to copy it to your Web server and create a link to it on a publicly-accessible Web page. Fortunately, it's not as bad as it sounds, and you can get some help from your company's Internet administrator in most cases.

Here's the basic procedure, which you can fill in with your own specifics:

1. Copy the presentation folder to your Web server. Contact your administrator to find out the appropriate place to put it.
2. Decide what Web page to place the link on. Your company probably already has several Web pages in place.
3. Place a link on that page to the file index.htm in the folder where you saved your HTML files. This is the "home page" for your presentation. Figure 15.16 shows what it will look like in your audience's browser.
4. With a Web browser, try out that link and see if your presentation runs satisfactorily from it. When you click on the Click Here to Start link, the presentation should begin. Figure 15.17 shows what it looks like if you selected a framed layout.

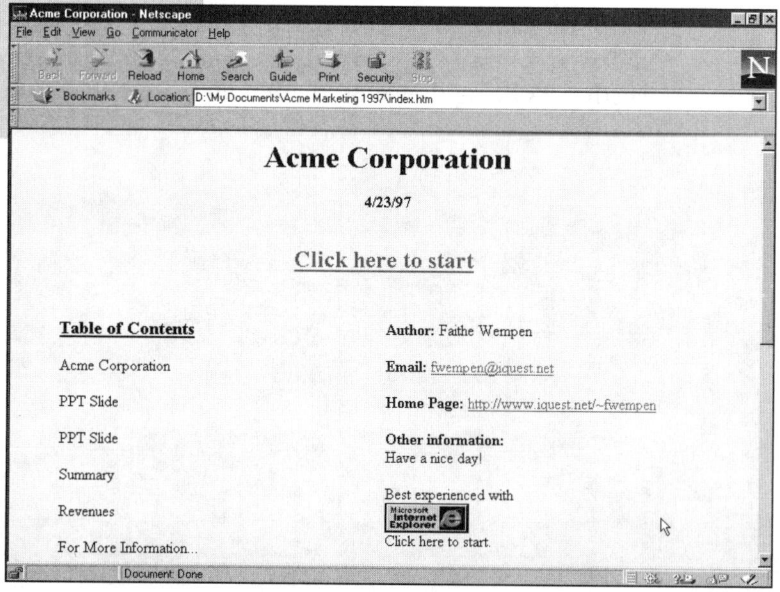

Figure 15.16 This is like the "cover sheet" for the presentation.

Figure 15.17
A multi-framed presentation.

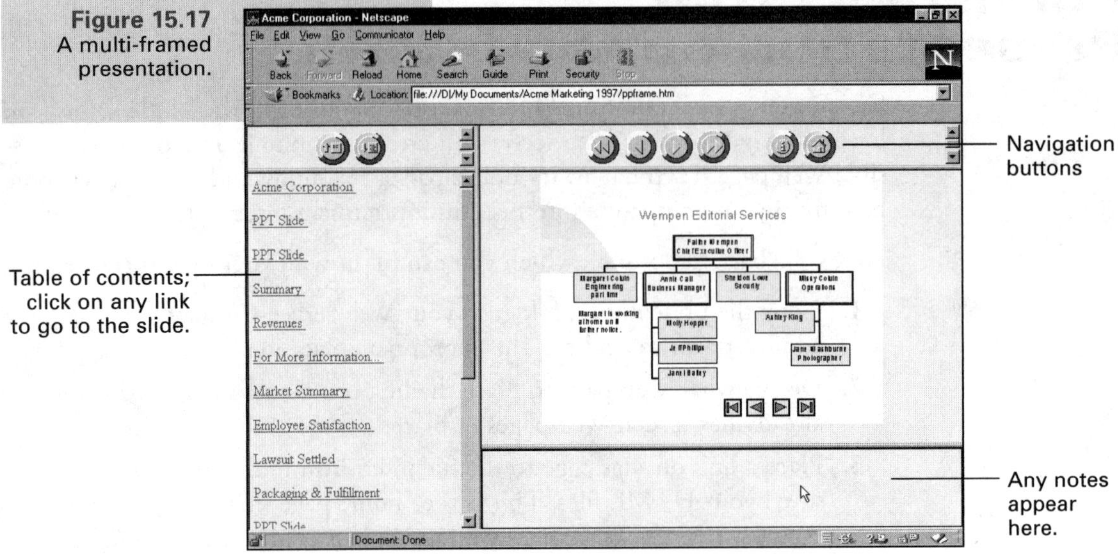

Summary

You may have come to this chapter expecting to learn how to create an Internet presentation. You did learn that—in the last part of the chapter—but I hope you came away with much more than that too. By now you should understand how to use hyperlinks to make your presentation more flexible, whether it's being shown on the Internet or on your own computer.

PART IV
Presenting Your Show!

16

Preparing to Give Your Slide Show

In This Chapter

- Finalizing Your Presentation's Slide Lineup
- Creating Handouts for Your Audience
- Developing Your Speaker Notes
- Copying the Presentation to Another Computer

Well, you've done it! You've created what may be the world's finest presentation. Now as the time draws near for presenting it, take a few minutes to put the finishing touches on your masterpiece.

Finalizing the Organization

While creating your presentation, you obviously gave some thought to the order in which the slides should appear, but now it's time to make some serious decisions. Run through your presentation now using Slide Show view, and make sure that everything is as it should be.

- Are the slides in the correct order?
- Do the transitions and animations look professional and consistent? If not, return to Chapter 14 to work on them.
- Do all your hyperlinks work that you created in Chapter 15?
- Are there certain slides that should be removed from the main presentation and used as backup?

Think carefully about these questions, and make the needed changes well in advance of the actual presentation. There is nothing worse than being rushed making last-minute changes as you are getting ready to give your presentation.

Rearranging Revisited

In Chapter 5, you learned to rearrange slides in both Slide Sorter and Outline view. I won't repeat all that detail here, but take a quick refresher:

- To move a slide in Outline view, select the slide text, and then drag it up or down in the outline. Alternatively, you can select the slide text and click on the Up or Down arrow button on the Outlining toolbar.
- To move a slide in Slide Sorter view, select the slide and then drag it where you want it.

Hiding Slides

If you go to all the trouble of creating a slide, why would you want to hide it? There are lots of good reasons. Probably the best reason is that, in the course of rearranging and pruning your presentation, you realize that a particular slide does not fit in with your main presentation very well. You don't want to delete it, because there's a chance that someone might ask a question relevant to it. If that happens, you'll be able to pull the slide out from the shadows with a flourish, and everyone will think you're wonderful!

Good presenters often come prepared with up to twice as many slides as they plan on showing. Lots of backup material makes it easier for you to maintain your confident, knowledgeable image in the face of tough questions.

You can hide a slide in a couple of different ways.

- From any view, you can select the slide and choose Slide Show, Hide Slide.
- From Slide Sorter view, you can click on the slide to hide and then click on the Hide Slide button on the Slide Sorter toolbar (see Figure 16.1).

In the multi-slide views (Slide Sorter and Outline) you can select more than one slide at once before issuing the Hide Slide command to hide several in one stroke.

So what does it mean when a slide is hidden? You can work on hidden slides the same as any other slide. It still shows up normally in every PowerPoint view except Slide Show. When you use Slide Show view to preview the presentation, the hidden slide will not be part of the flow. You can access it in indirect ways, as you'll learn in Chapter 18, but you won't see it by simple clicking the mouse or pressing Page Down.

To unhide a slide, just reissue the command to hide it. It's a toggle that turns the hidden attribute on/off.

Figure 16.1
You can hide a slide to keep it out of the main presentation.

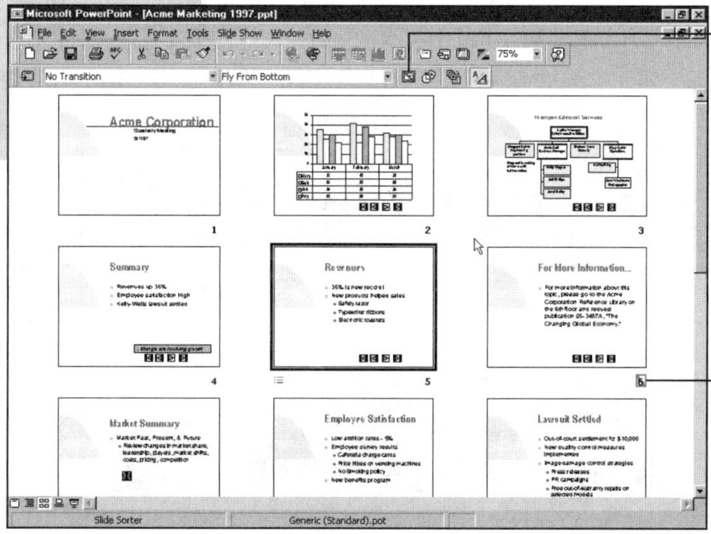

Creating Custom Shows

Custom shows are subsets of the presentation's slides that you create for special purposes. Some people put their backup slides in a custom show. Others devise different shows for different audiences, all made up of the same basic set of slides. For example, suppose you have a presentation on widget manufacturing. You want to give the presentation to three groups: engineers, managers, and factory workers. Each of these groups wants a different level of detail; with custom shows, you can pick and choose which slides to show to each group.

To save a group of slides in their custom show, follow these steps:

1. Choose Sli<u>d</u>e Show, <u>C</u>ustom Shows. The Custom Shows dialog box opens.
2. Click on the <u>N</u>ew button. The Define Custom Show dialog box opens (see Figure 16.2). All the slides in the current presentation appear on the left.
3. In the Slide Show <u>N</u>ame field at the top of the dialog box, enter a name for the show (for example, Engineering).
4. Click on the first slide you want in the custom show and click on the Add button. It is copied to the Custom Show column on the right.
5. Keep adding slides to the custom show until your show is the way you want it. If you need to rearrange the slides on the Custom Show list, click on the slide to move and then use the up and down arrow buttons to the right of the list. To remove a slide from the custom show, click on <u>R</u>emove.
6. Click on OK. You're returned to the Custom Shows dialog box (see Figure 16.3).
7. Click on <u>C</u>lose to return to editing the presentation.

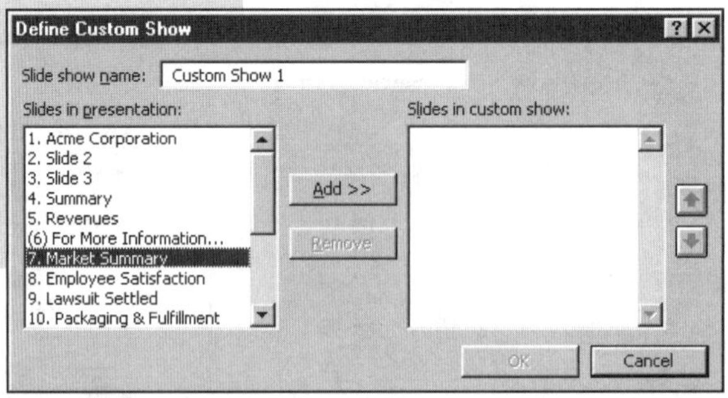

Figure 16.2 Here you'll choose which of the slides in your presentation belong in the custom show.

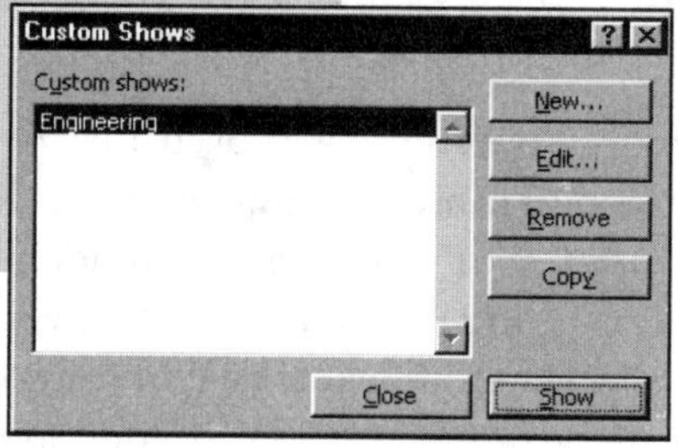

Figure 16.3 The custom show(s) you have set up appear here.

You may have noticed several other buttons in the Custom Shows dialog box. You can return to the dialog box at any time and do any of the following:

- *Edit.* Click on this to change what slides are included in the selected custom show.
- *Remove.* Click on this to delete the selected custom show.
- *Copy.* Select a custom show and then click on this to make a copy of it that you can then modify. Use this to base one custom show on another.
- *Show.* Click on this to actually present the custom show. You'll return to this dialog box and click on the Show button every time you want to use one of the custom shows as a presentation.

Creating Your Audience Handouts

You have probably been to a presentation before where the speaker gave you handouts to take home with you. These typically show all the slides in the main presentation and provide a place for the audience members to write notes. Sometimes speakers will include all their backup slides in the handouts too, so the audience will have the information if they need it later.

Choosing When and How to Use Handouts

There is a fierce debate among presentation professionals about the proper use of handouts. Here are some of the many conflicting viewpoints. I can't say who is right or wrong, but each of these brings up issues you will want to consider. Each one of them, at the bottom line, is an opinion on how much power and credit to give to the audience.

You should give handouts at the beginning of the presentation. The audience can absorb the information better if they can follow along on paper.

This makes a lot of sense—research has proven that people do absorb more facts if presented with them in more than one medium. It also gives your audience "free will;" they can listen to you, or they can not listen and still have the information. It's their choice, and this can be extremely scary for less-confident speakers. It's not just a speaker confidence issue in some cases, however. If you are going to give a lot of extra information in your speech that's not on the handouts, people might miss it because they're reading if you give the handouts at the beginning.

You shouldn't give the audience handouts, because they won't pay as close attention to your speech if they know that the information is already written down for them.

This philosophy falls at the other end of the spectrum. It gives the audience the least power, and shows the least confidence in their ability to pay attention to you in the presence of a distraction (handouts). If you truly don't trust your audience to be professional and listen, this may be your best option. However, don't let insecurity as a speaker drive you prematurely to this conclusion. The fact is that people won't take away as much knowledge about the topic without handouts as they would if you had provided some. So ask yourself: is my ultimate goal to fill the audience full of knowledge, or to make them pay attention to me?

You should give handouts at the end of the presentation, so that people will have the information to take home but not be distracted during the speech.

This attempts to solve the dilemma with compromise. The trouble with it, as with all compromises, is that it does an incomplete job from both angles. Because audience members can't follow along on the handouts during the presentation, they miss the opportunity to jot down notes on the handouts as they go. And because the audience knows that handouts are coming, they might nod off and miss something important that's not on the handouts. The other problem with this one is that, if you don't clearly tell people that handouts will be coming later, some people will spend the entire presentation frantically trying to copy down each slide on their own note paper.

In the end, each speaker must decide for him or herself whether handouts are appropriate for a particular topic and audience and when they are best distributed.

Deciding on a Handout Format

PowerPoint offers a variety of handout formats, each one appropriate for a certain situation. You can see samples of them in Figures 16.4 through 16.6.

The two-slide-per-page layout in Figure 16.4 prints two big slides on each page. This is good for slides that have a lot of fine print and small details, or for situations where you are not confident that the reproduction quality will be good. There is nothing more frustrating for an audience than not being able to read the handouts!

Figure 16.4 Two-slides-per-page handout format.

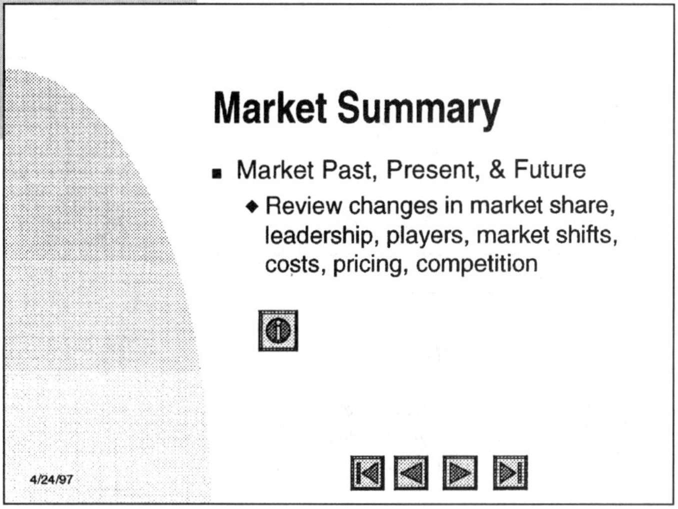

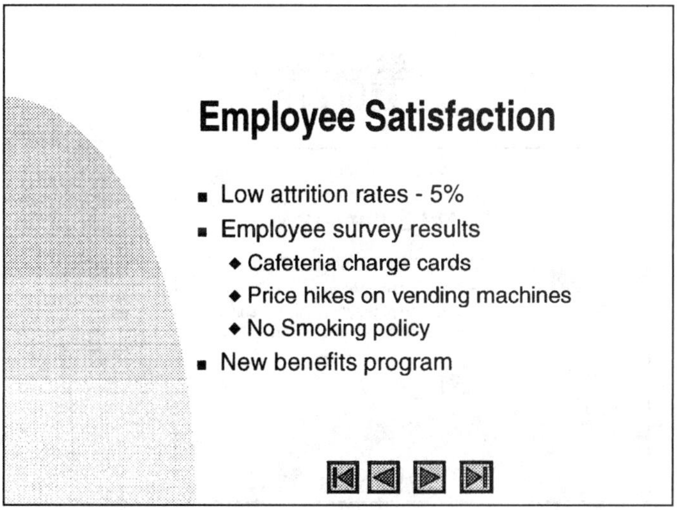

The three-slide-per-page layout shown in Figure 16.5 makes the slides much smaller (less than 1/3 the size of the ones in Figure 16.4), but you get a nice bonus—lines to the side of each slide for note-taking. This layout works well for presentations where the slides are big and simple and the speaker is providing a lot of extra information not on the slides. That way audience members can write the extra information in the blanks provided.

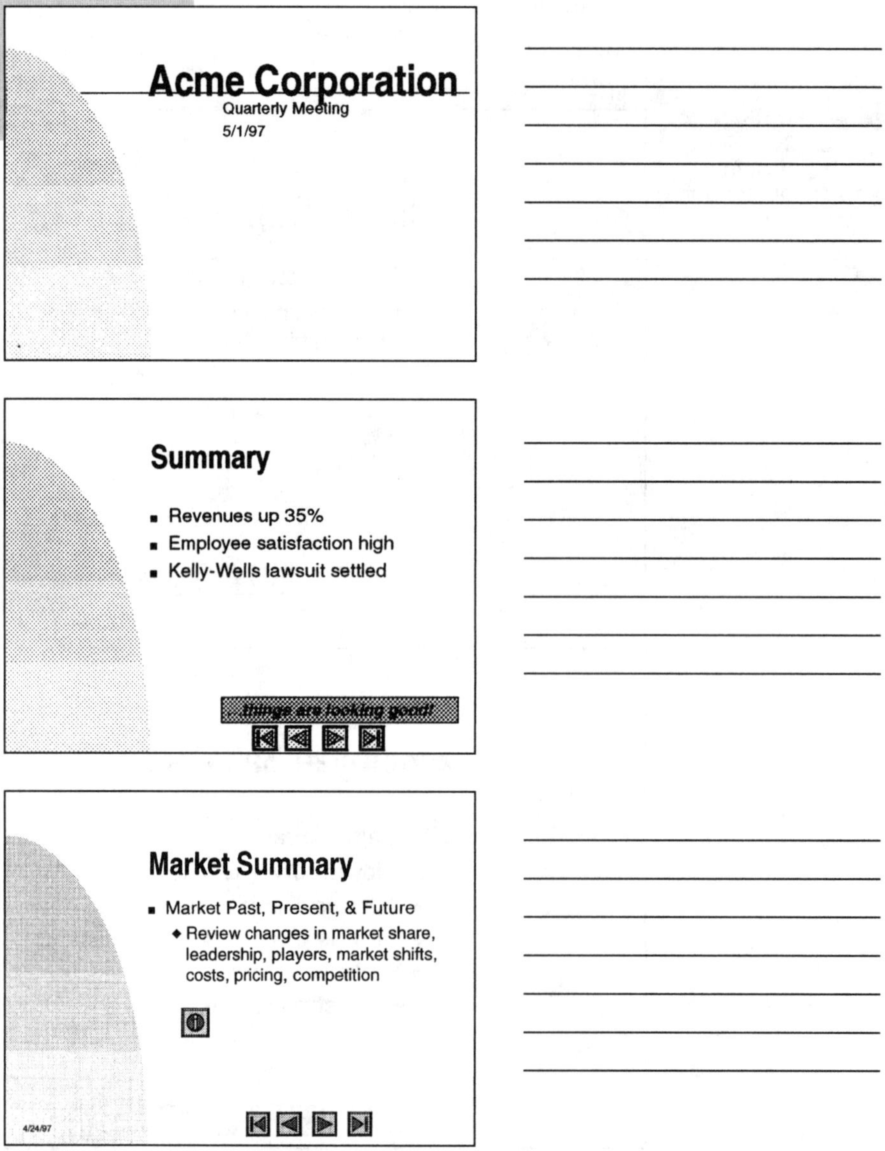

Figure 16.5 Three-slides-per-page handout format.

The six-slides-per-page layout in Figure 16.6 uses slides the same size as in Figure 16.5, but omits the notes lines to fit more slides on the page. This is good for presentations with big, simple designs where the audience does not need to take notes. If you are not sure whether the audience will even benefit from handouts in a certain situation, consider whether this six-per layout would be a good compromise.

Figure 16.6 Six-slides-per-page handout format.

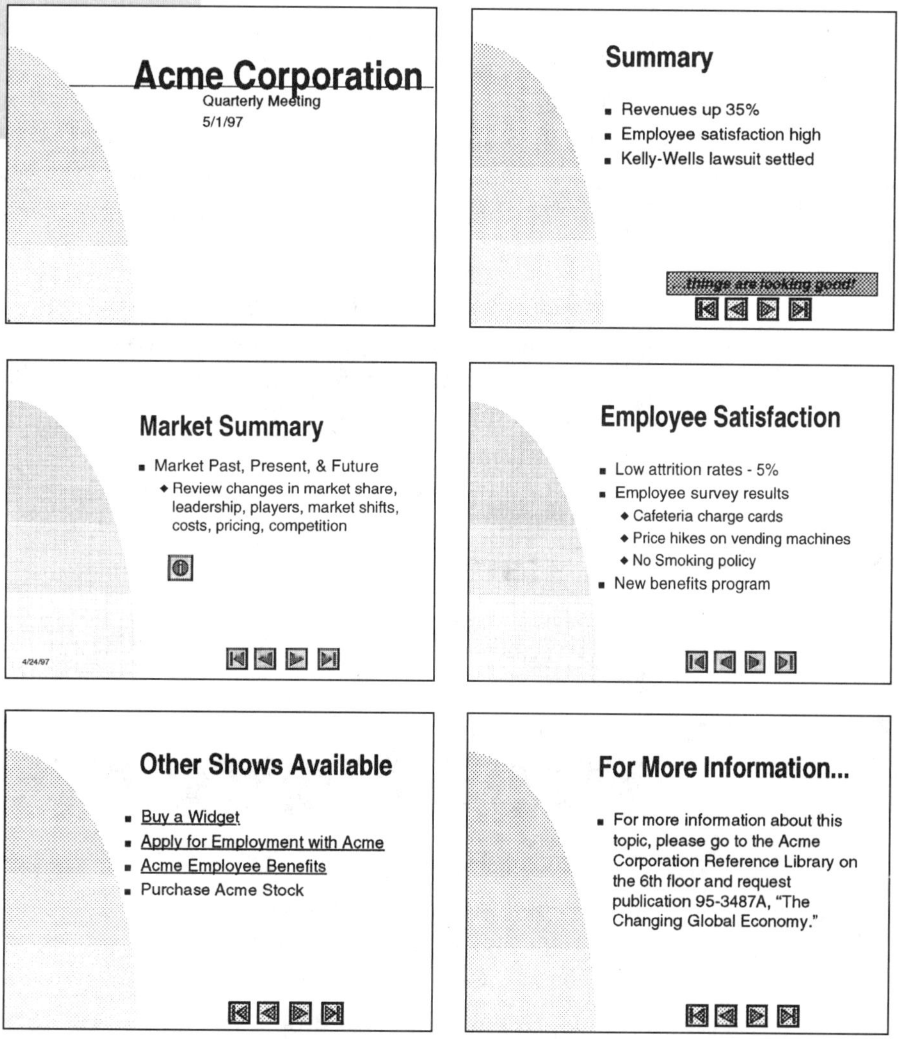

A Handout Nightmare Story

I was at a publishing conference last week where many of the most important people in the publishing industry were giving presentations. One man had a great-looking presentation; he (or someone) had obviously spent a lot of time on it. Unfortunately, the slides had a lot of small print on them. He had chosen a three-slides-per-page layout, as in Figure 16.5, which made the type on the slides very tiny. He also had a colored background for the slides, so that further degraded the quality of the handouts. As a result, the handouts were virtually useless to the attendees. Many of us used the space to the left of each slide to copy down the small print from the slide off the projection screen as quickly as we could.

Apparently some people complained, because they made an announcement later in the day that the handouts would be reprinted—in color—and mailed to all attendees within a few weeks. This satisfied the participants but it was an embarrassing situation for the speaker!

Printing your Handouts

I'm going to spend the entire next chapter on printing, so I won't get into it too deeply here. But in case you want a jump on things, here's how you print handouts.

Hands On: Printing Handouts

1. Choose File, Print. The Print dialog box opens (see Figure 16.7).
2. In the Print Range area, leave All selected, or choose a custom show from the Custom Show drop-down list.
3. Set a number of copies in the Number of Copies text box.
4. Open the Print What drop-down list and choose Handouts (6 per page), Handouts (3 per page) or Handouts (2 per page).
5. If you've got a black-and-white printer, make sure the Black & White check box is marked. (Leave the Pure Black & White check box blank.)

Figure 16.7
Use the Print dialog box to print handouts.

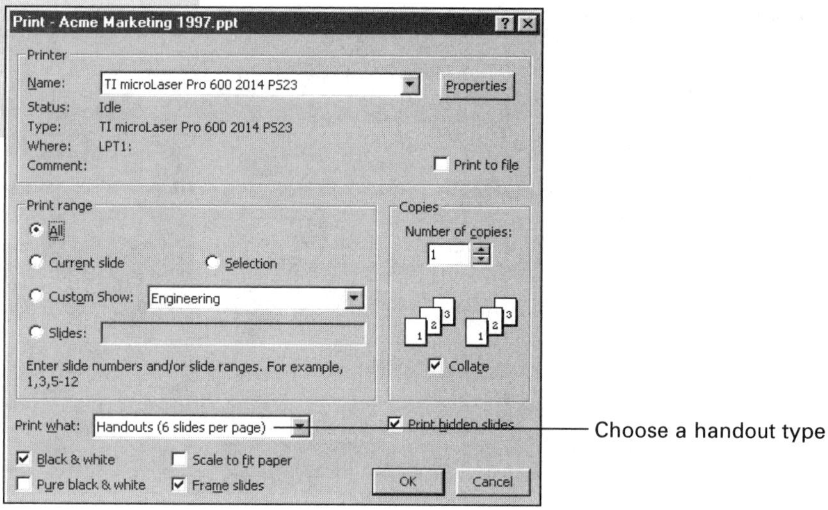

6. If you want to include hidden slides in the handouts, make sure the Print Hidden Slides check box is marked.
7. Click on OK. Your handouts print.

Creating Your Speaker Notes

Speaker notes are like handouts for yourself. There's only one printout format for them: the slide on the top (the same size as in Figure 16.4) and a blank area below it for your notes to yourself about the speech you'll give while that slide is on-screen.

Speaker notes are better than your traditional 3x5 note cards for several reasons. For one thing, you can type your notes right into the computer and print them out on regular paper. No jamming a note card into a typewriter and no messy correction fluid or erasers to make changes! The other benefit is that each note page has a miniature of the slide on it to which the notes refer, so it's not as easy to get lost.

Typing Your Notes

To type your notes into the computer, switch to Notes Page view, as shown in Figure 16.8.

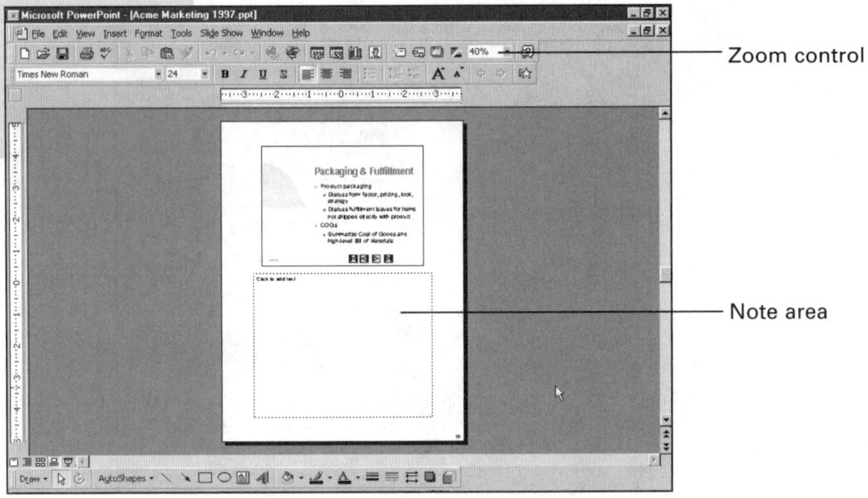

Figure 16.8
Type your notes into the Notes Page view for each slide.

Use the [Page Up] and [Page Down] keys to move to the slide for which you want to type notes. You may find it easiest to start with the first slide in your presentation and work forward.

Tip

Use the Zoom controls to zoom in or out until you find the optimal view for you where the text you type is large enough to be clear but small enough that you can see across the entire width of the note area. I find that 100% works well on my screen, but yours may vary.

Then just type your notes in the notes area, the same as you would in any text box. Press [Enter] to start a new paragraph. The lines with a paragraph wrap automatically. When you're done, press [Page Down] to move to the next slide.

Printing your Notes

When you're ready to print your notes, follow these steps:

1. Choose File, Print. The Print dialog box opens (refer to Figure 16.7).
2. In the Print Range area, leave All selected, or choose a custom show from the Custom Show drop-down list.
3. Set a number of copies in the Number of Copies text box. This is usually 1, because there is only one of you giving the presentation, but you may need an extra set for some reason.

4. Open the Print What drop-down list and choose Notes Pages.
5. If you've got a black-and-white printer, make sure the Black & White check box is marked. (Leave the Pure Black & White check box blank.)
6. If you want to include hidden slides in the handouts, make sure the Print Hidden Slides check box is marked.
7. Click on OK. Your handouts print.

If you print notes pages for hidden slides, you may want to arrange your printouts so that the hidden slides are at the bottom of the pile. That way you won't get confused when giving the presentation.

Copying the Presentation to Another Computer

If you want to give the presentation using a different computer, you would think that you'd just copy the PowerPoint file (.ppt) to the other computer and be done with it. However, if you use graphics, animation, links to other files, and so on, it's not that simple. Not all of the elements in a PowerPoint presentation are always contained in the .ppt file. Where are they? Unless you kept careful track when you imported and added objects, who knows.

That's where Pack and Go comes in. This feature takes a look at your presentation, makes a list of every file needed in order to give it on another computer, and packs all the needed files up neatly for travel.

Try it. Use the following Hands On to get your presentation ready for a journey. Never mind if you aren't going anywhere—this is just for practice.

Hands On: Packing a Presentation for Transport

1. Open the presentation that you want to transport.
2. Choose File, Pack and Go. The Pack and Go Wizard opens.
3. Click on Next to begin. You're asked whether you want to pack up the active presentation or a different once.
4. Make sure Active Presentation is marked, and then click on Next.
5. A screen appears asking which drive to pack to (see Figure 16.9). Choose the appropriate drive and click on Next. For this example,

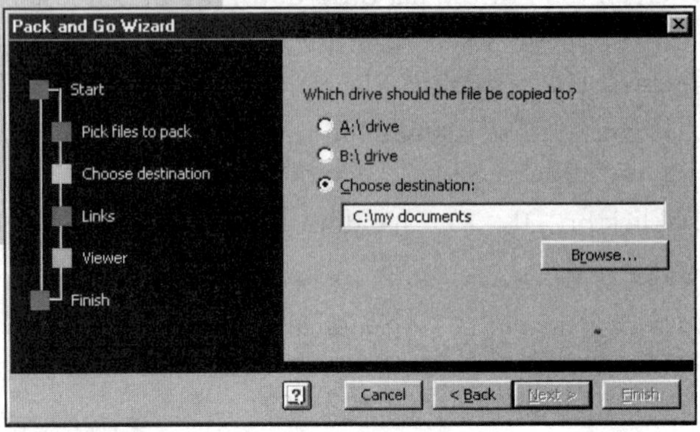

Figure 16.9 The Pack and Go Wizard needs to know where the packed presentation should reside.

put a blank disk in drive A and choose that, or click on Choose Destination and in the text box, type the name of the folder you want (for example, C:\My Documents).

6. Next you see two check boxes. Make your selections and click on Next.
   - *Include Linked Files.* Mark this check box if the linked files should be included as separate files, or deselect it if the links should be broken and simple copies of the objects included in the packed version.
   - *Embed TrueType Fonts.* Mark this check box if you want the fonts used in the presentation to be packed too. This is useful if the machine to receive the presentation does not have the fonts that the presentation needs.
7. Next you're asked whether you want to also pack the PowerPoint Viewer. You'll need this if the destination machine does not have PowerPoint installed. Click on the appropriate answer and then click on Next.
8. Click on Finish. Pack and Go does its work.
9. When you see a message that Pack and Go has successfully packed your presentation, click on OK. You're done!

Summary

In this chapter, you learned about the finishing touches you can put on your presentation. You learned how to rearrange and hide slides, how to create custom shows, and how to create and print audience handouts and speaker notes.

17

Printing Your Work

In This Chapter

- What Can You Print?
- Simple Printing
- Printing with Special Options
- Creating Page Headers and Footers

When you think about it, PowerPoint provides two products for you. First, it lets you create presentations that you can give on-screen, where you can add animations and transitions, sound and video, dress it up with colored and shaded objects, and all the other wonders you've learned about so far in this book. Second, it lets you create hard-copy printouts, to use as overhead transparencies, to hand out to the audience, or to organize your own notes.

When you print a presentation, it opens a whole new can of options. What size should the slides be? What information should be repeated on every page? How many slides should print per page? In this chapter, you'll learn to take your beautiful on-screen presentation and turn it into a beautiful hard copy.

What Can You Print?

PowerPoint lets you specify exactly what you want to print. You can print the entire presentation, a custom show, a single slide, or selected slides that you choose yourself. You also can print in a variety of formats:

Handouts and speaker notes are covered in Chapter 16.

- *Handouts.* Pages to give to your audience for their reference.
- *Speaker notes.* Pages with your own notes on them, for your use.
- *Copies of the slides themselves.* These are simply replicas of what you see onscreen, with no fancy stuff.
- *Outlines.* Text-only outlines of your slides. Slides that don't contain any text don't appear, nor do objects (like charts and pictures).

Simple Printing from the Toolbar

The easiest way to print is to click on the Print button on the Standard toolbar. It doesn't get much simpler than that. When you click on this button, the active presentation prints on the default printer, one copy of it. Each slide prints on a separate page, filling the entire page. It doesn't matter what view you were in when you clicked the Print button. Even if you click on Print in Notes Pages or Outline view, you'll still get Slide view type printouts.

How do you tell what the default printer is? Point the mouse at the Print button on the toolbar, and a ScreenTip pops up. It tells you that it's the Print button, and it also tells you what the default printer is. If you have more than one printer, you can change which printer is the default in the Print dialog box, which you'll learn about in the following section.

Printing with Options

The default print options work well if you want just the default settings, but many times you will want more than one copy, only certain slides, a different type of printout, or some other special settings when you print. To set your print options, use the Print dialog box:

1. Choose File, Print or press Ctrl+P. The Print dialog box appears (see Figure 17.1).
2. Set any options in the Print dialog box that you want. (These are covered in the following sections.)
3. Click on OK to print.

Printer Properties

The first thing to do in the Print dialog box is check whether the printer that you want to use appears in the Name text box. If it doesn't, open the drop-down list and select it.

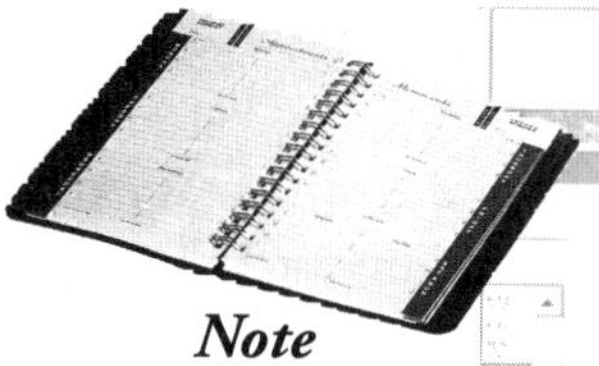

Note

If the printer you want to use doesn't appear on the drop-down list, it has not yet been set up in Windows 95, and you will need to set it up through the Control Panel before you can use it in any Windows program.

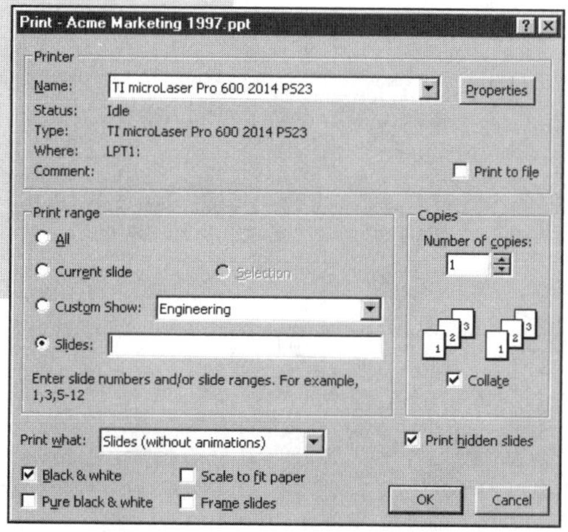

Figure 17.1 The Print dialog box enables you to choose nonstandard print settings like a different number of copies or pages.

If the printer you want appears, the next thing to be concerned about is the printer settings. You don't have to check these every time you print, because once you set them the way you want them, they stay set. But the first time you use a particular printer, it is worth a look to make sure that everything is the way you like it. Click on the Properties button next to the Name text box to display the printer's properties. Different printers show different tabs in the Properties dialog box; the ones for my printer (a PostScript laser model) appear in Figure 17.2.

Following are some of the settings you may see on your printer's Properties dialog box and what to do with them:

- *Paper Size.* Choose what size of paper you are using in your printer. If your printer can't handle a certain size, it appears with a red circle and line (the international symbol for "anti"), as you can see in Figure 17.2.
- *Orientation.* You can choose between Portrait and Landscape. Beware, however, that if you set this to Landscape, you may get unintended Landscape printouts in other programs besides PowerPoint; most people leave this set for Portrait and then set up Landscape for individual presentations as needed within PowerPoint. (You'll learn to do this later in the chapter.) Some PowerPoint items print in landscape by default (slides, for instance, do this).
- *Copies.* As noted in the preceding sidebar, "Print or Properties: What's the Difference?," unless you always want more than one copy of every

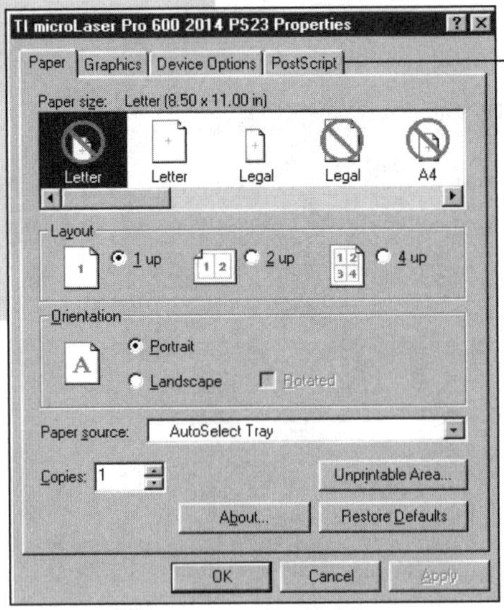

Figure 17.2 Here are my printer's properties; yours may look somewhat different.

Print or Properties: What's the Difference?

Some options can be set in two places: in the Properties dialog box for your printer and in PowerPoint's Print dialog box. Examples of this include page orientation and number of copies. It may seem like the same thing to set these in either spot, but it's not.

Keep this firmly in mind: when you make changes in the Properties dialog box for your printer, you are making base-level changes to the way that printer operates in Windows in general—and in all Windows-based programs. For example, if you set the number of copies to 2, your printer will print two copies of every single thing you print in every Windows program. If you set the orientation to Landscape, Landscape becomes the default orientation for every program that doesn't specify a particular orientation.

In contrast, when you set options in the Print or Page Setup dialog boxes in PowerPoint, the settings are applicable only in PowerPoint, and in some cases only in the active presentation.

Some settings build upon each other in ways you might not intend. For example, if you specify two copies in the Properties dialog box, and two copies in the Print dialog box, you will get a total of four copies. That's because PowerPoint sends two copies of your work to the printer driver, and when they get there, the printer driver says "let's see, you want two copies of everything, so here's two copies of each of the two things you sent me."

Be mindful when making changes to the Properties dialog box for your printer! The settings are easy enough to change back if you decide you're unhappy with your settings (just click on the Restore Defaults button), but if you forget you made those setting changes, you may find yourself with a problem that's hard to diagnose (like the extra copies issue just described or a printer that will print only in Landscape orientation).

document you print in every program, leave this set to 1. You can always specify more than one copy of a particular printout in the Print dialog box.

- *Graphics Tab.* Almost all printers show a Graphics tab in their Properties dialog box, but the controls on it vary widely. Color printers have color controls; PostScript printers have Scaling. Most printers have something about halftoning too, which means how grayscale images are represented using black ink (with little screens of dots that represent shades of gray). You may also see settings for Resolution, Dithering, and Intensity. If you don't understand a setting, leave it as-is.
- *Device Options Tab.* Nearly all printers also have a Device Options tab, and again the options are different depending on the printer type. Again, if you don't understand a setting, it's best to leave it alone.

Tip

Some printers include a Print TrueType as Graphics check box or option button in their Properties. This has to do with the way that TrueType fonts are sent to the printer. If you are running into problems such as TrueType fonts not printing correctly or not thick or dark enough, or if you are getting `Out of Memory` error messages on your printer, try changing this setting to see whether it corrects the problem.

When you're finished with your printer's Properties dialog box, click on OK to close it and return to the Print dialog box in PowerPoint.

There is one last control in the Printer section of the Print dialog box: a little check box called Print To File. When you select this check box, instead of printing when you click on OK, PowerPoint opens a Print To File dialog box where you can specify a file name (with the extension .prn) to print to (see Figure 17.3). This is a handy feature if the printer that you want to print from is

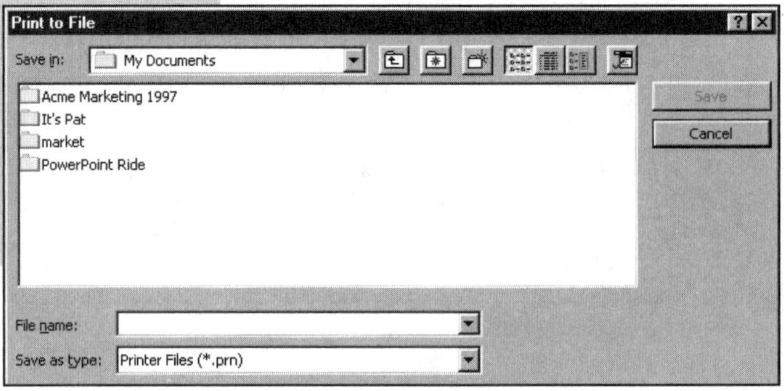

Figure 17.3 When you mark the Print To File check box, this dialog box appears when you click on OK to print.

More About Printing to a File

Notice under the Name list in the Print dialog box, there are some settings you cannot change, like Status, Type, Where, and Comments. Where tells what port the printer is installed on, such as LPT1 or COM2. You can't change these from within PowerPoint.

If it says FILE rather than a port, that means that someone has set up that printer to always print to a file. It's as if the Print To File check box in the Print dialog box were permanently marked (even though it may not appear to be marked at all when that printer is selected). If a particular printer is never directly available to your computer, for example, it would be appropriate for that printer to be set up this way.

If you need to change the port that a printer is on, you must change it from Windows 95. Choose Start, Settings, Printers to display a window with icons for each installed printer. Then right-click on the printer and choose Properties. You'll see the Properties dialog box again, but this time with more tabs to choose from. Click on the Details tab, and then choose a different port from the Print to the Following Port drop-down list, as shown below.

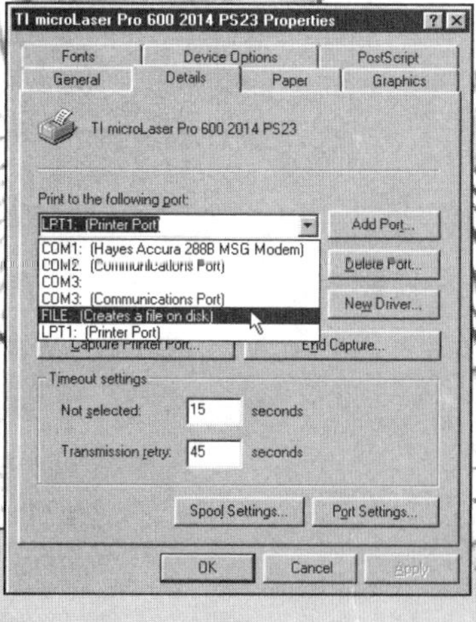

After you have printed to a file, copy the file onto a diskette or other portable medium and take it to a computer that's attached to that printer. Then in Windows 95, open the Printers window (Start, Settings, Printers), open a window for the disk (My Computer, double-click on the drive), and then drag the file to the printer icon and drop it there. This adds the file to that printer's queue.

not attached to your computer or not available at the moment, but the computer to which the correct printer is attached does not have PowerPoint. You print to a file, take the file on a floppy disk to a computer attached to that printer, and then copy the file to the printer.

Print Range

The Print Range area of the Print dialog box enables you to specify a certain number of pages to print from your presentation. The default is All, which prints everything. You can enter a range of slides, if you prefer, in the From and To boxes. You also can choose Current Slide to print just the active slide. If you have selected more than one slide (for example, in Slide Sorter) when you issued the Print command, the Selection option button will be available as well, which prints the selected slides.

Custom shows are covered in Chapter 16.

You also can print a custom show, if you have one set up. Just choose Custom Show and then choose the show from the drop-down list.

Note

Note that "slides" is not the same thing as "pages." True enough, some things that you print (like slides or notes pages) print one slide per page. But other things (like handouts) print multiple slides per page. In the Slides text box, you are entering the slides you want, not the number of pages in the printout.

Print What

The Print What section lets you choose what you want to print and how you want it. The first choice to make is from the Print What drop-down list:

- *Slides.* You can choose Slides With Animations or Slides Without Animations. No, the animations don't jump off the page and dance! It simply wants to know whether animated object should print or not.
- *Handouts.* As you learned in Chapter 16, you can print 2, 3, or 6 handouts per page. Just select what you want from the list here.
- *Notes Pages.* You learned about these in Chapter 16 too; notes pages are your speaker reminders that will help get you through the presentation.
- *Outline.* This is just a text-based outline of the presentation, very similar to what you see on-screen in Outline view.

Copies

The Copies options are pretty straightforward. How many copies do you want? One is the default. What's a little less straightforward is the Collate check box underneath. This feature is applicable only if both of the following are true:

- You are printing more than one copy.
- The selection you are printing has more than one page.

Collating means printing the copies so that they're ready to distribute, like this: Copy 1 page 1, Copy 1 page 2; Copy 2 page 1, Copy 2 page 2. If you deselect this check box, all the copies of each page will print in a row, like this: Copy 1 page 1, Copy 2 page 1; Copy 1 page 2, Copy 2 page 2.

Portrait or Landscape?

Remember, you saw some orientation controls in the Properties dialog box for your printer, and I promised you would be able to set this in PowerPoint instead? This is the place.

- *Portrait.* Taller than it is wide. This is the normal orientation for most business letters and textual reports. It's normally used for speaker notes and handouts.
- *Landscape.* Wider than it is tall. It's normally used for full-page slide printouts.

To set portrait or landscape, follow these steps:

1. Choose File, Page Setup. The Page Setup dialog box appears (see Figure 17.4).

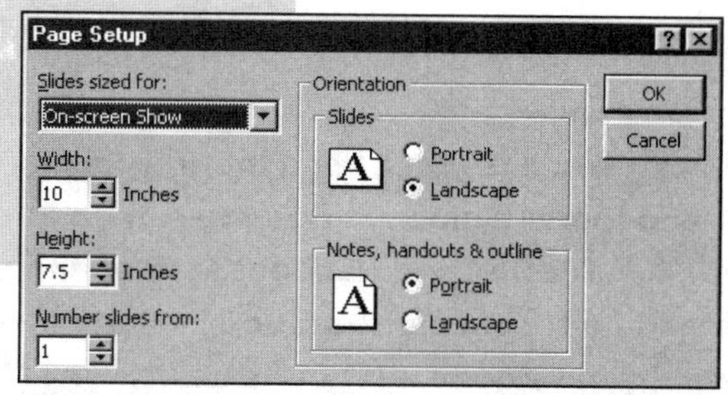

Figure 17.4 The Page Setup options include portrait and landscape settings.

2. For Slides, click on Portrait or Landscape. Landscape is the default for slides because they are wider than they are tall, so portrait orientation is not the most efficient use of the page.
3. For Notes, Handouts, and Outline (as a group), click on Portrait or Landscape. These are a set; you can't choose a different orientation for each.

Tip

It's easy enough to change this setting before you print if you need a special printout with a different orientation. For example, if you want portrait-style notes but landscape-style handouts, simply set up the notes here, print, set up the handouts, and print again.

4. Click on OK to accept your settings.

Headers and Footers

You have no doubt seen headers and footers in use, everywhere from your daily newspaper to the novel that you're reading. They run across the top and bottom of each page, telling the name of the publication, the page number, and often extra information like the date of publication and the author's name. Including these on your PowerPoint printouts adds a touch of class and also makes it much easier to reassemble a dropped stack of papers in the correct order (which you can't truly appreciate the value of until it's happened to you!). Figure 17.5 shows a page that uses a header and a footer.

You set up headers and footers in the Header and Footer dialog box (surprise!), which you open with the View, Header and Footer command. Figure 17.6 shows the Header and Footer dialog box.

Use the following Hands On to create a header and footer for your presentation printouts.

Note

It may not seem like you have a lot of flexibility in placing the header and footer elements. But you can go into the Notes Master, Slide Master, and Handout Master and move the header and footer elements around like any other objects, so you actually have quite a bit of flexibility.

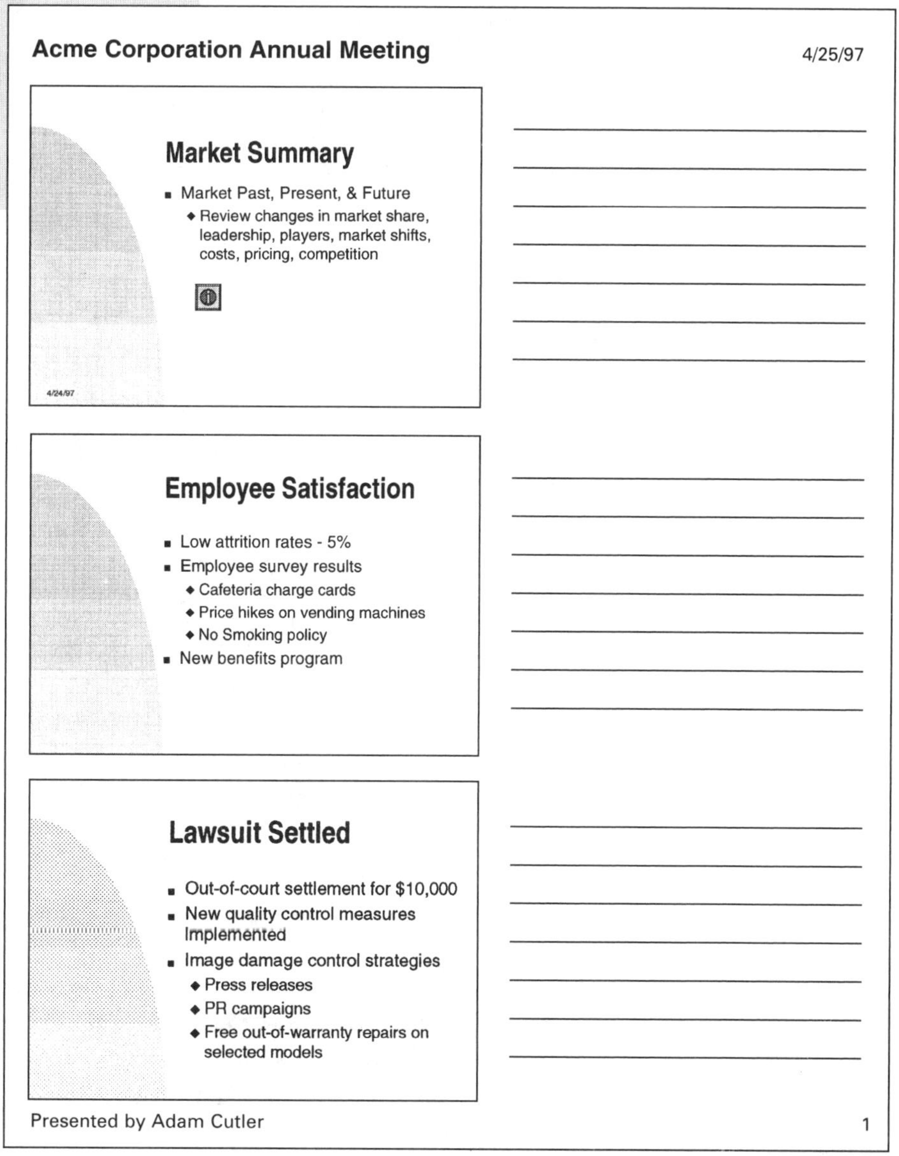

Figure 17.5 This page is made more useful and attractive by its header and footer.

Hands On: Headers and Footers

1. Choose View, Header and Footer. The Header and Footer dialog box opens.
2. You'll start with the Notes and Handouts tab. Make sure the Date and

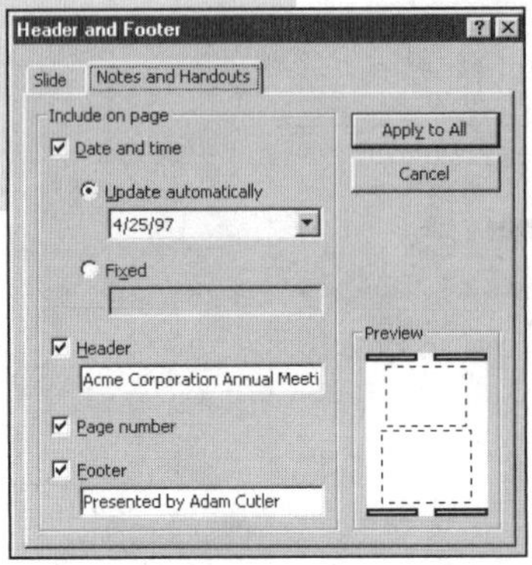

Figure 17.6 Create your headers and footers here.

Time check box is marked. The date will appear in the upper right corner of the printout.

3. Click on the Update Automatically option button so the current date will always appear on your printout.

   OR

   Click on the Fixed option button if you always want a certain date.
4. Make sure the Header check box is marked.
5. Type the text for the header in the Header text box. This will appear in the upper left corner of the printout.
6. Make sure the Page Number check box is marked. This will appear in the bottom right corner of the printout.
7. Make sure the Footer check box is marked.
8. Type the text for the footer in the Footer text box. This will appear in the bottom left corner of the printout.
9. Click on the Slide tab and set the same options for slide printouts. If you don't want the title slide to have a header or footer, select the Don't Show on Title Slide check box on the Slide tab.
10. Click on Apply to All. Now you'll have headers and footers on whatever you print!

Summary

In this chapter, you learned some tips and tricks that will help you produce the best printouts possible. You can now set your print options, change printers, and even tack headers and footers onto the printouts! Congratulations, you have done all the preparation. You're ready to give that presentation. In the next chapter, you'll learn how.

18

The Big Moment: Giving the Presentation

In This Chapter

- Controlling Slide Show View
- Displaying the Slides You Want
- Viewing Your Notes
- Drawing On-Screen
- Using Meeting Minder to Take Notes
- Giving Special Types of Presentations

Every chapter in this book has been preparing you for the moment when you will present your presentation to your audience. If you created a self-running presentation, the actual show will be somewhat anti-climactic; you will simply copy it to a Web site or set up a kiosk.

But if you are going to give the presentation "live," the big moment is yet to come. In this chapter, you'll learn how to survive that big moment, and find out about some PowerPoint features that can make it easier.

Practicing Beforehand

How do you get to the front of the boardroom? Practice, practice, practice. Now that your slide show is ready to go, you need to go over it and over it until you can do it in your sleep. Imagine frightening scenarios, like people asking tough questions, and plan how you'll handle them. Here are some ideas.

Speaker notes, hiding slides, and custom shows are all covered in Chapter 16.

- Present the presentation to your family and friends, and ask for feedback.
- Make a list of the questions that key listeners might ask, and prepare hidden backup slides.
- Create detailed speaker notes, and print two copies of them in case one gets lost.
- Prepare custom shows with special slides that will help if the discussion moves off on a related tangent.
- Practice drawing with your mouse pointer (covered later in this chapter), so your hand isn't shaky during the presentation.
- Experiment with the Meeting Minder beforehand (also covered later in this chapter), so you can use it with confidence when the time comes.

Rehearsing the Slide Show

The first step is to try out the slide show again. Yes, I know you've probably viewed the slide show before, but this time go through the entire thing, making sure that everything is in the right order.

Hands On: Running Through the Show

Follow these steps to view the entire show, start-to-finish:

1. Select the first slide in the presentation (in any view).
2. Click on the Slide Show button at the bottom left corner of the screen, or choose View, Slide Show.
3. To move to the next slide, press Page Down or click on the mouse button.

Note

If you have animations set up for a slide, pressing Page Down or clicking will move to the next animated part of the slide, rather than to the next slide, until you have seen every animated object on the slide do its thing.

4. Continue through your slide show until you reach the end and return to the view you started out with.
5. Repeat the entire process until you are thoroughly familiar with the flow of the presentation.

Jumping to Specific Slides

In the preceding Hands On, you showed the presentation in its most basic form—straight through. But you can also jump around and show any slide at any time. For example, suppose you are in the middle of the corporate overview when your boss says, "We're running out of time here; could you please get to your main point?" With PowerPoint, you can say "No problem!" and jump quickly to the last few slides.

The key to jumping around in the presentation is the shortcut menu in Slide Show view. When you move the mouse in Slide Show view, you see a rather large up-pointing arrow that looks like embossed text. When you click on that arrow, a shortcut menu appears. That's the shortcut menu. You can also see it by right-clicking anywhere on the slide. Point to the Go command, and a submenu appears, as shown in Figure 18.1.

Figure 18.1
Use the Slide Show menu to control the flow of your presentation.

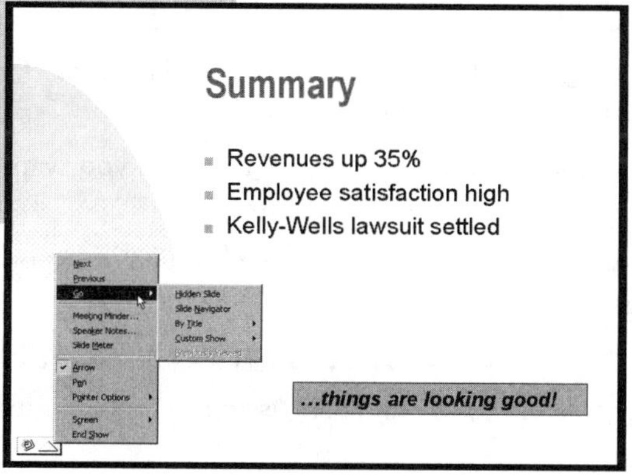

Tip

You can hide the mouse pointer and arrow button temporarily by pressing Ctrl+H. They will reappear the next time you move the mouse. To turn them off completely, press Ctrl+L.

From the Go menu, you can choose:

- *Hidden Slide.* If the next slide in the presentation is hidden, this command is available. You can show the hidden slide by selecting that command. In order to use this, you have to know where the hidden slides are in the presentation, so you have to become very familiar with the presentation before giving it!
- *Slide Navigator.* This command opens a dialog box that you can use to choose the slide you want. You'll look at it shortly.
- *By Title.* This command opens a submenu containing the titles of all the slides in the presentation. You can jump to a specific slide by selecting it from that list.
- *Custom Show.* If you have custom shows set up, this menu command is available, and its submenu lets you choose the custom show you want.
- *Previously Viewed.* This command takes you back to the last slide you viewed.

Custom shows are covered in Chapter 16.

Hands On: Using Slide Navigator

One of the commands on the Go submenu, Slide Navigator, offers some useful features for working with slides during a presentation. Use these steps to try it out.

1. From Slide Show view, move the mouse so that the control arrow appears in the bottom left corner.
2. Click on the arrow to display the Slide Show shortcut menu.
3. Point to Go, and then click on Slide Navigator. The Slide Navigator dialog box opens (see Figure 18.2).
4. On the Slide Titles list, click on the slide you want to go to. Hidden slides' numbers appear in parentheses.
5. Click on the Go To button. The chosen slide appears and the Slide Navigator box closes.

Tip

A quick way to return to the first slide is to hold down both mouse buttons for 2 seconds.

Figure 18.2
You can quickly jump to any slide from the Slide Navigator box.

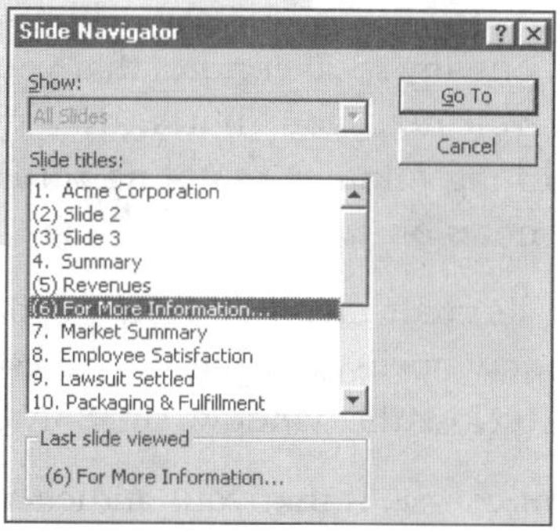

Other Ways to Control the Slide Show

Some people are more comfortable using a keyboard than a mouse. It's true, believe it or not! That's why PowerPoint offers a host of shortcut keys you can use to navigate in your slide show. You may think that you will never need these, but you may someday have to give a presentation using a computer that does not have a mouse attached or available, so keep their existence in the back of your mind. Table 18.1 gives an overview of them.

Table 18.1 Navigation Keys in Slide Show View

To	Press
Go to the next slide	N, Enter, or Spacebar
Go to the previous slide	P or Backspace
Go to a certain slide	Type the slide number and press Enter
Stop or restart an auto-running show	S
End a slide show	Esc
Go to next hidden slide	H
Display the shortcut menu	Shift + F10

Tip

If you forget any of the shortcuts in Table 18.1, you can press F1 during a slide show to see a list of them.

Viewing Your Notes

You have probably printed out any speaker notes that you've created, but Murphy's Law says that when you need your notes, they will be nowhere to be found. Rather than spend long minutes fumbling through your papers, you may want to refer to your notes on-screen.

To do so, just display the shortcut menu and then choose Speaker Notes. A simple Speaker Notes window opens showing the notes for the current slide, as shown in Figure 18.3. To close the window, click on Close.

The disadvantage to this, of course, is that your audience reads your notes on-screen along with you. But if you have the presentation set up to display on two screens (covered later in this chapter), the speaker notes appear only on the presenter screen, not the audience one.

Drawing On-Screen

Have you ever seen a coach in a locker room, drawing out football plays on a chalkboard? Well, you can do the same thing in PowerPoint. You can have impromptu discussions of concepts illustrated on slides, and punctuate the discussion with your own freehand circles and arrows and lines.

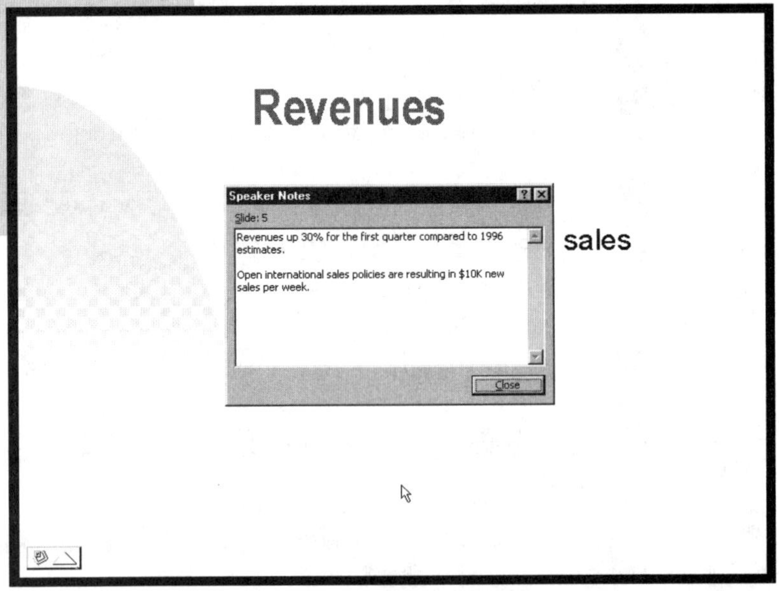

Figure 18.3 You can view speaker notes on-screen if you can't find your printout and need the information.

All you have to do is turn your mouse pointer into a pen. Sounds difficult, but with PowerPoint it's easy. Just open the shortcut menu and choose Pen, or press Ctrl+P. Now drag the mouse on the slide. A line! Practice drawing lines, arrows, or whatever; it takes awhile to get good at it. To erase your lines and try again, press the E key (for Erase).

When might this be useful? Well, perhaps during the discussion portion of your presentation, it was decided that one point on the slide is not important. You could use the pen to cross it out. Or perhaps a certain point becomes really important during a discussion and you want to emphasize it. You could circle it or underline it with the pen. Figure 18.4 shows how I've punctuated a key point in my presentation and crossed out another.

Tip

As you can see from Figure 18.4, the on-screen pen is not all that attractive. If you know in advance that you're going to emphasize a certain point, build the emphasis into the presentation by making that point larger, more bold, or a different color.

To change the pen back to a pointer again, reopen the shortcut menu and choose Arrow, or press Ctrl+A.

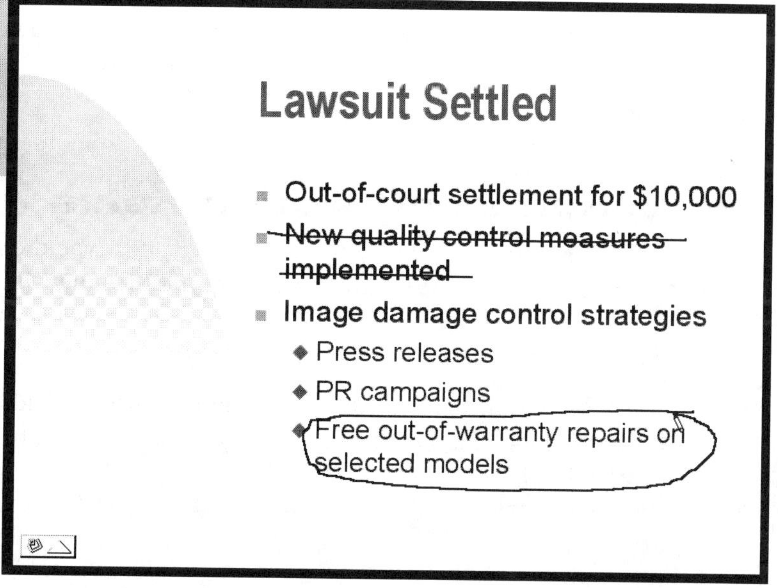

Figure 18.4 An on-screen pen is available to help emphasize key points.

There may be times when you want to draw on a totally blank screen instead of an existing slide. To blank out the screen for drawing, press the [B] key for a black screen or the [W] key for a white one. The pen color adjusts to be visible (black on white or white on black).

> **Tip**
>
> If you want to clear the screen of slides while a side discussion takes place during the presentation, the [B] and [W] keys work well. They blank out the current slide. You do not have to draw anything with the pen in order to take advantage of these blanks. When you want your regular slide back, just advance the presentation.

Using Meeting Minder to Take Notes

During most meetings, someone takes minutes and distributes them to participants later. Sometimes action items (things to do) are assigned to various people as well. You can take the minutes and assign the action items directly from PowerPoint.

Although you can't actually take the minutes or assign the action items until the actual presentation, you should practice using the Meeting Minder feature ahead of time so you will appear confident with it when the time comes.

To display the Meeting Minder, display the shortcut menu in Slide Show view and choose Meeting Minder. The Meeting Minder dialog box appears (see Figure 18.5).

Entering Minutes and Action Items

The Minutes tab is pretty straightforward. Just type the minutes into the dialog box as they happen. You must close the Meeting Minder to advance to the next slide, but you can reopen it whenever you need it. (You probably will not need it for every slide.)

On the Action Item tab, you can assign tasks to individuals (see Figure 18.6). Use the following Hands On to assign an action item to yourself.

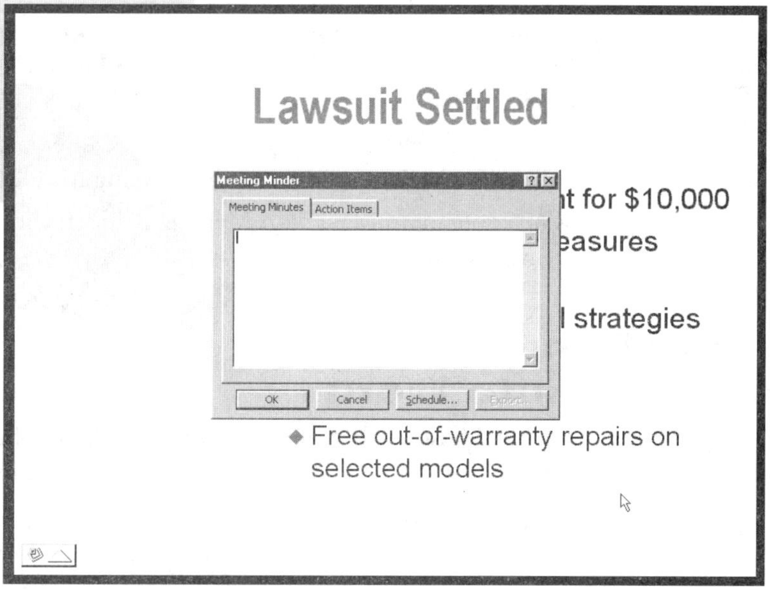

Figure 18.5 The meeting minder provides a space for taking minutes and assigning action items.

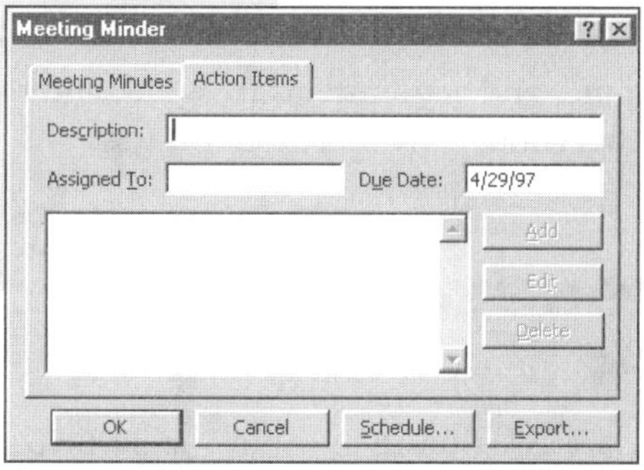

Figure 18.6 Use the Action Items tab to assign duties to people based on the presentation proceedings.

Hands On: Assigning Action Items

1. Open the Meeting Minder and display the Action Items tab.
2. In the Des<u>c</u>ription field, type the description. For example, type **Distribute Meeting Minutes**.
3. In the Assigned <u>T</u>o field, type your own first name.
4. In the D<u>u</u>e Date field, type the date when the task is due. Today's date is displayed by default; set it to 3 days from now.

5. Click on the Add button to add the action item.
6. If you use Microsoft Outlook and want to schedule the action item in Outlook, click on the Schedule button. Outlook opens with a new appointment started.
7. Fill in the details of the appointment in Outlook, then close Outlook and return to PowerPoint and the Meeting Minder.
8. When you are finished with Meeting Minder, click on OK to return to giving the presentation.

Exporting Minutes and Action Items into Word

If you have Microsoft Word on your system, when you finish the presentation, follow these steps to export the minutes and action items into Word:

1. Click on the Export button in the Meeting Minder.
2. In the dialog box that appears, choose Send Meeting Minutes and Action Items to Microsoft Word.
3. Click on Export Now. Word opens and displays the minutes, complete with the date and the name of the presentation.
4. Save the minutes and action items in Word, and then close Word and return to PowerPoint.

Giving Your Presentation over a Network

When you have a presentation to give but the participants can't all be in one room, you can use the Presentation Conference Wizard to run a presentation over a network or on the Internet. All participants must have PowerPoint 97 in order to see the presentation, because everyone needs access to the Presentation Conference Wizard. The wizard supports participants who connect directly to the Internet or who use a modem to dial in to their Internet service provider.

Note

To set up a conference with those who connect through a proxy server or firewall, see your network administrator.

Showing a presentation this way has some limitations. Your audience won't be able to see or hear these items:

- Multimedia objects such as sound or video clips. (However, sound effects applied to transitions and animations can be heard if the audience member has a sound card and speakers.)
- Embedded objects, such as a chart from Microsoft Graph or Microsoft Organization Chart.

As a presenter, you'll have access to the Stage Manager tools, which only you can see and use during the show. All audience members can use the pen to draw on the slides.

Receiving a Presentation Conference

Your audience members must set up their screens before you can set up yours. (Or at least, they must click on Finish to end the Wizard before you do.) Ask each of the audience members to perform these steps:

1. If you are connecting to the presenter through the Internet, start your Internet connection.
2. Start PowerPoint.
3. Choose Tools, Presentation Conference.
4. Click on Next to begin.
5. Click on the Audience button and then click on Next.
6. Click on the option button to describe how you are connecting: Local Area Network or Dial In to Internet. Then click on Next.
7. If you chose Internet in step 6, a message appears reminding you to connect to the Internet if needed. Click on Next.
8. On the next screen, a message appears telling you that the presenter needs to know your Internet address, and listing an address, as shown in Figure 18.7. Copy down that address, and call your presenter on the telephone to let him or her know the address.
9. Click on Next, and then click on Finish.
10. Wait for the presenter to start the presentation.

When the presenter starts the show, you will see each slide full-screen on your monitor. You can right-click on the slide to access the shortcut menu, but the only thing you can do from it is change the pointer to a pen and change the pen color. You can draw on the slide, and all other participants will see it. You cannot erase. Only the presenter can erase.

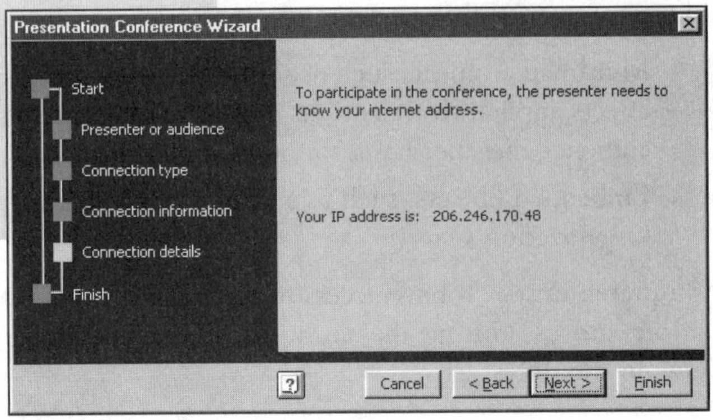

Figure 18.7 Copy down the address that you see on your screen; your presenter needs it.

You can end the show by right-clicking and choosing End Show, but you cannot return to the show still in progress. When you end the show, the entire presentation appears in PowerPoint, and you can edit and save your copy of it.

Presenting a Presentation Conference

If you are the presenter, it's a little bit different. You must wait until all the audience members have their machines set up and have provided you with their online addresses. Then follow these steps.

1. If you are connecting to your audience through the Internet, start your Internet connection. If you are presenting only over a network, or if your network connection is your Internet connection, you can skip this step.
2. Open the presentation you want to run.
3. Choose Tools, Presentation Conference. The Presentation Conference Wizard opens.
4. Click on Next to begin.
5. Make sure the Presenter button is selected, and then click on Next.
6. A message appears telling you that all slides will be shown; click on Next.
7. A message appears reminding you to connect to the network or Internet; click on Next.
8. A dialog box appears where you should enter the addresses of your participants (see Figure 18.8). Enter each one in turn and click on Add; then click on Next.

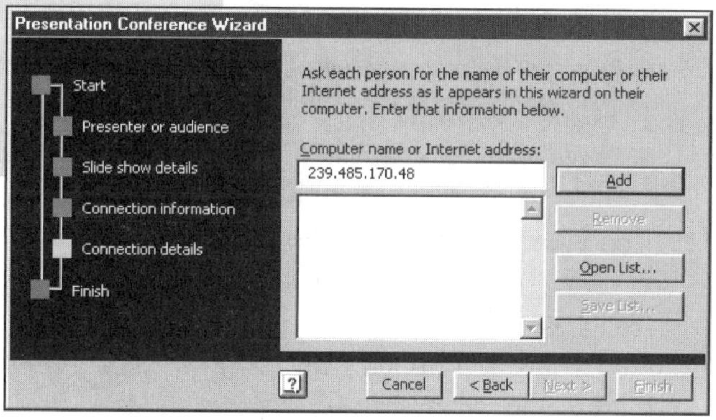

Figure 18.8 Type in the addresses of your participants.

9. If you are sure that all audience members have clicked Finish already, click on Finish yourself. The Presentation Conference Wizard checks the connections with all the addresses, and if all is well, it moves to the next screen.
10. Click on Finish to begin the presentation. When you start the presentation, several windows appear on-screen, as shown in Figure 18.9.
    - *PowerPoint Slide Show window.* This is your regular Slide Show view but it's in a window that takes up only about 1/3 of the screen.
    - *Slide Navigator window.* Same as usual.

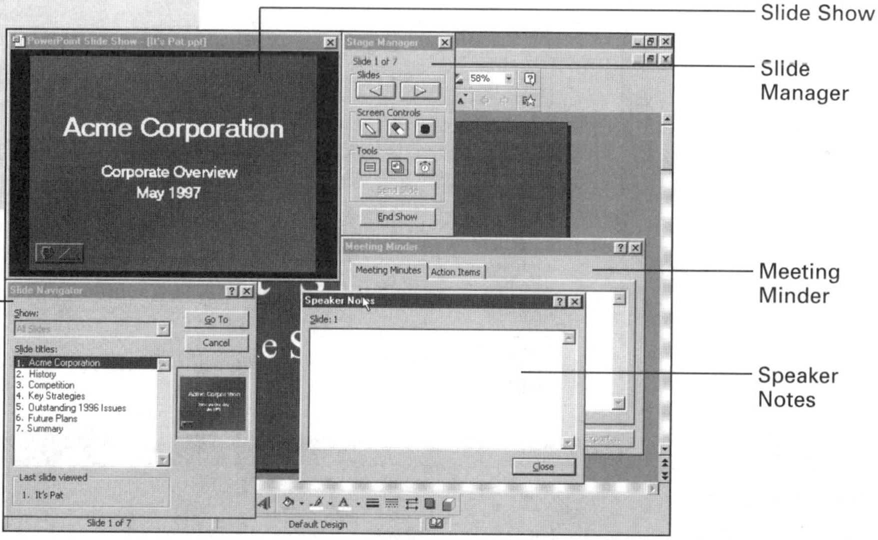

Figure 18.9 When you're the presenter, you have a whole host of controls at your disposal.

- *Speaker Notes window.* Also same as usual, except it appears by default here.
- *Meeting Minder window.* Ditto. Same as usual, except it appears by default.
- *Stage Manager window.* This is a totally new palette of controls. They're described in Table 18.2.

11. Run your slide show by advancing from slide to slide with the arrow buttons in the Stage Manager or by selecting slides from the Slide Navigator.
12. When you are finished with the show, click on the End Show button on the Stage Manager.
13. If necessary, close your Internet connection.

Table 18.2 Stage Manager Buttons

Icon	Purpose
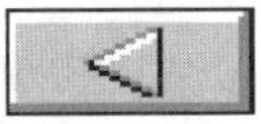	Go to the previous slide
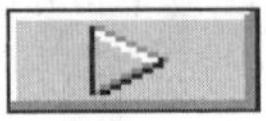	Go to the next slide
	Draw on the slide
	Erase the drawings on the slide
	Black out the screen temporarily
	Display/hide the Meeting Minder and Speaker Notes
	Display/hide the Slide Navigator
	Display/hide the Slide Meter

Gradient Texture Pattern Picture

Working with Two Screens

You can also view a presentation on one computer while you control it from another. For example, you might have a laptop computer but want to show the presentation on a computer with a large-screen monitor. You can connect the laptop to the computer and then view the presentation on the large screen. The controlling computer has access to the same tools that are available during a presentation conference.

To set this up, follow these steps:

1. With both computers off, connect the two computers through their serial ports with a null modem cable. (If you don't know what this is, go to a computer store and ask for one or ask your company's computer support department.)
2. Turn on both computers.
3. On the computer that will be the one the audience sees, start PowerPoint and choose Slide Show, View on Two Screens.
4. Click on the Audience option button.
5. Open the Select the Port You Want to Use drop-down list and choose the COM port that the cable is connected to (usually 1 or 2).
6. Click on OK.
7. On the computer that will be the one the presenter uses, start PowerPoint and choose Slide Show, View on Two Screens.
8. Click on the Presenter option button.
9. Open the Select the Port You Want to Use drop-down list and choose the COM port that the cable is connected to.
10. Click on OK. Now you can run the presentation from one machine and it will show up on both screens.

Running a Kiosk Presentation

Kiosk presentations are the generic name for presentations that are self-running and unattended. I talked about the need for security for this type of presentation in Chapter 14. When you've got one ready to go, here's how to set it up:

1. In any view except Slide Show, choose Slide Show, Set Up Show. The Set Up Show dialog box appears (see Figure 18.10).

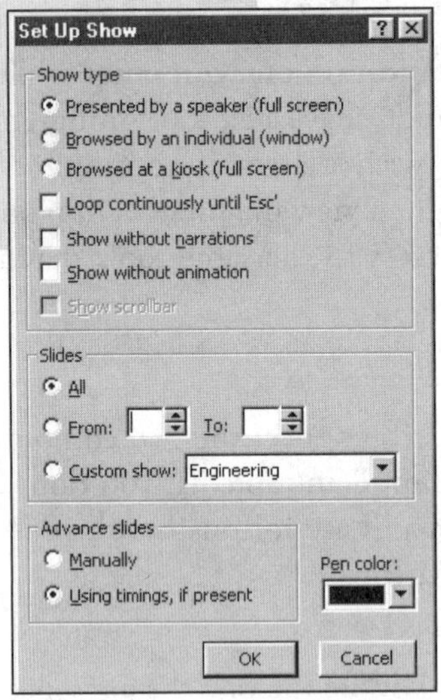

Figure 18.10 Use this dialog box to set up a self-running kiosk presentation.

You learned about timing between slides in Chapter 14.

2. Click on the Browsed at a Kiosk option button.
3. Select the Loop Continuously Until Esc check box.
4. Make sure the Use Timings If Present option button is selected if the presentation is supposed to run by itself. If the presentation is user-controlled with on-screen buttons, choose the Manually option button instead.
5. Click on OK.
6. Set up your kiosk, providing users with what they need to access your presentation (monitor, mouse if needed, keyboard if needed).

Summary

In this chapter, you learned how to give a presentation with PowerPoint. Congratulations! You've finished the book. Now go out there and be a success.

PART V
Appendixes

A

Installing PowerPoint on Your Computer

In This Chapter

- Understanding the Installation Process
- Installing PowerPoint
- Installing PowerPoint as Part of Microsoft Office
- Adding and Removing PowerPoint Components
- Installing Internet Explorer

If you're lucky, you'll find that someone else has already installed PowerPoint on your computer for you. But if you've turned to this appendix in the book, you probably aren't having such luck today.

PowerPoint 97 may come to you in one of two ways: as a stand-alone product or as a part of the Microsoft Office 97 package. In this appendix, you'll look at both possibilities as well as how to install extra components you may need eventually.

What Does Installing Do?

In the old days (1985 or so), a computer program could fit—uncompressed—on a single floppy disk. That was good because most computers didn't have hard disks back then. You just popped the floppy into your drive and ran the program right from there.

Today, of course, that could never happen. Big, feature-rich programs like PowerPoint take up tens of megabytes of space. You can't just pop in the disk PowerPoint came on and run it—you first have to run the setup program.

The installation program (called "setup") does several things:

- It decompresses the compressed files. (Files on the installation CD are squashed so that more of them will fit on the disc.)
- It creates the appropriate folder structure on your hard disk.
- It copies the files needed to run PowerPoint onto your hard disk.
- It adds a shortcut to PowerPoint to your Start menu.

Office 97 and PowerPoint 97 do provide an option to run the applications directly from the CD-ROM, saving disk space on your computer. (It runs slower that way, but it does work.) This works well for people who have limited space on their hard drive, or who use PowerPoint only very rarely. However, to set this up, you must still run the setup program, as you learn to do later in this appendix.

PowerPoint or Office?

Some people buy PowerPoint as a stand-alone product; others acquire it as part of the Microsoft Office suite of programs. The installation program works pretty much the same way no matter which version you have. The real difference is in what gets installed.

If you bought the Microsoft Office 97 version, when you run the setup program it installs all the Office components, not just PowerPoint. Office comes with a variety of tools, including Word (a word processor), Excel (a spreadsheet program with very good graphing capabilities), and Outlook (a scheduling and planning tool). The professional edition also comes with Access (a database). Installing all these tools is fine if you have enough disk space, but if you don't, you will want to use the Custom setup procedure described in the following section to exclude the components you won't ever use.

Installing PowerPoint

As I said, the installation procedure itself is the same no matter whether you have the Office 97 or PowerPoint 97 version. That's because the same tasks need to be done no matter what is getting copied to your hard disk: the Setup program needs to know who you are, what components you want, and where you want them stored. The following steps walk you through the procedure—follow them, or just follow along with the prompts on your screen.

1. Close all open applications.
2. Insert the Microsoft Office 97 or Microsoft PowerPoint 97 CD-ROM in your CD-ROM drive, or the first disk in your floppy disk drive. A dialog box opens automatically.

Note

If you don't see a dialog box automatically when you insert the CD-ROM, your computer may not be set up to Autorun CD-ROMs. Just double-click on the My Computer icon on the Desktop and double-click on the CD-ROM drive's icon. Locate and double-click on the Setup icon; then catch up to the rest of us at step 4.

3. Click on the Install Microsoft Office button (or the Install Microsoft PowerPoint button, if you're installing the stand-alone version).
4. At the Welcome dialog box, click on Continue.
5. In the Name and Organization Information dialog box, enter your name and organization. If you don't have an organization, leave that box empty. Click on OK.
6. When asked to confirm your name and organization, click on OK again.
7. If you're asked for the CD-ROM key, find it on the sticker on the back of the jewel case and enter it. Then click on OK.

8. Next you see your product ID number. It consists of your version number plus the CD-ROM key number that you just entered. Write it down on your registration card and then click on OK.
9. At this point, if you bought an upgrade version, the program may want to search your system for a qualifying product. Follow the on-screen instructions, which may involve inserting a disk from a qualifying product into your computer. When the installation program is satisfied that you are a legitimate upgrader, it lets you go on to selecting the drive and folder where you want to install.
10. Choose the drive and folder into which Microsoft Office is installed (or PowerPoint, if installing the stand-alone version). The default is the Program Files folder on the same drive that Windows is installed on (see Figure A.1). Click on OK to accept that (recommended), or click on Change Folder and select a new location.
11. Choose the type of installation you want by clicking on the appropriate button:
    - *Typical.* Installs the most common components. This is the easiest method, and most users will be happy with the options installed.
    - *Custom.* Enables you to choose exactly which components you want. This is for experienced users and those who are installing Office and don't use certain Office products at all.
    - *Run from CD-ROM.* Sets up the program(s) to run mostly from the CD-ROM. Because it copies very few files to your hard disk, it's ideal for users who are very short on disk space; however, it requires that the CD-ROM be in the drive whenever PowerPoint (or another Office component) is running.

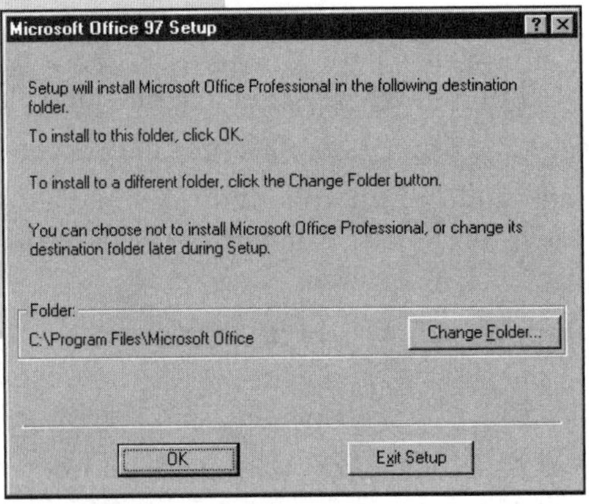

Figure A.1 Accept the directory chosen by the installation program by clicking on OK, or click on Change Folder and choose your own.

Figure A.2
Click on the check boxes to select or deselect categories and options.

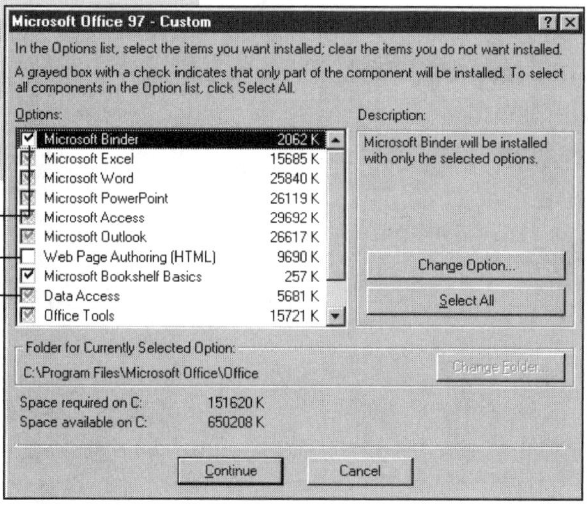

If you chose Typical or Run from CD-ROM, skip to step 14. If you chose Custom, the Microsoft Office 97 Custom dialog box appears (see Figure A.2).

12. You see a series of components with check boxes. A check in a white-background box means all options for that component will be installed. A check in a gray-background box means that only some of the component's options will be installed. Use these methods to choose which components and options you want:
    - To select all components, click on the Select All button. This is the best way to go if you have plenty of disk space and aren't sure which features you'll be using.
    - To deselect an entire component, click on its check box to remove the check mark. For instance, if you are using the Microsoft Office version and you don't want PowerPoint to be installed at all, remove the check mark next to PowerPoint. Do the same for any other Office components you don't want.
    - To choose which options of a component are installed, click on the component and then click on Change Option. A dialog box appears, showing the options for that component, each with its own check box that you can use to turn it on or off. Click on OK to return to the main screen. Refer to Table A.1 (in the next section) for some ideas about what to select.
13. When you finish selecting options, click on Continue.

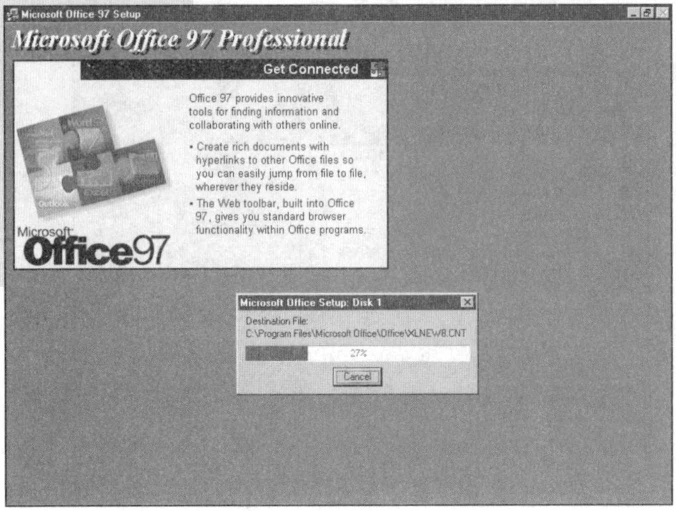

Figure A.3 It takes several minutes for the setup program to copy its files; a progress bar at the bottom of the screen shows how far it has progressed.

14. If the installation program finds old Office or PowerPoint components, it asks whether you want to remove them. Click on Yes. (Any data files you had will remain, even if you delete the old program.)
15. Wait for the setup program to copy the files (see Figure A.3). When you see the message "Microsoft Office 97 Setup was completed successfully" (or PowerPoint, as the case may be), click on OK. You are now ready to use Microsoft PowerPoint.

On some computers, you may be asked to restart before using the software. If you see a dialog box asking whether you want to restart now, click on Yes. Do not try to use the software without restarting the computer if restarting has been suggested; it will not work properly.

Custom Installation: Some Advice

It's hard to know exactly which options to choose in a Custom installation if you're a beginner. Table A.1 provides some ideas of some components you might want that are not installed by default. Table A.1 is based on the Office version of the software, but the options are similar for the stand-alone version.

Table A.1 PowerPoint Options Not Installed by Default That You Might Want

Component	Option	Comments (Office version)
PowerPoint	Content Templates	The Additional Content Templates are not installed by default, but you may find them useful.
PowerPoint	Animation Effects Sounds	These take up rather a lot of space, but are fun. They are sounds that go with your built-in animation effects.
PowerPoint	Presentation Translators	These are converters that let you open presentations from other products, such as Harvard Graphics.
PowerPoint	Genigraphics Wizard	If you plan to export your slides to the Genigraphics slide printing service, you'll need to install this setup wizard for that feature.
Web Page Authoring (HTML)	(No options)	If you plan to create Web pages, you definitely will need these tools. PowerPoint is not the best tool for creating Web pages, but you may need to publish a presentation in HTML format to include on your company's Web site.
Office Tools	Microsoft Office Shortcut Bar	(Office version only) This is not installed by default, although it was in previous releases of Office. If you're accustomed to using it, install it.
Converters	Text	I recommend that you and Filters install all of these. You never know what text file formats you may encounter.
Converters	Graphics	I also recommend that you and Filters install all of these.

Installing Internet Explorer

If you use the Internet (or if you want to learn), you may find Microsoft's *Web browser*, Internet Explorer 3.0, useful. After you run the PowerPoint or Office installation program, an icon appears on your desktop called Setup for Microsoft Internet Explorer 3.0 (or some variation of that, such as 3.01, 3.02, and so on). That icon makes it easy to install the program.

Note

A *Web browser* enables you to view graphical content on the Internet. To use it, you must have an Internet connection. You can get an Internet connection by subscribing to the Microsoft Network; the easiest way to get that subscription is to double-click on the Microsoft Network icon on your Desktop and follow the prompts.

Follow these steps to install Internet Explorer:

1. Double-click on the Setup for Microsoft Internet Explorer 3.0 icon on your Desktop.
2. A dialog box asks whether you want to install the program. Click on Yes.
3. Read the licensing agreement and then click on I Agree.
4. Wait for the setup program to install the files you need. If you see the Version Conflict dialog box asking you whether you want to keep an existing file, click on Yes.
5. At the message "Do you want to restart your computer now?", click on Yes.

After your computer restarts, you are ready to use Internet Explorer. You can use it through your Microsoft Network account or with any other Internet connection. For more information about the Internet, see Chapter 14.

B

Using the IntelliMouse with PowerPoint 97

In This Chapter

- Understanding the IntelliMouse
- IntelliMouse Operations in PowerPoint 97
- Exploring Additional IntelliMouse Functions

The Microsoft IntelliMouse is a pointing device that's like a regular mouse, but with some special features that make it easier to use Microsoft Office and some other Windows-based products that support its enhancements. If you use it with a product that doesn't recognize its special features, it works just like any other regular mouse. You can buy it along with the Microsoft Office 97 upgrade, or you can purchase it separately for about $70. Many new computer manufacturers are also including it with their new systems.

In PowerPoint 97, the IntelliMouse is used to scroll and zoom on the slide. It also can be used to collapse and expand outline levels in Outline view.

Note

To use the wheel on the IntelliMouse, you must install the IntelliPoint software that comes with it. Otherwise the IntelliMouse will work just like any other mouse, but it won't have the special wheel capabilities.

How to Use the IntelliMouse in PowerPoint

Like any other mouse, the IntelliMouse includes a primary (left) and secondary (right) mouse button. The difference between the IntelliMouse and a standard mouse is the wheel located between the left and right mouse buttons.

You can either rotate or click (press and release) the IntelliMouse wheel depending on what feature you want to use. Rolling the wheel forward or back scrolls up and down by small increments, as if you had clicked on the up or down arrow at the ends of the vertical scroll bar. When you click on the wheel and drag, the display scrolls continuously, as if you were clicking and holding on one of the scroll bar arrows.

To use the IntelliMouse to zoom rather than scroll, hold down the Ctrl key as you operate it. To zoom in, roll the wheel upward; to zoom out, roll it downward. The IntelliMouse can zoom the display between 10 and 100 percent.

Table B.1 describes how the IntelliMouse operates with PowerPoint 97.

Controlling How the IntelliMouse Operates

With the IntelliPoint 2.0 software, you can adjust how the IntelliMouse works. These changes are not directly connected to PowerPoint, but they can make your overall computer experience easier.

Table B.1 IntelliMouse Operations in PowerPoint 97

PowerPoint Operation	Mouse Motion
Scroll continuously in a presentation	Click and hold the wheel and drag the mouse pointer in the direction that you want to scroll. When you drag, the mouse pointer changes to a directional arrow with dot to indicate which way you are scrolling.
Scroll up or down on a slide	Rotate the wheel forward (without clicking on anything) to scroll up or down.
Speed up scrolling on a slide	Click and release the wheel button and move the mouse pointer in the direction that you want to go to.
Zoom in on a worksheet	Hold down the [Ctrl] key and move the wheel forward.
Zoom out on a worksheet	Hold down the [Ctrl] key and move the wheel back.
Show/hide levels in Outline view	Point to a heading, and then hold down [Shift] as you rotate the wheel forward or backward.

Hands On: Exploring the IntelliMouse Settings

To begin using some additional IntelliMouse capabilities, follow these steps:

1. Choose Start, Settings, Control Panel, and double-click on the Mouse icon. The Mouse Properties dialog box appears.
2. Select the Wheel tab (see Figure B.1). This tab contains the two check boxes for enabling the wheel and wheel button. These are on by default, but you can deselect either check box to turn the features off. If you do so, the IntelliPoint mouse will work the same as a normal mouse.

Note

If the check boxes are grayed out on the Wheel tab, it means the IntelliMouse is not functioning properly and the system does not recognize it.

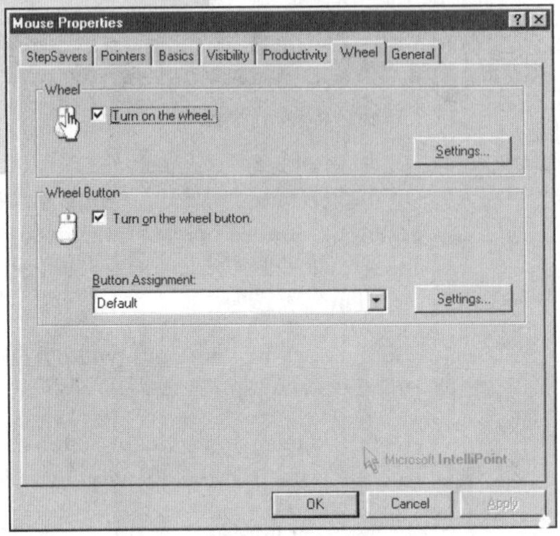

Figure B.1 Turn the wheel functionality on or off on the Wheel tab.

3. Select the Basics tab (see Figure B.2). This is where you set the speed and sensitivity of the mouse.
4. Slide the bar in the Pointer Speed section, and then test the new speed. When you are happy with your new setting, leave it there.
5. In the Button Selection area, notice that the Left button is selected. That's the button you use when you click and double-click. If you would prefer to use the right mouse button (for example, if you are left-handed), click on the Right button instead.

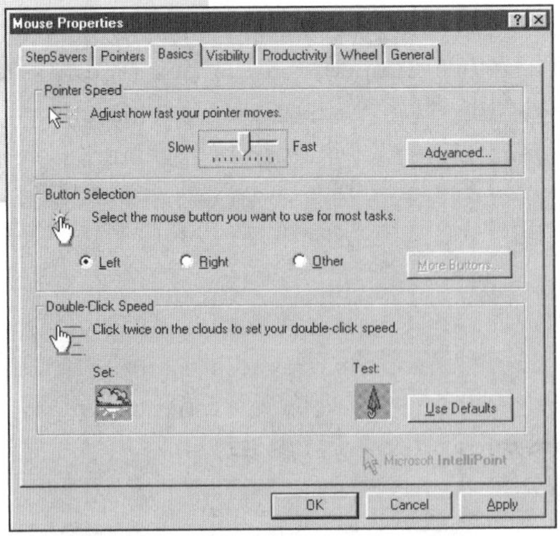

Figure B.2 Use the Basics tab to control the basic mouse sensitivity and movement.

6. To set a different double-click speed (that is, a minimal speed that you must click for two clicks to be recognized as a double), double-click on the left picture in the Double-Click Speed section. Then test your setting by double-clicking on the right picture.
7. Click on the StepSavers tab, and select any of the check boxes there that look helpful to you. (Descriptions appear next to each check box, as shown in Figure B.3.)
8. Click on the other tabs and see what's there. Change any settings that look interesting; you can always change them back if you don't like them. Here is some of what you'll find:
   - On the Pointers tab you can choose different mouse pointers. For example, you might want to choose a larger mouse pointer so you can see it better, especially on a laptop computer.
   - On the Visibility tab you can set various options that make your pointer easier to find and see on-screen. The Sonar feature is especially cool—with it on, you can press the Ctrl key to see a circle light up around the pointer, signaling where it is.
   - On the Productivity tab you can set the orientation for the mouse (the default is that the cord or "tail" is up.)
   - Also on the Productivity tab you can turn on the ClickLock feature, which enables you to click once and have the mouse button "lock down" as if you were holding it down. You click again to release it. This sounds like a good idea but can get annoying really quickly.

Figure B.3
The StepSavers tab contains some unusual but sometimes helpful features.

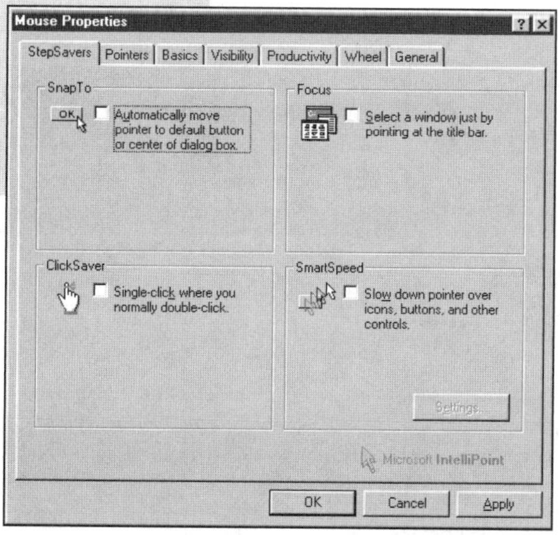

9. When you are finished, click on OK to close the dialog box.
10. If you don't like the settings, reopen the dialog box and change things back. On some tabs there is a Use Defaults or Reset button that will enable you to restore the original settings for that tab.

Note

If you have swapped the mouse buttons (i.e. made the right one function as the left one), remember that when you're trying to reenter the dialog box and change it back. You can no longer click with the left; you must click with the right until you restore the old setting.

C

Customizing PowerPoint Settings

In This Chapter

- Changing the Toolbar Buttons
- Creating Your Own Toolbars
- Changing How PowerPoint Operates
- Specifying File Locations

Some people are happy using the factory settings—on everything from their waffle irons to their VCRs. "If it works, why mess with it?" is these people's philosophy. If you're one of those people, feel free to skip this appendix. This chapter is for the dial-turners, the button-tweakers, the folks (like me!) who aren't content until every little control is set to their exact specifications.

In this appendix, you'll take a peek at the control panel behind PowerPoint's friendly interface and learn how to change the system settings for your own preferences. Necessary? No. But extremely handy. In many cases, a simple change you make to a setting can save you precious minutes of time later.

Customizing Toolbars and Menus

See Chapter 1 to learn how to use toolbar buttons for common tasks like printing, saving, and so on.

The toolbars you see at the top of the screen change in PowerPoint depending on what you're doing. Most of the time, the Standard and Formatting toolbars appear; when you do special things like edit charts (see Chapter 14), other toolbars appear instead containing tools appropriate to the task at hand. In Chapter 2, you learned to display and hide toolbars. (Remember: right-click on any visible toolbar and then select the toolbar you want to display or hide from the menu that appears.)

Changing What Buttons Appear on a Toolbar

Not all PowerPoint users use the program in the same way, and you may find that you frequently use a few commands for which there are no buttons on the default toolbars. In cases like that, you may want to add a button to one of the default toolbars that will perform the action you need.

To add a new toolbar button, the general procedure is this:

1. Right-click on any toolbar and choose Customize from the shortcut menu that appears. The Customize dialog box opens.
2. Click on the Commands tab.
3. Select a menu or toolbar from the Categories list. All the buttons, commands, and options available from that menu or toolbar appear on the Commands list to the right (see Figure C.1). For example, many commands on the Format menu open dialog boxes full of options. When you select Format in the Categories list, a complete list of all the options from all those dialog boxes appears on the Commands list.
4. Scroll through the Commands list and select the command you want. Some of the commands have ellipses (. . .) after their names. If you choose one of these, the button you add to the toolbar will open a dialog box. Others (for example, Font in Figure C.1) have a drop-down list after their names. Choosing one of these will place the drop-down list on the toolbar.

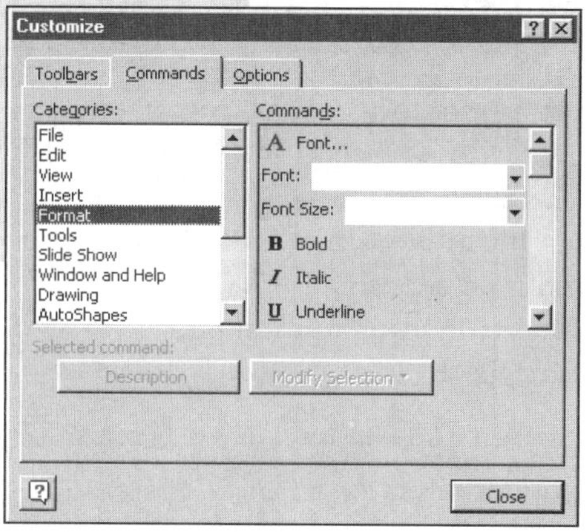

Figure C.1 From the Commands tab, you choose what command you want to make into a button.

5. Drag the command you want from the Comman<u>d</u>s list to a toolbar. As you drag onto a toolbar, your pointer becomes a bold vertical line that indicates where the new button will go. When you release the mouse button, the command becomes a button on that toolbar.
6. Repeat steps 3 through 5 to add more buttons if you want. Click on Close when you're finished.

When the Customize dialog box is open (refer to Figure C.1), you can not only add buttons to toolbars but also remove them simply by dragging them off the toolbar. You also can rearrange buttons by dragging them from one toolbar to another or from one spot to another on the same toolbar.

When the Customize dialog box is open, none of the menu commands and toolbars work normally—instead they respond to your dragging them around. So don't try to use any of the menus when the Customize dialog box is open (for instance, don't try Edit, Undo to reverse a button-dragging action you just performed), or you might accidentally make a change to the menu itself.

The easiest way to learn how to add and remove buttons to a toolbar is to "just do it," so perform the steps in the following "Hands On" section to try one out.

Hands On: Full Justify Button

Say your boss wants you to format some paragraphs on the slides with full justification (alignment with both right and left margins). There is no Justify button on either of the default toolbars, so each time you want that format, you have to go through the arduous process of opening the Format menu, choosing Alignment, and then choosing Justify. A much easier way to go is to add a Justify button to the Formatting toolbar, right next to the Align Right button. Follow these steps to do it:

1. Right-click on any toolbar and choose Customize.
2. Select the Commands tab.
3. Scroll down the Categories list and select Format.
4. On the Commands list, scroll down and select Justify.
5. Drag the word "Justify" up to the Formatting toolbar and drop it immediately to the right of the Align Right button.
6. Click on Close. Your new button appears on the toolbar, as shown in Figure C.2.

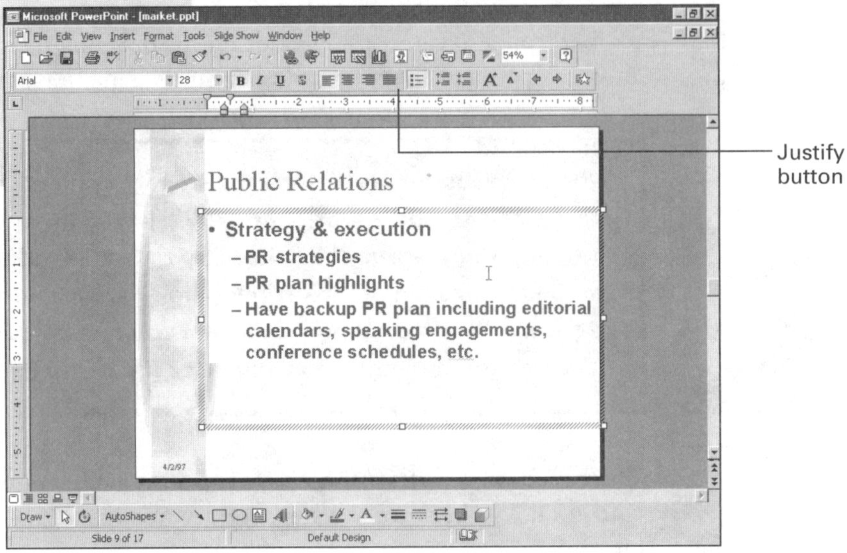

Figure C.2 The Justify button has been added to the Formatting toolbar.

To try out your button, type some text in a paragraph (more than one line), and then click on the new Justify button. It changes the paragraph alignment to full justification.

Suppose that you want to place that Justify button elsewhere—perhaps at the far right end of the toolbar. Continue the steps to do so.

7. Right-click on any toolbar and choose Customize.
8. Drag the Justify button from its current location to the right end of the toolbar (see Figure C.3).
9. Release the mouse button. The button moves to its new location.
10. Click on Close.

Now say you change your mind and you don't want that Justify button anymore. (Perhaps you get a new boss who doesn't care about full justification!) Continue the steps to get rid of the button.

11. Right-click on any toolbar and choose Customize.
12. Drag the Justify button down and away from the toolbar. Your mouse pointer turns into a gray box with an X when the button is far enough away from the toolbar to be removed (see Figure C.4).
13. Release the mouse button. The button disappears.
14. Click on Close.

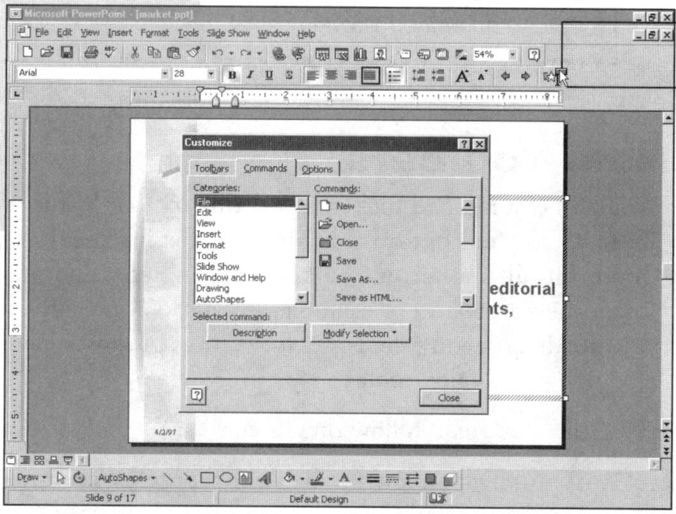

Figure C.3 You can move a button by dragging it to a different spot while the Customize dialog box is open.

Figure C.4
Drag a button away from the toolbars to remove it.

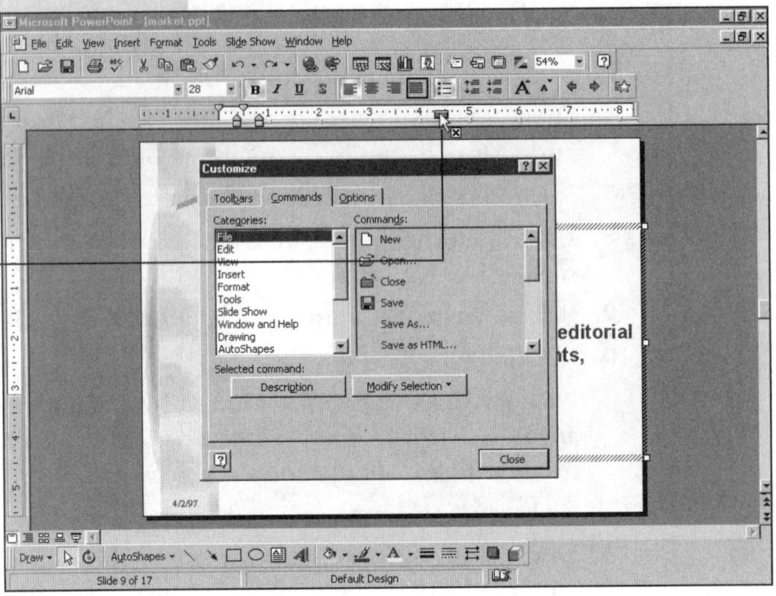

Mouse pointer shows an X under it.

If you make mistakes in customizing one of PowerPoint's toolbars, you can undo your changes by selecting the toolbar from the Toolbars tab of the Customize dialog box and then clicking on the Reset button. This works only with the toolbars that come with PowerPoint, not with toolbars you have created yourself (which you'll learn to do in the following section).

Creating New Toolbars

Sometimes a nip and tuck at an existing toolbar just isn't enough. Perhaps you need to add ten buttons to a toolbar, for instance—there won't be enough room for all the buttons on one line! In cases like that, it's best to create a brand-new toolbar. For example, if you do a lot with multiple presentations, frequently arranging the panes for various purposes, you might want to create a window-arranging toolbar.

To create a toolbar, follow these steps:

1. Right-click on any toolbar and choose Customize.
2. Select the Toolbars tab (see Figure C.5).
3. Click on the New button. A New Toolbar dialog box appears.

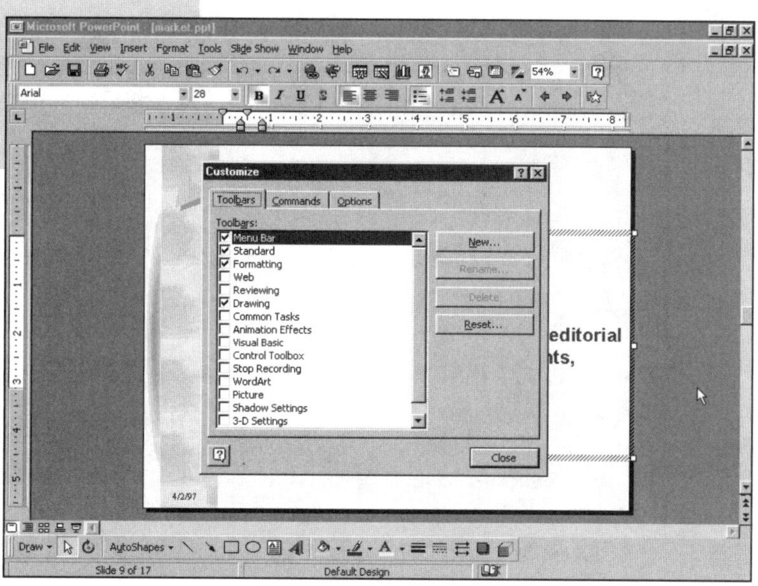

Figure C.5 You can create your own toolbars from here.

4. Type the name for the new toolbar in the Toolbar Name text box (for example, **Window Controls**) and click on OK. A little floating window appears alongside the Customize dialog box. This is your new toolbar (see Figure C.6).

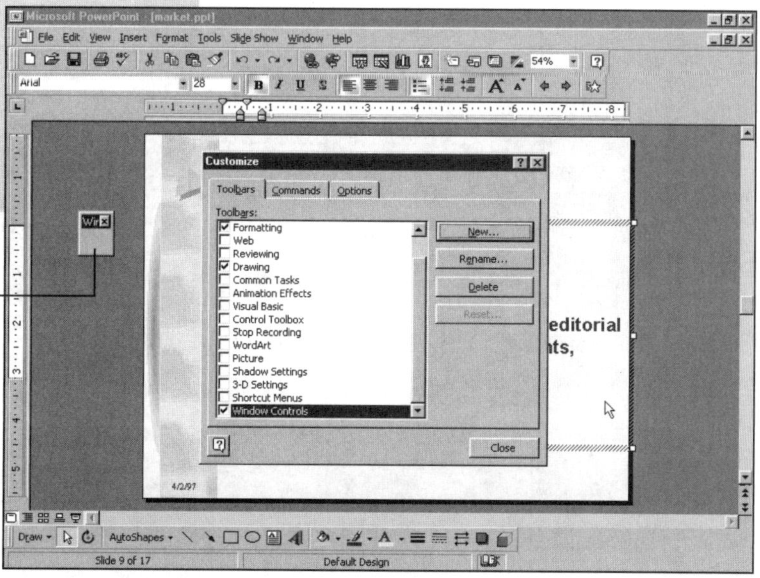

New toolbar

Figure C.6 Your new toolbar is empty, so it is very small. It will get bigger as you add buttons to it.

Note

If you don't see the new toolbar floating alongside the dialog box, drag the title bar on the dialog box to move it slightly to the left. The floating toolbar may be behind it.

5. (Optional) If you want the toolbar to be anchored at the top of the screen, like the other toolbars, drag its title bar up to the position where you want it (see Figure C.7).

Tip

If you plan on using the toolbar in its docked position at the top or bottom of the screen, drag it into place (step 5) first, before you add buttons to it (step 6). That way you can gauge how many buttons will fit on the toolbar without running off-screen.

6. Add buttons to the new toolbar, as you learned earlier in this chapter.
7. When you are finished, click on Close.

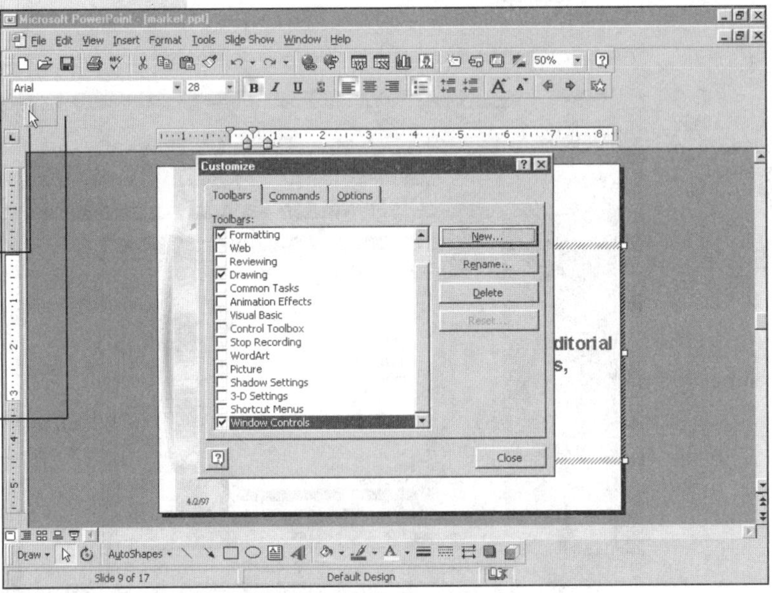

Figure C.7 When the toolbar is anchored at the top, it no longer has a title bar.

You can move the toolbar by dragging this tab.

New toolbar

Choosing Which Toolbars to Display

You have already learned how to display and hide toolbars—just right-click on any toolbar and select the one you want to display or hide. A check mark means the toolbar is displayed.

In Figure C.5, you saw another way to choose which toolbars to display or hide. Each toolbar listed on the Toolbars tab of the Customize dialog box has a check box beside it. Click on to place or remove check marks to display or hide each toolbar.

Deleting a Toolbar

You cannot delete the toolbars that come with PowerPoint, but you can delete the custom toolbars you have created yourself. To do so, click on the check box next to the toolbar's name on the Toolbars tab of the Customize dialog box and then click on the Delete button.

Renaming a Toolbar

Like deleting, renaming works only with toolbars you've created yourself. To rename a toolbar, select it from the Toolbars tab of the Customize dialog box and then click on the Rename button. The Rename Toolbar dialog box appears. Type a new name in the Toolbar Name text box and click on OK.

Customizing Menus

Customizing menus is a lot like customizing toolbars, but for some reason many people are more afraid of doing it. It's not complicated, really. When the Customize dialog box is open, the menus become customizable, just like the toolbars. With the Customize dialog box open, you can:

- Drag a menu from one spot to another to rearrange the order in which menus appear.
- Drag a menu away from the menu bar to remove it (not recommended because you won't have access to its commands anymore if you do that).
- Click on a menu to open it, and then drag a command to a different spot on the menu (or off the menu completely to remove it).
- Rename a menu by right-clicking on it and typing a new name in the Name text box on the shortcut menu.

You also can create your own menus and add commands to them. To create a new menu, follow these steps:

1. If the Customize dialog box is not open, right-click on any menu and choose Customize to open it.
2. Click on the Commands tab.
3. Select New Menu at the bottom of the Categories list.
4. Drag the words "New Menu" from the Commands list to the spot on the menu bar where you want the new menu. The new menu appears with the name New Menu.
5. To change the menu name, right-click on it and type a new name in the Name text box, pressing Enter when finished.
6. To add commands to the menu, locate the command you want to add on the Commands list (after choosing a different category) and drag it up to the new menu. When the mouse pointer touches the new menu, the menu opens so that you can drag the command onto it. Release the mouse button.
7. Repeat step 6, filling your new menu with the commands you want.
8. Click on Close when finished.

Tip

If you right-click on one of PowerPoint default menu's names, you can see that the name of a menu has an ampersand (&) in it. The ampersand precedes the letter that should appear underlined. (Remember, the underlined letter can be pressed along with Alt to open the menu.) For example, *F&ormat* means that the *o* will appear underlined. When you are naming menus that you create yourself, don't forget to add an ampersand in the name to indicate which letter should be underlined. Make sure you choose a letter that none of the other menu names are currently using as their underlined letter.

Setting Your Toolbar and Menu Options

Take a quick look at the Options tab of the Customize dialog box before moving on (see Figure C.8). There are a few options here you might find useful.

- Select the Large Icons check box to make the buttons on the toolbars larger. This is helpful if you have poor eyesight, but it makes fewer icons fit on the screen at once.
- Deselect the Show ScreenTips on Toolbars check box if you don't want the ScreenTips popping up whenever you position your mouse pointer over a toolbar button.

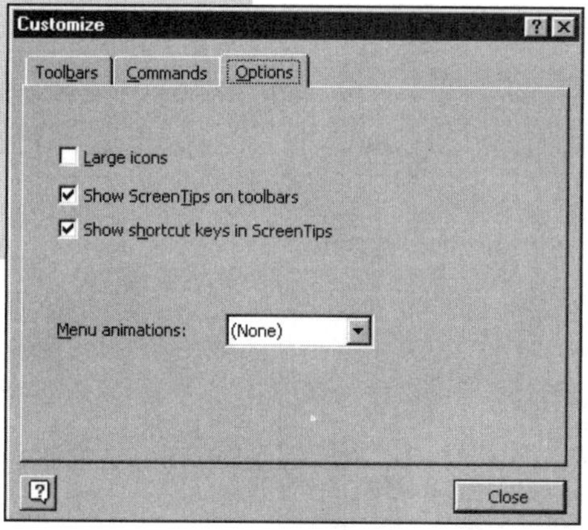

Figure C.8 The Options tab contains a few miscellaneous settings for menus and toolbars.

- Deselect the Show Shortcut Keys in ScreenTips check box if you don't want the ScreenTips to include any shortcut key equivalents for the button being pointed at.
- Open the Menu Animations drop-down list and choose an animation type if you like. (The default is None.) This makes the menus open with more of a flourish, but it may make slower computers run even more slowly.

Setting PowerPoint Options

Besides the settings for menus and toolbars that you've seen so far in this chapter, there are many, many other settings you can choose. Some of them are purely cosmetic, whereas others enable timesaving or safety features. Think of this dialog box as PowerPoint's "control panel," where you can adjust the default settings to your own preferences.

To access the options, you must open the Options dialog box by choosing Tools, Options. The Options dialog box has seven tabs, each with a different category of settings on it; look at each tab individually.

View Options

The View tab contains options that affect how PowerPoint appears on-screen (see Figure C.9). They are divided into two types: the Show items, which control what PowerPoint controls appear on-screen as you are building the

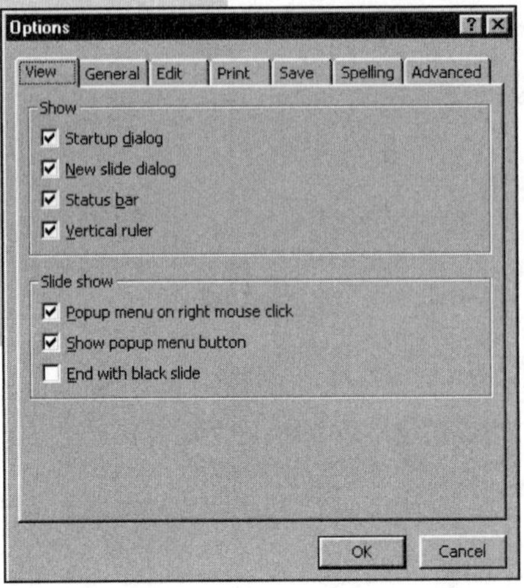

Figure C.9 The View tab of the Options dialog box controls which elements are visible on-screen.

presentation, and the Slide Show items, which control the way an on-screen slide show behaves.

Show

- *Startup Dialog.* Deselect this if you do not want the PowerPoint dialog box to appear each time you start PowerPoint.
- *New Slide Dialog.* Deselect this if you do not want the New Slide dialog box to appear each time you create a new slide. Since you will not be selecting an AutoLayout from that dialog box, all new slides will be blank.
- *Status Bar.* Deselect this to suppress the display of the status bar.
- *Vertical Ruler.* Deselect this to suppress the display of the vertical ruler.

Slide Show

- *Popup menu on right mouse click.* During the slide show, if you do not want the person running the show to access the shortcut menu by right-clicking, deselect this check box.
- *Show popup menu button.* Deselect this check box to suppress the arrow button and attached menu that normally appear when you move the mouse during a slide show.
- *End with black slide.* Deselect this if you do not want a black slide after the last one in the show.

General Options

Most of the customization I personally do to PowerPoint is done on the General tab (see Figure C.10). It contains the features that I most want to tinker with. This may be the case for you too! Take a look at what the General tab offers:

- *Provide Feedback with Sound to Screen Elements.* When this feature is on, PowerPoint plays the sounds associated with various system events. (You set these up from the Windows 95 Control Panel's Sound feature.) Most people find these annoying after the first ten minutes and leave this feature turned off.
- *Recently Used File List.* As you learned in Chapter 3, one way to open a file that you have recently used is to select it from the bottom of the File menu. The File menu, by default, lists the four most recently used files. To increase or decrease this number, change the number in this text box. Or turn off the feature completely by deselecting the check box.
- *Macro Virus Protection.* Some computer viruses embed themselves in PowerPoint macros or customized toolbars or menus. If you open a presentation that contains any of these items, PowerPoint will warn you of that fact if you leave this feature turned on.
- *Link Sounds with File Size Greater Than.* When you place a sound file in a presentation, PowerPoint creates a link to it if it is larger than the size you list here. This keeps the presentation file from growing too large. For sounds smaller than the listed size, it embeds a copy of the actual sound right into the presentation.

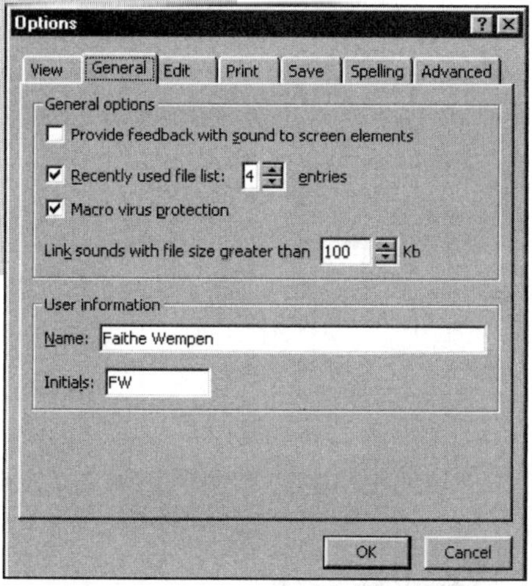

Figure C.10 General options affect the way PowerPoint operates in general, rather than in a specific area.

- *User Name* and *Initials*. Fill in your name here if it doesn't already appear. PowerPoint uses this information in several ways, including placing it on the Properties sheet (File, Properties) and filling it in on certain forms and templates.

Editing Options

On the Edit tab, you'll find a variety of options that affect the way PowerPoint works as you create and change objects on slides (see Figure C.11). Setting these options the way you feel most comfortable with can be a big time-saver and frustration-eliminator. Some examples:

- *Replace Straight Quotes with Smart Quotes.* If you leave this check box marked, PowerPoint will replace straight quotation marks (") with curly ones that face inward toward the text it modifies, like "this."
- *Automatic Word Selection.* If this check box is marked, when you select part of a word, the entire word will become selected, along with the white space after it.
- *Use Smart Cut and Paste.* When this feature is enabled, and you move things around with the Cut, Copy, and Paste commands, PowerPoint automatically removes excess spaces and adds spaces when needed.
- *Drag and Drop Editing.* Drag and drop is a great feature that enables you to move text from place to place by dragging with the mouse. Most people leave this feature turned on; however, if you don't use the feature and find yourself accidentally moving things when you didn't mean to, turn off the feature.

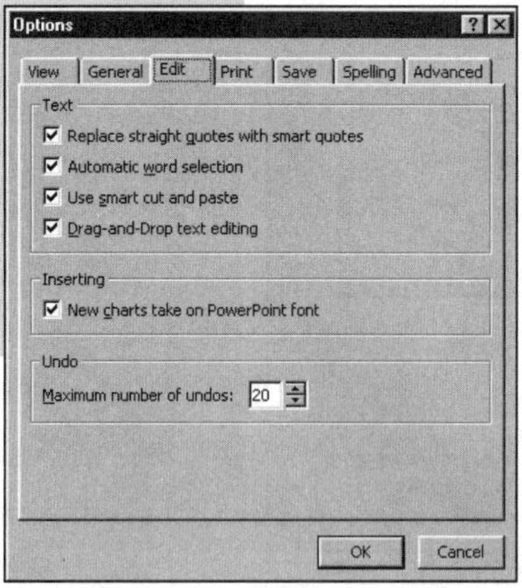

Figure C.11 Use the Edit tab's options to set up how PowerPoint will behave when you are entering and editing information on slides.

- *New Charts Take on PowerPoint Font.* This sets the font for inserted charts at 18-point Arial. Clear the check box to use the chart's own fonts.
- *Maximum Number of Undos.* This is the number of actions that PowerPoint "remembers" so you can undo them with the Edit, Undo command or the Undo toolbar button.

Printing Options

PowerPoint can print a variety of handouts, notes, and other items, and the Print tab lets you fine-tune the printing process (see Figure C.12).

- *Background Printing.* If you deselect this check box, you won't be able to continue to use PowerPoint after issuing the Print command until the print job has been completely sent to the printer. I recommend that you leave this on.
- *Print TrueType Fonts as Graphics.* This sends your presentation's TrueType fonts to the printer as pictures rather than as outline font images. If you are having trouble with your printer running out of memory during a print job, experiment with this setting; sometimes changing it can make a difference.
- *Print Inserted Objects at Printer Resolution.* If an inserted object has a higher graphic resolution than your printer supports, this option "dumbs down" the object to match the printer's capabilities, thereby decreasing the size of the print file and making it print faster.

Figure C.12 The Print tab controls determine how your printouts will print.

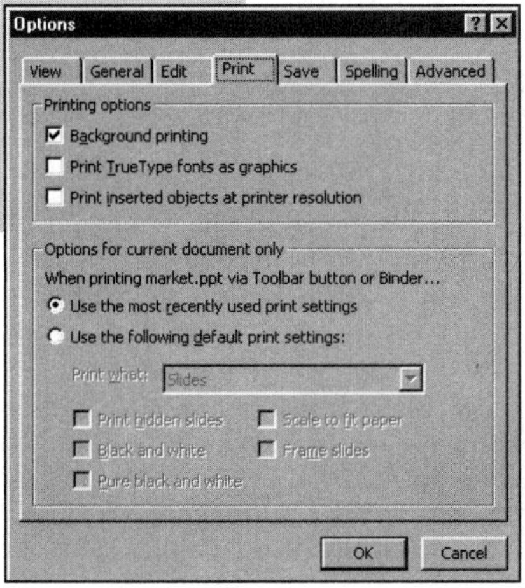

- *When Printing Via Toolbar Button or Binder.* This controls what happens when you click on the Print button on the Standard toolbar. There are two choices here: Use the Most Recently Used Print Settings, and Use the Following Default Print Settings. If you choose the latter, several additional controls become available at the bottom of the dialog box to enable you to specify your preferences.

Save Options

On the Save tab you'll find a number of settings that specify what happens when you save your work in PowerPoint (see Figure C.13).

- *Allow Fast Saves.* Fast saves speeds up the saving process by saving only the changes to the presentation each time you save. When you are ready to save the presentation for the final time, if you clear this check box temporarily, you will get a full re-save of the entire file, which may result in a smaller file size.
- *Prompt for File Properties.* If this box is selected, the first time you save a file, the File Properties dialog box appears, prompting you to enter extra information about the file. Some organizations manage their documents based on this extra information; most people ignore it.
- *Full Text Search Information.* Stores full text search information with your presentation, so if you search for this file using Windows 95's Find command, and specify that the file you are looking for contains certain text, the Find program can quickly look through this file to see if it matches the criteria. This slows down each save operation slightly.

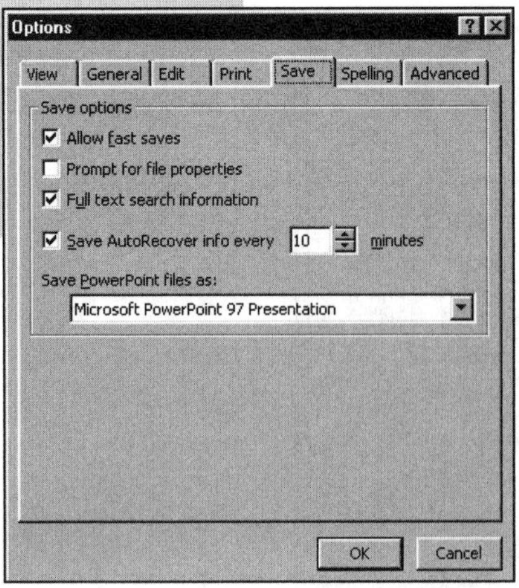

Figure C.13 The Save tab controls how your presentation is saved.

- *Save AutoRecover Info Every.* PowerPoint periodically saves your work in an AutoRecover file, so that if the power goes out before you have saved your work, all will not be lost. You can specify the interval at which this occurs; 10 minutes is the default.
- *Save PowerPoint Files As.* You can save your PowerPoint files by default in any of several PowerPoint versions. If you need to exchange presentation files with other people who use older versions of PowerPoint, you should set this to the oldest version that you have to exchange with. Newer versions will open older files, but not the other way around.

Spelling Options

On the Spelling tab, you'll find settings that control the way the Spelling Checker program works in PowerPoint (see Figure C.14).

The Spelling Checker was discussed in Chapter 6.

- *Check Spelling as You Type.* There are two check boxes under this heading. Spelling controls whether or not spelling is checked as you type. Hide Spelling Errors makes errors appear red-underlined on-screen. To see a list of suggested spellings, you right-click on the red lines.
- *Suggest.* The single check box here, Always, controls whether spelling suggestions are always offered or not. If this is turned off, you must click on the Suggest button in the Spelling Checker to see suggestions. This speeds up the spell check process somewhat.
- *Ignore.* The two check boxes here specify what kinds of words the spelling checker should ignore: Words in UPPERCASE and Words with Numbers.

Figure C.14 The Spelling tab lets you fine-tune the Spelling Checker program.

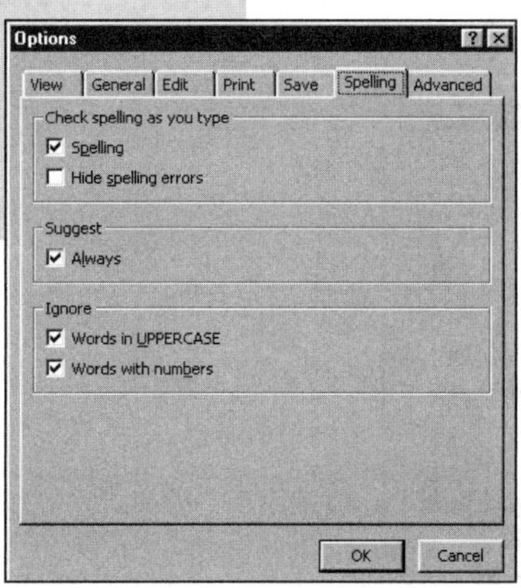

Advanced Options

Finally you come to the Advanced tab (see Figure C.15). The Advanced tab options don't really have anything in common, except that they're options that an advanced user would worry about and that don't typically need to be changed very often.

- *Render 24-bit Bitmaps at Highest Quality.* 24-bit images have lots of colors in them—millions, in fact. Displaying such images at the highest possible quality on your screen will make the images look their best but may slow down the display somewhat. You can start with this check box marked, and deselect it if you run into problems with a sluggish display.
- *Export Pictures.* This controls whether exported pictures are optimized for on-screen viewing or for hard copy printouts. The default is Best for Printing.
- *Default File Location.* This is the one setting that I always change immediately in every Office application! It controls where your data files will be stored by default, and what folder your Save As and Open dialog boxes will show to by default. Set this to the folder where you want to keep your PowerPoint data files. By default it is \My Documents (or \Windows\Personal if you are using a later release of Windows 95).

All Microsoft Office applications have a default file location of \My Documents. But I always set the default file location to a different folder for each application, to keep my data files better organized. Also, when I am working on a specific project, such as this book, I typically create a special folder just for that project's files, and change the Default File Location to that folder.

Figure C.15 On the Advanced tab, you can set the default file location, plus a few other settings.

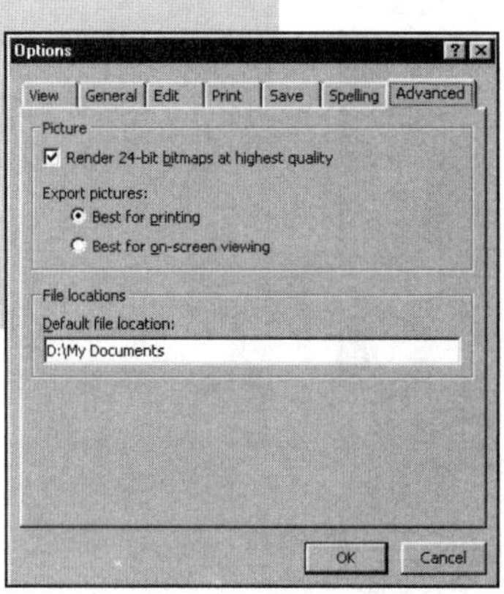

Glossary

3-D An effect used with pictures and charts to add the appearance of depth (three dimensions) using shading.

A

Action buttons Buttons you place on slides that hyperlink to other parts of the presentation or other locations. Also called Navigation buttons.

Active slide The slide that is currently selected (in multi-slide views) or visible (in single-slide views).

Alignment The arrangement of text or an object in relation to a document's margins or the edges of a text box. Alignment can be left, right, centered or justified.

Animation Effects Movement you can assign to individual objects on a slide (for example, having it appear dropped in from the top).

Applet A small software program provided with PowerPoint that allows you to perform additional operations, such as WordArt for enhanced text effects.

Aspect ratio The ratio of height to width on a graphic. When resizing a graphic, you want to keep the aspect ratio the same to avoid distortion.

AutoContent Wizard A series of dialog boxes that help you build your basic presentation by answering questions.

AutoCorrect A feature of PowerPoint that corrects common spelling mistakes (such as "teh" for "the") automatically.

AutoFormat A feature of PowerPoint that applies generic, moderately attractive formatting to save you time.

AutoLayouts A group of pre-designed slide layouts you can choose (for example, a slide with a title and bullet list is one of them).

AutoShape A set of automated drawing shapes.

Axis (pl. axes) In a graph, one of two value sets (see also y-axis and x-axis).

B

Bar chart A type of chart that uses horizontal bars of varying lengths to represent values. When the bars are vertical, it's called a *Column chart*; however, some people call both kinds Bar.

Bitmap A type of graphic image made up of individual colored dots that form a picture.

Bold A style applied to text to make the font lines thicker.

Border A visible line surrounding text or objects.

C

Chart Also called Graph. A visual representation of numerical data.

Click To press and release the left mouse button once.

Clip Art A ready-made drawing that can be inserted in a PowerPoint presentation.

Clip Gallery PowerPoint's clip management program, enabling you to categorize and organize pictures, clip art, video clips, and sound files.

Clip Gallery Live Microsoft's Web page devoted to providing free downloadable extra clips for use in Office programs.

Clipboard A holding area in Windows where material that is *Cut* or *Copied* is placed until you are ready to *Paste* it.

Color scheme A pre-designed set of colors in a template.

Column chart A type of chart that uses vertical bars of varying lengths to represent values. This is sometimes called a *Bar chart.*

Command Button A button in a dialog box that issues a command (like Close or Save) or opens another dialog box.

Contrast The amount of black and white in a picture that can be adjusted to modify the image's seeming brightness.

Copy To copy the contents of cells or an object to the *Clipboard.*

Crop To trim off one or more edges of an image or hide it from view.

Custom Animation Animation effects that you can assign to individual objects. Compare to Preset animation, which you apply to entire slides only.

Custom show A subset of slides from a slide show that you can save as a mini-show within the main show.

Cut To move the contents of cells or an object to the *Clipboard.*

D

Data Information, which can be either numerical or textual.

Data table A grid accompanying a chart that shows the data on which the chart was based.

Demote To make a paragraph a lower level in Outline view (move it toward the right).

Desktop The main area of Windows where you can open and manage files and programs.

Dialog box A window that appears during some procedures in PowerPoint that allows you to make settings by entering text, selecting things from lists or checking boxes or buttons.

Docked A toolbar that is "fastened" at the top or bottom of the PowerPoint window. Docked toolbars have no title bar of their own. Compare to *Undocked.*

Double-click To press and release the left mouse button twice quickly in succession.

Doughnut Chart A variation of a pie chart that shows the data as percentages of a whole ring-shaped object.

Drag To press and hold the left mouse button down while moving the mouse.

Drag and drop A method of moving text or objects by clicking on an object with a mouse, dragging it to a new location and releasing the mouse button to drop it into its new location.

E

Ellipses Three dots. Whenever you see ellipses after a command, it means that the command opens a dialog box.

E-mail Electronic mail. Messages distributed and received over a computer network or system of networks, such as the Internet.

Embossed text Text that looks like it is raised or stamped into the background rather than created with ink. This is a screen effect, and the text isn't really raised on the printout.

F

Fill To place a color or line pattern in the interior of an object, such as a square or background of a text box.

Flip To reverse an image so it looks like you flipped it over. For example, if you have a transparency, and you turn it over so you are seeing it from the back, it is flipped.

Font A design set of letters, symbols and numbers.

Footer Text entered in a footer placeholder, which is the automatically placed at the bottom of each document page.

Format To add settings for font, font style, color and line style to text or an object.

Format Painter A feature of PowerPoint that allows you to easily copy all formatting applied to one set of text to any other.

Free Rotate See *Rotate.*

G

GIF A graphic format, the default format for saving graphics when you save your presentation in HTML format. GIF stands for *Graphic Interchange Format.*

Gradient A shading effect that moves from lighter to darker in such a way that it suggests a light source shining on the object containing the gradient.

Graph Also called Chart. A graph is a visual representation of numerical data.

Graphics A file containing visual data, such as a line drawing, rather than text.

Graphics file format Individual systems of storing graphics file data. Graphics file filters are required to read various graphics file formats; PowerPoint comes with several built in.

Grayed out Unavailable. Commands and buttons that cannot be used immediately appear gray or dimmed (instead of normal black) to indicate this.

Grayscale A process of used in printing documents that utilizes shades between white and black to enhance computer graphics printouts.

Gridlines Lines that help you align on-screen elements precisely. On a chart, gridlines help your eye follow the data series to determine its value.

Group To tell PowerPoint that you want two or more objects to be considered a single object for the purpose of selecting, moving, and resizing.

H

Handle Small squares that appear when you select an object that allow you to resize it. Also called a selection handle or resizing handle.

Handout Master A screen where you can make global settings for all handout pages.

Header Text entered in a header placeholder, which is the automatically placed at the top of each document page.

Highlight A feature that places colored highlighting on-screen for selected text.

Home Page The hypertext document on the World Wide Web that will display when you first open your Web browser. Also refers to the top page on someone's Web site.

HTML Hypertext Markup Language. The language used to create hypertext.

Hyperlink Any underlined text or hyperlink object created using hypertext that a computer user can click on with a mouse, causing a different hypertext document to display.

I

Image Control A PowerPoint feature used to adjust the appearance of pictures relative to grayscale settings.

Indent To set text away from a margin by a specific distance, as at the beginning of a paragraph.

Insertion Point The blinking vertical line that indicates where typed text will appear.

IntelliPoint Mouse A new mouse from Microsoft that has a rolling wheel in the center that controls Zoom and some other features.

Internet A globally connected system of computer networks allowing online access to various types of documents such as graphics and hypertext documents.

Italic A font style that applies a slanted effect to text.

J

JPEG A graphics format, more flexible than GIF format, that you can choose to save your images in when you export your presentation to HTML format.

Jump Within a hypertext system, to move from one hypertext document to another using hyperlinks.

Justify One type of alignment that spreads letters on a line so that they are spaced out between the left and right margin.

K

Kiosk A generic term for any self-running presentation. Also, more specifically, a little booth in a public space where a video screen shows a presentation.

L

Label A descriptive text element added to a chart to help the reader understand a visual element.

Landscape Orientation of a document so that, when printed, text runs from left to right along the longer edge of a piece of paper.

Layout The arrangement of the text boxes and other objects on a slide.

Legend In a chart, a feature that defines the relationship of the graphic symbols to the data elements for the reader.

Line style Effects using width, arrows, and dashes that can be applied to a line.

Loop To repeat a sound or video clip from the beginning when it reaches the end.

M

Margin A border that runs around the outside of a document page, in which nothing will print.

Master A template slide that controls the appearance of a group of other slides in a presentation.

Maximize To expand a window to fill the entire screen.

Media Player A Microsoft Windows accessory program for playing multimedia files.

Meeting Minder A PowerPoint feature that enables you to take notes and record action items as you are giving a presentation.

Menu A list of commands you can choose from.

Minimize To shrink a window to an icon on the Desktop or in the application window.

Multimedia An overused term that means, in its simplest form, more than one medium(for example, both pictures and sound used in a presentation).

N

Narration A voice-over description of each slide that you can record to play with your presentation, if you can't be there to speak yourself when your audience views it.

Navigation buttons See *Action buttons.*

Notes Master A screen where you can set global settings for all notes pages.

Notes Page view A PowerPoint view where you can type the notes that will appear on your notes pages printouts.

O

Object Any graphic, drawing, text, chart or other file placed within a PowerPoint slide.

Office Assistant A feature of PowerPoint 97 that allows you to enter questions in natural English language sentences.

OLE Object Linking and Embedding. Microsoft Corporation's standards built into Windows that allows you to embed a document created in one software application in a document created in another software application. OLE also allows you to establish a relationship (link) between the embedded data in one document to the original data.

Online templates Templates that are designed to help you create self-running presentations with navigation buttons. Compare to Standard templates.

Option Buttons A set of buttons in a dialog box from which only one may be selected at a time. Also called *Radio Buttons.*

Org Chart Short for *Organizational Chart*; a chart consisting of linked boxes that shows how employees work together in a company or other data.

Orientation A setting that designates whether a document will print with text running along the long or short side of a piece of paper (portrait or landscape).

Outline View A PowerPoint view where you see all the text in the presentation as an outline. You do not see other objects, like pictures, in Outline view.

P

Pack and Go A PowerPoint feature that enables you to transfer all the files needed for your presentation onto a disk.

Page Setup The collection of settings that relate to how the pages of your document are set up, including the size of the slide and the page orientation.

Paste To place text or an object onto a slide from the Windows Clipboard.

Paste Link To place a copy of a file in a PowerPoint presentation while establishing a link with the original file.

Pattern An arrangement of dots or lines that can be used to fill the center of an object.

Pie chart A round chart type in which each pie wedge represents a value.

Portrait An orientation that places text from left to right along the shorter side of a piece of paper.

PowerPoint Central A built-in presentation that contains links to additional materials (like extra clip art) and helpful information for using PowerPoint (like a tutorial).

Presentation Design Template A template that provides a color scheme and Slide Master layout but no sample slides.

Presentation Template A template that provides not only a color scheme and Slide Master layout, but also sample slides.

Preset Animation Pre-fabricated animation settings that apply to all objects on a slide.

Promote To increase a paragraph's outline level in Outline view, moving it to the left.

Properties Characteristics or settings for a device, file, or program.

R

Radio Buttons See *Option Buttons.*

Raster image An image consisting of individual pixels. Also called bitmap image.

Redo To restore an action you have undone using the Undo command.

Restore To change a minimized or maximized window back to its original size (opened but not filling the entire screen).

Right aligned Text that is lined up with the right side of a tab setting or document margin, as with a set of numbers in a column.

Right-click To press and release the right mouse button once.

Right-drag To press and hold the right mouse button down while you move the mouse.

Rotate To move an object along a 360 degree path. When the rotation can be any amount, PowerPoint refers to it as *Free Rotate.*

S

Save As To save a previously saved presentation with a new name or properties.

Scan To electronically record a hard copy image as a graphics file; this file can then be opened and manipulated within software such as Paint.

ScreenTip A Help feature that displays the name of a tool in a small box when you move your cursor over the tool.

Scroll To move the on-screen display to view different parts of the presentation.

Scroll bar A mechanism used with a mouse for navigating around a document horizontally or vertically.

Shading A pattern ranging between white and black that fills an object.

Shadow A drawing effect that appears to place a shadow alongside an object.

Shortcut An icon that refers to a program or data file in Windows.

Shortcut Keys Keys you can press as a shortcut to choosing a command from a menu—for example, Ctrl+C is the shortcut key combination for the Edit, Copy command.

Shortcut Menu The menu that appears when you right-click on an object in PowerPoint (or in Windows 95 itself).

Slide layout See *Layout.*

Slide Master A screen where you can set global settings for all slides in the presentation.

Slide Miniature A small window that appears in Outline view to show you how the selected slide will appear in Slide view. In other views it shows you alternate color settings, like black-and-white if your presentation is in color on-screen.

Slide Navigator A dialog box that enables you to switch to any slide while giving the presentation.

Slide Show view A PowerPoint view that lets you practice and give your presentation.

Slide Sorter View A PowerPoint view that shows all the slides in the presentation in miniature form, so you can sort and organize them.

Slide View A PowerPoint view that lets you work intensively on one slide at a time.

Sound Recorder A Microsoft Windows accessory program that can be used to record, edit and play back sound files.

Spelling checker A feature of PowerPoint that checks the spelling of words in your document against a dictionary and flags possible errors for correction.

Standard Templates Templates that are used to create presentations designed to be presented by a live speaker, rather than shown in a kiosk or online.

Status Bar An area at the bottom of PowerPoint that provides information about the document, such as what page, line and column your cursor is currently resting in.

Submenu A menu within a menu.

Summary slide A slide that summarizes two or more other slides, with those slides titles as bullets on it.

Symbol A typeface that uses graphics like circles, percent signs or smiling faces in place of letters and numbers.

T

Tabs Markers at the top of a dialog box that represent the pages available for viewing.

Template A pre-defined collection of formatting and style settings on which you can base a new presentation.

Texture A pre-designed background that comes with PowerPoint that makes your objects appear to be sitting on a surface like brick, marble, wood, or some other material.

Text wrap This feature forces newly entered text to wrap to the next line when the insertion point reaches the right edge of the text box.

Tile To arrange multiple windows so that each window fits on-screen without overlap.

Timing The amount of time a slide appears on-screen in the presentation before the next slide automatically replaces it.

Title Bar The colored bar across the top of a window that tells the program's name.

Title Master A screen where you set the global settings for all slides formatted with the Title AutoLayout in your presentation.

Toolbar A group of buttons (tools) representing commonly used commands—toolbars can be *docked* or *undocked.*

Toolbar Button A graphic representation used on toolbars to represent the various functions performed when those buttons are pressed with a mouse.

Transition An animation that moves you from one slide to the next.

Transparent Color A color in an image that is set to "see-through" so whatever is behind the image shows through.

U

Undo To reverse the last action performed.

Undocked Toolbars that are not fastened to the top or bottom of the screen, but float freely in their own window, are undocked.

Uppercase A capital letter.

URL Uniform Resource Locator, another name for the address of an Internet Web page or file downloading site.

V

Vector image An image created with mathematical formulas rather than individual pixels. Clip art is vector format art.

View In software, various displays of documents or information that allow you to perform different tasks or see different perspectives on information. PowerPoint has several views: Slide, Slide Show, Slide Sorter, Notes Page, and Outline.

Virus A computer program that attaches itself to other programs and replicates and/or causes system problems.

W

Watermark A shading effect for pictures which makes them appear to be a background impression, like a watermark impression on fine stationary.

Web See *World Wide Web.*

What's This? A part of the PowerPoint help system; once you select What's This? your cursor changes to a question mark and you can click on any on-screen element to receive an explanation of that element.

Wizard A feature that walks you through certain procedures, producing something, such as an HTML version of your presentation, based on answers you give to questions and selections made in Wizard dialog boxes.

WordArt An applet included with PowerPoint used for adding special effects to text, such as curving the text.

World Wide Web A hypertext system of documents transmitted and accessed over the Internet.

Wrap See *Text Wrap.*

X

X-axis In a chart, the vertical value axis.

Y

Y-axis In a chart, the horizontal value axis.

Z

Zoom To modify view settings so that what you are seeing on your screen is a percentage (larger or smaller) of a document page's actual size.

Index

Symbols/Numbers

A

B

C

D

E

G

H

I

J

K

L

M

N

O

P

Q

R

S

T

U

Z

Send Us YOUR COMMENTS

Dear Reader:

Thank you for buying this book. In order to offer you more quality books on the topics ***you*** would like to see, we need your input. At Prima Publishing, we pride ourselves on timely responsiveness to our readers needs. If you'll complete and return this brief questionnaire, ***we will listen!***

Name: (first) ______ (M.I.) ______ (last) ______

Company: ______ Type of business: ______

Address: ______ City: ______ State: ______ Zip: ______

Phone: ______ Fax: ______ E-mail address: ______

May we contact you for research purposes? ❑ Yes ❑ No

(If you participate in a research project, we will supply you with your choice of a book from Prima CPD)

❶ How would you rate this book, overall?

- ❑ Excellent
- ❑ Very Good
- ❑ Good
- ❑ Fair
- ❑ Below Average
- ❑ Poor

❷ Why did you buy this book?

- ❑ Price of book
- ❑ Content
- ❑ Author's reputation
- ❑ Prima's reputation
- ❑ CD-ROM/disk included with book
- ❑ Information highlighted on cover
- ❑ Other (Please specify): ______

❸ How did you discover this book?

- ❑ Found it on bookstore shelf
- ❑ Saw it in Prima Publishing catalog
- ❑ Recommended by store personnel
- ❑ Recommended by friend or colleague
- ❑ Saw an advertisement in: ______
- ❑ Read book review in: ______
- ❑ Saw it on Web site: ______
- ❑ Other (Please specify): ______

❹ Where did you buy this book?

- ❑ Bookstore (name) ______
- ❑ Computer Store (name) ______
- ❑ Electronics Store (name) ______
- ❑ Wholesale Club (name) ______
- ❑ Mail Order (name) ______
- ❑ Direct from Prima Publishing
- ❑ Other (please specify): ______

❺ Which computer periodicals do you read regularly? ______

❻ Would you like to see your name in print?

May we use your name and quote you in future Prima Publishing books or promotional materials?

❑ Yes ❑ No

❼ Comments & Suggestions: ______

PLEASE
PLACE
STAMP
HERE

PRIMA PUBLISHING
Computer Products Division
3875 Atherton Road
Rocklin, CA 95765

---

8 Where do you use your computer?

Work	❑ 100%	❑ 75%	❑ 50%	❑ 25%
Home	❑ 100%	❑ 75%	❑ 50%	❑ 25%
School	❑ 100%	❑ 75%	❑ 50%	❑ 25%

Other ______________________

9 How do you rate your level of computer skills?

❑ Beginner
❑ Advanced
❑ Intermediate

10 What is your age?

❑ Under 18
❑ 18-24
❑ 25-29
❑ 30-39
❑ 40-49
❑ 50-59
❑ 60-over

11 I would be interested in computer books on these topics

❑ Word Processing
❑ Networking
❑ Desktop Publishing
❑ Database:
❑ Spreadsheets
❑ Web site design

Other ______________________

SAVE A STAMP

Visit our Web Site at: **http://www.primapublishing.com**
and simply fill in one of our online Response Forms

OTHER BOOKS FROM PRIMA PUBLISHING

Computer Products Division

ISBN	Title	Price	Release Date
0-7615-0801-5	ActiveX	$40.00	Available Now
0-7615-0680-2	America Online Complete Handbook and Membership Kit	$24.99	Available Now
0-7615-0915-1	Building Intranets with Internet Information Server and FrontPage	$40.00	Available Now
0-7615-0417-6	CompuServe Complete Handbook and Membership Kit	$24.95	Available Now
0-7615-1083-4	Corel WordPerfect 8 Visual Learning Guide	$16.99	Spring '97
0-7615-0849-X	Corporate Intranet Development	$45.00	Available Now
0-7615-0692-6	Create Your First Web Page in a Weekend	$29.99	Available Now
0-7615-0743-4	Create FrontPage Web Pages in a Weekend	$29.99	Available Now
0-7615-0428-1	The Essential Excel 97 Book	$27.99	Available Now
0-7615-0969-0	The Essential Office 97 Book	$27.99	Available Now
0-7615-0695-0	The Essential Photoshop Book	$35.00	Available Now
0-7615-0752-3	The Essential Windows NT 4 Book	$27.99	Available Now
0-7615-0427-3	The Essential Word 97 Book	$27.99	Available Now
0-7615-1008-7	Excel 97 Visual Learning Guide	$16.99	Available Now
0-7615-1013-3	Hands On Java	$40.00	Spring '97
0-7615-1046-X	Hands On Visual Basic 5	$40.00	Spring '97

ISBN	Title	Price	Release Date
0-7615-1005-2	Internet Information Server 3 Administrator's Guide	$40.00	Available Now
0-7615-0815-5	Introduction to ABAP/4 Programming for SAP	$45.00	Available Now
0-7615-0901-1	Leveraging Visual Basic with ActiveX Controls	$45.00	Available Now
0-7615-0690-X	Netscape Enterprise Server	$40.00	Available Now
0-7615-0691-8	Netscape FastTrack Server	$40.00	Available Now
0-7615-0852-X	Netscape Navigator 3 Complete Handbook	$24.99	Available Now
0-7615-0759-0	Professional Web Design	$40.00	Available Now
0-7615-0773-6	Programming Internet Controls	$45.00	Available Now
0-7615-0914-3	Programming ISAPI with Visual Basic 5	$40.00	Available Now
0-7615-0780-9	Programming Web Server Applications	$40.00	Available Now
0-7615-0063-4	Researching on the Internet	$29.95	Available Now
0-7615-0686-1	Researching on the World Wide Web	$24.99	Available Now
0-7615-0769-8	VBScript Master's Handbook	$45.00	Available Now
0-7615-0684-5	VBScript Web Page Interactivity	$40.00	Available Now
0-7615-0903-8	Visual FoxPro 5 Enterprise Development	$45.00	Available Now
0-7615-0814-7	Visual J++	$35.00	Available Now
0-7615-0726-4	Webmaster's Handbook	$40.00	Available Now
0-7615-0751-5	Windows NT Server 4 Administrator's Guide	$50.00	Available Now
0-7615-1007-9	Word 97 Visual Learning Guide	$16.99	Available Now

TO ORDER BOOKS

Please send me the following items:

Quantity	Title	Unit Price	Total
________	______________________________	$________	$________
________	______________________________	$________	$________
________	______________________________	$________	$________
________	______________________________	$________	$________
________	______________________________	$________	$________

Subtotal	$________
Deduct 10% when ordering 3–5 books	$________
7.25% Sales Tax (CA only)	$________
8.25% Sales Tax (TN only)	$________
5.0% Sales Tax (MD and IN only)	$________
Shipping and Handling*	$________
TOTAL ORDER	$________

Shipping and Handling depend on Subtotal.

Subtotal	Shipping/Handling
$0.00–$14.99	$3.00
$15.00–29.99	$4.00
$30.00–49.99	$6.00
$50.00–99.99	$10.00
$100.00–199.99	$13.00
$200.00+	call for quote

Foreign and all Priority Request orders:
Call Order Entry department for price quote at 1-916-632-4400

This chart represents the total retail price of books only (before applicable discounts are taken).

By telephone: With Visa or MC, call 1-800-632-8676. Mon.–Fri. 8:30–4:00 PST.

By Internet e-mail: sales@primapub.com

By mail: Just fill out the information below and send with your remittance to:

PRIMA PUBLISHING
P.O. Box 1260BK
Rocklin, CA 95677-1260

http://www.primapublishing.com

Name________________________________ Daytime Telephone______________

Address ____

City ______________________ State ________ Zip ______________

Visa /MC# ________________________ Exp. ______________

Check/Money Order enclosed for $______________ Payable to Prima Publishing

Signature ____